The ARRL
Ham Radio License Manual

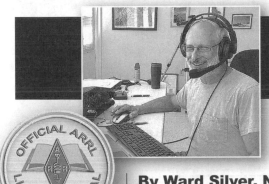

All You Need to Become an Amateur Radio Operator!

Fourth Edition
For use with *ARRL's Online Exam Review for Ham Radio*

By Ward Silver, NØAX

Contributing Editor
Mark Wilson, K1RO

Production Staff

Maty Weinberg, KB1EIB, Production Coordinator

David Pingree, N1NAS, Senior Technical Illustrator

Jodi Morin, KA1JPA, Assistant Production Supervisor: Layout

Sue Fagan, KB1OKW, Graphic Design Supervisor: Cover Design

Michelle Bloom, WB1ENT, Production Supervisor: Layout

Top Left Photo: Whether it is a contest operation, or just a casual conversation, Tom Tate, WA7NPX, is always happy to be on the air!
[Jack Reed, WA7LNW, photo]

Bottom Right Photo: Amateur Radio isn't necessarily a solo experience. Friends often meet to enjoy radio together.

ARRL The national association for **AMATEUR RADIO®**
225 Main Street, Newington, CT 06111-1400
www.arrl.org

i

Feedback: We're interested in hearing your comments on this book and what you'd like to see in future editions. Please e-mail comments to us at **pubsfdbk@arrl.org**, including your name, call sign, e-mail address, and the title, edition and printing of this book.

This book may be used for Technician license exams given beginning July 1, 2018.

QST and the ARRL website (**www.arrl.org**) will have news about any rules changes affecting the Technician class license or any of the material in this book.

We strive to produce books without errors. Sometimes mistakes do occur, however. When we become aware of problems in our books (other than obvious typographical errors), we post corrections on the ARRL website. If you think you have found an error, please check **www.arrl.org/ham-radio-license-manual** for corrections. If you don't find a correction there, please let us know by sending e-mail to **pubsfdbk@arrl.org**

Contents

Foreword

Welcome to the diverse group of individuals who make up Amateur Radio! There are nearly 750,000 amateurs, or "hams," in the United States alone and 3,000,000 around the world. Hams come from all walks of life, all ages, and every continent. Hams are busily communicating without regard to the geographic and political barriers that often separate humanity. This is the power of Amateur Radio — to communicate with each other directly, without any other commercial or government systems.

Hams come to Amateur Radio from many walks of life and many interests. Perhaps you intend to engage in public service for yourself and your community. Technical experimentation might be your interest or you might be one of the many "makers" who are building, testing, using, and learning. Making new friends via the radio, keeping in touch as you travel, or exploring where a wireless signal can take you — these are all valuable and valued parts of the Amateur Service.

As you read this book, getting ready to pass your first ham radio licensing exam, be sure to take advantage of the additional material on the ARRL's website — **www.arrl.org/ham-radio-license-manual**. You can also review and take practice exams at **www.arrl.org/examreview**. That's the ARRL way of going the extra mile to help you learn about Amateur Radio. "Of, By, and For the Amateur" is the ARRL's motto. By providing this extra information, you will be better prepared to get on the air, have more fun, and be a more effective operator.

After you get your "ticket," be sure to explore your local and online ham radio clubs and groups. This is where you'll find answers to your questions and help in getting on the air. You can start by asking the hams who administer your exam session — their organization can be your first mentor. One of ham radio's strongest traditions is helping other hams learn and grow, just like you.

Most active radio amateurs in the United States are ARRL members. They realize that since 1914, the ARRL's training, sponsorship of activities, and representation both nationally and internationally are second to none. The book you're reading now, *The ARRL Ham Radio License Manual* is just one of many publications for all levels and interests in Amateur Radio. You don't need a license to join the ARRL — just be interested in Amateur Radio and we are interested in you. It's as simple as that!

Ward Silver, NØAX
St. Charles, Missouri
March 2018

New Ham Desk
ARRL Headquarters
225 Main Street
Newington, CT 06111-1494
(860) 594-0200

Prospective new amateurs call:
800-32-NEW-HAM (800-326-3942)
You can also contact us via e-mail: **newham@arrl.org**
or check out **ARRLWeb: www.arrl.org**

About ARRL

The seed for Amateur Radio was planted in the 1890s, when Guglielmo Marconi began his experiments in wireless telegraphy. Soon he was joined by dozens, then hundreds, of others who were enthusiastic about sending and receiving messages through the air — some with a commercial interest, but others solely out of a love for this new communications medium. The United States government began licensing Amateur Radio operators in 1912.

By 1914, there were thousands of Amateur Radio operators — hams — in the United States. Hiram Percy Maxim, a leading Hartford, Connecticut inventor and industrialist, saw the need for an organization to unify this fledgling group of radio experimenters. In May 1914 he founded the American Radio Relay League (ARRL) to meet that need.

ARRL is the national association for Amateur Radio in the US. Today, with approximately 167,000 members, ARRL numbers within its ranks the vast majority of active radio amateurs in the nation and has a proud history of achievement as the standard-bearer in amateur affairs. ARRL's underpinnings as Amateur Radio's witness, partner, and forum are defined by five pillars: Public Service, Advocacy, Education, Technology, and Membership. ARRL is also International Secretariat for the International Amateur Radio Union, which is made up of similar societies in 150 countries around the world.

ARRL's Mission Statement: To advance the art, science, and enjoyment of Amateur Radio.
ARRL's Vision Statement: As the national association for Amateur Radio in the United States, ARRL:

- Supports the awareness and growth of Amateur Radio worldwide;
- Advocates for meaningful access to radio spectrum;
- Strives for every member to get involved, get active, and get on the air;
- Encourages radio experimentation and, through its members, advances radio technology and education; and
- Organizes and trains volunteers to serve their communities by providing public service and emergency communications.

At ARRL headquarters in the Hartford, Connecticut suburb of Newington, the staff helps serve the needs of members. ARRL publishes the monthly journal *QST* and an interactive digital version of *QST*, as well as newsletters and many publications covering all aspects of Amateur Radio. Its headquarters station, W1AW, transmits bulletins of interest to radio amateurs and Morse code practice sessions. ARRL also coordinates an extensive field organization, which includes volunteers who provide technical information and other support services for radio amateurs as well as communications for public service activities. In addition, ARRL represents US radio amateurs to the Federal Communications Commission and other government agencies in the US and abroad.

Membership in ARRL means much more than receiving *QST* each month. In addition to the services already described, ARRL offers membership services on a personal level, such as the Technical Information Service, where members can get answers — by phone, e-mail, or the ARRL website — to all their technical and operating questions.

A bona fide interest in Amateur Radio is the only essential qualification of membership; an Amateur Radio license is not a prerequisite, although full voting membership is granted only to licensed radio amateurs in the US. Full ARRL membership gives you a voice in how the affairs of the organization are governed. ARRL policy is set by a Board of Directors (one from each of 15 Divisions). Each year, one-third of the ARRL Board of Directors stands for election by the full members they represent. The day-to-day operation of ARRL HQ is managed by a Chief Executive Officer and his/her staff.

Join ARRL Today! No matter what aspect of Amateur Radio attracts you, ARRL membership is relevant and important. There would be no Amateur Radio as we know it today were it not for ARRL. We would be happy to welcome you as a member! Join online at **www.arrl.org/join**. For more information about ARRL and answers to any questions you may have about Amateur Radio, write or call:

ARRL — The national association for Amateur Radio®
225 Main Street
Newington CT 06111-1494
Tel: 860-594-0200
FAX: 860-594-0259
e-mail: **hq@arrl.org**
www.arrl.org

Prospective new radio amateurs call (toll-free):
800-32-NEW HAM (800-326-3942)
You can also contact ARRL via e-mail at **newham@arrl.org**
or check out the ARRL website at **www.arrl.org**

ARRL Members Get it All!

Members-Only Web Services

- **QST Digital Edition**
  In addition to the printed copy of *QST*, all members have access to the online, monthly digital version at no additional cost. *QST* apps are also available.

- **Archives**
  ARRL members can browse ARRL's extensive online *QST* archive, including downloading and viewing *QST* product reviews. *QST* Product Reviews help our members make smarter, more informed purchasing decisions for Amateur Radio equipment.

- **E-Mail Forwarding Service**
  E-mail sent to your arrl.net address will be forwarded to any e-mail account you specify.

- **E-Newsletters**
  Subscribe to the weekly ARRL Letter and a variety of other e-newsletters and announcements: ham radio news, radio clubs, public service, contesting and more!

FREE Book Offer!

Join ARRL Today!

Go to **www.arrl.org/join/HRLM**
to become a member and select your free gift

Make your gift choice from a selection of books chosen for new hams. Family memberships do not qualify. Please allow 4-6 weeks for delivery.

Membership Application

☑ Membership options (circle your choice/s)

	1 Year	2 Years	3 Years	
US	$49	$95	$140	Monthly *QST* via standard mail for US members
Youth	$25			Must be 21 years old or younger AND the oldest licensed Radio Amateur in the household
Canada	$62	$120	$177	Monthly *QST* via standard mail for Canadian members
International	$76	$147	$217	Monthly *QST* via standard mail for international members
International/Canada – no print *QST*	$49	$95	$140	Digital *QST* only
Family	$10	$20	$30	Must reside with primary member and have corresponding membership dates; no extra copies of *QST*

Additional membership options are available at www.arrl.org/join Membership includes $21 per year for subscription to *QST*. Dues subject to change without notice and are nonrefundable.

Name _____ Call Sign _____

Street _____ City _____ State _____ ZIP _____

E-mail _____ Phone _____ Date of Birth _____

Family Member Name _____ Call Sign (if any) _____

☑ Payment Options

- ☐ Total enclosed payable to ARRL $ _____
- ☐ Visa ☐ MasterCard ☐ Amex ☐ Discover ☐ Check Enclosed

☐ I do not want my name and address made available for non-ARRL related mailings.

Card Number _____ Expiration Date _____

Cardholder's Signature _____

 ARRL, 225 Main St. Newington, CT 06111   **1-888-277-5289** 🖱 **www.arrl.org/join**

HRLM 2018

When to Expect New Books

A Question Pool Committee (QPC) consisting of representatives from the various Volunteer Examiner Coordinators (VECs) prepares the license question pools. The QPC establishes a schedule for revising and implementing new question pools. The current question pool revision schedule is as follows:

Question Pool	Current Study Guides	Valid Through
Technician (Element 2)	*The ARRL Ham Radio License Manual*, 4th Edition *ARRL's Tech Q&A*, 7th Edition	June 30, 2022
General (Element 3)	*The ARRL General Class License Manual*, 8th edition *ARRL's General Q&A*, 5th Edition	June 30, 2019
Amateur Extra (Element 4)	*The ARRL Extra Class License Manual*, 11th Edition *ARRL's Extra Q&A*, 4th Edition	June 30, 2020

As new question pools are released, ARRL will produce new study materials before the effective date of the new Pools. Until then, the current Question Pools will remain in use, and current ARRL study materials, including this book, will help you prepare for your exam.

As the new question pool schedules are confirmed, the information will be published in *QST* and on the ARRL website at **www.arrl.org**.

Online Review and Practice Exams

Use this book with the online *ARRL Exam Review for Ham Radio* to review material you are learning chapter-by-chapter. Take randomly generated practice exams using questions from the actual examination question pool. You won't have any surprises on exam day! Go to **www.arrl.org/examreview**.

The ARRL Ham Radio License Manual ON THE WEB

www.arrl.org/ham-radio-license-manual

Visit *The ARRL Ham Radio Class License Manual* home on the
web for additional resources.

How to Use this Book

The ARRL Ham Radio License Manual is designed to help you learn about every topic in the Technician exam question pool. Every page presents information you'll need to pass the exam and become an effective operator. This book goes well beyond the answers to exam questions — it also contains explanations, guidelines, and helpful information to help you remember and use what you learn on the air.

The book is organized to help you learn about radio and operating in easy-to-understand, bite-sized steps. You'll begin by learning about the basics of radio signals and simple ham radio equipment. The next steps cover the principles of electricity and an introduction to electrical components. You'll then learn how a simple station is assembled and some basic operating procedures. At that point, you'll be ready to understand and remember the rules and regulations of ham radio. The final section is about ham radio safety and related topics.

In each section of the book, the exam questions are included for easy reference. The material most directly answering the question is followed by the question's ID in bold text, such as **[T1A01]**. This will help you learn exactly what you need to pass the exam with material that addresses each question. The question pool in Chapter 11 also includes a page reference where each topic is discussed.

At the back of this book you'll also find a large glossary of ham radio words and a selection of advertisements from some vendors of ham radio equipment and supplies.

Conventions

Throughout your studies keep a sharp eye out for words in *italics*. These words are important so be sure you understand them. Many of them are included in the glossary. Another thing to look for is the web mouse symbol, indicating that there is supplemental information on the *Ham Radio License Manual* website (**www.arrl.org/ham-radio-license-manual**) to support and extend what you learn. If a web or e-mail address is included, it will be printed in **boldface type**.

Question IDs are shown in square brackets, such as **[T1A01]**. These are the identifying num-ber for each question in the exam's question pool. This will help you find the material answering each question.

The Exam Question Pool

The complete Technician exam question pool is included at the back of this book. The 35 questions you'll answer on the exam will be drawn from this question pool. Yes, these are the actual questions on the exam but resist the temptation to just memorize the answers! Memorizing without learning the subject is likely to leave you "high and dry" when you begin using your new operating privileges. Do yourself a favor and take the time to understand the material.

When using the question pool for exam practice, each question also includes a cross-reference back to the page of the book covering that topic. If you don't completely understand the question or answer, please go back and review that material. The question IDs in bold, for example **[T1A01]**, will help you find the answers quickly

Self-Study and Classroom Tips

For self-study students, the material in the book is designed to be studied in order from beginning to end. Read the material and then test your understanding by answering the questions at the end of each section. Use the supplemental material on the *Ham Radio License* Manual website if you need extra help.

The ARRL's *New Ham Desk* can answer questions emailed to **newham@arrl.org**. Your question may be answered directly or you might be directed to more instruction material. The *New Ham Desk* can also help you find a local ham to answer questions. Studying with a friend makes learning the material more fun as you help each other over the rough spots and you'll have someone to celebrate with after passing the exam!

If you are taking a licensing class, the instructors will guide you through the material. Help your instructors by letting them know where you need more assistance. They want you to learn as thoroughly and quickly as possible, so don't hold back your questions. Similarly, if you find their explanations particularly clear or helpful, tell them that, so it can be used in the next class!

At the end of each section is a good time to pause for a short review session. Be sure you understand the material by answering the questions before moving to the next section. It is a lot easier to learn the material section-by-section than by rushing ahead and you'll remember it more clearly. For a focused discussion on each exam question, pick up a copy of the *ARRL's Tech Q&A*. Every question is included with the correct answer and a short explanation.

To make the best use of the on-line reference material, bookmark the *Ham Radio License Manual* website to use as an online reference while you study. The web page includes

Choosing Your First Ham Radio

After you pass your exam, you'll need a radio so the ARRL has provided *Choosing Your First Ham Radio*, a guide to making that first selection. It is available on this book's website for downloading and will answer a lot of questions you have about important features and some of the terms you'll need to know as you look over the different models. Your mentor will help you along the way, too!

other resources organized by section and chapter to follow the book. Browse these links for extra information.

Online Practice Exams

As you complete each chapter of this book, use ARRL's online Exam Review for Ham Radio to help prepare for exam day. This web-based service uses the question pool to construct chapter-by-chapter reviews. Once you've finished this book, use the online service to take practice exams with the same number and variety of questions that you'll encounter on exam day. You can practice taking the test over and over again in complete privacy (even print practice exams!).

These exams are quite realistic and you get quick feedback about the questions you missed. When you find yourself passing the online exams by a comfortable margin, you'll be ready for the real thing.

 To begin using ARRL Exam Review for Ham Radio, go to **www.arrl.org/examreview**.

Chapter 1

Welcome to Amateur Radio

In this chapter, you'll learn about:

- **What makes Amateur Radio unique**
- **Why the FCC makes the rules**
- **What activities you'll find in Amateur Radio**
- **Where you can find other hams**
- **The Technician license — what it is and how to get it**
- **Ready? Set? Go!**

When you see the mouse, you'll find more information at www.arrl.org/ham-radio-license-manual

Welcome to the *Ham Radio License Manual*, the most popular introduction to Amateur Radio of all! In this study guide, not only will you learn enough to pass your Technician license exam, you'll also learn what ham radio is all about and how to jump right in once you're ready to get on the air.

If you want to know more about amateur or "ham" radio before you start preparing to get a license, you'll find your answers in sections beginning with "What is Amateur Radio?" If you already know about ham radio and are anxious to get started, you're in good company — there are thousands of other folks getting ready to become a ham radio operator. Jump ahead to section 1.4 — "Getting Your Ham Radio License" and get started!

1.1 What is Amateur Radio?

Amateur Radio will surprise you with all its different activities. If you've encountered Amateur Radio in a public service role or if someone you know has a ham radio in their home or car, then you already have some ideas. Maybe you have seen ham radio in a movie or read about it in a book. Are you a part of a maker community? If so, you'll really enjoy getting involved with one of the most "hands-on" hobbies of all. Amateur Radio is the most powerful communications

Jerry Clement, VE6AB, demonstrates that you don't need much equipment to make contacts through a ham radio satellite.

What's an Elmer?

As someone learning about Amateur Radio, you'll hear the term "Elmer" and "Elmering" a lot! A ham radio "Elmer" is someone who personally guides and tutors a new ham, both before and after getting a license. It doesn't refer to anyone in particular, just the more experienced hams who help newcomers.

Using the word "Elmer" to mean "mentor" is unique to ham radio. Rick Lindquist, WW1ME traces the origin of the term to the March 1971 issue of *QST* magazine; the term appeared in a "How's DX" column by Rod Newkirk, W9BRD. Rod's mentor was a ham named Elmer and Rod thought every new ham should have an Elmer of their own. The name stuck and since then, "Elmering" has meant "helping."

Every ham has at least one Elmer at some point. You will, too, and if someone refers to you as "their Elmer," you can be proud.

Ham operators (from left) Rochelle, AE7ZQ, Kevin, N2LGN, Greg, NF7H, and ICS Commander Tina Birch staffed the Multnomah County (Oregon) EOC during a recent Simulated Emergency Test. [Nathan Hersey, N9VCU, photo]

Who Made the "Ham"?

How did "amateur" become "ham"? The real answer is unknown! Even before radio, telegraphers referred to a poor operator as a ham. Perhaps this was derived from a poor operator being "ham-fisted" on the telegraph key — an operator's "fist" referred to his or her distinctive style over the wires. With all radio stations sharing the same radio spectrum in the early days, commercial and military operators would sometimes refer to amateurs as hams when there was interference. Regardless, amateurs adopted the term as a badge of honor and proudly refer to each other as "hams" today.

service available to the private citizen anywhere on Earth — or even above it!

Amateur Radio is a recognized national asset, providing trained operators, technical specialists and disaster response communications in time of need. It was created for people just like you who have an interest in radio communications. Some hams prefer to focus on the technology and science of radio. Competitive events and award programs hold the interest of others. Some train to use radio in support of emergency response efforts, to provide public service, or to keep in touch with family. There are many hams who simply like to talk with other hams, too. This introductory section of the *Ham Radio License Manual* will give you a broad overview of Amateur Radio so you can understand how radio works and why hams do what they do. Let's start at the beginning, shall we?

BEGINNINGS OF HAM RADIO

Amateur Radio has been around since the beginning of radio communications. It wasn't long after Marconi spanned the Atlantic in 1901 before curious folks began experimenting with "wireless." Amateur Radio more or less invented itself, right along with broadcasting and wireless telegraphy. The very first amateur licenses were granted back in 1912 and the number of hams grew rapidly. Early stations used "spark," literally a vigorous and noisy electrical arc, to generate radio waves. Inefficient and hazardous, spark was soon replaced by far more effective vacuum tube transmitters. By the end of the 1920s both voice and Morse code could be heard on the airwaves. Radio became very popular, instantly connecting communities and individuals as they had never been before.

As radio communication became widespread, the Federal Communications Commission (FCC) was created to regulate the competing radio uses, including broadcasting, commercial message and news services, military communications, and public safety. The Amateur service (the legal name for Amateur Radio) was created in 1934 and has expanded in size and capability ever since.

Amateurs, skilled in the ways of radio, played crucial roles during World War II as operators and radio engineers. After the war, thousands of hams turned to radio and electronics as a profession, fueling the rapid advances in communications during the 1950s and 60s. Amateur Radio evolved right along with industry — spanning the globe was commonplace! With Morse code as popular as ever, the amateur airwaves were also filling with voice and radioteletype signals. Hams even invented a new form of picture transmission called slow-scan television that used regular voice transmitters and receivers. The first satellite built by amateurs, called OSCAR-1, was launched in 1961, transmitting a simple Morse message back to Earth for several weeks.

Through the 1970s amateurs built an extensive network of relay "repeater" stations to provide regional communications with low-power mobile and handheld radios. In the 1980s and 1990s, microprocessors were quickly applied to radio, greatly increasing the capabilities of amateur equipment and ushering in a new era of digital communications. Packet radio, an adaptation of computer network technology, was developed by hams and is now widely used for commercial and public safety communications.

The personal computer, as in many other fields, gave amateurs a powerful new tool for design, modeling, station automation, and recordkeeping, as well as making Amateur

Hams have been building "OSCAR" satellites for decades. OSCAR stands for Orbiting Satellite Carrying Amateur Radio. These photos show Lance Ginner, K6GSJ, holding the first OSCAR launched in 1961 and a flight model of a modern satellite — FUNcube-1.

That's Why It's Called "Amateur" Radio

In order to keep businesses or municipalities from unfairly exploiting the amateur bands, amateurs are strictly forbidden from receiving compensation for their activities. That means you can't talk with a co-worker about an assignment, for example. If you provide communications for a parade or charity activity, you can't accept a fee. This keeps radio amateurs free to explore and improve and train — it's worked well for many years.

Radio computer networks a reality. Finally, the internet arrived and hams quickly adapted the new technology to their own uses just as they had many times before. At each step in the development of today's communication-intensive world, hams have contributed either as part of their profession or as individuals pursuing a personal passion.

HAM RADIO TODAY

Here more than a century later and wireless is still very much at the forefront of communications technology. Far from being eclipsed by the internet, ham radio continues its tradition of innovation by combining the internet with radio technologies in new ways. Hams have created their own wireless data networks, position reporting systems, and even a radio-based e-mail network that enables the most solitary ham to "log in" from anywhere in the world. Voice communications hop between internet and radio links to connect hams on the opposite sides of the globe using only handheld transmitters less powerful than a flashlight!

Don't let anyone tell you that Morse code is finished. It's still very much alive in Amateur Radio where its simplicity and efficiency continue to make it popular. Amateurs also speak to each other directly using sophisticated radios that are grown-up versions of the Citizen's Band (CB) and Family Radio Service (FRS) radios available at local electronics stores. Computers are a big part of ham radio today as hams chat "keyboard-to-keyboard" or send pictures via radio. You'll even find some hams assembling their own TV stations and transmitting professional-quality video!

In step with the telecommunications industry, hams also look to the skies for their communications. Amateur Radio satellites whirling through orbit connect hams on the ground by voice, Morse code, and data signals. There is a ham station on the International Space Station used by astronauts (most astronauts have ham licenses) and ground-based

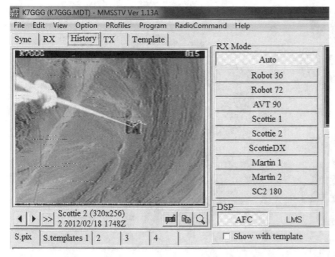

Hams perform experiments with Amateur Radio, too, such as this high-altitude balloon that carried a slow-scan TV transmitter to 88,000 feet! [Courtesy Gary Miller, K7GGG]

Edison High School (Queens, NY) students Kolsuma Begum, KD2DME, and Karl Anthony Singh, KD2DMF, are holding CSCEs that document they just passed their Technician exams! Their mentor (or Elmer) at left is Fred, N2EGQ, and the Volunteer Examiner team (left to right) are Rich, W2RB, Pete, K2IQK, and Mike, W2RT.

The Goldfarb Scholarship winner for 2015 was Jacob Nunez-Kearney, KF7DSY, of Mesa, Arizona. Jacob is studying aerospace engineering at Purdue University and has been an intern with NASA's Johnson Space Center in Houston, Texas.

Operating with a portable station as part of a hike or camping trip is a lot of fun. Tommy, W4TZM, operated from the summit of Wesser Bald (North Carolina) during the North Carolina QSO Party. [Tom Mitchell, photo]

hams. Ham-written software allows signals to be bounced off the Moon and even meteor trails in the Earth's atmosphere.

When disaster strikes, you will find hams responding quickly and capably in support of public safety agencies and relief organizations such as the Red Cross and the National Hurricane Center. Amateur Radio is an important part of many response and relief efforts. Hams also turn out in great numbers to provide communications for parades, sporting events, festivals, and other public occasions.

While Amateur Radio got its start long ago as a collection of tinkerers in basements and backyard "shacks" — the origin of the term "radio shack" — it has grown to become a worldwide communications service with millions of licensees. The tinkerers are very much still with us, of course, creating new and useful ways of putting radio to work. You will find that ham radio has more facets than you could imagine and they're growing in number every day.

WHO CAN BE A HAM?

Are you ready to join us? Anyone can become a ham! It doesn't matter how old you are or how much you know about radio when you begin. One of ham radio's most enjoyable aspects is that you're on a first-name basis with every other ham, whether you're an elementary school student, a CEO, an astronaut, or a long-distance truck driver. There are also thousands of people with disabilities for whom ham radio is a new window to the world.

Hams range in age from six to more than one hundred years old. While some are technically skilled, holding positions as scientists, engineers, or technicians, all walks of life are represented on the airwaves.

Musicians? Try Joe Walsh, WB6ACU, guitarist for the Eagles. Nobel Prize winner? Meet Joe Taylor, K1JT. Athlete? Now active in radiosport competitions, Joe Rudi, NK7U,

Handihams — No Barriers to Ham Radio

Amateur Radio presents an opportunity to communicate and participate for those with disabilities. Disabled hams often use their unique talents to make valuable contributions over the airwaves, even though they might not be physically present or active. The Courage Kenny Rehabilitation Institute sponsors the Courage Kenny Handiham Program (**www.handiham.org**) to help people with physical disabilities obtain amateur licenses. The system provides materials and instruction to persons with disabilities interested in obtaining ham licenses. The Program also provides information to other hams, dubbed "verticals," who wish to help people with disabilities earn a license.

is a retired major league outfielder and MVP! Why not imagine your name and call sign up there in lights?

The photo nearby shows Glenn Johnson, WØGJ, operating from Desecheo Island as K5D. Glenn is a pediatric surgeon and sometimes combines ham radio with his travels to donate medical services. He has been the ARRL's Humanitarian of the Year and has operated from many far-away places such as Bhutan and the Andaman Islands.

Rachel Finerman, KI6PJY, and Christina Soltero, KI6QLR, worked together as a two-student team to help build an Elecraft K2 HF transceiver kit at Granite Bay Montessori School in California. The 4th through 8th-grade students also assembled and installed a GAP Titan vertical antenna and operate the K6GBM repeater on the UHF band of 70 centimeters. As part of learning about science, more than 20 students have earned their Technician license and several have upgraded to General.

One of radio contesting's most enjoyable challenges is operating mobile or portable, putting rare counties or other locations on the air. At VHF and UHF, "hilltopping" is a popular way of greatly extending a station's range. Microwave enthusiasts like the Jacobsens, Tammy, KI7GVT, and Kevin, AD7OI, look for DX (long-distance) contacts from special locations that offer regular tropospheric paths over dozens or hundreds of miles, such as a southern California ridge overlooking the deserts below.

Developing a world-wide ham community of students and young adults, YOTA (**www.ham-yota.com**) organizes on-the-air and in-person events. The annual get-together in 2018 is being held in South Africa. The accompanying photo shows the Estonian team operating in one of the competitions held at a recent YOTA conference. Watch for special call signs ending in YOTA during "YOTA months!"

Glenn, WØGJ, took a break from his surgery practice to operate from Desecheo Island as K5D.

Microwave contesters such as Tammy, KI7GVT, and Kevin, AD7OI, often travel to special locations to make long-distance contacts. [Kevin Jacobson, AD7OI, photo]

Richard, W5WKQ, made hundreds of contacts from orbit aboard the International Space Station (ISS).

Estonian hams Keijo, ES1XQ, Tauri, ES5HTA, Keven, ES6AXS, and Lithuanians Simonas, LY2EN, and Linas, LY5AT joined numerous other young hams in a recent Youngsters On the Air (YOTA) conference featuring competitions, seminars, and socializing. [Martti Laine, OH2BH, photo]

Rachel, KI6PJY (left), and Christina, KI6QLR, helped build a radio from kit with the rest of the Granite Bay Montessori School students.

Taking ham radio to new heights, astronaut Richard Garriott, W5WKQ, operated from aboard the International Space Station (ISS), using the call sign NA1SS. Richard contacted more than 500 different hams from the ISS in a 12-day visit to space. Richard's father Owen, W5LFL, was the first ham in space from aboard the Space Shuttle in 1984. Nearly all of the US and Russian astronauts have ham licenses, contacting both individual hams and students in school classrooms from orbit.

Picnic, Training, or Contest? It's ARRL Field Day!

The most popular ham radio event of all is called ARRL Field Day, held on the fourth full weekend of June every year. More than 30,000 hams participate across the United States, Canada, and the Caribbean. (European clubs hold their own Field Day on different weekends.) The goal is to exercise your abilities to set up and operate radio equipment "in the field" as if an emergency or disaster occurs. Field Day takes on all the aspects of a competition, emergency exercise and club picnic — it's all three! Visitors, particularly prospective hams like you, are welcome at these events and there's no better way to learn about ham radio. See the ARRL website for more information.

Members of the Ski Country Amateur Radio Club of Carbondale, Colorado, had a great time on the Western Slope during the ARRL Field Day. [Peter Buckley, NØECT, photo]

WHAT DO HAMS DO?

There are so many things that hams do that it's almost easier to tell you what they don't do! The image most people have of a ham is someone with headphones hunched over a stack of glowing radios, listening to crackling voices from around the globe. We certainly do that — thousands of contacts span the oceans every day — but there is so much more!

Talking

Hams talk, literally, more than any other way of communicating. After all, it's the way humans are built. For that reason, most ham radios are made for voice communication. Relay stations called repeaters allow hams using low-power radios to talk with each over a wide region, 50 miles or more. Hams also bounce signals off the upper layers of the atmosphere, making contacts around the globe. Even computer-to-computer speech is available on ham radio, across town or to a distant repeater system on another continent.

Byte-ing

Hams also use digital "codes" to communicate. By connecting a computer to a radio, digital information can be sent over the air waves. This is one of the most exciting facets of 21st-century ham radio. One popular style is simple "keyboard-to-keyboard" communications similar to mobile-phone texting. Hams are busy devising and using new techniques of making contacts using state-of-the-art modulation and encoding. Not only are hams sending digital data, they're inventing new ways of doing it, too!

Sending

The oldest method hams use is the venerable Morse code, now well into its second century of use. Far from being a useless antique, Morse transmissions are simple to generate and very efficient. Hams also love the musicality of "the code" and have devised many ways to generate Morse, from the original "straight key" to fancy electronic versions and even via computer keyboards. Morse has a language all its own, both in its clear, pure tones and in the mannerisms with which hams connect and converse.

Building

Unlike many other radio communication services, you are allowed — no, encouraged — to build and repair your own equipment, from the radio itself to the antennas and any accessory you can think of. Hams call this build-it-yourself ethic "homebrewing" and are proud to use equipment and accessories they built themselves. You'll find hams constructing anything from high-power, signal-boosting amplifiers to a miniature hand-built radio that fits in a metal candy tin! Hams have been responsible for numerous advances in the state of the antenna art as they tinker and test, too. If you like to know what's "under the hood" you'll find many like-minded friends in ham radio.

Watching

Hams have devised many ways of exchanging pictures and video. Many years ago, hams used teletype to send pictures made from text characters. Today a ham can set up a video camera and transmit pictures every bit as good as professional video. This is called ATV for amateur television, and there are even ATV transmitters flying in model aircraft and balloons that ascend to the edge of space! Hams pioneered the use of regular voice transmitters to send still photographs as "slow-scan television" over long-distance paths to hams thousands of miles away.

Hams Respond in Times of Need

Hurricanes Harvey, Irma, and Maria wreaked havoc on Texas, Puerto Rico, the US Virgin Islands, and across the Caribbean in the fall of 2017. Before, during, and after the storms, ARRL Amateur Radio Emergency Service (ARES)® volunteers were active and worked closely with the National Weather Service and the National Hurricane Center to report on local conditions. Since mobile and landline telephones, electrical power, cable TV, and internet service were knocked out, amateur voice and digital links were put to work at EOCs (Emergency Operations Centers), Red Cross shelters, and supported numerous other agencies and facilities in the affected areas. The amateur response lasted well beyond the duration of the storms and continued as the Caribbean communities struggled to rebuild.

While these major storms were incredibly damaging and costly, amateurs respond to many other events that can be just as devastating on a local scale. Hams are called when tornados strike in the Midwest and Southeast. In the West, hams support wildfire responders in the rugged mountain terrain that stretches from San Diego to Colorado and Montana. Around the world, hams were there when earthquakes leveled cities in China and monsoons flooded cities and created landslides in Southeast Asia.

These stories offer just a tiny glimpse of how Amateur Radio operators respond when their communities are damaged or destroyed. You'll find that becoming a radio amateur gives you an opportunity to learn the skills and techniques necessary to be of service when called upon. It's one of the most valued features of the Amateur service.

Emergency Communications and Public Service

One of the reasons Amateur Radio continues to enjoy its privileged position on the airwaves is the legendary ability of hams to organize and respond to disasters and emergencies. Because ham radio doesn't depend on extensive support systems, ham stations are likely to be able to operate while the public communications networks are recovering from a hurricane or earthquake. Hams are also self-organized in teams that train to respond quickly and provide communications wherever it's needed. It's not necessary to have a big emergency for hams to pitch in. We also provide public service by assisting with communications at parades and sporting events, or by serving as weather watchers.

Hams recognize the value of Amateur Radio to their communities and have created training programs such as the ARRL Amateur Radio Emergency Service (ARES®) that promote readiness. The ARRL offers emergency communications training classes over the internet. Hams often work closely with other citizen volunteer teams. Many are also certified as emergency response workers with a wide variety of skills such as first aid, search-and-rescue and so forth. Hams hone their message-handling skills in nets so that they'll be ready when called upon for real.

AMATEUR RADIO CLUBS AND ORGANIZATIONS

Helping newcomers is one of ham radio's oldest traditions. After all, we are all "amateurs," learning and training together. Nearly every ham has mentored or *Elmered* another ham at one time or another. You'll be amazed at the amount of sharing within the ham community. Your ham radio support group comes in many forms — a fellow student or classmate, a nearby ham, a club or even a nationwide organization. All of them are resources for you, not only during your studies for the licensing exam, but also after you have your call sign and are learning how to be a ham.

If you haven't already found a local radio club, you can find one by using the ARRL's *Affiliated Club Search* on the ARRL website. There are several types of clubs; some specialize in one type of operating or public service. Most are "general interest" clubs for the members to socialize, learn, and help each other out — a good first choice. Don't hesitate to make use of the contact info and attend a meeting! Many clubs make an extra effort to offer special assistance to aspiring and new hams.

Once you decide on a club, you'll get a lot more than just study help by participating

Eagle Scout Carey, N5RM, demonstrates ham radio to another Scout at the John Nickels Scout Ranch (Oklahoma) during the Jamboree On the Air (JOTA).

Ross, KR4USA, and his daughter Hope look for some contacts on the "magic band" — 6 meters — during Field Day at K4PJ, the Oak Ridge (Tennessee) Amateur Radio Club.

in the club activities. Log on to the club website. Take advantage of open houses, work parties, or operating events, and maybe attend those informal lunches or breakfasts. Be sure to introduce yourself to the club officers and let them know you're a visitor or new member. Is there another new member? Buddy up! Soon you'll be one of the regulars.

WHAT MAKES AMATEUR RADIO DIFFERENT?

There are lots of other types of two-way radios you can buy in a store — Citizen's Band, handheld FRS/GMRS "walkabouts," marine radio for boaters — what is it about Amateur Radio that sets it apart? In a word — variety. You'll find that each of the radio types listed in **Table 1.1** is designed for just a few purposes and they might do that well. Amateur Radio, on the other hand, is tremendously flexible with many different types of signals and radio bands. As a ham, you're not restricted to any one combination; you can experiment and try different things as much as you want to get the job done.

Unlicensed Personal Radios

The most popular personal radios are the FRS/GMRS handheld radios that are seemingly sold everywhere. FRS stands for Family Radio Service and GMRS stands for General Mobile Radio Service. These radios use a set of 22 channels in a narrow frequency band best suited for short-range, line-of-sight communications. (You may be unaware that using the GMRS channels and features of the radio requires a license! It's in the manual's fine print.) Without the GMRS license, your maximum 1/2 watt of transmitter output power limits you to communications over a few hundred yards to a couple of miles. You can't extend your range with repeaters, nor can you use more powerful mobile radios.

Citizens Band remains popular in the applications for which it was originally intended. Mobile radios in vehicles, boats, and farm equipment provide useful, medium-range radio communications to other vehicles or with radios at home or at work. Handheld radios are also popular. CB radios have 40 channels (more with selectable sidebands) and communication is fairly reliable over a range of several miles.

Boaters will be familiar with marine VHF radios used for boats to communicate with each other and with stations on shore. These radios can use up to 50 channels for communicating around harbors and for short-range needs during both fresh and salt-water travel.

All three of these radios are designed to use a set of channels selected for a single type of communications as shown in Table 1.1. They do their designated job well. Amateurs have access to a much broader range of communications options and create new ways of communicating that are more powerful and flexible than those of the unlicensed radio services. If you find your personal radio interesting, but limited, then Amateur Radio is definitely the place for you.

Business and Public Safety Radio

Table 1.1

Types of Personal Radio

Service	Channels	Intended Use	Range
Citizens Band (CB)	40	Private/Business	10 miles +
Marine VHF	50	Maritime	20 miles +
Family Radio Service (FRS)	22	Personal	2 miles
Multi-Use Radio Service (MURS)	5	Personal	5 miles+

ARRL — The National Association for Amateur Radio®

The American Radio Relay League (ARRL) has been an integral part of Amateur Radio from the very beginning. The ARRL offers more assistance to potential and licensed hams than any other organization, including operating the largest of the Volunteer Examiner Coordinators and working on behalf of all hams with the FCC and Congress. The core missions of the ARRL are:

• Public Service

The ARRL actively promotes the public service aspects of Amateur Radio, a tradition that has earned respect through decades of service. The ARRL's legacy of public service began in 1935 with the creation of the Amateur Radio Emergency Service, better known as ARES, to provide communication support during natural and man-made disasters.

• Advocacy

The ARRL represents Amateur Radio at the local, state, federal and international levels. Thanks to the efforts of the ARRL, Amateur Radio has been able to thrive despite repeated attempts to restrict its growth. The ARRL serves as a voice for Amateur Radio before regulatory agencies such as the Federal Communications Commission (FCC) and the International Telecommunication Union (ITU).

• Education

The educational mission of the ARRL is twofold. (1) To recruit new amateurs, the ARRL publishes books and study guides such as this one for Amateur Radio license exams, maintains a mentor program for new hams and much more. (2) The ARRL also promotes ham radio in school classrooms, advocating its use as a tool to teach science and technology. To that end, the ARRL assists teachers with appropriate instructional materials and training.

• Technology

The ARRL promotes technical skills and training for all amateurs. It publishes more Amateur Radio technical material — in print and online — than any other amateur organization in the world. The *ARRL Handbook* and *ARRL Antenna Book* have been amateur and professional references for decades. The ARRL's online *Technical Information Service* provides numerous resources on technical topics. *QEX* is the ARRL's magazine for advanced technology and presents state-of-the-art information in each issue.

• Membership

The majority of active amateurs belong to the ARRL, and for good reason! In addition to all the member services listed above, ARRL members receive *QST* magazine each month and can subscribe to an entire roster of e-mailed newsletters and bulletins. Members also have full access to the extensive ARRL website. The ARRL also sponsors the largest *radiosport* program in the world with an event for every mode of operating. Membership does not require a license and costs about the same as a couple of large pizzas, with considerably longer-lasting benefits!

• *QST* — The Amateur's Magazine

QST is the authoritative source for news and information on any topic that's part of, or relates to, Amateur Radio It is available in print and digital formats, whichever you prefer. In each colorful issue you'll find technical articles and informative Product Reviews of the newest radios and accessories from handheld and mobile FM radios, to home station transceivers, antennas, and even shortwave radios. Each month's Convention and Hamfest Calendar shows you who's getting together at hamfests, conventions, and swap meets in your area. Whether you're interested in radiosport contests, DXing, or radios, accessories and antennas you can build at home, *QST* covers them all: New trends and the latest technology, news, club activities, rules and regulations, special events and much more.

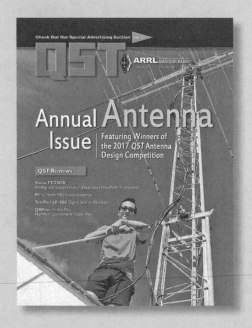

Every day you can see police and firemen using handheld and mobile radios as part of their jobs. Many businesses also have their employees use similar radios. How do these relate to Amateur Radio? The FCC has created radio services for public agencies and private businesses. These organizations, public and private, are all licensed, just like hams must be, although the individual users need not have a license. The electronics in these radios are very similar to those of radios that hams use, sometimes identical. In fact, many a ham has converted a surplus commercial or public safety radio to ham radio use. While business and public safety radio users are restricted to just a few "channels," though, hams can use their radios on hundreds of channels and for far more varied uses.

1.2 The FCC and Licensing

The Federal Communications Commission (FCC) is charged with administering all of the radio signals transmitted by US radio stations. The FCC also coordinates these transmissions with other countries as part of the International Telecommunication Union (ITU). While you may not need a license to use an FRS or CB radio, the vast majority of radio users must have a license or be employed by a company that has a license. This section explains how licensing works for Amateur Radio.

WHY GET A LICENSE?

Amateurs are free to choose from many types of radios and activities — that's what you get in return for passing the license exam. If you can learn the basics of radio and the rules of Amateur Radio, then the opportunities of ham radio are all yours! Just remember that the license is there to ensure that you understand the basics before transmitting. This helps keep Amateur Radio useful and enjoyable to everyone.

Why don't people just buy radios and transmit anyway? (This is called "bootlegging" or "pirating.") First of all, it's quite apparent to hams who has and who hasn't passed a license exam. You'll find yourself attracting the attention of the FCC but more importantly, you won't fit in and you won't have fun.

One of the most important benefits to being licensed is that you have the right to be protected from interference by signals from unlicensed devices, such as consumer electronics. Your right to use the amateur bands is similarly protected. The protection doesn't work perfectly all the time, but nevertheless, as a licensed amateur operator, your license is recognized by law. This is a big improvement over unlicensed radio users. It's definitely worth the effort to get that license!

LICENSING OVERVIEW

The FCC has a different set of rules for each type of radio use. These uses are called *services*. Each service was created for a specific purpose — Land Mobile, Aviation, and Broadcasting, for example. Nearly all services require that a license be obtained before transmissions are made. These are called *licensed services* and the Amateur service is one such service.

Most services do not require an examination to be licensed. This is because the FCC sets strict technical standards for the radio equipment used in these services and restricts how those radios may be used. This tradeoff reduces the training required for those radio users. Licensing in these services is primarily a method to control access to the airwaves.

Amateurs, on the other hand, have great latitude in how we use radios. We can build and repair our own radios. The procedures we use to communicate are completely up to us. We can operate however we want, with few restrictions. This flexibility requires that amateurs be more knowledgeable than the typical user in other services so we don't cause interference to them. That is why amateurs have to pass a licensing examination.

Amateur Licenses

Once upon a time, the FCC gave the exams for Amateur Radio licenses. In those days, hams often had to travel long distances to get to a regional Federal Building, stand in lines for hours, sit on uncomfortable chairs, and sweat their way through exams graded by grim-faced proctors. It's a wonder any of them survived the experience!

Today, amateurs give and grade the exams ourselves under the guidance of a Volunteer Examiner Coordinator (VEC). There are currently 14 different clubs or organizations recognized as VECs by the FCC. These make up the National Conference of Volunteer Examiner Coordinators (NCVEC). The NCVEC elects representatives to write the questions used for the license exam *question pool*. The representatives make up the Question Pool Committee. There is one question pool for each class of amateur license.

Each VEC also certifies Volunteer Examiners (VEs) who actually administer the exam sessions. The VEC then handles the paperwork for each license exam and application. That doesn't mean you won't sweat a little bit, but the examination process is not as imposing as it seems.

The result of passing the exam is an *operator license* (or "ticket") granted by the FCC after it receives the necessary paperwork from the VEC that administered your exam session. The license also specifies a call sign that becomes your radio identity.

There are three classes of license being granted today: the Technician, General, and Amateur Extra. The exam for each of the three license classes is called an *element*. Passing each of the elements grants the licensee more and more *privileges* allowed by the FCC's Amateur service rules. **Table 1.2** shows the elements and privileges for each of the Amateur license classes as of early 2018.

You'll learn the privileges of the Technician class license as you study this book. For now, all you need to remember is that Technician licensees are granted privileges on the radio airwaves referred to as the "VHF and UHF bands" and a few privileges on the "HF bands." You'll learn what those terms mean as you study.

Table 1.2
Amateur License Class Examinations

License Class	Exam Element	Number of Questions	Privileges
Technician	2	35 (passing grade is 26 correct)	All VHF and UHF privileges, with some HF privileges
General	3	35 (passing grade is 26 correct)	All VHF, UHF and most HF privileges
Amateur Extra	4	50 (passing grade is 37 correct)	All amateur privileges

1.3 Amateur Radio Activities

Ham radio has a lot to offer, but the many activities can be confusing. To help you understand why we operate in certain ways or why rules are written the way they are, this section presents some basics of ham radio. Later, you'll learn more details, but this introduction present some of the fundamentals that are present in almost all ham radio communications.

IDENTIFICATION AND CONTACTS

On the airwaves, your everyday identity gets something new — a *call sign* and your radio identity becomes "Steve WB8IMY" or "Mary K1MMH." Hams become known by their call signs and often keep them for life. Your call sign or *call* is completely unique among all the radio users anywhere in the world! There is only one N6BV (Dean in USA)

Hams use repeaters to relay signals from low-power radios over a wide area. Repeaters are a popular on-the-air meeting place for hams.

just like there is only one G4BUO (Dave in England) and one PP5JR (Sergio in Brazil) and one JE1CKA (Tack in Japan). By transmitting your call, other hams know who you are and your nationality. Identifying yourself with your call sign is known as signing. Because you can't see other hams except when using video transmissions, your call sign is very important. In fact, you're required to transmit your call regularly during every contact so that everyone knows whose transmissions are whose.

Speaking of contacts, any conversation between hams over the air is called a *contact* and starting a conversation is *making contact*. Attempting to make contact by transmitting your call sign is making a call or calling. If you're making a "come in anybody" call to which any station can respond, that's calling CQ. ("CQ" means "a general call.")

Once you establish contact, the next step is to exchange more information such as a *signal report* that lets the other station know how well you are receiving or copying them. Name and location are exchanged after that — then you're off to whatever business is at hand. A long conversation is known as a *ragchew*. At the end of a contact, you sign off.

Ham Shorthand

Like any activity that has been around for a while, such as sailing or flying, radio has a special jargon of its own. Many of these conventions originate from the days of the telegraph. In those days, every word took up precious time so the operators developed an extensive series of abbreviations and special characters (called *prosigns*) that kept the information (or traffic) flowing quickly and smoothly. For example, you may have heard the word "break" or "breaker" used over the radio. The word originally referred to a telegraph operator disconnecting or breaking the telegraph line so that no characters could be sent. This got the attention of every other operator along the line and to do so was called breaking in. The word is still in use 150 years later!

Later, as radio became a worldwide tool, operators that didn't speak the same language were aided by the creation of *Q-signals*. For example, "QTH?" means "What is your location?" and in response "QTH Seattle" means "I am located in Seattle." Many of these procedures and abbreviations are still in place today, because they work!

USING YOUR VOICE

By far, the most popular method or *mode* of making contacts is by voice. There are a number of ways to transmit voices via radio signals and you'll learn about those in the next chapter. It's easy and natural to converse this way, using the proper procedures. Voice is widely used by amateurs for short-distance and long-distance contacts. It is the most popular mode for hams on the go and during public service or emergency response.

As a Technician licensee, you'll be able to make voice contacts directly with other hams and also by using stations called *repeaters* that relay signals from low-power mobile or handheld transmitters across a wide area. Hams have also built internet-linked repeater systems that send digitized voices around the world so that local repeater users can communicate worldwide with just a low-power, handheld radio!

Hams typically use English as a common language when making international contacts, although when communicating within a country hams use their native languages. Voice contacts can be a good way to learn or polish your foreign language skills.

EXCHANGING DIGITAL DATA

Inexpensive sound card hardware and signal processing software for personal computers has created a surge of interest in the *digital modes* in which the conversation is carried out as streams of characters sent over the airwaves. A *data interface* is used to connect the radio to the computer. Most digital contacts are *keyboard-to-keyboard*, meaning that the operators take turns typing, just like text messaging.

Hams have been blazing trails in developing new methods of converting the computer characters into radio signals and back again. The methods are called *protocols* and are referred to by their initials, such as RTTY, PSK31, or FT8. Different protocols are used to get the most effective communications possible.

One of the digital radio systems developed by hams exchanges e-mail over Amateur Radio. It's called Winlink and it looks a lot like regular e-mail on the computer screen. It's used daily by thousands of hams who are unable to access the internet while traveling, at sea, or camping in remote locations. It's also used for emergency and disaster response communications.

USING MORSE CODE

Morse or "CW" is still quite popular in Amateur Radio. Because all of a signal's energy is concentrated in a single on-and-off signal, Morse works very well in the presence of interference or when signals are weak. Morse signals can be generated by extremely simple transmitters — all you need is something to generate a radio signal and something else to turn it on and off. Receiving and decoding Morse (called copying the code) requires only a basic receiver and a human ear.

Many operators enjoy the rhythm and musicality of "the code." It's a skill like playing a musical instrument that you can enjoy for its own sake. Listening to a seasoned Morse operator is quite a treat!

EMERGENCIES AND PUBLIC SERVICE

One of the reasons ham radio is so valuable (and maybe a reason you're reading this book) is that hams are good at helping. Communications is key to making any kind of organized effort work, whether it's a small parade or major response to a natural disaster. While the day-to-day telecommunication systems are recovering, hams quickly set up temporary networks that support public safety and government operations. Why does this work? Because there are lots of hams and we are skilled in basic communication techniques that don't depend on any other telecommunications system.

Table 1.3

Emergency Response Organizations

ARES®	Amateur Radio Emergency Service® — organized by the ARRL
RACES	Radio Amateur Civil Emergency Service (works with civil defense agencies)
SATERN	Salvation Army Team Emergency Radio Network
HWN	Hurricane Watch Net — works with the National Hurricane Center
SKYWARN	Severe weather watch and reporting system — works with the National Weather Service

Can Technician class licensees help out? You bet they can! By learning how to use your radio and taking some simple training classes, such as the ARRL's Introduction to Emergency Communication training course, you'll be ready to join and practice with other hams. The largest ham public service organization is the Amateur Radio Emergency Service (ARES) which is organized by the ARRL. You can join a local ARES team to receive training and practice providing emergency communications support. **Table 1.3** lists several ham radio emergency response groups.

Hams can pitch in and help in many ways. Not everyone has to be on-site to make a contribution. Whatever your personal capabilities and license class, there is a need you can fill.

• From home — Use base station radios and antennas to provide long distance communications, relay messages, and act as a net control to coordinate communications.

• From a vehicle — From a personal vehicle or a communications-equipped van, portable stations provide valuable relay and coordination functions in the field.

• On foot — Go where the action is to provide status reports and relay supply and operations messages between the control centers and workers in the field.

One of the most important functions, repeated three times in the list above, is to relay communications. It is no coincidence that the third letter in ARRL stands for "relay," one of the oldest and most highly valued radio functions. Relaying information requires accuracy and efficiency. Hams pride themselves on both.

AWARDS AND CONTESTS

Hams keep their skills sharp not only by training, but by getting on the air and having fun! Just as sports and recreational activities keep your body fit and in good health, there are competitive radio activities, as well. There are many suitable for Technician license holders.

Worked All States (WAS) is a popular first major award pursued by hams around the world.

There are operating achievement awards for almost anything you can imagine, such as *working* (contacting) every state or different countries, contacting satellites, and making low-power contacts. **Table 1.4** shows several examples of awards and operating events, but thousands of awards are available. Collecting these colorful certificates and other prizes can be addictive!

Contests, also called *radiosport*, fill the ham bands with rapid-fire contacts as amateurs strive to make as many short contacts as possible within a limited time. There is a tremendous variety of contests, from sprints lasting only a few hours to international contests that last for 48 hours.

Table 1.4

Awards and Operating Events for Technician Licensees

OSCAR Satellite Communications Achievement Award: Contact 20 different states, Canadian provinces, or countries using amateur satellites. Sponsored by AMSAT.

ARRL VHF/UHF Century Club (VUCC): Contact grid squares using VHF and UHF bands (100 grids on 50 and 144 MHz; 50 grids on 222 and 432 MHz; fewer on the higher bands)

ARRL and CQ VHF Contests: Several contests throughout the year that make use of the VHF and UHF bands

ARRL Field Day: The largest on-the-air event in ham radio, held annually in June

ARRL 10 Meter Contest: Held annually in December, there is plenty of activity in the Technician portions of the band

Working hard to compete and improve provides a strong incentive to become skilled in both technical and operating capabilities.

NOVEL ACTIVITIES

As if all this wasn't interesting enough, hams are famous for pushing the envelope and either inventing an entirely new technology or adopting a commercial technology in an unexpected way. It was mentioned before that hams have their own satellites and radio/internet networks, but that's just the start. Here are some examples:

SSTV and ATV

Slow-scan television (SSTV) was invented by hams to send pictures over regular voice radios. Black-and-white or color pictures and images can be sent and received by a computer with a sound card. Broadcast TV-style video is the domain of the amateur TV (ATV) enthusiasts. They hook up a regular video camera to an ATV transmitter and *voila!* they're on the air, beaming video that looks just like a professional signal. Both ATV and SSTV are increasingly used in emergencies.

The Automatic Packet Reporting System (APRS) was invented by hams to show location and travel path by using ham radio.

Packet Radio and Broadband Hamnet

Amateurs have long built data networks using the AX.25 adaption of commercial computer network protocols. A special kind of data interface called a *terminal node controller* (TNC) takes characters from a computer and re-packages them into data packets which are transmitted by a regular, unmodified radio, usually on the VHF or UHF bands. Hams have also adapted WiFi routers, reprogramming them to form "mesh" networks automatically, creating regional networks Packet stations and networks are used to support emergency communications and a variety of other uses.

APRS — Automatic Packet Reporting System

Invented by Bob Bruninga, WB4APR, APRS integrates GPS position data and other information with packet radio. Amateurs with a GPS and a mobile radio can send their position to a local APRS relay point or gateway and on to internet-based servers. Other users can log on to the APRS servers and find the location of anyone sending position data by tracking their movements on maps of various detail levels. It's fascinating!

Meteor Scatter and EME

Perhaps the most exotic of all ham activities is making contacts via meteor scatter or Earth-Moon-Earth (EME) reflections. The trail of a meteor can reflect radio signals during the few seconds it lasts. A skilled amateur can use that trail to make short contacts! The biggest reflector in the sky is the Moon and hams can bounce their signals off the Moon and hear them when they complete the round trip back to Earth. Nobel Prize-winner Joe Taylor, K1JT, wrote software that uses a computer's sound card to both send and receive data in a highly specialized code that enables even modest stations to operate both meteor scatter and EME and at extremely low power levels. Does that sound exciting? It is!

1.4 Getting Your Ham Radio License

THE TECHNICIAN LICENSE

The Technician license is the first license for newcomers to ham radio. There are more Technician licensees than of any other class, about 50% of all US hams. You'll be able to communicate with thousands of other hams in many of the ways amateurs use the airwaves.

Once you gain some experience, you'll be ready to *upgrade* your license to General class and beyond to the top-of-the-line Amateur Extra class. These licensees gain more privileges on the traditional HF or "shortwave" bands of Amateur Radio. They all started just like you, taking the basic exams and getting on the air.

OBTAINING A LICENSE

The first step is in your hands right now! To get your license, you'll need to pass a 35-question, multiple-choice exam on the rules of ham radio, simple operating procedures, and basic electronics. You can study on your own or you can enroll in a licensing class. Log on to the ARRL website where you can search for classes being held near you. There are more than 2000 instructors throughout the United States who are part of the ARRL-sponsored training program. By joining a class, you can take advantage of the experience of these ham radio experts and learn in the company of other students.

When you are ready to take your exam, it will be time to locate an exam session. If you're part of a study class, the instructor will make the necessary

Want More Information?

Looking for more information about ham radio in your local area? Interested in taking a ham radio class? Ready for your license exam? Call 1-800-32 NEW HAM (1-800-326-3942). Do you need a list of ham radio clubs, instructors or examiners in your local area? Just let us know what you need!

You can also contact us via e-mail: **newham@arrl.org**

Or check out our website: **www.arrl.org**

Find some special content just for *Ham Radio License Manual* readers at **www.arrl.org/ham-radio-license-manual**

You can even write to us at:
New Ham Desk
ARRL Headquarters
225 Main St
Newington, CT 06111-1494

Books to Help You Learn

As you study the material on the licensing exam, you will have lots of other questions about the hows and whys of Amateur Radio. The following references, available from your local bookstore or the ARRL will help "fill in the blanks" and give you a broader picture of the hobby:

• *Ham Radio for Dummies* by Ward Silver — written for the prospective and new ham wondering "What do I do now?." It supplements the information in study guides with an informal, friendly approach to the hobby — your "desktop Elmer."

• *ARRL Operating Manual* — in-depth chapters on the most popular ham radio activities. Learn about nets, award programs, DXing and more.

• *Understanding Basic Electronics* — for students who want more technical background about radio and electronics. The book covers the fundamentals of electricity and electronics that are the foundation of all radio.

arrangements. For solo students, you can find an exam session by visiting the ARRL website. Use the exam search page to find exam sessions near you, including complete contact information. All Amateur Radio exams are given by ham radio operators acting as volunteer examiners.

After you pass your exam, the examiners will give you a *Certificate of Successful Completion of Examination* (CSCE) that documents your achievement. They will also file all of the necessary paperwork so that your license will be granted by the Federal Communications Commission (FCC). In a few days, you will be able see your new call sign in the FCC's database via the ARRL's website. Congratulations — you're authorized to get on the air! You print a copy of your license, or you can contact FCC to request a paper copy of your license by mail.

WHAT WE ASSUME ABOUT YOU

The only thing you'll really need to succeed is a strong interest in Amateur Radio and a willingness to learn. You don't have to be a technical guru to get your license. As you progress through the material, you'll encounter some basic science about radio and electricity. There will be a bit of simple math here and there. When we get to the rules and regulations you'll have to learn some new words and maybe memorize a few numbers. That's it! It will help if you have regular access to the internet. You should have a simple calculator — you'll be allowed to use it during the license exam.

ADVANCED STUDENTS

Perhaps you've used other types of radios, such as Citizen's Band or a business band radio at work. You might have a technical background or have experience as a radio operator. If so, we suggest that you jump to the questions listed at the start of each section. If you find it easy to answer the questions correctly, you can skim or skip the corresponding section of the book. Regardless of your background, be sure to review the chapters on Licensing Regulations and Operating Regulations since ham radio rules and procedures are probably different than what you're used to.

ONLINE PRACTICE EXAMS

When you feel like you're nearly ready for the actual exam you can get some good practice by taking Amateur Radio practice exams using the online ARRL Exam Review for Ham Radio (a link is listed on this book's web page). The Exam Review website uses the question pool to construct an exam with the same number and variety of questions that you'll encounter on exam day. You can take them over and over again in complete privacy.

These exams are quite realistic and you get quick feedback about the questions you missed. When you find yourself passing the online exams by a comfortable margin, you'll be ready for the real thing.

A note of caution: If you use a different online practice exam service, be sure that the questions used are current — the Technician question pool is completely rewritten every four years. The set of questions put in place in July of 2018 will be replaced in 2022. (A new set of General questions will go into effect in 2019 and a new set of Extra questions will go into effect in 2020.)

TESTING PROCESS

The final step is to find a *test session*. If you're in a licensing class, the instructor will help you find and register for a session. Otherwise, you can find a test session by using the ARRL's web page for finding exams. If you can register for the test session in advance, do so. Other sessions, such as those at hamfests or conventions, are available to "walk-ins," that is anyone who shows up. You may have to wait for an available space though, so go early!

Bring two forms of identification including at least one photo ID, such as a driver's license, passport or employer's identity card. Also know your Social Security Number (SSN). You can bring pencils or pens and a calculator, but any kind of computer or online device is prohibited. (If you have a disability and need these devices to take the exam, contact the session sponsor ahead of time.) Once you're signed in, you pay the test fee (check with the test session administrator) and get ready.

Amateur Radio licensing test sessions are administered by volunteer examiners — hams just like you will be. They grade the exams, help you fill out the necessary forms, and take care of all the paperwork for your ham radio license.

The Technician test usually takes less than an hour. You will be given a question sheet and an answer sheet. As you answer each question, mark a box on the answer sheet. Once you've answered all 35 questions, the volunteer examiners (VE) will grade and verify your test results. Assuming you've passed (congratulations!) you'll fill out a Certificate of Successful Completion of Examination (CSCE) and a NCVEC Form 605. The exam organizers will submit your results to the FCC while you keep the CSCE as evidence that you've passed your Technician test. As soon as your name and call sign appear in the FCC's database of licensees, typically a week to ten days later, you can start transmitting. (You can listen any time.)

If you don't pass, don't be discouraged! You might be able to take another version of the test. Ask the session organizers about a second try. Even if you decide to take the test again at a later date, you now know just how the test session feels — you'll be more relaxed and ready next time. The ham bands are full of hams that took their tests more than once before passing. You'll be in good company!

The Upgrade Trail

Successfully obtaining your Technician license is a great achievement — enjoy it! After you get some experience on the air and interact with your fellow hams, it's likely that you'll become interested in using more of the shortwave HF bands that support communication over long distances. The accompanying US Amateur Bands chart shows the additional privileges available to General and Amateur Extra ticket holders enable them to make contacts over really long distances on a wide variety of frequencies. (A full-size version of the chart is available at **www.arrl.org/graphical-frequency-allocations**.)This is where digital mode experimentation is the most active.

It's a whole different experience on the "short waves." Fortunately, there are a lot of resources available as you hit the "upgrade trail." The ARRL offers study guides and local clubs often sponsor classes.

The important thing is to just get started and keep going. Read some of the books listed as resources. Keep a study guide available. Ask questions and visit stations where you can use the HF bands. Be sure to attend a Field Day event where all of ham radio is often on display. Just like studying for your Technician license, soon it starts making sense and your scores on the practice exams will soar.

TIME TO GET STARTED!

By following these instructions and carefully studying the material in this book, soon you'll be joining the rest of us on the air! Each of us at the ARRL Headquarters and every ARRL member looks forward to the day when your signals join ours on the ham bands. "73" (best regards) and good luck!

US Amateur Radio Bands

ARRL The national association for AMATEUR RADIO®

US AMATEUR POWER LIMITS

FCC 97.313 An amateur station must use the minimum transmitter power necessary to carry out the desired communications.

(b) No station may transmit with a transmitter power exceeding 1.5 kW PEP.

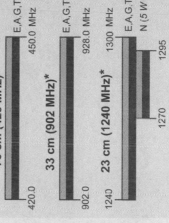
Amateurs wishing to operate on either 2,200 or 630 meters must first register with the Utilities Technology Council online at **https://utc.org/plc-database-amateur-notification-process/**. You need only register once for each band.

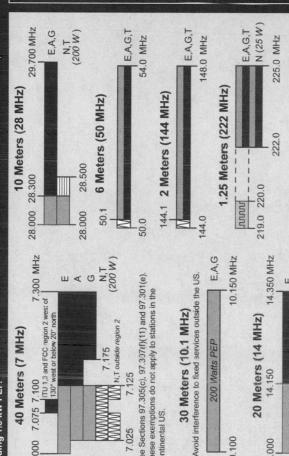

2,200 Meters (135 kHz)
135.7 kHz   1 W EIRP maximum   137.8 kHz
E,A,G

630 Meters (472 kHz)
5 W EIRP maximum, except in Alaska within 496 miles of Russia where the power limit is 1 W EIRP.
472 kHz   479 kHz
E,A,G

160 Meters (1.8 MHz)
Avoid interference to radiolocation operations from 1.900 to 2.000 MHz
1.800   1.900   2.000 MHz
E,A,G

80 Meters (3.5 MHz)
3.500   3.600   3.700   3.800   4.000 MHz
E
A
G
N,T (200 W)
3.525   3.600

60 Meters (5.3 MHz)
CW, Dig   5332   5348.5   5358   5373   5405 kHz
E,A,G (100 W)
USB   5330.5   5346.5   5357.0   5371.5   5403.5 kHz
2.8 kHz

General, Advanced, and Amateur Extra licensees may operate on these five channels on a secondary basis with a maximum effective radiated power (ERP) of 100 W PEP relative to a half-wave dipole. Permitted operating modes include upper sideband voice (USB), CW, RTTY, PSK31 and other digital modes such as PACTOR III. Only one signal at a time is permitted on any channel.

40 Meters (7 MHz)
7.000   7.075   7.100   7.300 MHz
E
A
G
N,T (200 W)
7.025   7.125   7.175
ITU 1,3 and FCC region 2 west of 130° west or below 20° north
7.175 N,T outside region 2

30 Meters (10.1 MHz)
See Sections 97.305(c), 97.307(f)(11) and 97.301(e). These exemptions do not apply to stations in the continental US.
200 Watts PEP
10.100   10.150 MHz
E,A,G

20 Meters (14 MHz)
Avoid interference to fixed services outside the US.
14.000   14.025   14.150   14.225   14.350 MHz
E
A
G
14.025   14.150   14.175

17 Meters (18 MHz)
18.068   18.110   18.168 MHz
E,A,G

15 Meters (21 MHz)
21.000   21.200   21.450 MHz
E
A
G
N,T (200 W)
21.025   21.200   21.225   21.275

12 Meters (24 MHz)
24.890   24.930   24.990 MHz
E,A,G

10 Meters (28 MHz)
28.000   28.300   28.500   29.700 MHz
E,A,G
N,T (200 W)

6 Meters (50 MHz)
50.0   50.1   54.0 MHz
E,A,G,T

2 Meters (144 MHz)
144.0   144.1   148.0 MHz
E,A,G,T

1.25 Meters (222 MHz)
219.0   220.0   222.0   225.0 MHz
E,A,G,T
N (25 W)

70 cm (420 MHz)*
420.0   450.0 MHz
E,A,G,T

33 cm (902 MHz)*
902.0   928.0 MHz
E,A,G,T

23 cm (1240 MHz)*
1240   1270   1295   1300 MHz
E,A,G,T
N (5 W)

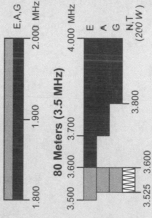

*Geographical and power restrictions may apply to all bands above 420 MHz. See *The ARRL Operating Manual* for information about your area.

All licensees except Novices are authorized all modes on the following frequencies:

2300-2310 MHz	10.0-10.5 GHz ‡
2390-2450 MHz	24.0-24.25 GHz
3300-3500 MHz	47.0-47.2 GHz
5650-5925 MHz	76.0-81.0 GHz

122.25-123.0 GHz
134-141 GHz
241-250 GHz
All above 275 GHz

‡ No pulse emissions

Chapter 2

Radio and Signals Fundamentals

In this chapter, you'll learn about:

- The radio spectrum
- Radio signals and waves
- The characteristics of radio signals
- Names and types of basic radio equipment
- Simple radio stations

When you see the mouse, you'll find more information at **www.arrl.org/ham-radio-license-manual**

This is the real beginning of your Amateur Radio adventure! The material in each chapter is presented in a "here's what you need to know" style. References will be provided so that you can learn more about topics that interest you. Start by bookmarking the ARRL's *Ham Radio License Manual* web page, **www.arrl.org/ham-radio-license-manual**. Don't forget that there's a comprehensive glossary in the back of the book for unfamiliar terms.

In this chapter, we dive into what makes radio work — starting with the signals themselves — and then basic radio equipment. We'll then go on to basic electronics, operating, rules, and safety in the following chapters.

Covering technical topics first makes it easier for you to understand operating rules and procedures. You'll be a better and safer operator. Relax — we'll start at the beginning and learn one step at a time!

2.1 Radio Signals and Waves

We'll start with the *signals* that travel back and forth between radios. All radio equipment is designed to generate or manipulate *radio signals*. A radio signal can be electrical energy inside radio equipment or a *radio wave* traveling through space. A radio wave begins at an *antenna* that turns an electrical signal into radio waves that travel at the speed of light. As the wave passes other antennas, it creates replicas of the original electrical signal. A radio then turns the received signal back into a voice, digital data, or even Morse code.

The process of turning the transmitter's output signal into radio waves that leave the antenna is called *radiating* or *radiation*. The word "radiation" should not concern you. Radiation from an antenna is not the same as *ionizing radiation* from radioactivity. You'll learn more about this subject in the **Safety** chapter.

Metric Prefixes — the Language of Radio

The units of measurement employed in radio use the *metric system* of prefixes. The metric system is used because the numbers involved cover such a wide range of values. **Table 2.1** shows metric prefixes, symbols, and their meaning. The prefixes expand or shrink the units, multiplying them by the factor shown in the table. For example, a *kilo*meter (km) is one thousand meters and a *milli*meter (mm) is one-thousandth of a meter.

The most common prefixes you'll encounter in radio are pico (p), nano (n), micro (μ), milli (m), centi (c), kilo (k), mega (M), and giga (G). It is important to use the proper case for the prefix letter. For example, M means one million and m means one-thousandth. Using the wrong case would make a big difference!

If you're already familiar with the metric system, review the following questions to be sure you have it mastered. If the metric system is unfamiliar to you, the *Ham Radio License Manual* web page has a detailed discussion of how the prefixes work and examples for you to learn from. Review that material until you are comfortable with the examples and definitions.

Table 2.1
International System of Units (SI) — Metric Units

Prefix	Symbol	Multiplication Factor	
Tera	T	10^{12} =	1,000,000,000,000
Giga	G	10^{9} =	1,000,000,000
Mega	M	10^{6} =	1,000,000
Kilo	k	10^{3} =	1000
Hecto	h	10^{2} =	100
Deca	da	10^{1} =	10
Deci	d	10^{-1} =	0.1
Centi	c	10^{-2} =	0.01
Milli	m	10^{-3} =	0.001
Micro	μ	10^{-6} =	0.000001
Nano	n	10^{-9} =	0.000000001
Pico	p	10^{-12} =	0.000000000001

T5B01 — How many milliamperes is 1.5 amperes? (1.5 A = 1,500 mA)

T5B02 — What is another way to specify a radio signal frequency of 1,500,000 hertz? (1,500,000 Hz = 1,500 kHz = 1.5 MHz)

T5B03 — How many volts are equal to one kilovolt? (1 kV = 1000 V)

T5B04 — How many volts are equal to one microvolt? (1 μV = one one-millionth of a volt)

T5B05 — Which of the following is equivalent to 500 milliwatts? (500 mW = 0.5 W)

T5B06 — If an ammeter calibrated in amperes is used to measure a 3000-milliampere current, what reading would it show? (3,000 mA = 3 A)

T5B07 — If a frequency display calibrated in megahertz shows a reading of 3.525 MHz, what would it show if it were calibrated in kilohertz? (3.525 MHz = 3,525 kHz)

T5B08 — How many microfarads are 1,000,000 picofarads? (1,000,000 pF = 1 μF)

T5B12 — Which of the following frequencies is equal to 28,400 kHz? (28,400 kHz = 28.4 MHz)

T5B13 — If a frequency display shows a reading of 2425 MHz, what frequency is that in GHz? (2425 MHz = 2.425 GHz)

FREQUENCY and PHASE

T5A12 — What describes the number of times per second that an alternating current makes a complete cycle?
T5C05 — What is the unit of frequency?
T5C14 — What is the proper abbreviation for megahertz?

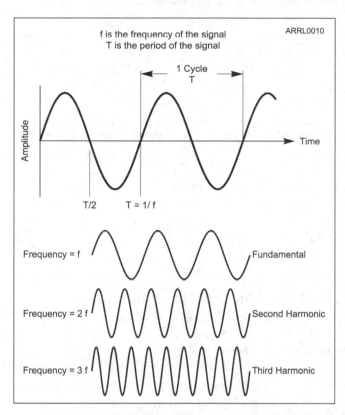

Figure 2.1 — The frequency of a signal and its period are reciprocals. Higher frequency means shorter period and vice-versa.

Like a water wave, a radio wave continually varies in strength or *amplitude* like the *sine wave* shown in **Figure 2.1**. This continual change is called *oscillating*. As the signal oscillates, each complete up-and-down sequence is called a *cycle*. The number of *cycles per second* is the signal's *frequency*, represented by a lower-case *f*. **[T5A12]** The unit of measurement for frequency is *hertz*, abbreviated Hz. **[T5C05]** The *period* of the cycle (represented by capital *T*) is its duration. The reciprocal of the period, 1/*T*, is the signal's frequency, *f*.

One cycle per second is one hertz or 1 Hz. As frequency increases, it becomes easier to use units of kilohertz (1 kHz = 1000 Hz), megahertz (1 MHz = 1000 kHz = 1,000,000 Hz), and gigahertz (1 GHz = 1000 MHz = 1,000,000,000 Hz). **[T5C14]**

For More Information

As shown at the bottom of Figure 2.1, a *harmonic* is a signal with a frequency that is some multiple (×2, ×3, ×4 and so on) of a *fundamental* frequency. The harmonic at twice the fundamental's frequency is called the *second harmonic*, at three times the fundamental frequency the *third harmonic*, and so forth. There is no "first harmonic."

Every cycle of the signal has the same basic shape: rising and falling and returning to where it started. Position within a cycle is called *phase*, illustrated in **Figure 2.2**. Phase is used to compare how sine wave signals are aligned in time.

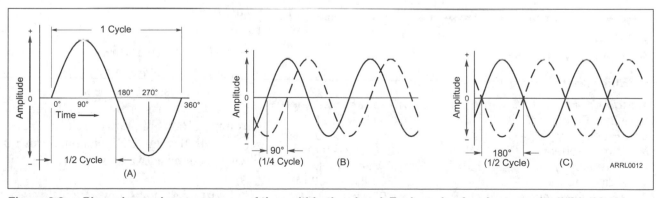

Figure 2.2 — Phase is used as a measure of time within the signal. Each cycle of a sine wave is divided into 360 degrees of phase (A). Parts (B) and (C) show two special cases. In (B) the two signals are 90 degrees out of phase, and in (C) they are 180 degrees out of phase.

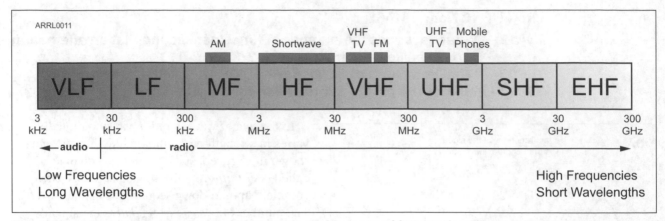

Figure 2.3 — The radio spectrum extends over a very wide range of frequencies. The drawing shows the frequency ranges used by broadcast stations and mobile phones. Amateurs can use small frequency bands in the LF and higher frequency regions of the spectrum.

Phase is measured in *degrees* and there are 360 degrees in one cycle of a sine wave. If two sine waves have a phase difference of 180 degrees so that one wave is increasing while the other is decreasing, they are *out of phase*. Waves that have no phase difference so that they are increasing and decreasing at the same time are *in phase*.

THE RADIO SPECTRUM

T3B08 — What are the frequency limits of the VHF spectrum?
T3B09 — What are the frequency limits of the UHF spectrum?
T3B10 — What frequency range is referred to as HF?
T5C06 — What does the abbreviation "RF" refer to?

If connected to a speaker, signals below 20 kHz produce sound waves that humans can hear, so we call them *audio frequency* or *AF* signals. Signals that have a frequency greater than 20,000 Hz (or 20 kHz) are *radio frequency* or *RF* signals. **[T5C06]**

The range of radio signal frequencies is called the *radio spectrum*. It starts at 20 kHz and continues through several hundred GHz, a thousand million times higher in frequency! For convenience, the radio spectrum of **Figure 2.3** is divided into ranges of frequencies that have similar characteristics as shown in **Table 2.2**.

A specific range of frequencies in which signals are used for a common purpose or have similar characteristics is called a *band*. The AM broadcast band extends from 550 to 1700 kHz and the FM broadcast band covers 88 to 108 MHz. Frequency bands used by amateurs are called *amateur bands* or *ham bands*.

Table 2.2
RF Spectrum Ranges

[T3B08-T3B10]

Range Name	Abbreviation	Frequency Range
Very Low Frequency	VLF	3 kHz – 30 kHz
Low Frequency	LF	30 kHz – 300 kHz
Medium Frequency	MF	300 kHz – 3 MHz
High Frequency	HF	3 MHz – 30 MHz
Very High Frequency	VHF	30 MHz – 300 MHz
Ultra High Frequency	UHF	300 MHz – 3 GHz
Super High Frequency	SHF	3 GHz – 30 GHz
Extremely High Frequency	EHF	30 GHz – 300 GHz

For More Information

Frequencies above 1 GHz are generally considered to be *microwaves*. Microwave ovens operate at 2.4 GHz, for example. Hams primarily use frequencies in the MF through UHF and microwave ranges, but have two bands in the LF region as well.

Figure 2.4 shows how a typical AM broadcast receiver "sees" the AM broadcast band. Starting at the lowest

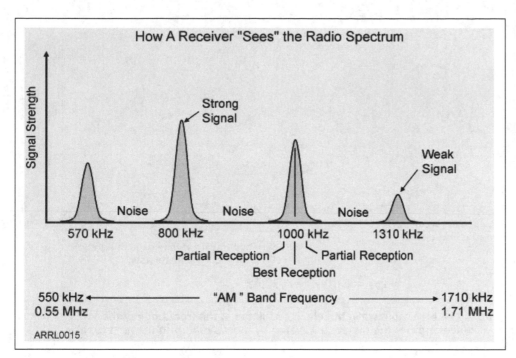

How A Receiver "Sees" the Radio Spectrum

Strong Signal

Weak Signal

Noise   Noise   Noise

570 kHz   800 kHz   1000 kHz   1310 kHz

Partial Reception   Partial Reception

Best Reception

550 kHz ←――――――――― "AM" Band Frequency ―――――――→ 1710 kHz
0.55 MHz   1.71 MHz

ARRL0015

Figure 2.4 — As a radio receiver is tuned across the AM broadcast band, starting at the left, it encounters each signal in turn. Between signals, only noise is received. Although signals can be received slightly lower and higher in frequency, the signal is received best when the receiver is tuned exactly to the signal's frequency.

frequency on the left, if the receiver is tuned higher in frequency it encounters first a signal at 570 kHz, tunes "past" it to find the next signal, and so forth. The receiver is designed to recover information (the station's programming) from only one signal at a time — the one with the right frequency.

Figure 2.4 also shows a new way of looking at signals. Instead of showing how the signal's amplitude varies with time from left to right, as in Figure 2.1, this *spectrum display* organizes the signals according to their frequencies. The horizontal axis represents frequency and the vertical axis shows signal strength. This is a common way to describe the radio spectrum or a specific signal.

WAVELENGTH

T3B01 — What is the name for the distance a radio wave travels during one complete cycle?

T3B04 — How fast does a radio wave travel through free space?

T3B05 — How does the wavelength of a radio wave relate to its frequency?

T3B06 — What is the formula for converting frequency to approximate wavelength in meters?

T3B07 — What property of radio waves is often used to identify the different frequency bands?

T3B11 — What is the approximate velocity of a radio wave as it travels through free space?

The *wavelength* of a radio wave is the distance that it travels during one complete cycle. [**T3B01**] Wavelength is represented by the Greek letter lambda, λ. **Figure 2.5** shows the relationship between the wave's frequency, wavelength, and speed.

All radio waves travel at the speed of light (represented by a lower-case c) in whatever medium they are traveling, such as air. [**T3B04**] The speed of light in space and air is very close to 300 million meters per second (300,000,000 or 3×10^8 meters per second) [**T3B11**]. Because radio waves travel at a constant speed, one wavelength, $\lambda = c / f$. This means that as frequency increases, wavelength decreases and vice-versa. [**T3B05**]

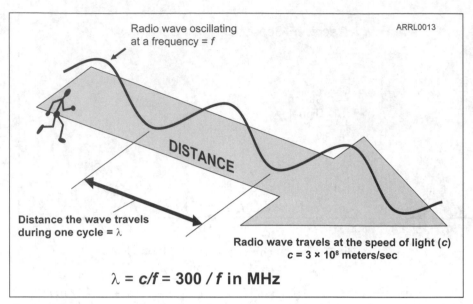

Figure 2.5 — As a radio wave travels, it oscillates at the frequency of the signal. Wavelength is the distance traveled by the wave during the time for one complete cycle.

A radio wave can be referred to by wavelength or frequency because the wave is moving at a constant velocity — the speed of light. If you know the frequency of a radio wave, you automatically know its wavelength!

$$\lambda \text{ in meters} = \frac{300}{f \text{ in MHz}}$$ **[T3B06]**

Because of this relationship, amateur bands are often referred to by wavelength. **[T3B07]** You'll often hear something like this, "I'll call you on 2 meters. Let's try 146.52 MHz." The frequency band is referred to as "2 meters" because the radio waves are all approximately that long. The exact frequency then tells you precisely where to tune in the band.

For More Information

A radio wave can be referred to by wavelength or frequency since the two are related by the speed of light. Because radio waves travel at a constant speed, one wavelength, $\lambda = c / f$. This can also be stated as $f = c / \lambda$.

A higher frequency wave takes less time to complete one cycle so it doesn't move as far during that time. Waves at very high frequencies have very short wavelengths — such as microwaves with frequencies above 1 GHz.

For waves in air or space, the formula for wavelength in meters is:

$$\lambda \text{ in meters} = \frac{300,000,000 \text{ meters per second}}{f \text{ in hertz}} = \frac{300 \times 1,000,000 \text{ meters per second}}{f \text{ in megahertz}} = \frac{300}{f \text{ in MHz}}$$

For example, the wavelength of a 1 MHz radio wave from an AM broadcast station is

$$\lambda = \frac{300}{1 \text{ MHz}} = 300 \text{ meters}$$

Clearly, the shorter form is more convenient when working with radio frequency signals.

To convert from meters to feet, multiply the wavelength in meters by 3.28. To get the wavelength in meters, divide feet by 3.28. To convert from meters to inches, multiply by 39.37. For example, the wavelength of an 80 meter signal in feet is:

80 meters × 3.28 feet per meter = 262.4 feet

and the wavelength of a 70 cm signal in inches is:

0.7 meters × 39.37 inches per meter = 27.6 inches

2.2 Radio Equipment Basics

You've used radios before, of course — at home, in the car, or at work. That means you're already familiar with some of the topics in this section. It's a good idea to review this material even if you have previously used two-way radios. In ham radio some terms might be used a little differently than what you're used to. We'll cover the operating details and procedures later.

BASIC STATION ORGANIZATION

T7A02 — What is a transceiver?

The three basic elements of an amateur station, big or small, are the transmitter, receiver, and antenna as shown in **Figure 2.6**. A *transmitter* (abbreviated XMTR) generates a signal that carries speech, Morse code, or data. A *receiver* (abbreviated RCVR) recovers the speech, Morse code, or data from a signal. (Figure 2.6 is a *block diagram* that shows how a system of equipment is organized without getting into the complex details of every connection and control.)

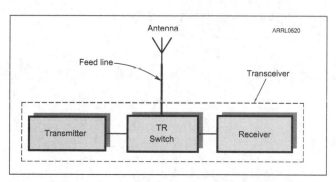

Figure 2.6 — A basic amateur station is made up of a transmitter and receiver connected to an antenna with a feed line. The transmit-receive (TR) switch allows the transmitter and receiver to share the antenna. A transceiver combines the transmitter, receiver, and TR switch in a single package.

Most amateur equipment combines the transmitter and receiver into a single piece of equipment called a *transceiver* (abbreviated XCVR). [T7A02] Transceivers are also called "rigs." For example, a transceiver intended for mounting in a vehicle is a "mobile rig."

An *antenna* turns the radio signals from a transmitter into energy that travels through space as a radio wave. An antenna also captures radio waves and turns them into signals for a receiver to work with. A *feed line* connects the antenna to the transmitter or receiver. Feed lines are also called *transmission lines*, just like power lines. A *transmit-receive (TR) switch* allows a transmitter and receiver to share a single antenna.

REPEATERS

T1F09 — What type of amateur station simultaneously retransmits the signal of another amateur station on a different channel or channels?

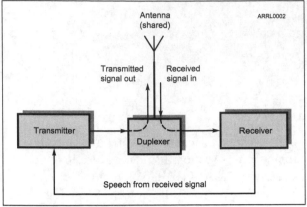

Figure 2.7 — In a repeater, the receiver's output is immediately retransmitted by the transmitter on a different frequency. The duplexer allows the transmitter and receiver to share a common antenna at the same time.

Repeaters consist of a receiver and transmitter that re-transmit the information from a received signal simultaneously on another frequency or channel. **[T1F09]** This is called *duplex communication*.

Figure 2.7 shows the basic elements of a repeater station. Because a repeater receives and transmits at the same time, instead of a transmit-receive switch it uses a *duplexer*. Repeaters are located on high buildings, towers or hills for maximum range.

Repeaters provide local and regional communications between low-power mobile and portable stations. The job of the repeater is to provide a strong, low-noise signal that everyone can hear and understand well, especially in emergencies. Most repeaters are designed to relay FM and digital voice signals. There are repeaters for data and video signals, too.

Chapter 3

Electricity, Components and Circuits

In this chapter, you'll learn about:

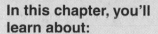

- **Fundamentals of electricity and circuits**
- **Voltage and current**
- **Resistance, capacitance and inductance**
- **Reactance, impedance and resonance**
- **Common types of electronic components**
- **Basic radio circuits**

When you see the mouse, you'll find more information at www.arrl.org/ham-radio-license-manual

3.1 Electricity

Although radios use sophisticated electronics, they are based on fundamental principles of electricity. In this chapter, you'll learn about the basic electrical concepts that apply to everything from the household wall socket to the latest radio or computer.

If you would like some assistance with the math in this chapter, tutorials are available on the book's website, and all exam math problems are worked out for you there, too.

CURRENT AND VOLTAGE

T5A01 — Electrical current is measured in which of the following units?
T5A03 — What is the name for the flow of electrons in an electric circuit?
T5A04 — What is the name for a current that flows only in one direction?
T5A05 — What is the electrical term for the electromotive force (EMF) that causes electron flow?
T5A09 — What is the name for a current that reverses direction on a regular basis?
T5A11 — What is the unit of electromotive force?
T7D01 — Which instrument would you use to measure electric potential or electromotive force?
T7D04 — Which instrument is used to measure electric current?

Electric *current* (represented in equations by the symbol *I* or *i*) is the flow of *electrons*. **[T5A03]** Electrons are negatively charged atomic particles. Current is measured in units of *amperes*, which is abbreviated as A or amps. **[T5A01]** Current is always measured as the flow through something, such as a wire or electronic component. An *ammeter* is used to measure current. **[T7D04]**

Voltage (represented in equations by the symbol *E* or *e*) is the *electromotive force* or *electric potential* that makes electrons move. **[T5A05]** Electrons move in the direction of a positive voltage difference. *Polarity* refers to the convention that determines which voltages are positive and negative.

Voltage is measured in units of *volts*, which are abbreviated as V. **[T5A11]** (Sometimes *V* or *v* is used in equations as a symbol for voltage, as well.) Voltage is measured with a *voltmeter*. **[T7D01]**

Voltage is always measured from one point to another or with respect to some reference voltage. If the Earth's surface is used as the reference voltage, it is called *earth ground*, *ground potential*, or just *ground*.

Direct and Alternating Current

Electrical current takes different forms, depending on how the electrons move. Current that flows in one direction all the time is *direct current,* abbreviated *dc*. **[T5A04]** Current that regularly reverses direction is *alternating current*, abbreviated *ac*. **[T5A09] Figure 3.1** shows the difference between ac and dc.

Just like current, a voltage that has the same *polarity* (the same direction from positive to negative voltage) all the time is a *dc voltage*. A voltage that regularly reverses polarity is an *ac voltage*. Batteries and solar cells are a source of dc voltage and current. Household power is supplied by an electrical utility in the form of ac voltage and current. A radio signal in a cable or wire is also ac. The frequency of household ac is 50 or 60 Hz, while radio signals used by amateurs have frequencies in the MHz and GHz range.

CIRCUITS

T5A13 — In which type of circuit is current the same through all components?

T5A14 — In which type of circuit is voltage the same across all components?

T5D13 — What happens to current at the junction of two components in series?

T5D14 — What happens to current at the junction of two components in parallel?

T5D15 — What is the voltage across each of two components in series with a voltage source?

T5D16 — What is the voltage across each of two components in parallel with a voltage source?

T7D02 — What is the correct way to connect a voltmeter to a circuit?

T7D03 — How is a simple ammeter connected to a circuit?

A *circuit* is any path through which current can flow. Electrical circuits are made from *components* and the connections between them. **Figure 3.3** illustrates the difference between series and parallel circuits. If two or more components such as light bulbs are connected in a circuit so that the same current must flow through all of them, that is a *series* circuit. **[T5A13]** If two or more components are connected so that the same voltage is present across all of them, that is a *parallel* circuit. **[T5A14]** A *short circuit* is a direct connection, usually unintentional, between two points in a circuit. An *open circuit* is made by breaking a current path in a circuit.

At the junction of two components in a series circuit, as in Figure 3.3A, you can see that the current is unchanged — the same current flows in each component. **[T5D13]** If two components are connected in parallel, however, the current divides between them. How much goes through each component depends on characteristics or value of the component. **[T5D14]**

When components are connected in parallel with a source of voltage, such as the battery in Figure 3.3B, the voltage across each is the same as that of the source. **[T5D15]** When the components are connected in series with the source of voltage, as in Figure 3.2A, the voltage divides between the components, depending on their type and value. [T5D16]

As shown in Figure 3.2, voltmeters are connected in parallel with or "across" a component or circuit to measure voltage. [T7D02] Ammeters are connected in series with a component or circuit to measure current. [T7D03]

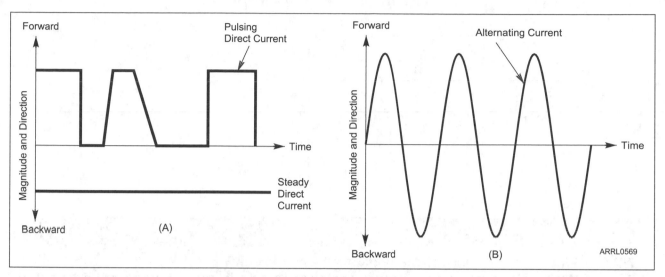

Figure 3.1 — Direct current (A) flows steadily in one direction — forward or backward. Pulsating direct current may stop and start, but always flows in the same direction. Alternating current (B) regularly reverses its direction.

Electrical Pressure and Flow

Figure 3.2 shows a time-tested analogy that helps newcomers to electricity understand what voltage and current are and how they act. Voltage acts like pressure in a water pipe and current acts like water flow. You can have lots of pressure with no flow — think of a pipe with the faucet closed. You can't have flow with no pressure, though. There must always be something pushing water molecules and electrons before they'll move.

Pressure is always measured between two points in the plumbing or between one point and the open air (atmospheric pressure). Voltage is the same — an electrical force that pushes electrons to flow from one point to another and is measured between these points. Water flow must go through something — a pipe or stream — and current must go through something as well, such as a wire.

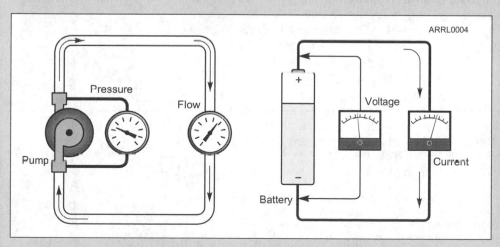

Figure 3.2 — Voltage acts similarly to pressure and current similarly to flow in a water system. Voltage between two points is what causes the electrons to move between those points. Current is a measure of how many electrons pass through the circuit per second.

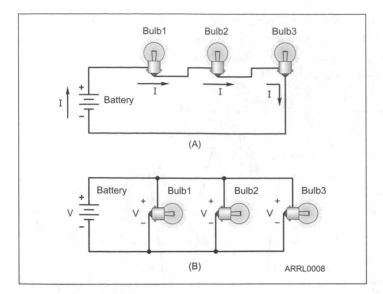

Figure 3.3 — Part A shows three light bulbs and a battery connected in a *series* circuit. The same current flows from the battery through all three light bulbs. Part B shows the same bulbs and battery connected in a *parallel* circuit. The same voltage from the battery is applied across each light bulb.

(A)

(B)   ARRL0008

Economies of Scale — The Multimeter

T7D06 — Which of the following might damage a multimeter?
T7D07 — Which of the following measurements are commonly made using a multimeter?
T7D10 — What is probably happening when an ohmmeter, connected across an unpowered circuit, initially indicates a low resistance and then shows increasing resistance with time?
T7D11 — Which of the following precautions should be taken when measuring circuit resistance with an ohmmeter?
T7D12 — Which of the following precautions should be taken when measuring high voltages with a voltmeter?

The basic electrical test instruments are simple meters: voltmeters, ammeters, and ohmmeters. So that a separate meter isn't needed for each parameter, the *multimeter* was invented — short for "multifunction meter." It measures all three electrical values of voltage, current, and resistance. **[T7D07]** A multimeters is also referred to as a *VOM* (volt-ohm meter) or *DVM* (digital volt meter). A typical digital multimeter is shown in **Figure 3.4A**. A switch and different sets of input connections select which parameter and range of values to measure.

It is important to use the meter properly and safely. Trying to measure voltage or connecting the probes to an energized circuit when the meter is set to measure resistance is a common way to damage a multimeter, for example. **[T7D06, T7D11]** You must also take heed of the meter's voltage rating as shown in Figure 3.4B. Voltages beyond the meter's rating can "flashover" to other pieces of equipment or to you, creating a serious shock hazard. Ensure that the voltmeter and leads are rated for use at the voltages to be measured! **[T7D12]**

You'll find unexpected ways to interpret a multimeter's readings, too. For example, if you are measuring the resistance of a circuit and the reading starts out low, but gradually increases, that indicates the presence of a large-value capacitor! **[T7D10]** (More information about the use of test equipment in general is available on the ARRL website's Technical Information Service.)

(A)

(B)

Figure 3.4 — A multimeter (A) combines three basic instruments into a single package: voltmeter, ammeter and ohmmeter. Stay within the voltage rating of the meter (B) to avoid shock hazards from arcs or "flashover."

RESISTANCE AND OHM'S LAW

T5A07 — Which of the following is a good electrical conductor?
T5A08 — Which of the following is a good electrical insulator?
T7D05 — What instrument is used to measure resistance?

All materials oppose the flow of electrons through them. This property is called resistance, represented by the symbol *R*. Resistance is measured in ohms, which are represented by the Greek letter omega, Ω. Resistance is measured with an *ohmmeter*. **[T7D05]**

Materials in which electrons flow easily in response to an applied voltage are *conductors*. Metals such as copper are good conductors. **[T5A07]** Materials that resist or prevent the flow of electrons are *insulators*, such as glass and ceramics, dry wood and paper, most plastics, and other non-metals. **[T5A08]**

T5D01 — What formula is used to calculate current in a circuit?
T5D02 — What formula is used to calculate voltage in a circuit?
T5D03 — What formula is used to calculate resistance in a circuit?

Ohm's Law states that the current through a material is directly proportional to the voltage across it and inversely proportional to the material's resistance. The higher the material's resistance, the lower the current through it will be in response to a voltage across the material.

As an equation, Ohm's Law is $I = E / R$. (You will also see this written as $I = V / R$ with *V* representing voltage.) If you know any two of *I, E,* or *R*, you can determine the missing quantity as follows:

$I = E / R$ **[T5D01]**

$E = I \times R$ **[T5D02]**

$R = E / I$ **[T5D03]**

The drawing in **Figure 3.5A** is a convenient aid to remembering Ohm's Law in any of these three forms. **Figure 3.6** shows several examples of how to use Ohm's Law.

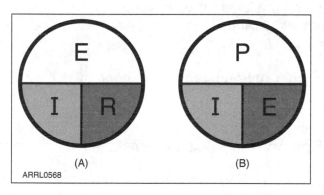

Figure 3.5 — These simple diagrams will help you remember the Ohm's Law (A) and power (B) relationships. If you know any two of the quantities, the equation to find the third is shown by covering up the unknown quantity. The positions of the remaining two symbols show if you have to multiply (side-by-side) or divide (one above the other).

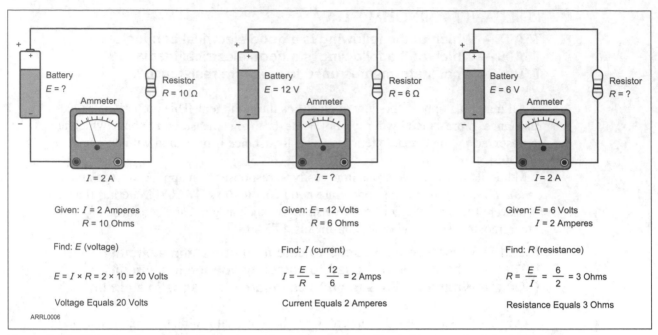

Figure 3.6 — This drawing shows three examples of how to use Ohm's Law to calculate voltage, current, or resistance.

T5D04 — What is the resistance of a circuit in which a current of 3 amperes flows through a resistor connected to 90 volts?
$R = E / I = 90 \text{ V} / 3 \text{ A} = 30 \, \Omega$

T5D05 — What is the resistance in a circuit for which the applied voltage is 12 volts and the current flow is 1.5 amperes?
$R = E / I = 12 \text{ V} / 1.5 \text{ A} = 8 \text{ W}$

T5D06 — What is the resistance of a circuit that draws 4 amperes from a 12-volt source?
$R = E / I = 12 \text{ V} / 4 \text{ A} = 3 \text{ W}$

T5D07 — What is the current in a circuit with an applied voltage of 120 volts and a resistance of 80 ohms?
$I = E / R = 120 \text{ V} / 80 \, \Omega = 1.5 \text{ A}$

T5D08 — What is the current through a 100-ohm resistor connected across 200 volts?
$I = E / R = 200 \text{ V} / 100 \, \Omega = 2 \text{ A}$

T5D09 — What is the current through a 24-ohm resistor connected across 240 volts?
$I = E / R = 240 \text{ V} / 24 \, \Omega = 10 \text{ A}$

T5D10 — What is the voltage across a 2-ohm resistor if a current of 0.5 amperes flows through it?
$E = I \times R = 0.5 \text{ A} \times 2 \, \Omega = 1 \text{ V}$

T5D11 — What is the voltage across a 10-ohm resistor if a current of 1 ampere flows through it?
$E = I \times R = 1\,A \times 10\,\Omega = 10\,V$

T5D12 — What is the voltage across a 10-ohm resistor if a current of 2 amperes flows through it?
$E = I \times R = 2\,A \times 10\,\Omega = 20\,V$

POWER

T5A02 — Electrical power is measured in which of the following units?
T5A10 — Which term describes the rate at which electrical energy is used?
T5C08 — What is the formula used to calculate electrical power in a DC circuit?

Power, represented by the symbol *P*, is the rate at which electrical energy is used. **[T5A10]** A device that consumes or dissipates power, such as a heater or a motor, is often referred to as a *load*. Power is measured in *watts* which are abbreviated as W. **[T5A02]** In a dc circuit, power is calculated as the product of voltage and current. **[T5C08]** (In ac circuits, other considerations must be taken into account when calculating power.)

As with Ohm's Law, if you know any two of P, E, or I, you can determine the missing quantity as follows:

$$P = E \times I \text{ or } E = P / I \text{ or } I = P / E$$

Here are some examples of how to use these power formulas:

T5C09 — How much power is being used in a circuit when the applied voltage is 13.8 volts and the current is 10 amperes?
$P = E \times I = 13.8\,V \times 10\,A = 138\,W$

T5C10 — How much power is being used in a circuit when the applied voltage is 12 volts DC and the current is 2.5 amperes?
$P = E \times I = 12\,V \times 2.5\,A = 30\,W$

T5C11 — How many amperes are flowing in a circuit when the applied voltage is 12 volts and the load is 120 watts?
$I = P / E = 240\,W / 12\,V = 20\,A$

What is the voltage in a circuit if a 50-watt load draws 5 amps?
$E = P / I = 50\,W / 5\,A = 10\,V$

3.2 Components and Units

Each component in an electrical circuit performs one or more functions such as storing or using energy, routing current, or amplifying a signal. In this chapter you'll learn about common components and their functions.

BASIC COMPONENTS

T5C01 — What is the ability to store energy in an electric field called?
T5C02 — What is the basic unit of capacitance?
T5C03 — What is the ability to store energy in a magnetic field called?
T5C04 — What is the basic unit of inductance?
T6A01 — What electrical component opposes the flow of current in a DC circuit?
T6A02 — What type of component is often used as an adjustable volume control?
T6A03 — What electrical parameter is controlled by a potentiometer?
T6A04 — What electrical component stores energy in an electric field?
T6A05 — What type of electrical component consists of two or more conductive surfaces separated by an insulator?
T6A06 — What type of electrical component stores energy in a magnetic field?
T6A07 — What electrical component usually is constructed as a coil of wire?
T6D06 — What component is commonly used to change 120V AC house current to a lower AC voltage for other uses?

The three most basic types of electronic components are resistors, capacitors and inductors (coils). These have their own units of measurement and have a different effect on voltage and current.

Resistors have a certain value of resistance specified in ohms (Ω), kilohms (kΩ), or megohms (MΩ). The function of a resistor is to oppose the flow of electrical current in an

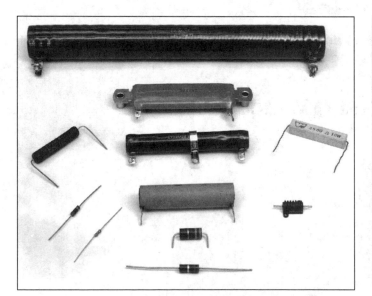

Figure 3.7 — This photograph shows some of the many types of resistors. Large, power resistors are at the top of the photo. The small resistors are used in low-power circuits.

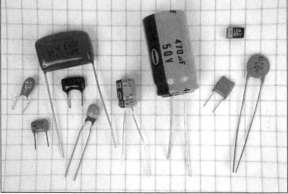

Figure 3.8 — This photograph shows a few styles of capacitors that are used in most common electronic equipment. Capacitors used in transmitters and high-power circuits are larger than those shown here.

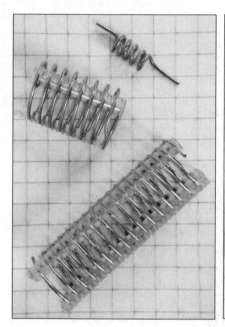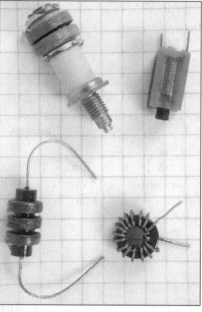

Figure 3.9 — Here are two types of inductors. On the left are air-core inductors. Those on the right wind the coiled around a magnetic material to concentrate the stored energy and increase inductance. At the lower right is an inductor wound on a toroid-shaped core.

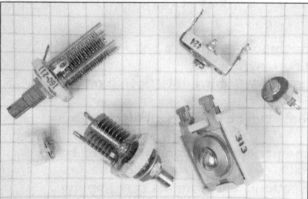

Figure 3.10 — Components with adjustable values are used to tune or calibrate circuits. This photograph shows variable resistors (top) and capacitors (bottom). Variable inductors can be seen at the top of the right-hand photo in Figure 3.9.

ac or dc circuit, just as a valve in a water pipe restricts the flow through the pipe. [T6A01] The electrical current flowing through the resistor loses some of its energy as heat, so resistors also dissipate energy, like an electrical brake. **Figure 3.7** shows different types of resistors.

Capacitors store electrical energy in the *electric field* created by a voltage between two conducting surfaces or *electrodes* [T6A04] that are separated by an insulator called a *dielectric*. [T6A05] Storing energy this way is called *capacitance*, and it is measured in farads (F). [T5C01, T5C02] Capacitors used in radio circuits have values measured in picofarads (pF), nanofarads (nF), and microfarads (μF). In most capacitors, the electrodes and dielectric are sealed inside a protective coating as shown in **Figure 3.8**.

Inductors store energy in the *magnetic field* created by current flowing in a wire. [T6A06] This is called *inductance* and it is measured in henrys (H). [T5C03, T5C04] Inductors have values measured in nanohenrys (nH), microhenrys (μH), millihenrys (mH), and henrys (H). Inductors are made from wire wound in a coil, sometimes around a *core* of magnetic material that concentrates the magnetic energy. [T6A07] **Figure 3.9** shows several common types of inductors.

All three types of basic components are also available as *adjustable* or *variable* models. A variable resistor is also called a *potentiometer* (poh-ten-chee-AH-meh-tur) or *pot* because it is frequently used to adjust voltage or potential, such as for a volume control. [T6A02, T6A03] **Figure 3.10** shows some examples of variable components.

Transformers are made from two or more inductors that share their stored energy. This allows energy to be transferred from one inductor to another while changing the combination of voltage and current. For example, a transformer is used to transfer energy from household 120 V ac voltage to a lower voltage for other uses such as in electronic equipment. [T6D06]

REACTANCE AND IMPEDANCE

T5C12 — What is impedance?
T5C13 — What is a unit of impedance?

In a resistor, ac voltages and currents are exactly in step, or *in phase*: As voltage increases, so does current and vice-versa. In capacitors and inductors, the relationship between ac voltage and current is altered so that there is an offset in time between changes in one and changes in the other as energy is stored, then released. That means voltage and current have a *phase difference*.

In a capacitor, the changes in current are a little ahead of, or *lead*, voltage changes because the capacitor's smoothing action works against changes in voltage. In an inductor, changes in the ac current *lag* a little behind changes in voltage because the inductor resists changes in current. The result is an opposition to ac current flow called *reactance*, represented by the capital letter *X*. Reactance is measured in ohms, as is resistance.

Reactance from a capacitor is called *capacitive reactance* and from an inductor, *inductive reactance*. The value of a component's reactance depends on the amount of capacitance or inductance and the frequency of the ac current.

The combination of resistance and reactance is called *impedance*, represented by the capital letter Z, and is also measured in ohms (Ω). **[T5C13]** Radio circuits almost always have both resistance and reactance, so impedance is often used as a general term to mean the circuit's opposition to ac current flow. **[T5C12]**

RESONANCE

T6D08 — Which of the following is combined with an inductor to make a tuned circuit?
T6D11 — Which of the following is a resonant or tuned circuit?

In a circuit with both capacitive and inductive reactance, at some frequency the two types of reactance will be equal and cancel each other out — a condition called resonance. The frequency at which resonance occurs is the resonant frequency.

Circuits that contain both a capacitor and an inductor are called *resonant circuits* or *tuned circuits*. **[T6D08]** If variable capacitors or inductors are used, the resonant frequency can be varied, *tuning* the circuit. A tuned circuit acts as a filter, passing or rejecting signals at its resonant frequency. **[T6D11]** Tuned circuits are important in radio because they help generate, pass, or reject signals based on their frequency.

DIODES, TRANSISTORS, AND INTEGRATED CIRCUITS

T6B01 — What class of electronic components uses a voltage or current signal to control current flow?
T6B02 — What electronic component allows current to flow in only one direction?
T6B03 — Which of these components can be used as an electronic switch or amplifier?
T6B04 — Which of the following components can consist of three layers of semiconductor material?
T6B05 — Which of the following electronic components can amplify signals?
T6B06 — How is the cathode lead of a semiconductor diode often marked on the package?
T6B07 — What does the abbreviation LED stand for?

T6B08 — What does the abbreviation FET stand for?

T6B09 — What are the names of the two electrodes of a diode?

T6B10 — Which of the following could be the primary gain-producing component in an RF power amplifier?

T6B11 — What is the term that describes a device's ability to amplify a signal?

T6D01 — Which of the following devices or circuits changes an alternating current into a varying direct current signal?

T6D07 — Which of the following is commonly used as a visual indicator?

T6D09 — What is the name of a device that combines several semiconductors and other components into one package?

T6D10 — What is the function of component 2 in Figure T1? (See Figure 3.16 later in this chapter.)

Some materials don't conduct electricity quite as well as a metallic conductor, nor are they a good insulator. These materials are called *semiconductors*. Some semiconductors, such as silicon, have the useful property that adding small amounts of certain impurities, called *doping*, changes their ability to conduct current. The impurities create *N-type* or *P-type* material, depending on the chemical properties of the impurity.

When N- and P-type material are placed in contact with each other, the result is a *PN junction* that conducts better in one direction than the other. This and other properties are used to create many useful electronic components, generally referred to as semiconductors. **Figure 3.11** shows several types of semiconductor components.

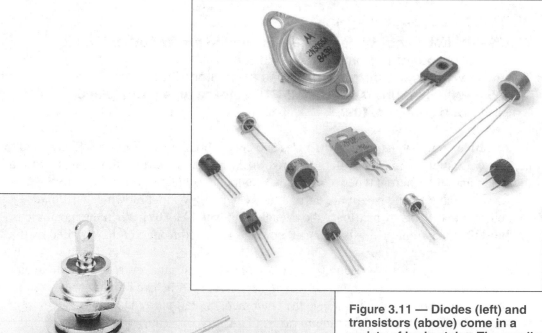

Figure 3.11 — Diodes (left) and transistors (above) come in a variety of body styles. The smaller types are used in low-power circuits to control very small signals. The larger types are used for controlling power and in transmitting circuits.

A semiconductor that only allows current flow in one direction is called a *diode*. [**T6B02**] Heavy-duty diodes that can handle large voltages and currents are called *rectifiers*. If an ac voltage is applied to a diode, the result is a pulsing dc current because current is blocked when the voltage tries to push electrons in the "wrong" direction. [**T6D01**] A diode has two electrodes, an *anode* and a *cathode*. [**T6B09**] As seen in Figure 3.11, on a diode the cathode is usually identified by a stripe marked on the component. [**T6B06**]

A special type of diode, the light-emitting diode or LED, gives off light when current flows through it. [**T6B07**] The material from which the LED is made determines the color of light emitted. LEDs are most often used as visual indicators. [**T6D07**] LEDs are often used instead of incandescent lamps or bulbs because they are smaller and use less power.

Transistors are components made of N- and P-layer patterns, and can have three layers of semiconductor material. [**T6B04**] The transistor's electrodes are contacts made to a certain piece of the pattern. Transistors use small voltages and currents to control larger ones. [**T6B01, T6D10**] With the appropriate external circuit and a source of power, transistors can amplify or switch voltages and currents. [**T6B03, T6B05**] Using small signal to control or amplify larger signals is called *gain*. [**T6B11**]

There are two common types of transistors: *bipolar junction transistors* (*BJT*) and *field-effect transistors* (*FET*). [**T6B08**] RF power transistors are used as the primary gain-producing component in RF power amplifiers. [**T6B10**]

An *integrated circuit* (*IC* or *chip*) is made of many components connected together as a useful circuit and packaged as a single component. [**T6D09**] ICs range from very simple circuits consisting of a few transistors all the way to complex microprocessors or signal-processing chips with many millions of components.

PROTECTIVE COMPONENTS

T6A09 — What electrical component is used to protect other circuit components from current overloads?

T0A04 — What is the purpose of a fuse in an electrical circuit?

T0A05 — Why is it unwise to install a 20-ampere fuse in the place of a 5-ampere fuse?

Protective components such as the fuses and circuit breakers in **Figure 3.12** are used to prevent equipment damage or safety hazards such as fire or electrical shock. It is important to understand the different types of protective components and use them correctly.

Fuses are rated by the maximum current they can carry without blowing. They interrupt current overloads by melting a short length of metal. [**T6A09**] When the metal melts or "blows," the current path is broken and power is removed from circuits supplied by the fuse. [**T0A04**]

When replacing a fuse or circuit breaker, use one with the same current rating to avoid creating a safety hazard. Using one with a higher current rating, even temporarily, could allow the fault to permanently damage the equipment or start a fire. Do not use a device with a higher current rating, even temporarily. [**T0A05**]

For More Information

"Slow-blow" fuses can withstand temporary overloads, but will blow if the overload is sustained. Fuses cannot be reused.

Circuit breakers act like fuses by *tripping* when current overloads occur. Tripping opens or *breaks* the circuit. Unlike fuses, circuit breakers can be *reset* once the current overload is removed, closing the circuit and allowing current to flow again.

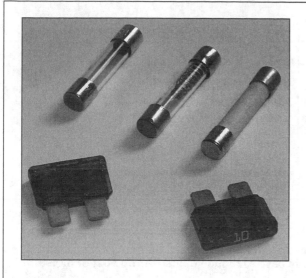

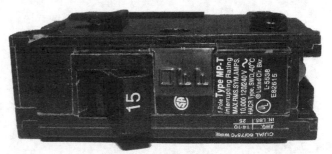

Figure 3.12 — Fuses (left) and circuit breakers (right) protect equipment by interrupting the current in case of an overload. Fuses "blow" by melting a metal wire or strip, seen in glass tube of the cartridge models. Circuit breakers can be reset once the problem creating the overload is removed.

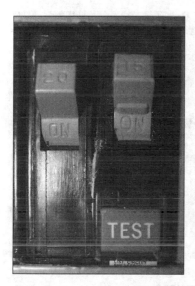

Figure 3.13 — The ground-fault circuit interrupter (GFCI) circuit breaker interrupts current flow when it senses imbalances between the hot and neutral circuits in ac wiring. The imbalance of currents indicates that a shock or other safety hazard exists in wiring supplied by the breaker. Electrical outlets with a built-in GFCI may be found in kitchens, bathrooms, basements, garages and other damp areas.

Used in ac power wiring, a *ground-fault circuit interrupter* (GFCI) circuit breaker shown in **Figure 3.13** trips if an imbalance is sensed in the currents carried by the hot and neutral conductors. Current imbalances indicate the presence of an electrical shock hazard.

Surge protectors limit temporary voltage *transients* above normal voltages by dissipating the excess energy of the transient as heat. Surge protectors are connected to a home's ac power circuits, often in power outlet strips, and to telephone lines. *Lightning arrestors* have a similar function in an antenna feed line. They are designed to handle the much higher voltages and currents of a lightning strike.

CIRCUIT GATEKEEPERS

T6A08 — What electrical component is used to connect or disconnect electrical circuits?

T6D02 — What is a relay?

T6D03 — What type of switch is represented by component 3 in figure T2? (See Figure 3.16 later in this chapter)

Switches and *relays* control current through a circuit by connecting and disconnecting paths for current to follow. **[T6A08]** Both can interrupt current — called *opening* a circuit — or allow it to flow — called *closing* a circuit. **Figure 3.14** shows different types of switches and a typical relay. A switch is operated manually while a relay is a switch controlled by an electromagnet. **[T6D02]**

Switches and relays are described by their number of *poles* and the number of *throws*. Each pole controls the path of one current. For example, a single-pole (SP) switch controls a single current flow and a double-pole (DP) switch controls two separate currents. Each throw refers to a different path for the current. A double-throw (DT) switch can route current through either of two paths while a single-throw (ST) switch can only open or

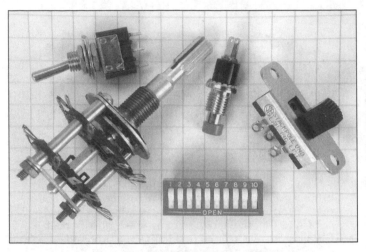

Figure 3.14 — Switches and relays control the path of current flow through a circuit. On the left are several types of switches. On the right is a typical relay, enclosed in a plastic case to reduce damage from dust or moisture.

Indicator, Meters and Displays

T6D04 — Which of the following displays an electrical quantity as a numeric value?

Indicators and displays are important components for radio equipment. An *indicator* is either ON or OFF, such as a power indicator or a label that appears when you are transmitting. A *meter* provides information as a value in the form of numbers or on a numeric scale. **[T6D04]** A *display* combines indicators, numbers, and labels. A *liquid crystal display* or LCD is used on the front panel of many radios and test instruments.

close a single path. **[T6D03]**

The combination of poles and throws describes the switch. For example, the simplest switch that opens or closes a single current path is an SPST (single-pole single-throw) switch. SPDT, DPST, and DPDT are other common configurations.

SCHEMATICS AND COMPONENT SYMBOLS

T6C01 — What is the name of an electrical wiring diagram that uses standard component symbols?

T6C02 through T6C11 — Refer to Figures 3.15 and 3.16 to learn the right type of component for each of the symbols in Exam Diagrams T1, T2, and T3.

T6C12 — What do the symbols on an electrical schematic represent?

T6C13 — Which of the following is accurately represented in electrical schematics?

If a circuit contains more than two or three components, trying to describe it clearly in words is very difficult. To describe complicated circuits, engineers have developed the *schematic diagram* or simply *schematic*. Schematics are a visual description of a circuit and its components that uses standardized drawings called *circuit symbols*. **[T6C01, T6C12] Figure 3.15** shows the schematic symbols for a number of common components.

Well-Grounded Symbols

Figure 3.15 includes four different symbols for "Grounds" which can be confusing. The upper right ground symbol in Figure 3.15 represents a connection directly to the Earth. Some circuits require a connection to the metal enclosure or *chassis*, the upper left-hand ground symbol. The chassis may or may not be connected to an earth ground.

Within a piece of equipment the triangular ground symbol on the bottom left generally indicates a connection for current to flow back to the power supply. This is usually referred to as *circuit common* or just *common*. If an A or D is added to the triangle, the circuit has digital (D) computing components (such as microprocessors) as well as circuits that handle analog signals (A). By keeping the return connection to the power supply separate for each type of circuitry, the analog signals are kept free of noise from the digital circuits.

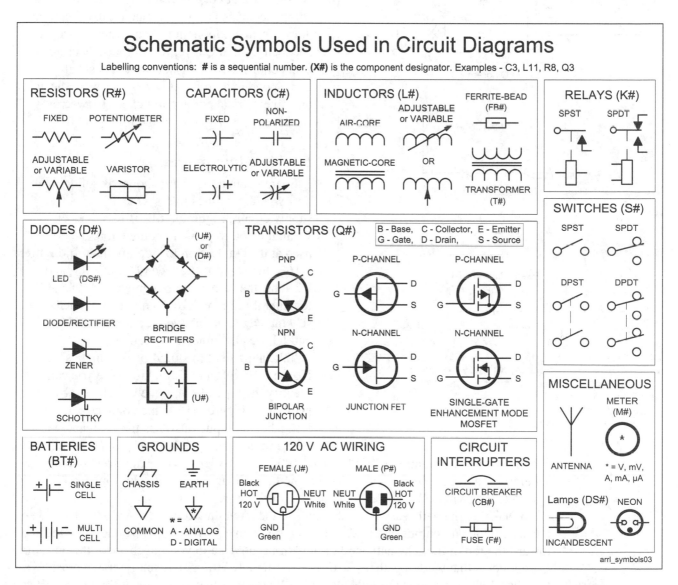

Figure 3.15 — Symbols are used when drawing a circuit because there are so many types of components. Radio and electrical designers use them as a convenient way of describing a circuit.

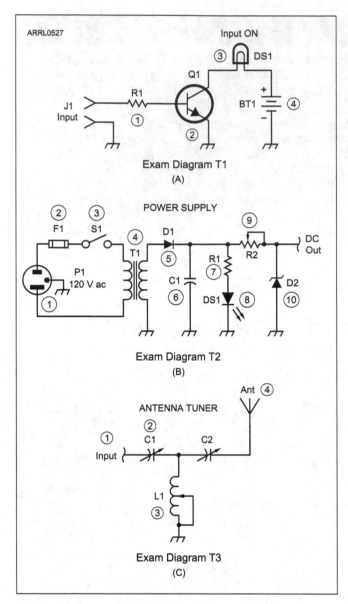

ARRL0527

Input ON

Exam Diagram T1
(A)

POWER SUPPLY

Exam Diagram T2
(B)

ANTENNA TUNER

Exam Diagram T3
(C)

Figure 3.16 — A schematic diagram describes complex circuits using symbols representing each type of component. Lines and dots show electrical connections between the components, but may not correspond to actual wires. These are diagrams T1 (A), T2 (B), and T3 (C) that are used on the Technician exam. The numbers enclosed in circles correspond to numbered components in the exam diagrams.

Don't worry that you aren't familiar with all of them! Look for and identify the circuit symbols for a resistor, capacitor, inductor, diode, and transistor. **[T6C02 to T6C11]**

Figure 3.16A shows the schematic for a simple transistor circuit. (These schematics are also used on the Technician exam.) Each component is assigned a unique *designator* within the circuit or a text label. Examples are BT1, R1, Q1 or a label may be added, such as "Input On" for the lamp's function. Resistors are designated with an R, capacitors with a C, inductors with an L, diodes with a D, transistors with a Q and so forth.

A schematic does not illustrate the actual physical layout of a circuit. (A *pictorial diagram* is used for that purpose.) It only shows how the components are connected electrically. The lines drawn from component to component, such as between R1 and Q1, represent those electrical connections. Each line does not necessarily correspond to a physical wire — it just indicates that an electrical connection exists between whatever is at each end of the line. **[T6C13]**

For More Information

Shared connections are shown as solid, black dots where two lines intersect as in the power supply circuit, Figure 3.16B. If two lines cross without a dot, there is no connection. No dots are used at the connection to a component. In Figure 3.16B, the two dots between D1, C1, R1, and R2 show that these components are connected together. In Figure 3.16C, an antenna tuner schematic, the dot above L1 shows that C1, C2, and L1 are all connected together.

Take a moment to study the schematics of Figure 3.16A, B and C, making sure you can identify the type of component indicated by each symbol. In Figure 3.16A, the connector at the left, labeled "Input" also has the designator J1, with J indicating a *jack* or *receptacle*. In Figure 3.16B, the ac *plug* symbol, P1, is labeled "120 V ac" to identify it as a power source. The schematic shows the important safety information that ac line voltage is connected to the fuse, F1, the switch S1, and the transformer, T1.

To make a schematic easy to read, inputs to the circuit are located toward the left side of the schematic and outputs are toward the right. Positive power supply voltages are located toward the top of the schematic and ground or negative supply voltages are at the bottom. Components that work together performing a single function are usually drawn close together. Labels are added to indicate circuit function. You can see this in Figure 3.16B as power from the ac line flows through the input components at left, through the transformer, and through the rectifier and regulator circuit components at the right. DC output voltage is available from the connection point at the right of the schematic labeled, "DC Out."

Remember that a schematic may have little resemblance to the actual physical layout of the circuit. It is just a convenient way to describe how the circuit is constructed electrically. The "First Steps in Radio" link on the *Ham Radio License Manual* web page will take you to a good article on reading schematics.

3.3 Radio Circuits

In Chapter 2, you learned about some of the terms that describe the functions of a radio signal used for communication — frequency, phase, modulation, bandwidth, sideband and so forth. In this section, we'll introduce some of the circuits that make those functions happen. The block diagrams that describe simple radios show how successive circuits, called *stages*, are arranged to construct basic radio transmitters and receivers.

OSCILLATORS AND AMPLIFIERS

T7A05 — What is the name of a circuit that generates a signal at a specific frequency?

An *oscillator* produces a steady signal at one frequency. **[T7A05]** Oscillators are used in both receivers and transmitters to determine the operating frequency. In a transmitter, the output signal from an oscillator is modulated (see Chapter 5) and amplified before actually being applied to an antenna.

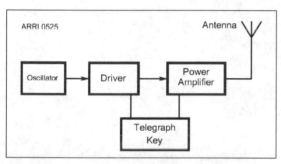

Figure 3.17 — A simple CW transmitter consists of an oscillator to generate a low-power signal and two amplifiers to increase the signal strength to a useful level. A telegraph key is used to turn the amplifiers on and off, creating the CW signal that is transmitted. The oscillator runs continuously so that its frequency remains stable.

For More Information

The output signal from the oscillator is not strong enough for reliable communication over long distances. An *amplifier* circuit called a *driver* allows the oscillator to operate continuously at low power so that its frequency remains stable. The output of the driver is then applied to a *power amplifier* which has an output strong enough for reliable communication with other stations. In order to turn the output signal on and off as Morse code, the driver and power amplifier stages are *keyed* (switched on and off) by a telegraph key. **Figure 3.17** illustrates how these stages are combined into a simple Morse code transmitter.

MODULATORS

T7A08 — Which of the following describes combining speech with an RF carrier signal?

The process of combining data or voice signals with an RF signal is *modulation*. A circuit that performs the modulation function is therefore called a *modulator*. **[T7A08]** The function of the modulator is to add the data or voice signal to an RF signal or carrier. The result is an RF signal that can be communicated by radio. A *demodulator* circuit extracts the information from a modulated signal. Modulation is discussed further in Chapter 5.

MIXERS

T7A03 — Which of the following is used to convert a radio signal from one frequency to another?

A *mixer* is closely related to a modulator. Mixers combine two RF signals and shift one of them to a third frequency. [T7A03] Mixers are used in both transmitters and receivers to shift signal frequencies for various purposes. (This circuit should not be confused with an *audio mixer* that combines audio signals for recording or live entertainment.)

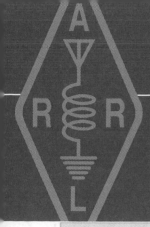

Chapter 4

Propagation, Antennas and Feed Lines

In this chapter, you'll learn about:
- How radio signals travel from place to place
- Basic ideas about antennas
- How feed lines are constructed and used
- What SWR is and what it means to you

When you see the mouse, you'll find more information at www.arrl.org/ham-radio-license-manual

No piece of equipment has as great an effect on the performance of a radio station, whether handheld or home-based, as the antenna. Experimenting with antennas has been a favorite of hams from the very beginning, contributing greatly to the development of antennas for all radio services. To choose and use an antenna effectively, it's important to understand some basics of *propagation* — how radio waves get from one place to another. For these reasons, knowledge of antennas and propagation is very important for amateurs.

4.1 Propagation

T3A01 — What should you do if another operator reports that your station's 2 meter signals were strong just a moment ago, but now they are weak or distorted?

T3A02 — Why might the range of VHF and UHF signals be greater in the winter?

T3A06 — What term is commonly used to describe the rapid fluttering sound sometimes heard from mobile stations that are moving while transmitting?

T3A08 — Which of the following is a likely cause of irregular fading of signals received by ionospheric reflection?

T3A10 — What may occur if data signals arrive via multiple paths?

T3A12 — How might fog and light rain affect radio range on 10 meters and 6 meters?

T3A13 — What weather condition would decrease range at microwave frequencies?

T3C05 — Which of the following effects might cause radio signals to be heard despite obstructions between the transmitting and receiving stations?

T3C06 — **What mode is responsible for allowing over-the-horizon VHF and UHF communications to ranges of approximately 300 miles on a regular basis?**

T3C08 — **What causes tropospheric ducting?**

T3C11 — **Why do VHF and UHF radio signals usually travel somewhat farther than the visual line of sight distance between two stations?**

Radio waves spread out from an antenna in straight lines unless reflected or diffracted along the way, just like light. Like light waves, the strength of a radio wave decreases as it travels farther from the transmitting antenna. Eventually the wave becomes too weak to be received because it has spread out too much or something along its path absorbed or scattered it. The distance over which a radio transmission can be received is called *range*.

Radio waves can be reflected by any sudden change in the path they are traveling, such as a building, hill, or even weather-related changes in the atmosphere. Obstructions such as buildings and hills also create radio *shadowing*, especially at VHF and UHF frequencies. Vegetation can also absorb VHF and UHF radio waves. This can result in greater range in the winter. **[T3A02]** Precipitation such as fog and rain can absorb microwave and UHF radio waves although it has little effect at HF and on the lower VHF bands. **[T3A12, T3A13]**

Figure 4.1 shows how radio waves can also be *diffracted* as they travel past sharp edges of large objects. This type of propagation is called *knife-edge diffraction*. **[T3C05]**

Refraction is another type of propagation — a gradual bending of VHF and UHF radio waves in the atmosphere. By bending signals slightly back towards the ground, refraction counteracts the curvature of the Earth and allows signals at these frequencies to be received at distances somewhat beyond the visual horizon. **[T3C11]**

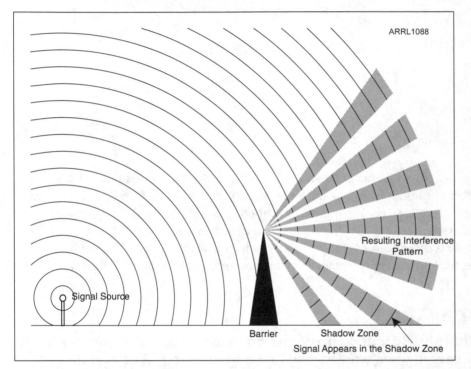

Figure 4.1 — VHF and UHF radio waves are diffracted by the edge of a solid object, such as a building, hill or other obstruction, bending them in different ways around the obstruction. The resulting interference pattern creates shadowed areas where little signal is present. If the edge of the object is small compared to a wavelength, the result is called "knife-edge diffraction."

Radio signals arriving at a receiver after taking different paths from the transmitter can interfere with each other if they are out of phase, even canceling completely! This phenomenon is known as *multipath* and can cause a signal to become weak and distorted. Multipath propagation of signals from distant stations results in irregular fading, even when reception is generally good. **[T3A08]** Moving your antenna just a few feet may avoid the location at which cancellation is occurring. Re-orienting the antenna may also help by making one of the interfering signals stronger or weaker. **[T3A01]**

Because "dead spots" from multipath are usually spaced about ½-wavelength apart,

VHF or UHF signals from a station in motion can take on a rapid variation in strength known as *mobile flutter* or *picket-fencing*. [T3A06] Distortion caused by multipath can also cause VHF and UHF digital data signals to be received with a higher error rate, even though the signal may be strong. [T3A10]

Propagation at and above VHF frequencies assisted by variations in the atmosphere is called *tropospheric propagation* or just "tropo." Variations such as weather fronts or temperature inversions create layers of air next to each other that have different characteristics. The layers form structures called *ducts* that can guide even microwave signals for long distances. [T3C08] Tropo is regularly used by amateurs to make VHF and UHF contacts that would otherwise be impossible by line-of-sight propagation. Tropo contacts over 300-mile paths are not uncommon. [T3C06]

THE IONOSPHERE

T3A11 — Which part of the atmosphere enables the propagation of radio signals around the world?

T3C01 — Why are direct (not via a repeater) UHF signals rarely heard from stations outside your local coverage area?

T3C02 — Which of the following is an advantage of HF vs VHF and higher frequencies?

T3C03 — What is a characteristic of VHF signals received via auroral reflection?

T3C04 — Which of the following propagation types is most commonly associated with occasional strong over-the-horizon signals on the 10, 6, and 2 meter bands?

T3C07 — What band is best suited for communicating via meteor scatter?

T3C09 — What is generally the best time for long-distance 10 meter band propagation via the F layer?

T3C10 — Which of the following bands may provide long distance communications during the peak of the sunspot cycle?

Above the lower atmosphere where the air is relatively dense and below outer space where there isn't any air at all lies the *ionosphere*. In this region, from 30 to 260 miles above the Earth, atoms of oxygen and nitrogen gas are exposed to the intense and energetic *ultraviolet* (UV) light from the Sun. UV light has enough energy to create positively charged *ions* from the gas atoms by knocking off some of their negatively charged electrons. The resulting ions and electrons cause the ionosphere to be weakly conducting.

The ionosphere forms in layers shown in **Figure 4.2**, called the D, E, F1 and F2 layers, with the D layer being the lowest. Depending on whether it is night or day and on the intensity of solar radiation, these layers can refract (E, F1 and F2 layers) or absorb (D and E layers) radio waves.

Radio waves can be completely bent back toward the Earth by refraction in the ionosphere's E and F layers as if they were reflected. This is called *sky wave* propagation or *skip*. The ability of the ionosphere to refract or bend radio waves also depends on the frequency of the radio wave. Higher frequency waves are bent less than those of lower frequencies.

Since the Earth's surface is also conductive, it can also reflect radio waves. This means that a radio wave can be reflected between the ionosphere and ground multiple times. Each reflection from the ionosphere is called a *hop*. Reflections from the ionosphere allow radio waves to be received hundreds or thousands of miles away. [T3A11]

Long-distance ionospheric propagation is the most common way for hams to make long-distance contacts on the HF bands. As illustrated in **Figure 4.3**, at VHF and higher

Figure 4.2 — The ionosphere is formed by solar ultraviolet (UV) radiation. The UV rays knock electrons loose from air molecules, creating weakly charged layers at different heights. These layers can absorb or refract radio signals, sometimes bending them back to the

Ionosphere   30 to 260 Miles Above the Surface

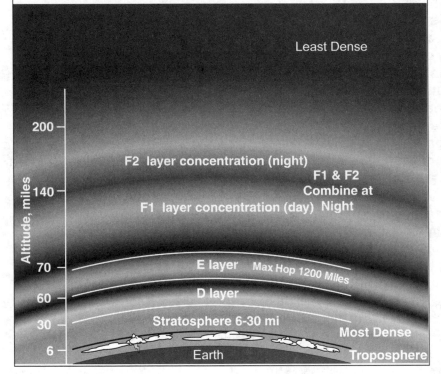

Least Dense

Altitude, miles

200 —

F2 layer concentration (night)

140 —   F1 & F2 Combine at

F1 layer concentration (day) Night

70 —   E layer Max Hop 1200 Miles

60 —   D layer

30 —   Stratosphere 6-30 mi

6 —   Most Dense

Earth   Troposphere

frequencies, the waves usually pass through the ionosphere with only a little bending and are lost to space. [T3C02] This is why UHF signals from stations beyond the radio horizon are rarely heard without being relayed by a repeater. [T3C01]

As sunspot activity increases, solar UV rays become more intense. This increases the peak level of ionization in the ionosphere, raising the highest frequency for signals to be returned to Earth along the path between stations. During the years of maximum solar activity, the upper HF bands, such as 10 meters, are likely to be open from dawn until shortly after sunset. Occasionally, the F layers can even reflect 6 meter (50 MHz) signals at the sunspot cycle's peak. [T3C09, T3C10]

At all points in the solar cycle, patches of the ionosphere's E layer can become sufficiently ionized to reflect VHF and UHF signals back to Earth. This is called *sporadic E* or E_s (or E-skip) propagation and it is most common during early summer and mid-winter months on 10, 6, and occasionally 2 meters. [T3C04]

Along with sporadic E propagation, the ionosphere is home to other radio wave reflectors. The aurora (northern lights) is the glow from thin sheets of charged particles flowing down through the lower layers of the ionosphere. Those thin sheets 50 miles or more above the Earth's surface reflect VHF signals. Because the aurora is constantly changing, the reflected signals change strength quickly and are often distorted. [T3C03]

The E region of the ionosphere is also home to meteor trails. A meteoroid burning up in the upper atmosphere results in a *meteor* with a *meteor trail* of ionized gas lasting up to several seconds that can reflect radio signals. Bouncing signals off of these ionized trails is called *meteor scatter* propagation. The best band for meteor scatter is 6 meters, and contacts can be made at distances up to 1200 to 1500 miles. [T3C07]

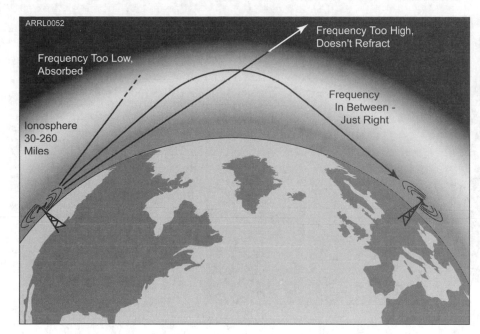

Figure 4.3 — Signals that are too low in frequency are absorbed by the ionosphere and lost. Signals that are too high in frequency pass through the ionosphere and are also lost. Signals in the right range of frequencies are refracted back toward the Earth and are received hundreds or thousands of miles away. Paths of this length generally require several ionospheric hops — the figure is intended only to illustrate the maximum and lowest usable frequencies.

Labels within figure: ARRL0052 · Frequency Too Low, Absorbed · Frequency Too High, Doesn't Refract · Frequency In Between - Just Right · Ionosphere 30-260 Miles

For More Information

The highest frequency signal that can be reflected back to a point on the Earth between the transmitter and receiver is the *maximum usable frequency* (MUF) along that path. The lowest frequency that can travel between those points without being absorbed is the *lowest usable frequency* (LUF). This is illustrated in Figure 4.3.

When sky wave propagation on an amateur band is possible between two points, the band is said to be *open*. If not, the band is *closed*. Because the ionosphere depends on solar radiation to form, areas in daylight have a different ionosphere above them than do those in nighttime areas. That means radio propagation may be supported in some directions but not others, opening and closing to different locations as the Earth rotates and the seasons change. This makes pursuing long-distance contacts (DXing) very interesting!

VHF and UHF operators also experience exciting ionospheric propagation. When solar radiation becomes sufficiently intense, such as during the peak of the 11-year sunspot cycle, the F layers of the ionosphere can bend even VHF signals back to Earth. When these conditions occur, the ionosphere supports long-distance VHF communication not possible under normal conditions.

4.2 Antenna and Radio Wave Basics

T3A04 — What can happen if the antennas at opposite ends of a VHF or UHF line of sight radio link are not using the same polarization?

T3A07 — What type of wave carries radio signals between transmitting and receiving stations?

T3A09 — Which of the following results from the fact that skip signals refracted from the ionosphere are elliptically polarized?

T3B02 — What property of a radio wave is used to describe its polarization?

T3B03 — What are the two components of a radio wave?

T5C07 — A radio wave is made up of what type of energy?

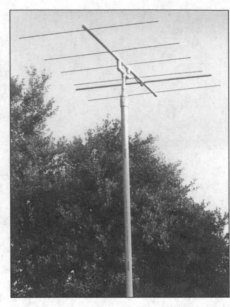

Figure 4.4 — The ground-plane antenna shown at the left radiates a signal from the vertical wire attached to the base. The vehicle's metal surface acts as an electrical mirror, creating the effect of another wire opposite to the one above the surface. On the right, the Yagi beam antenna uses parasitic elements to direct the signal in one direction and reject signals in the opposite direction.

An antenna is a conductor, usually a wire, rod, or pipe, that radiates and receives radio signals. For an antenna to do that job efficiently, its dimensions must be an appreciable fraction of the signal's wavelength. **Figure 4.4** shows two examples of antennas commonly used by Technician class hams.

RF current in an antenna creates radio waves that travel away from the antenna, spreading out into space like ripples traveling across water. The radio wave contains both electrical and magnetic energy supplied by the electrons moving back and forth in the antenna. The wave's electric and magnetic fields oscillate at the same frequency as the RF current in the antenna. The wave is a combination of an electric and a magnetic field. **[T3B03]** Because a radio wave is made up of both types of fields, it is called an *electromagnetic wave*. **[T5C07, T3A07]**

Polarization refers to the orientation of the radio wave's electric field. **[T3B02]** A *horizontally polarized* antenna radiates a radio wave with an electric field oriented horizontally. When the electric field of the radio wave and the element of the antenna have the same polarization, the maximum amount of signal is created in the antenna by the wave. That is why it is important to hold your handheld radio so that its antenna is aligned with the antenna of the receiving station.

When the polarizations of transmit and receive antennas aren't aligned the same, the received signal can be dramatically reduced. Because the polarization of the radio wave doesn't match that of the receiving antenna, less current is created in the antenna. **[T3A04]**

As a radio wave travels through the ionosphere its polarization changes from vertical or horizontal to a combination of the two, called *elliptical polarization*. As a result, a receiving antenna of any polarization will respond to the incoming wave at least partially. This means both vertical and horizontal antennas are effective for receiving and transmitting on the HF bands where skip propagation is common. **[T3A09]**

For More Information

A *feed line* is used to deliver the radio signals to or from the antenna. The connection of antenna and feed line is called the *feed point* of the antenna. Just like Ohm's Law in Chapter 2, the ratio of radio frequency voltage to current at an antenna's feed point is the antenna's *feed point impedance*. An antenna is *resonant* when its feed point impedance is all resistance with no reactance.

An antenna's feed point impedance at a specific frequency depends on how its physical dimensions compare to the wavelength at that frequency. Feed point impedance changes with frequency because wavelength changes but the physical dimensions don't. An antenna's feed point impedance is also affected by nearby conductors and its height above ground.

The conducting portions of an antenna by which the radio signals are transmitted or received are called *elements*. An antenna with more than one element is called an *array*. The element connected to the feed line is called the *driven element*. If all of the elements are connected to a feed line, that's a *driven array*. Elements that are not directly connected to a feed line, but that influence the antenna performance, are called *parasitic elements*.

If you could feel what an electron in an antenna element feels as a radio wave passes by, you would feel both an electric force and a magnetic force. The forces are caused by the radio wave's electric field and magnetic field and oscillate at the frequency of the radio wave's signal. These forces cause electrons in the receiving antenna element to move back and forth, creating an RF current that can be detected by a receiver.

ANTENNA GAIN
T9A11 — What is the gain of an antenna?

Concentrating an antenna's radiated signals in a specific direction is called *gain*. Antenna gain increases signal strength in a specified direction when compared to a reference antenna. **[T9A11]** Gain aids communication in the preferred direction by increasing transmitted and received signal strengths.

An antenna creates gain by radiating radio waves that add together in the preferred direction and cancel in others. Gain can also be created by reflecting radio waves so that they are focused in one direction. Gain only focuses power — it does not create power. The focusing effect makes the signal seem more powerful in the favored direction. Gain also increases the strength of received signals in the focused direction.

For More Information

An *isotropic* antenna has no gain because it radiates equally in every possible direction. Isotropic antennas do not exist in the real world — they are only used as imaginary references. An *omnidirectional* antenna radiates a signal equally in every horizontal direction. An antenna with gain in a single direction is called a *beam* or *directional* antenna. Omnidirectional antennas are useful for communicating over a wide region while beam antennas are used when communication is desired in one direction.

An antenna's gain is measured in decibels (dB) with respect to some type of reference antenna. For example, the abbreviation dBi means gain in decibels with respect to an isotropic antenna. The abbreviation dBd means gain with respect to a dipole antenna's peak gain (discussed below). Gain, like voltage, is a relative measurement between an antenna and some reference antenna, most often an isotropic or dipole antenna.

The easiest way to describe how an antenna distributes its signals is a graph showing the antenna's gain in any direction around the antenna. That graph is called a *radiation pattern*. An antenna transmits and receives with the same pattern.

The most common type of radiation pattern is an *azimuthal* pattern that shows the antenna's gain in horizontal directions around the antenna. An azimuthal pattern can be imagined as looking down on the antenna from above as in **Figure 4.5**. An *elevation* pattern shows the strength of the radiated energy in vertical directions as if the antenna is viewed from the side, as shown in **Figure 4.6**. An antenna's radiation pattern may change as frequency changes for the same reasons that feed point impedance changes with frequency — changes in frequency change the wavelength, while the physical dimensions remain fixed, causing the antenna to behave differently electrically.

The region of the radiation pattern in which the antenna's gain is greatest is called the

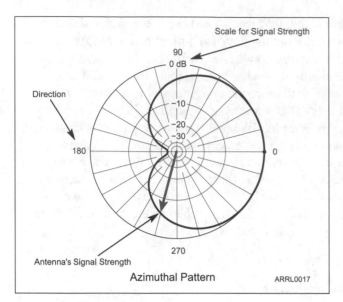

Azimuthal Pattern

ARRL0017

Figure 4.5 — As if looking down on the antenna from above, the azimuth radiation pattern shows how well the antenna transmits or receives in all horizontal directions. The distance from the center of the graph to the solid line is a measure of the antenna's ability to receive or transmit in that direction.

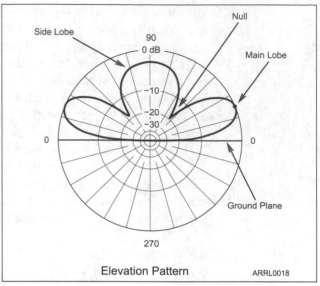

Elevation Pattern

ARRL0018

Figure 4.6 — The elevation pattern looks at the antenna from the side to see how well it receives and transmits at different angles above a horizontal plane.

Decibels — Bringing Large and Small Together

T5B09 — What is the approximate amount of change, measured in decibels (dB), of a power increase from 5 watts to 10 watts?

T5B10 — What is the approximate amount of change, measured in decibels (dB), of a power decrease from 12 watts to 3 watts?

T5B11 — What is the amount of change, measured in decibels (dB), of a power increase from 20 watts to 200 watts?

Radio signals vary dramatically in strength. At the input to a receiver, signals are frequently smaller than one ten-billionth of a watt. When they come out of a transmitter, they're often measured in kilowatts! Antennas, propagation and electronic circuits change signal strengths by many factors of ten. These big differences in value make it difficult to compare signal sizes. Enter the *decibel*, abbreviated dB and pronounced "dee-bee." The decibel measures the ratio of two quantities as a power of 10. The formula for computing decibels is:

dB = 10 log (power ratio)

dB = 20 log (voltage ratio).

Positive values of dB mean the ratio is greater than 1 and negative values of dB indicate a ratio of less than 1. For example, if an amplifier turns a 5-watt signal into a 10-watt signal, that's a change of 10 log (10 / 5) = 10 log (2) = 3 dB. **[T5B09]** An increase in power from 20 to 200 watts is a change of 10 log (200 / 20) = 10 log (10) = 10 dB. **[T5B11]** Turning up an audio amplifier to increase output voltage from 1 to 5 volts is a change of 20 log (5 / 1) = 20 log (5) = 14 dB.

On the other hand, if an amplifier's output is reduced from 12 watts to 3 watts, that's a change of 10 log (3 /12) = 10 log (0.25) = −6 dB. **[T5B10]** Reducing the audio output signal voltage from 2 volts to 0.1 volts is a change of 20 log (0.1 / 2) = 20 log (0.05) = −26 dB.

A complete discussion of the decibel, its history, and examples of how to work out the answers to exam questions about decibels are available on the *Ham Radio License Manual* web page. Look for the section on Chapter 4.

main lobe. Regions of lower gain are called *side lobes* and *nulls* are where gain is a minimum. The ratio of gain in the preferred or *forward* direction to that in the opposite direction is called the *front-to-back ratio*. The ratio of gain in the forward direction to that at right angles is called the *front-to-side ratio*. Antennas with high front-to-back and front-to-side ratios are useful in rejecting interference and noise from unwanted directions.

4.3 Feed Lines and SWR

T7C07 — What happens to power lost in a feed line?
T9B02 — What is the impedance of most coaxial cables used in amateur radio installations?
T9B03 — Why is coaxial cable the most common feed line selected for amateur radio antenna systems?
T9B05 — In general, what happens as the frequency of a signal passing through coaxial cable is increased?
T9B11 — Which of the following types of feed line has the lowest loss at VHF and UHF?

Feed lines are used to connect a radio to an antenna. They are also used when an RF signal must be conducted from one piece of equipment to another. Feed lines are made from two conductors separated by an insulating material such as plastic. The radio signal is carried on the conductors and in the space between them. Feed lines used at radio frequencies use special materials and construction methods to minimize power being dissipated as heat by *feed line loss* and to avoid signals leaking in or out. **[T7C07]** Feed line loss increases with frequency for all types of feed lines. **[T9B05]**

COAXIAL CABLE

The most popular feed line used by amateurs to connect radios and antennas is *coaxial cable* or *coax*. It is easy to use and requires few special installation considerations. **[T9B03]** Figure 4.7 shows how coaxial cable is constructed. A wire *center conductor* is surrounded by insulation (the *center insulator* or *dielectric*). The insulation is covered with a tubular *shield* of braided wire or foil. Finally, the cable is covered with a plastic sheath called the *jacket*. The name "coaxial" comes from the common central axis of the center conductor and the shield.

Coaxial cable carries the radio signal on the surface of the center conductor and the inside surface of the shield. That means it can be placed next to other cables or conducting surfaces such as conduit or antenna support masts without affecting the signal inside.

A special type of coaxial feed line is called *hardline* because its shield is made from a semi-flexible solid tube of aluminum or copper. This limits the amount of bending the cable can do, but hardline has the lowest loss of any type of coaxial feed line. **[T9B11]**

CHARACTERISTIC IMPEDANCE

Feed lines have a *characteristic impedance* which is denoted by Z_0, a measurement of how energy is carried by the feed line. This is not the same as the resistance of the conductors if measured from end to end of the feed line.

The dimensions of feed line conductors, the spacing between them, and the insulating material determine characteristic impedance. Most coaxial cable used in ham radio has a characteristic impedance of 50 ohms. **[T9B02]** Coaxial cables used for video and cable television have a Z_0 of 75 ohms. Open-wire feed lines have a Z_0 of 300 to 600 ohms.

Figure 4.7 — This drawing illustrates some common types of open-wire and coaxial cables used by amateurs. Open-wire line (A and B) has two parallel conductors separated by insulation. "Coax" (C-F) has a center conductor surrounded by insulation. The second conductor, called the *shield*, covers the insulation and is in turn covered by the plastic outer *jacket*.

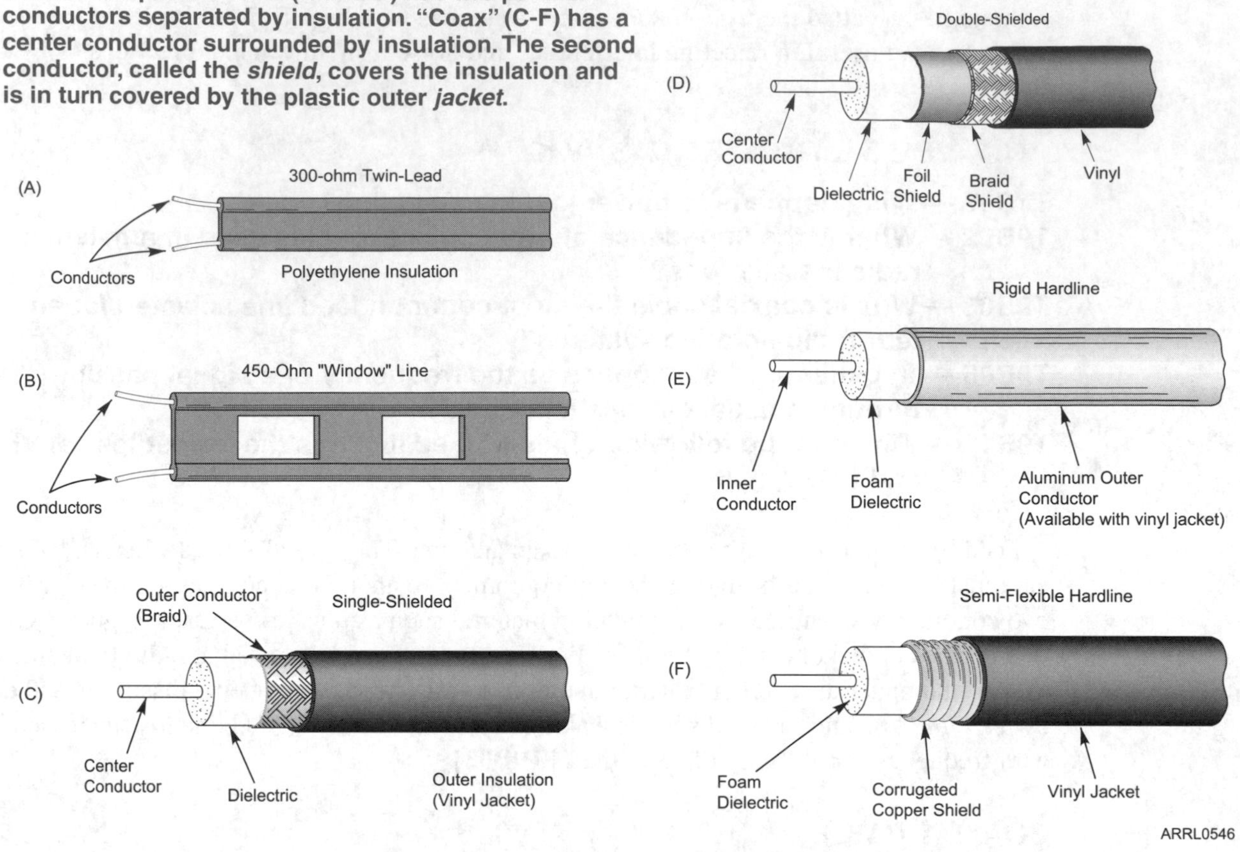

(A) 300-ohm Twin-Lead
Conductors
Polyethylene Insulation

(B) 450-Ohm "Window" Line
Conductors

(C) Single-Shielded
Outer Conductor (Braid)
Center Conductor
Dielectric
Outer Insulation (Vinyl Jacket)

(D) Double-Shielded
Center Conductor
Dielectric
Foil Shield
Braid Shield
Vinyl

(E) Rigid Hardline
Inner Conductor
Foam Dielectric
Aluminum Outer Conductor (Available with vinyl jacket)

(F) Semi-Flexible Hardline
Foam Dielectric
Corrugated Copper Shield
Vinyl Jacket

ARRL0546

For More Information

A feed line of two parallel wires separated by insulating material has several names; *open-wire*, *ladder line*, *window line*, or *twin-lead*. This type of feed line, also shown in Figure 4.7 (parts A and B), has less insulating material and greater spacing between its conductors, so it has less loss than coaxial cable. Since the radio energy is not shielded by an outer tube, the signals in parallel conductor feed lines can be affected by nearby conductors. Open-wire feed lines cannot be buried or installed in metal conduits and must be kept clear of nearby conducting surfaces.

STANDING WAVE RATIO — SWR

T7C03 — What, in general terms, is standing wave ratio (SWR)?

T7C04 — What reading on an SWR meter indicates a perfect impedance match between the antenna and the feed line?

T7C05 — Why do most solid-state amateur radio transmitters reduce output power as SWR increases?

T7C06 — What does an SWR reading of 4:1 indicate?

T9B01 — Why is it important to have low SWR when using coaxial cable feed line?

T9B09 — What can cause erratic changes in SWR readings?

The power carried by a feed line is transferred completely to a load, such as an antenna, when the load and feed line impedances are identical or *matched*. If the feed line and load impedances do not match, some of the power is *reflected* by the load. Power traveling toward the load is *forward power*. Power reflected by the load is *reflected power*. The greater the difference between the feed line and load impedances, the more power is reflected by the load. In the worst case where the feed line is connected to or *terminated* in an open or short circuit, all of the forward power is reflected.

Reflected and forward power traveling in opposite directions create a stationary wave-like interference pattern in the feed line called a *standing wave*. The ratio of the maximum value to minimum value of the interference pattern is called the *standing wave ratio* or *SWR*. SWR is the same everywhere along a feed line, but it is usually measured at the transmitter's connection to the feed line. (This is illustrated in an excellent video from the AT&T Archives at **techchannel.att.com/play-video.cfm/2011/3/7/AT&T-Archives-Similarities-of-Wave-Behavior.**)

Because SWR is determined by the amounts of forward and reflected power, SWR in an antenna system is also a measure of the how well the antenna (or load) and feed line impedances are matched. **[T7C03]**

SWR is equal to the ratio of antenna-to-feed line or feed line-to-antenna impedances, whichever ratio is greater than 1. When there is no reflected power there is no interference pattern and the SWR is 1:1. This condition is called a *perfect match*. **[T7C04]** As more power is reflected, SWR increases. SWR is always greater than or equal to 1:1. SWR greater than 1:1 is called an *impedance mismatch* or just *mismatch*. **[T7C06]** Since an antenna's feed point impedance changes with frequency while that of the feed line does not, SWR also changes with frequency.

Why does SWR matter? Low SWR indicates efficient transfer of power from the feed line because less power is reflected by the antenna. That means there is less loss from reflected power in the feed line traveling back and forth between the antenna and transmitter. **[T9B01]** With each pass through the feed line, some of the power is transferred to the antenna, but some is also lost as heat. As SWR increases, more power is reflected and more power is lost.

Another effect of high SWR is that the interference pattern causes voltages to increase in the feed line and at the transmitter's output where the feed line is connected. The higher voltages can damage a transmitter's output circuits. Most amateur transmitting equipment is designed to work at full power with an SWR of 2:1 or lower. SWR greater than 2:1 may cause the transmitter's protection circuits to reduce power automatically to avoid damage to the output transistors. **[T7C05]**

What causes high SWR? Antennas that are much too short or too long for the frequency being used often have extreme feed point impedances, causing high SWR. A faulty feed line or feed line connectors can also raise SWR. Erratic SWR usually indicates a loose connection in the feed line or antenna. **[T9B09]**

4.4 Practical Antenna Systems

T9A02 — Which of the following describes a type of antenna loading?

T9A03 — Which of the following describes a simple dipole oriented parallel to the Earth's surface?

T9A04 — What is a disadvantage of the "rubber duck" antenna supplied with most handheld radio transceivers when compared to a full-sized quarter-wave antenna?

T9A05 — How would you change a dipole antenna to make it resonant on a higher frequency?

T9A07 — What is a disadvantage of using a handheld VHF transceiver, with its integral antenna, inside a vehicle?

T9A08 — What is the approximate length, in inches, of a quarter-wavelength vertical antenna for 146 MHz?

T9A09 — What is the approximate length, in inches, of a half-wavelength 6 meter dipole antenna?

T9A10 — In which direction does a half-wave dipole antenna radiate the strongest signal?

T9A12 — What is an advantage of using a properly mounted ⅝ wavelength antenna for VHF or UHF mobile service?

DIPOLES AND GROUND-PLANES

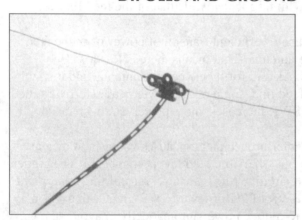

Figure 4.8 — The center of a basic dipole antenna with the balanced feed line connected to a center insulator and the legs of the dipole extending to the left and right.

The simplest type of antenna is a *dipole*, meaning essentially "two electrical parts." Dipoles are made from a straight conductor of wire or tubing one-half wavelength (½ λ) long with a feed point somewhere along the antenna, usually in the middle. Dipoles are easy to make, easy to use, and work quite well in a variety of environments. Most are oriented horizontally, particularly on the lower frequency bands, and radiate a horizontally polarized signal. **[T9A03]** Dipoles can also be installed vertically, sloping or even drooping from a single support in the middle (the *inverted-vee* or *inverted-V*). **Figure 4.8** shows the central portion of a typical wire dipole.

A dipole radiates strongest broadside to the antenna and weakest off the ends. The radiation pattern for a dipole isolated in space looks like a donut as seen in **Figure 4.9**. **[T9A10]** The figure shows both two- and three-dimensional patterns. The two-dimensional pattern is a cross-section of the three-dimensional pattern.

Another popular antenna is the *ground-plane* antenna. The most common type of ground-plane antenna is one-quarter wavelength long (¼ λ) with the feed point at the base of the antenna (see **Figure 4.10**) The ground-plane acts like one-half of a dipole with the missing portion made up by the electrical mirror formed by the ground plane. The ground plane is made from sheet metal or a screen of wires called *radials* that extend out from the base of the antenna. The ⅝-λ ground-plane antenna offers some improvement over the ¼-λ version. Due to its extended length, the ⅝-λ vertical focuses a bit more energy toward the horizon, improving range. **[T9A12]**

On the HF bands below 24 MHz, the increasing wavelength makes a ¼-λ ground-plane less practical for portable and mobile operation. To reduce the physical size of the antenna, it is often constructed with some of the radiating conductor wound into a coil or a separate

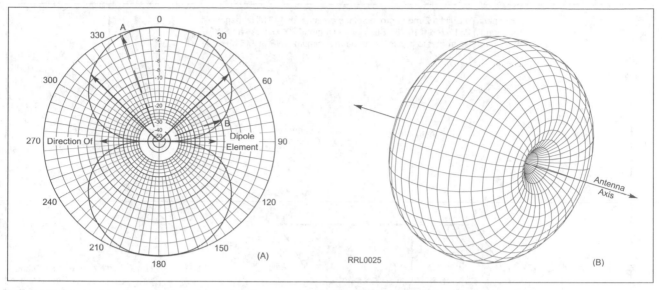

Figure 4.9 — The radiation pattern of a dipole far from ground (in free-space). At (A) the pattern is shown in a plane containing the dipole. The lengths of the arrows indicate the relative strength of the radiated power in that direction. The dipole radiates best broadside to its length. At (B) the 3-D pattern shows radiated strength in all directions.

How Long is That Antenna?

If a resonant dipole antenna is ½-λ long, how long is that in feet? This traditional formula for thin wire dipoles that are lower than one-half wavelength above ground is often used, even though the estimate is usually too short at HF:

Length (in feet) = 468 / frequency (in MHz)

or

Length = 468 / f

Example: At 50.1 MHz (in the 6 meter band), dipole length is calculated as 468 / 50.1 = 9..33 feet = 112 inches long **[T9A09]**

The value of the constant used in the formula accounts for effects that cause an antenna to act like it is a little longer electrically than it is physically. The actual resonant length is affected by height above ground, its electrical properties, and nearby conductive objects.

Make the dipole a few percent longer at first (use 490 instead of 468), then use an SWR meter or antenna analyzer to determine the resonant frequency. Assuming the resonant frequency is too low because the dipole is too long, shorten it until the dipole is resonant at the desired frequency. **[T9A05]** This allows you to compensate for the effects of ground or nearby conductors that might affect the antenna. For dipoles made out of wire, be sure to add a little extra wire to fasten it to insulators and supports.

The length of a ground-plane antenna is half that of a dipole and is often estimated as: length (in feet) = 234 / frequency (in MHz).

Example: At 146 MHz, a λ/4 ground-plane is 234 / 146 = 1.6 feet = 19¼ inches long. **[T9A08]** At HF, a longer length is often required as discussed above.

inductor inserted in the antenna. This technique is called *inductive loading* and it makes the antenna longer electrically than it is physically. **[T9A02]**

For More Information

Figure 4.10 also illustrates what is meant by "electrical mirror." Have you ever watched as someone put their face at the end of a mirror, the reflection recreating the face's missing half? A ground-plane works in much the same way. The more complete the ground-plane plane, the better the reflection and more dipole-like the result. A good ground-plane should extend at least ¼-λ from the base of the antenna in all directions. As you might expect, since a ground-plane antenna emulates a dipole, it radiates strongest perpendicular to the axis of the antenna and weakest off its end.

Ground-plane antennas are often called *verticals* because it is easiest to mount them so they are

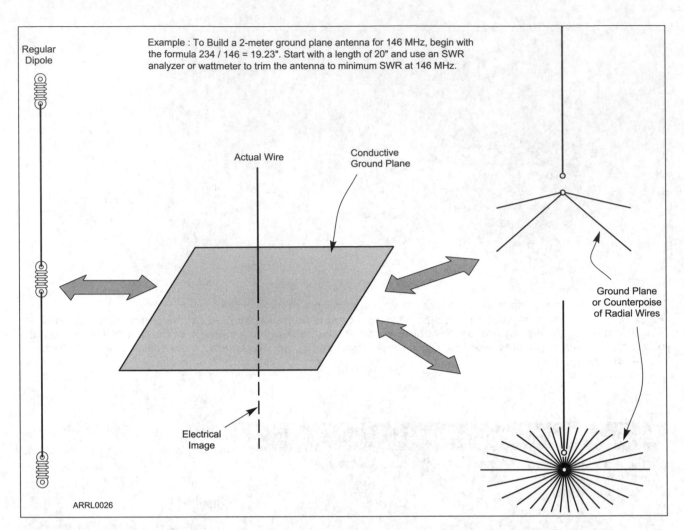

Regular Dipole

Example : To Build a 2-meter ground plane antenna for 146 MHz, begin with the formula 234 / 146 = 19.23". Start with a length of 20" and use an SWR analyzer or wattmeter to trim the antenna to minimum SWR at 146 MHz.

Actual Wire

Conductive Ground Plane

Electrical Image

Ground Plane or Counterpoise of Radial Wires

ARRL0026

Figure 4.10 — A ground-plane makes up an electrical mirror that creates an image of the missing half of a ground-plane antenna. The result is an antenna that acts very much like a dipole. The ground plane can be made up of a screen of wires (often used at HF) or a metal surface at VHF and UHF. For VHF and UHF antennas mounted on masts, a counterpoise of a few wires serves the same purpose.

perpendicular to the ground, with the ground-plane on or parallel to the ground. When mounted this way, the radiation pattern of the single-element ground-plane is *omnidirectional*, transmitting and receiving equally well in all directions. This type of pattern is used when there is no preferred direction of communications.

Antennas for Handheld Radios

The flexible antenna used with most handheld radios is called a *rubber duck.* It's a ground-plane antenna shortened by coiling the conductor inside a plastic coating. The body of the radio and the operator form the antenna's ground plane. The rubber duck is conveniently sized, but doesn't transmit or receive as well as a full-sized ground-plane antenna. **[T9A04]** For best performance while using a rubber duck antenna, hold the transceiver so that the antenna is vertical as shown in **Figure 4.11**. This aligns the handheld antenna with those of repeaters and most other handhelds so that signal strength is maximized.

When using a handheld transceiver inside a vehicle, a rubber duck may not be an effective antenna. The vehicle's metal roof and doors act like shields, trapping the radio waves inside. Some of the signal gets out through the windows (unless they're tinted with a thin metal coating), but it's as much as 10 to 20 times weaker than an external mobile antenna. **[T9A07]**

A handheld radio can also be connected to a full-size or external base-style antenna for better performance, replacing the rubber duck. The radio usually has a standard RF connector that allows a mobile antenna to be used in a vehicle or with base station-style antennas at home.

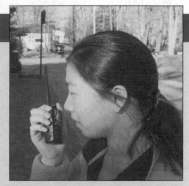

Figure 4.11 — To get the best range from a handheld radio, hold it so that the antenna is vertical. This aligns your antenna with those of a repeater or another handheld user. Also, turn the microphone slightly away from your face when talking so that your breath does not blow directly into it.

DIRECTIONAL ANTENNAS

T3A03 — What antenna polarization is normally used for long-distance weak-signal CW and SSB contacts using the VHF and UHF bands?

T3A05 — When using a directional antenna, how might your station be able to access a distant repeater if buildings or obstructions are blocking the direct line of sight path?

T9A01 — What is a beam antenna?

T9A06 — What type of antennas are the quad, Yagi, and dish?

Simple dipoles, ground-planes, and loops work well, but they have little gain. That is, their radiation patterns don't have strongly preferred directions. In many situations, it is

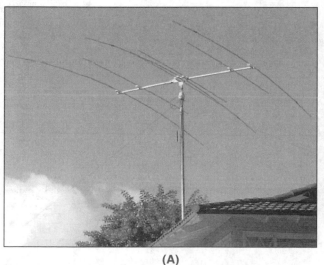

(A)

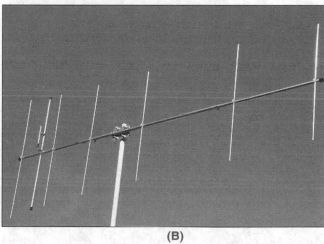

(B)

Figure 4.12 — Yagi antennas are beam antennas that focus radiated power along their axis. Yagi elements are tubes or rods and can be oriented for horizontal polarization (A) or vertical (B).

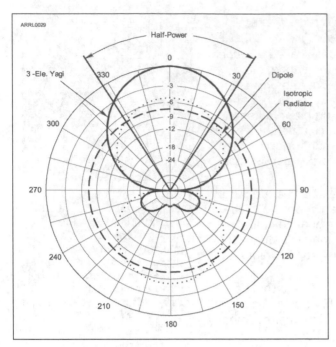

Figure 4.13 — The radiation pattern of a typical, three-element Yagi antenna with a driven element, reflector, and director shows that most of the antenna's energy is focused in one direction along the boom of the antenna (along the 0-180 axis of the graph.) Smaller amounts are radiated toward the side and back. This antenna also rejects noise and interference from the side and back. The round pattern of the isotropic antenna and the figure-eight pattern of a dipole are included for reference.

desired to focus transmitted power and get the best reception in one direction, so a directional *beam* antenna is used. **[T9A01]** Beams can be used to increase signal level at a distant station or to reject interference or noise. On VHF and UHF, if a direct signal path is blocked by building or other obstruction, a beam antenna can be used to aim the signal at a reflecting surface to bypass the obstruction. **[T3A05]**

Beams are created from arrays of multiple elements. (Dipoles and ground-planes are *single-element* antennas.) The most widely used type of beam antennas used by hams are *Yagis* (named for one of its inventors), shown in **Figure 4.12**. The radiation pattern for a typical beam is shown in **Figure 4.13**.

Horizontally polarized Yagis are usually used for long-distance communications, especially for weak signal SSB and CW contacts on the VHF and UHF bands. Horizontal polarization is preferred because it results in lower *ground losses* when the wave reflects from or travels along the ground. **[T3A03]**

As frequency increases and the size of Yagi elements become smaller, it becomes more difficult to construct practical antennas. At frequencies above 1 GHz, a different style of antenna becomes practical — the *dish* seen in **Figure 4.14**. **[T9A06]** Amateur dish antennas work very much like the satellite TV dishes often seen on residences.

Figure 4.14 — N7CFO's dish antenna operates on 10 GHz and is portable enough to be taken on contest outings.

T7C09 — Which of the following is the most common cause for failure of coaxial cables?

T7C10 — Why should the outer jacket of coaxial cable be resistant to ultraviolet light?

T7C11 — What is a disadvantage of air core coaxial cable when compared to foam or solid dielectric types?

T7D08 — Which of the following types of solder is best for radio and electronic use?

T7D09 — What is the characteristic appearance of a cold solder joint?

T9B06 — Which of the following connectors is most suitable for frequencies above 400 MHz?

T9B07 — Which of the following is true of PL-259 type coax connectors?

T9B08 — Why should coax connectors exposed to the weather be sealed against water intrusion?

T9B10 — What is the electrical difference between RG-58 and RG-8 coaxial cable?

Feed Line Selection and Maintenance

Popular types of coax used by amateurs are shown in **Table 4.1**. Next to characteristic impedance, the most important characteristic of coax is feed line loss. Loss is specified in dB per 100 feet of cable at a specific frequency. Table 4.1 gives cable loss at 30 MHz (close to the 10 meter band) and at 150 MHz (close to the 2 meter band). In general, a larger diameter cable such as RG-8 will have less loss than a small cable such as RG-58. **[T9B10]**

The performance of coaxial cable depends on the integrity of its outer jacket. Nicks, cuts, and scrapes can all breach the jacket allowing moisture contamination, the most common cause of coaxial cable failure. **[T7C09]** Prolonged exposure to the ultraviolet (UV) in sunlight will also cause the plastic in the jacket to degrade, causing small cracks that allow water into the cable. **[T7C10]** To protect the cable against UV damage the jacket usually contains a pigment that absorbs and blocks the UV. Coax should also not be bent sharply, lest the center conductor be forced gradually through the soft center insulation, eventually causing a short circuit to the outer braid.

Table 4.1

Common Types of Coaxial Cable

Type	Impedance Ω	Loss per 100 feet (in dB) at 30 MHz	Loss per 100 feet (in dB) at 150 MHz
RG-6	75	1.4	3.3
RG-8	50	1.1	2.5
RG-8X	50	2.0	4.5
RG-58	50	2.5	5.6
RG-59	75	1.8	4.1
RG-174	50	4.6	10.3
RG-213	50	1.1	2.5
LMR-400	50	0.7	1.5

Values in this table were calculated using the online calculator at the Times-Microwave website. (**www.timesmicrowave.com/calculator**).

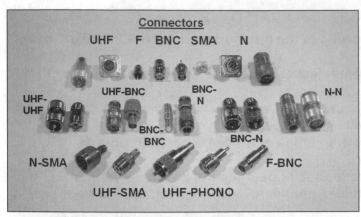

Connectors

UHF F BNC SMA N

UHF-UHF

UHF-BNC

BNC-N

N-N

BNC-BNC

BNC-N

N-SMA

UHF-SMA UHF-PHONO

F-BNC

Figure 4.15 — The photo shows a variety of common coaxial connectors that hams use. The larger connectors are used for higher power transmitters and antennas. The most common are the UHF and N styles. Special *adapters* are used to make connections between cables and equipment that have different styles of connectors.

Melting Metal — In a Good Way

As you assemble your antenna system, if you don't know how already this is the time to learn the basics of soldering. Some coax connectors can be installed without soldering by crimping or compression fittings, but many cannot. Learning how to install your own coax connectors not only saves money but allows you to make repairs at home and under emergency conditions! Start by reading the ARRL Technical Information Service's online article "The Art of Soldering." (**www.arrl.org/circuit-construction**) Follow up with "Connectors For All Occasions, Parts 1 and 2". You'll learn what kind of solder to use for electronics (rosin-core), what a "cold" solder joint looks like (it has a grainy or dull surface), and many other useful tips to get you melting metal like a pro! **[T7D08, T7D09]**

Coaxial Feed Line Connectors

Connectors for coaxial cable ("coax connectors") are required to make connections to radios, accessory equipment and most antennas. In a "pigtail" connection, the braid and center conductor are separated and attached to screw terminals or soldered directly to the antenna. Pigtails are generally unsuitable at UHF and higher frequencies. They are also difficult to seal and expose the inside of the cable to water which increases feed line loss.

Figure 4.15 shows several common types of coaxial connectors. The figure also shows *adapters* that make connections from one type of connector to another. Which connector to use depends on the signal frequency. The UHF series of connectors — PL-259 plugs and SO-239 receptacles — are the most widely-used for HF equipment. (UHF does not stand for "ultra-high frequency" in this case.) **[T9B07]** Above 400 MHz, the Type N connectors are used. **[T9B06]** You'll find both UHF and N connectors on 6, 2 and 1¼ meter equipment.

Coax connectors exposed to the weather must be carefully waterproofed. Water in coaxial cable degrades the effectiveness of the braided shield and dramatically increases losses. **[T9B08]** If you use low-loss air-core or "open-cell foam" coax, special techniques are required to prevent water absorption by this cable. **[T7C11]** You must pay extra attention to waterproofing the connectors for this type of cable.

Complete information on common coax connectors, including assembly instructions, is available in any edition of the *ARRL Handbook* and *ARRL Antenna Book*.

SWR Meters and Wattmeters

T4A05 — What is the proper location for an external SWR meter?

T7C02 — Which of the following instruments can be used to determine if an antenna is resonant at the desired operating frequency?

T7C08 — What instrument other than an SWR meter could you use to determine if a feed line and antenna are properly matched?

T9B04 — What is the major function of an antenna tuner (antenna coupler)?

To measure the SWR in a feed line the *SWR meter* is used. The meter is placed in series with the feed line, usually right at the output of the radio as shown in **Figure 4.16.** **[T4A05]** This makes it easy to see exactly what SWR is being presented to the radio by the antenna system. Many radios include a built-in SWR meter.

Instead of SWR meters, many amateurs prefer a *wattmeter* and better yet, a *directional*

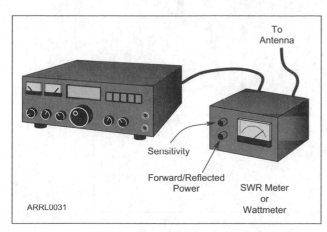

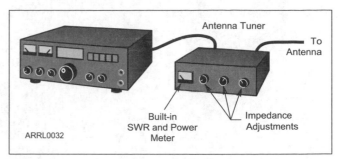

Figure 4.17 — By adjusting an antenna tuner's controls, the impedance present at the end of the feed line can be converted to the impedance that best suits the transceiver's output circuits, usually 50 ohms.

Figure 4.16 — The SWR meter measures power flowing toward the antenna (forward) and toward the transmitter (reflected or reverse). The meter is calibrated to show SWR or power. A wattmeter does not measure SWR, just power, and the SWR can be calculated from the power readings.

Figure 4.18 — The popular MFJ series of antenna analyzers are used to adjust and troubleshoot antenna systems. The instrument contains a low-power signal source with an adjustable frequency and an SWR meter. The LCD display shows the operating frequency and information about the antenna impedance. The meters show SWR and feed point impedance.

wattmeter. Wattmeters measure power in a feed line and can be placed in the line to read power flowing in either direction. Directional wattmeters can measure power flowing toward the antenna and power reflected from the antenna by rotating a sensing element or turning a switch. The operator can then convert the forward and reflected power readings to SWR by using a table or formula. **[T7C08]**

Antenna Tuners

If the SWR at the end of the feed line is too high for the radio to operate properly, devices called *impedance matchers* or *transmatches* or *antenna tuners* are used. They are connected at the output of the transmitter as shown in **Figure 4.17**. An antenna tuner is adjusted until the SWR measured at the transmitter output is acceptably close to 1:1. This means the antenna system's impedance has been matched to that of the transmitter output. **[T9B04]**

Despite the name, the antenna is not really tuned — the impedance at the output of the feed line is converted to some other value. This allows the transmitter to deliver full power output without damage from the high SWR. For convenience, most tuners combine the functions of impedance matcher, directional wattmeter and antenna switch. There are also *automatic tuners* that sense when SWR is high and make the necessary adjustments under the control of a microprocessor to match the impedances.

Antenna Analyzers

Figure 4.18 shows an *antenna analyzer*. This instrument contains a very low-power signal source with an adjustable frequency and one or more meters to show the impedance and SWR. It is used to measure an antenna system without using a transmitter whose signal might cause interference. **[T7C02]** Antenna analyzers are very handy and can be used for many types of antenna and feed line measurements.

Chapter 5

Amateur Radio Equipment

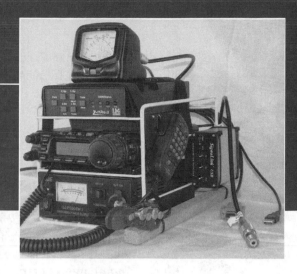

In this chapter, you'll learn about:

- **Modulation — how information combines with RF**
- **Basic operation of transmitters, receivers, and amplifiers**
- **Digital mode characteristics**
- **Power supplies and batteries**

When you see the mouse, you'll find more information at www.arrl.org/ham-radio-license-manual

Previous chapters have introduced basic equipment used by hams and fundamentals of electronics and radio ideas that make the equipment go. We are now ready to start learning about Real Ham Radio, where knobs and dials get turned, meters jump, and signals crackle back and forth over the airwaves!

This chapter begins by explaining how information is added to radio signals so that it can be transmitted. Then we'll cover how radio equipment works and how to operate it, including the digital modes that are an important part of ham radio today. Finally, we'll study some important supporting accessories.

5.1 Modulation

A simple radio signal just sitting there on the radio spectrum not doing anything isn't very useful and doesn't do much communicating. To communicate, information must be added to the radio signal. How does that happen?

Modulation is what enables us to communicate information using radio signals. While the modulation section might seem rather technical, understanding its basics also helps you understand how to operate a radio properly. The online supplement for this chapter provides additional details. You can also save this section for future reference as you learn more about Amateur Radio.

BANDWIDTH

You know that a signal can have both a frequency and a strength or amplitude. Actual signals are spread out over a range of frequencies. That range is the signal's *bandwidth*. Your voice is made up of many individual signals occupying frequencies from less than 300 Hz to more than 3000 Hz. That makes the bandwidth of a typical voice a bit more than $3000 - 300 = 2700$ Hz.

A *composite signal* such as speech is made up of many individual signals. The individual signals are called *components*. Most radio signals that are used to carry information are composite signals. The bandwidth of these radio signals is the difference between their highest and lowest frequency component. For example, by tuning a receiver across the AM broadcast band (see Figure 2.3 in Chapter 2) you might find the signal of a station playing music occupies frequencies from 870 to 890 kHz. The bandwidth of that signal is 890 − 870 = 20 kHz.

MODULATION

Adding information to a signal by changing it in some way is modulation. A signal that doesn't carry any information is called *unmodulated*. Recovering the information from a modulated signal is called *demodulation*.

If speech is the information used to modulate a signal, the result is a *phone* or *voice mode* signal. If data characters modulate a signal, the result is a *data mode* or *digital mode* signal. *Analog* modes carry information that can be understood directly by a human, such as speech or Morse code. Digital or data modes carry information as individual characters that are read or displayed by computers.

The three characteristics of a signal that can be modulated are the signal's amplitude or strength, its frequency, and its phase. All three types of modulation are used in ham radio. You already know of two forms of modulation — the AM and FM signals from broadcast stations.

CONTINUOUS WAVE (CW)

The simplest radio signal with a strength and frequency that never change is called a *continuous wave*, abbreviated CW. The simplest type of modulation is a continuous wave

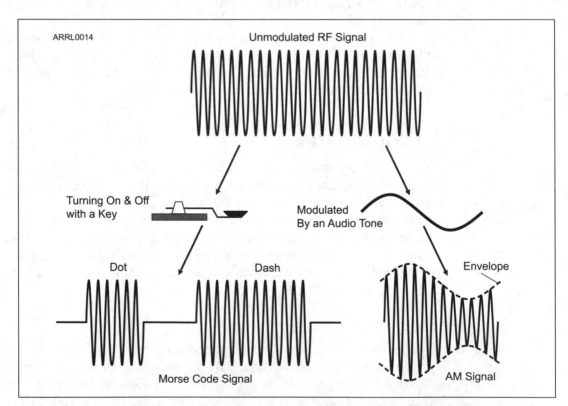

Figure 5.1 — Information can be added to an RF signal by modulating the signal's amplitude. Turning the signal on and off in a pattern such as Morse code is a very simple form of amplitude modulation. A tone or speech can also be used to modulate the signal, resulting in a signal whose shape or envelope contains the information from the tone or speech.

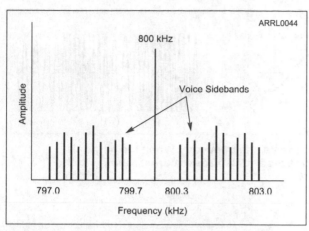

Figure 5.2 — An 800 kHz AM signal modulated by voice has an unmodulated carrier at 800 kHz. Above and below the carrier are the sidebands. Each sideband contains all of the voice signal information.

turned on and off in a coded pattern, such as Morse code in **Figure 5.1**. In fact, Morse code radio signals are called CW for that reason.

AMPLITUDE MODULATION

Varying the power or amplitude of a signal to add speech or data information is called *amplitude modulation* or *AM*. (Morse code is the simplest form of AM.) If you have watched a meter jump in response to your voice or music, an AM signal's amplitude changes in the same way to carry the information in your voice. An AM transmitter adds your voice to the unmodulated signal by varying its amplitude. The information is contained in the outline or *envelope* of the resulting signal. Figure 5.1 shows the result of using a tone to create an AM signal.

All a receiver has to do to recover your voice from an AM signal is to follow the signal's amplitude variations. Recovering speech or music from the envelope of an AM signal is called *detection*.

An actual AM signal is made up of three separate signals working together — a *carrier* and two *sidebands*. (See **Figure 5.2**) The carrier is a steady, unmodulated signal. The *upper sideband* or *USB* signal is higher in frequency than the carrier by the frequency of the tone. The *lower sideband* or *LSB* signal is lower in frequency than the carrier.

SINGLE-SIDEBAND (SSB)

T8A01 — Which of the following is a form of amplitude modulation?

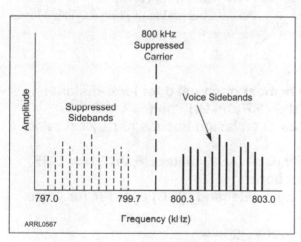

Figure 5.3 — Removing or *suppressing* the carrier and one sideband of an AM signal creates a single-sideband (SSB) signal. All of the signal's power then is concentrated in one sideband. SSB signals are effective for long-distance and weak-signal voice contacts.

In an AM signal the carrier doesn't carry any information. In addition, each sideband contains a copy of the modulating signal. Only one sideband is needed to transmit the information and that's just what *single-sideband* or *SSB* signals are. **Figure 5.3** shows a single-sideband signal — the same AM signal as shown in Figure 5.2 with the carrier and one sideband removed or *suppressed*.

[T8A01] All of the SSB signal's power is concentrated in the one sideband. The upper sideband (USB) is used on VHF and UHF. Both USB and LSB are used on the MF and HF bands.

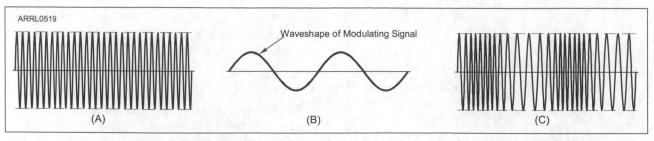

Figure 5.4 — At (A), each cycle of the unmodulated carrier has the same frequency. When the carrier is frequency modulated with the signal at (B), its frequency increases and decreases corresponding to the increases and decreases in amplitude of the modulating signal.

FREQUENCY AND PHASE MODULATION

T8A02 — What type of modulation is most commonly used for VHF packet radio transmissions?

T8A04 — Which type of modulation is most commonly used for VHF and UHF voice repeaters?

The remaining two signal characteristics that can be varied to carry information are frequency and phase. Modes that vary the frequency of a signal to add speech or data information are called *frequency modulation* or *FM*. The frequency of an FM signal varies with the amplitude of the modulating signal as shown in **Figure 5.4**. *Phase modulation* or *PM* is very similar to FM. Phase modulation varies a signal's phase instead of changing its frequency. (FM and PM signals are nearly identical. For the rest of this book, "FM" will apply to both FM and PM unless noted.) Because of FM's excellent noise-rejection qualities, it the mode used by most VHF and UHF repeaters. **[T8A04]**

FM is also commonly used for packet radio on VHF and UHF. **[T8A02]** The data is exchanged as audio tones by using the FM radio's speech input and audio output. This allows inexpensive FM voice radios to be used.

BANDWIDTH OF MODULATED SIGNALS

T8A03 — Which type of voice mode is most often used for long-distance (weak signal) contacts on the VHF and UHF bands?

T8A05 — Which of the following types of emission has the narrowest bandwidth?

T8A06 — Which sideband is normally used for 10 meter HF, VHF, and UHF single-sideband communications?

T8A07 — What is an advantage of single sideband (SSB) over FM for voice transmissions?

T8A08 to T8A11 — Bandwidth of different signals

Because the SSB signal's power is concentrated into a narrow bandwidth, it is possible to communicate with SSB over much longer ranges and in poorer conditions than with FM or AM, particularly on the VHF and UHF bands. **[T8A03, T8A07]** That is why the VHF and UHF "DXers" and contest operators use SSB signals. **Table 5.1** shows the bandwidth of different types of signals.

For even better range, extremely narrow CW signals are the easiest for a human operator to send and receive, particularly in noisy or fading conditions. Even though the signals can be quite strong, hams refer to CW and SSB as *weak signal* modes because they are more effective than FM at low signal strengths. Newer digital modes, such as JT65 and FT8,

Table 5.1

Signal Bandwidths

[T8A05, T8A08 to T8A11]

Type of Signal	Typical Bandwidth
CW	150 Hz (0.15 kHz)
SSB digital	500 to 3000 Hz (0.5 to 3 kHz)
SSB voice	2 to 3 kHz
AM voice	6 kHz
AM broadcast	10 kHz
FM voice	10 to 15 kHz*
FM broadcast	150 kHz
Commercial video broadcast	6 MHz

*On 10 meters below 29.0 MHz, FM voice must be narrowband (6 kHz max). As of early 2018, most VHF/UHF FM voice repeater signals are approximately 15 kHz wide although there is some narrowband equipment using 5-6 kHz.

require a computer to decode but provide even better performance when signals are weak.

If an SSB signal can use either an upper or lower sideband — which one should you use? Although USB and LSB perform identically, ham radio has standardized on the following conventions:

- Below 10 MHz, LSB is used
- Above 10 MHz, USB is used — including all of the VHF and UHF bands **[T8A06]**

There is one exception: amateurs are required to use USB on the five channels of the 60 meter band (5 MHz).

5.2 Transmitters and Receivers

This section introduces common radio controls and functions with examples in figures and photos. Your radio will be different, of course, so read the owner's manual for complete information. You can learn more about radios from this book's supplement "Choosing a Ham Radio". User's manuals can also be downloaded from manufacturers' websites.

You'll get a look at how antennas, feed lines and power supplies are used. We'll also cover the basics of dealing with interference. Knowing these practical techniques will get you started on the right foot as a ham. It also simplifies learning about operating conventions, rules and regulations that follow in upcoming chapters. Ready? Let's find that power switch and get to it!

SELECTING BAND, FREQUENCY AND MODE

T4B02 — Which of the following can be used to enter the operating frequency on a modern transceiver?

T4B04 — What is a way to enable quick access to a favorite frequency on your transceiver?

Whether you use a transceiver (most likely) or a separate receiver and transmitter, there are two functions that are the same for all three — control of frequency and mode. Amateur Radio is unique among the other radio services: we can tune anywhere in our assigned bands and are not required to use channels pre-assigned by the FCC, except in the 60 meter band. Repeaters operate on fixed channels, but that is for

BAND Buttons   MODE Buttons

BAND Button   MODE Button

Figure 5.5 — The frequency and mode controls are shown for a pair of HF radios, the Kenwood TS-590SG (left) and Yaesu FT-991A (right). On the TS-590SG, bands are selected by pressing the appropriate button on the front panel (1.8, 3.5 and so on). On the FT-991A, pressing the BAND button brings up choices on the touchscreen display. Frequency within a band can be adjusted with the large tuning knob. If a computer is connected to the radio, frequency may be changed by the computer software. Pressing the MODE key button on the FT-991A brings up available mode choices on the touchscreen display. On the TS-590SG, there are separate mode buttons for USB/LSB, CW/FSK, FM/AM, and DATA.

convenience and the channel frequencies are assigned by amateurs.

Amateurs can also use many different modes, a few of which we covered in a previous chapter. Most other radio services are restricted to a single mode. With this flexibility and freedom comes the obligation to know how to choose and set a frequency and select a mode.

Figure 5.5 shows the typical frequency and mode controls of two common transceivers. If the radio is a transceiver, frequency and mode settings will apply to both transmit and receive.

Start by selecting the band if your radio operates on multiple bands. For example, you might have a *dual-band* handheld transceiver for the 2 meter and 70 cm bands or a *multiband* HF rig that covers 160 through 10 meters. The band selection controls may be labeled in terms of frequency or wavelength. **Table 5.2** shows how the labels on your radio may indicate the band.

Then a frequency is selected within the band — this is called *tuning*. The control you use for tuning is the *VFO*, an abbreviation for *variable frequency oscillator*. In older radios, the VFO knob changes the frequency of an oscillator circuit that in turn determines the radio's operating frequency. In most newer radios, the VFO control is read by a microprocessor that controls the radio's frequency.

Some radios also have a keypad that you can use to enter frequencies directly. **[T4B02]** The keypad will be on the radio's front panel or on the microphone. Numeric keys are used to enter the exact frequency. The radio's manual will show you how to use the keypad.

On *multimode* radios, the operator also selects the signal mode:
- SSB (USB or LSB)
- AM
- FM
- CW or Morse code
- Data (for RTTY or other digital modes)

Radios that cover HF and the all-band radios that cover HF/VHF/UHF are multimode. Most handheld and mobile transceivers designed to be used with repeaters are single-mode radios that use only FM or a single digital mode.

Table 5.2
Band Selection Labels

Frequency (MHz)	Wavelength (meters or cm)
HF and MF	
1.8	160 meters
3.5	80
5	60
7	40
10	30
14	20
18	17
21	15
24	12
28	10
VHF	
50	6 meters
144	2
222	1.25
UHF	
440	70 cm
902	33
1240	23
2300	13

Memories or *memory channels* are used to store frequencies and modes for later recall. Memories are provided so that you can quickly tune to frequently used or favorite frequencies. **[T4B04]**

TRANSMITTER FUNCTIONS

T7A07 — What is meant by "PTT"?
T7C01 — What is the primary purpose of a dummy load?
T7C12 — What does a dummy load consist of?
T8D14 — What is an electronic keyer?

In radios that operate using AM/SSB and CW, the transmitter output power is controlled by an RF power control. A typical RF power control is shown in **Figure 5.6**. (This may be a menu option or a knob shared by several features.) FM hand-held and mobile radios have selectable fixed power levels.

Microphone gain (MIC GAIN or MIC as seen in Figure 5.6) controls the level of speech audio that is applied to the modulator circuit of an SSB transmitter. FM transmitters usually have a fixed microphone gain.

Switching between receive and transmit on voice can be performed manually with a *push-to-talk* (PTT) switch or an automatic *voice-operated transmitter* control circuit (VOX). **[T7A07]**

For sending Morse code, a *key* is used to turn the transmitter output signal on and off. Morse code's dots and dashes are known as the *elements* of the code. When using a *straight key*, the operator generates the dots and dashes manually. This is called *hand keying*.

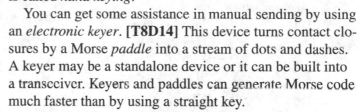

Figure 5.6 — The maximum output power of this HF transceiver is set by an RF PWR knob. This control does not affect MIC GAIN or other audio settings. On mobile rigs, output power is varied between several preset levels with a button or key.

You can get some assistance in manual sending by using an *electronic keyer*. **[T8D14]** This device turns contact closures by a Morse *paddle* into a stream of dots and dashes. A keyer may be a standalone device or it can be built into a transceiver. Keyers and paddles can generate Morse code much faster than by using a straight key.

Peak envelope power (PEP) is the measure of an AM or SSB signal's power. PEP is the transmitter output power when speech into the microphone is the loudest. CW, FM, and most digital mode transmissions have a constant power output, so PEP is the same as that constant level.

To avoid interfering with other stations while you're adjusting your transmitter or measuring its output power, it's a good idea to use a *dummy load*. A dummy load is a heavy-duty resistor that can absorb and dissipate the output power from a transmitter. **[T7C01, T7C12]**

Watch That Band Edge!

T1B09 — Why should you not set your transmit frequency to be exactly at the edge of an amateur band or sub-band?

Amateurs are allowed to use any frequency in a band, but you have to be careful when operating near the edge of the band. You must keep *all* of your signal inside the band. Since your radio displays the *carrier frequency*, you have to remember to leave room for the signal's sidebands. For example, when using FM voice, your signal is 15 kHz wide. That means your carrier frequency (in the center of the signal) should never be less than 7.5 kHz from the band edge. To give yourself some margin, 10 kHz from the edge would be even better. **[T1B09]**

T2B05 — What might be the problem if a repeater user says your transmissions are breaking up on voice peaks?

T4B01 — What may happen if a transmitter is operated with the microphone gain set too high?

T7B01 — What can you do if you are told your FM handheld or mobile transceiver is over-deviating?

DSP and SDR — Radios Made with Software

DSP stands for *digital signal processing*, the technique of using software to perform filtering and other functions. DSP operates on a received signal converted to digital form. A microprocessor performs the filtering and other functions on the digital data before it is converted back to a signal you can hear or see.

Common DSP functions in amateur radios include:
- Noise reduction
- Variable signal filtering
- Automatic notch filtering
- Audio equalizing

SDR stands for *software defined radio* — an even more advanced use of DSP to do nearly *all* of the radio functions. Except for higher power amplification, SDR techniques can change the radio signal to digital form directly from the antenna. The rest of the radio is software!

SDR and DSP have enabled many innovations in the way a radio operates and the signals it can generate and receive. SDR radios are becoming very popular and you will find more and more models with these features.

Excessive modulation results in distortion of transmitted speech and unwanted or *spurious* transmitter outputs on adjacent frequencies where they cause interference. Those unwanted transmitter outputs have lots of names, but the most common is *splatter*. Generating those outputs is called *splattering*, as in, "You're splattering 10 kHz away!"

An overmodulated FM signal has excessive deviation and is said to be *overdeviating*. Overdeviation is usually caused by speaking too loudly into the microphone and may cause interference on adjacent channels. It often generates noise or distortion on voice peaks, called "breaking up." To reduce overdeviation, speak more softly or move the microphone farther from your mouth. **[T2B05, T7B01]**

Overmodulation of an AM or SSB signal is caused by speaking too loudly or by setting the microphone gain or speech compression too high, possibly resulting in distortion of the transmitted signal. **[T4B01]** To eliminate overmodulation, speak more softly or reduce microphone gain or speech compression.

RECEIVER FUNCTIONS

T4B03 — What is the purpose of the squelch control on a transceiver?

T4B11 — What is the function of automatic gain control, or AGC?

The receiver has a difficult task — picking just the one signal you want out of all the other signals. Nevertheless, modern receivers do a great job as long as they're adjusted properly. Knowing how a receiver's controls work makes a big difference, as you will see when you start tuning the bands! **Figure 5.7** shows where you might find receiver controls on a typical transceiver.

Most familiar is the *AF gain* or *volume* control. Just like on

Figure 5.7 — The front panel of this Yaesu FT-840 transceiver has some of the receiver controls you'll use every day. AF GAIN (labeled AF) is the volume control. CLAR (RIT) and SHIFT vary the receiver frequency without changing your transmit frequency. ATT adds attenuation to reduce the strength of very strong received signals.

a home or car radio, this sets the speaker or headphone listening level. On an HF rig, the *RF gain* control will be nearby. RF gain adjusts the sensitivity of the receiver to incoming signals. An *attenuator* reduces the strength of signals to prevent them from overloading the receiver.

A receiver's *automatic gain control (AGC)* circuitry constantly adjusts the receiver's sensitivity to keep the output volume constant for both weak and strong signals. **[T4B11]**

To keep from having to listen to continuous noise when no signal is present, the *squelch* circuit was invented. The squelch circuit (sometimes called *carrier squelch*) mutes the receiver's audio output when no signal is present. **[T4B03]**

Selectivity and Sensitivity

T7A01 — Which term describes the ability of a receiver to detect the presence of a signal?

T7A04 — Which term describes the ability of a receiver to discriminate between multiple signals?

T7A11 — Where is an RF preamplifier installed?

Receivers are compared on the basis of two primary characteristics: *sensitivity* and *selectivity*. A receiver's sensitivity determines its ability to detect signals. **[T7A01]** Sensitivity is specified as a *minimum detectable signal* level, usually in microvolts (μV). The lower the MDS, the more sensitive the receiver. If a receiver is not sensitive enough, a *preamplifier* or "preamp" can be used. The preamp is connected between the antenna and receiver. **[T7A11]**

Selectivity is the ability of a receiver to discriminate between signals, retrieving only the information from the desired signal in the presence of unwanted signals. **[T7A04]** High selectivity means that a receiver can operate properly even in the presence of strong signals on nearby frequencies.

Filtering and Tuning

T4B05 — Which of the following would reduce ignition interference to a receiver?

T4B06 — Which of the following controls could be used if the voice pitch of a single-sideband signal seems too high or low?

T4B07 — What does the term "RIT" mean?

T4B08 — What is the advantage of having multiple receive bandwidth choices on a multimode transceiver?

T4B09 — Which of the following is an appropriate receive filter bandwidth for minimizing noise and interference for SSB reception?

T4B10 — Which of the following is an appropriate receive filter bandwidth for minimizing noise and interference for CW reception?

T4B12 — Which of the following could be used to remove power line noise or ignition noise?

A receiver rejects unwanted signals through the use of *filters*. At the receiver input, a filter passes only signals from the selected band. Those signals then pass through filters narrow enough to reject all but the desired signal. ("Narrow" means smaller bandwidth and "wide" means greater bandwidth.) Wide filters (around 2.4 kHz) are used for SSB reception. **[T4B09]** Narrow filters (around 500 Hz) are used for CW and data mode reception. **[T4B10]** Having multiple filters available allows you to reduce noise or interference by selecting a filter with just enough bandwidth to pass the desired signal. **[T4B08]**

Receiver incremental tuning (RIT) is a fine-tuning control used for SSB or CW operation. RIT allows the operator to adjust the receiver frequency without changing the transmitter frequency. **[T4B07]** This allows you to tune in a station that is slightly off frequency or to adjust the pitch of an operator's voice that seems too high or low. **[T4B06]** On some radios, the RIT is called a *clarifier* which is labeled CLAR.

There are lots of types of noise in the radio spectrum. Special circuits are employed to get rid of noise or at least limit its effect. A *noise blanker* (NB) senses the sharp pulses from arcing power lines, motors, or vehicle ignition systems and temporarily mutes the receiver during the pulse. **[T4B05, T4B12]**

For More Information

Receivers usually have a way to indicate signal strength, such as a meter with a moving needle or a variable-length bar at the side or bottom of the display. On the rig in Figure 5.7, the meter shows signal strength in *S-units*. Although not strictly calibrated, a change of one S-unit corresponds to about a factor of four in signal strength. S-units are numbered from S-1 to S-9, with S-9 being the strongest. The strength of signals stronger than S-9 is reported as the number of dB (decibels) greater than S-9. For example, "Your signal is 20 dB over S-9!"

AGC can respond quickly or slowly to changes in signal strength. A *fast AGC* response is used for CW and data. *Slow AGC* response is used for AM and SSB signals. FM receivers don't use AGC.

The *squelch threshold*, controlled by the squelch control, is the signal level at which muting is turned off and the signal becomes audible. If the receiver's output is not muted, squelch is *open*. If the signal is muted, squelch is *closed*. Raising the squelch threshold is called *tightening the squelch*.

A *notch filter* removes a very narrow range of frequencies from a receiver's audio output. This is useful when an interfering tone is encountered. The tone is removed, leaving the desired speech, code, or data relatively unaffected.

Receivers may also provide *noise reduction* (NR) functions. Noise reduction is special software that removes audio noise by using digital signal processing.

VHF/UHF RF POWER AMPLIFIERS

T7A09 — What is the function of the SSB/CW-FM switch on a VHF power amplifier?

T7A10 — What device increases the low-power output from a handheld transceiver?

Handheld transceivers or *handhelds* are incredibly popular and offer a variety of useful features. They can only output a few watts, however. If you have difficulty accessing distant repeaters or making simplex contacts, an RF power amplifier can be used to increase the output power by a factor of five or more. **[T7A10]** To use an amplifier with a handheld, you'll also need a connecting cable between the handheld's antenna jack and the power amplifier's input connector.

Amplifiers can also be used with SSB and CW radios for contesting and working distant stations. Many VHF/UHF power amplifiers can be used on all modes but need to be set to the right mode to operate properly. On most amplifiers, this is controlled by a CW/SSB switch on the front panel. **[T7A09]** You can use the amplifier in the CW position to operate on FM. Be sure your antenna is capable of handling the higher power, such as a mag-mount whip or mast-mounted vertical or beam antenna. Be sure you learn about RF exposure in the RF Management and Safety chapter before using an RF power amplifier.

TRANSVERTERS

T7A06 — What device converts the RF input and output of a transceiver to another band?

By using mixers (see Chapter 3), it is possible to convert an entire transceiver to operate on a different band. The mixers are part of equipment called a *transverter*. Low-power transmitter output signals are shifted to the new output frequency where they are amplified for transmission. A *receiving converter* mixer shifts input signals to the desired band where they are received as regular signals by the transceiver. Transverters allow one main transceiver to be used on one or more new bands. **[T7A06]** For example, with few transceivers available for CW and SSB operation on 222 MHz, a transverter is used to convert 222 MHz signals to and from the 28 MHz band on an HF radio.

5.3 Digital Communications

T4A02 — How might a computer be used as part of an amateur radio station?
T8D09 — What code is used when sending CW in the amateur bands?

What is That Signal?

With so many different digital modes active on the air, it can be difficult to tell what type of signal you're listening to. After a while, you'll find that it's easy to learn to recognize the most common modes by ear or even by eye on a band scope or waterfall display. In the meantime, a collection of sound samples from several popular modes is available online at **www.arrl.org/resources-for-license-instruction** under "Digital Modes: Audio Files."

Before we begin this section, it's important to mention the one piece of equipment that applies to just about every part of Amateur Radio — the computer! Just about any function or capability of the ham radio experience has the potential to involve a computer: bookkeeping chores such as logging contacts, operating on the digital modes, and even sending and receiving CW. **[T4A02]** Without the computer becoming such a central part of the station, digital communications would still be a specialized interest and not widespread.

Why use digital modes, anyway? Voice and CW are quite effective but they don't have the ability of digital systems to automatically correct errors caused by noise and interference. Special codes and characters embedded in the stream of data allow the receiving modem to detect, and sometimes correct, errors. The result is that some digital modes offer error-free communications at speeds that adjust automatically to propagation and noise. Protocol design is an area in which amateur experimentation is definitely advancing the state of the radio art.

Amateurs have developed or adapted techniques for exchanging digital data by transforming the 1s and 0s of data into tones that are in the same frequency range as the human voice. Radios designed for voice transmission can then transmit and receive the tones as either AM or FM signals. *Digital* or *data modes* combine modulation (the addition of information to a radio signal) with a *protocol*, the rules by which data is packaged and exchanged. The protocol also controls how the transmitter and receiver coordinate the exchange of data. The method used to represent each character as digital 1s and 0s is called a *code* and yes, Morse is a digital code. **[T8D09]**

AMATEUR DIGITAL MODES

T8D01 — Which of the following is a digital communications mode?

Different combinations of protocols, codes, and modulation, such as SSB or FM, are used to create *digital modes*. Each mode has its own advantages and disadvantages for

Wi-Fi and Broadband Hamnet

T8D12 — Which of the following best describes Broad band-Hamnet, also referred to as a high-speed multi-media network?

Wi-Fi, described by the IEEE 802.11 standard, shares some channels in the 2.4 GHz and 5.6 GHz band with the amateur service. Hams have modified the firmware of some commercial Wi-Fi routers so they automatically connect to each other forming data networks. This system is called *Broadband Hamnet* or *High-Speed Multimedia* (HSMM). **[T8D12]** These networks have proven very useful in public service and emergency communications. (For more information, see **www. broadband-hamnet.org**.)

The WSJT Modes

T8D10 — Which of the following operating activities is supported by digital mode software in the WSJT suite?
T8D13 — What is FT8?

Many of today's most popular digital modes are part of the *WSJT Suite*, a package of open-source software available at **physics.princeton.edu/pulsar/k1jt**. The software was initially developed by Joe Taylor, K1JT, using techniques he developed as part of his Nobel-winning career as an astrophysicist. A team maintains and extends the software today, including modes designed for special types of communication such as JT65 for moonbounce (or Earth-Moon-Earth, EME), weak-signal propagation beacons (WSPR), and meteor scatter (MSK144). **[T8D10]** The latest invention, FT8, is capable of operating in low signal-to-noise conditions by transmitting special code sequences on 15-second intervals. **[T8D13]** The advanced capability of these modes enables amateurs to communicate in ways not possible before.

speed, error rate, and how it is used. The FCC rules also place different limits on how fast digital data may be transmitted on the different bands. This means the different modes are more popular on different bands.

On HF, where SSB modulation and ionospheric or "skip" propagation is the norm, popular digital modes include:
- Radioteletype (RTTY) using the 5-bit Baudot code
- Keyboard-to-keyboard modes such as PSK31
- Weak-signal modes such as FT8 and WSPR
- PACTOR or WINMOR modes for Winlink system messaging

On VHF/UHF, the popular digital modes include: **[T8D01]**
- Packet radio based on the AX.25 protocol
- B2F protocol for Winlink system messaging
- JT65 for moonbounce and MSK144 for scatter paths
- IEEE 802.11 (Wi-Fi) adapted to amateur use on microwave bands

Amateurs are also using digital protocols to communicate by voice — these are *digital voice* modes. On HF, the AOR and FreeDV modes are the most popular. There are several choices used on VHF/UHF: D-STAR, System Fusion (C4FM), DMR (Digital Mobile Radio), and P25 are the most widely used as of early 2018. Digital voice is discussed in more detail in Chapter 6.

Packet and Packet Networks

T8D08 — Which of the following may be included in packet transmissions?
T8D11 — What is an ARQ transmission system?

On VHF and UHF, the most common digital mode is *packet radio*. Packet signals are often found on simplex channels from 145.01 to 145.09 MHz. Information on packet radio can be found in the *ARRL Handbook* and the manuals for TNC data interfaces.

Data characters are transmitted in groups called *packets*. *Frequency-shift keying* (FSK) is used to transmit the individual characters as a series of rapidly alternating audio tones. A receiving modem and terminal node controller (TNC) then reassemble the data from the received packets. On VHF and UHF, the packet is transmitted at 1200 or 9600 baud, so that the overall *throughput* of a packet system is about 400 or 3000 bits per second. (Packet radio is limited to 300 baud on HF as of early 2018.)

Each packet consists of a *header* and *data*. The header contains information about the packet and the call sign of the destination station. The header also includes a *checksum* that allows the receiver to detect errors. If an error is detected, the receiver automatically requests that the packet be retransmitted until the data is received properly. This is called ARQ for *automatic repeat request*. [**T8D08, T8D11**] The rules of the packet radio protocol, AX.25, ensure that data accepted by the receiver is error-free.

Keyboard-to-Keyboard

T8D06 — What does the abbreviation "PSK" mean?

Digital modes that are designed for real-time person-to-person communication are called *keyboard-to-keyboard* modes. They are most popular on the HF bands. Most are generated by computer software using a sound card and an interface to a transceiver's audio input and output. Many software packages such as *fldigi* from W1HKJ Software (**www.w1hkj.com**) are free or low-cost, making it easy to get on the air with numerous digital modes.

Radioteletype (RTTY) is the oldest keyboard-to-keyboard mode, invented in the 1930s. It uses the *Baudot code* (pronounced *baw-DOH*), which is where the term *baud* comes from.

The most popular keyboard-to-keyboard mode today is PSK31, which stands for *phase shift keying, 31 baud*. [**T8D06**] PSK31 uses precise signal timing to recover the signal from noise and interference. Although it sends data at a low rate, it works very well in noisy conditions. A typical operating program for PSK31 is shown in **Figure 5.8**.

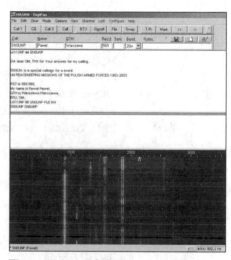

Figure 5.8 — PSK31 is a popular keyboard-to-keyboard mode on HF. Many amateurs use the *DigiPan* software shown here (www.digipan. net). At the top is a window that shows the decoded text. The bottom shows a *waterfall display* that is a visual presentation of what the computer's sound card is receiving from the radio.

APRS

T8D02 — What does the term "APRS" mean?

T8D03 — Which of the following devices is used to provide data to the transmitter when sending automatic position reports from a mobile amateur radio station?

T8D05 — Which of the following is an application of APRS (Automatic Packet Reporting System)?

The *Automatic Packet Reporting System* (APRS) uses packet radio to transmit the position information from a moving or portable station. An APRS station is basically a packet radio station combined with a *Global Positioning System* (GPS) receiver. [**T8D02, T8D03**]

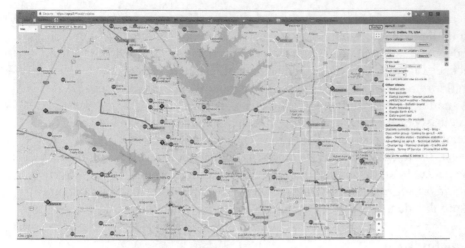

Figure 5.9 — APRS, the Automatic Packet Reporting System, uses packet radio signals to display the positions of fixed and mobile stations on a computer-generated map.

The GPS receiver outputs a stream of position data that is then transmitted in packet form. Along with position information, you can also transmit weather information and short text messages.

Digipeaters and gateways forward the APRS packets, position information, and call sign to a system of server computers via the internet. Once the information is stored on the servers, websites access the data and show the position of the station on maps in various ways. A typical APRS tracking map is shown in **Figure 5.9**. A common public service application of APRS is to provide maps of station locations while they are providing real-time tactical communications. **[T8D05]**

SETTING UP FOR DIGITAL MODES

T4A04 — Which computer sound card port is connected to a transceiver's headphone or speaker output for operating digital modes?

T4A06 — Which of the following connections might be used between a voice transceiver and a computer for digital operation?

T4A07 — How is a computer's sound card used when conducting digital communications?

Figure 5.10 shows an example of how a station is configured to use digital modes. If a standalone TNC is used, it is connected to one of the computer's digital data ports via a

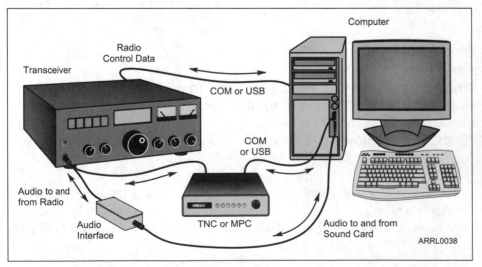

Figure 5.10 — Data interfaces are connected between the transceiver's audio inputs and outputs and the computer's data connections (USB or COM ports) or sound card jacks. A TNC or MPC (multi-protocol controller) converts between data and audio. An audio interface isolates the computer sound card from the radio to prevent hum.

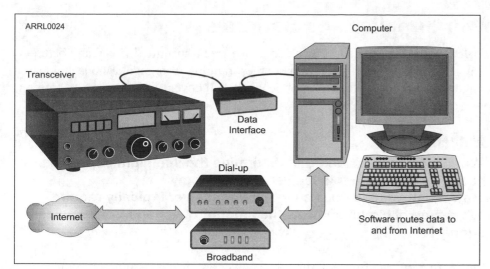

Figure 5.11 — An internet gateway station is a regular digital mode station and also runs software that relays data to and from the internet. The most common example of gateway stations are APRS gateways and Winlink RMS stations.

COM port or USB interface. The TNC is then connected to the radio's microphone input (for transmit audio) and speaker or headphone output (for receive audio). If a sound card is used instead, its output is connected to the radio's microphone input and the speaker or headphone output is connected to the sound card input. If you use a sound card, you may need a digital communications interface to supply the PTT (push-to-talk) signal for keying the transmitter. **[T4A04, T4A06, T4A07]**

GATEWAYS

T8C11 — What name is given to an amateur radio station that is used to connect other amateur stations to the Internet?

The *gateway* shown in **Figure 5.11** is a special kind of digital station that provides a connection to the internet via Amateur Radio. **[T8C11]** Most gateways are set up to *forward* messages. The most common examples are APRS gateways and the Winlink RMS stations described previously.

Caution! All of the rules and regulations about commercial and business-related messages and communications apply to internet gateways. For example, it is definitely not okay to exchange e-mails for your employer or to access websites with third-party advertising. Because so much of the internet is associated with commercial activity, take extra care to follow the Amateur Radio rules.

5.4 Power Supplies and Batteries

A solid power source is important for a clean, noise-free transmitted signal and better reception. Hams use a wide variety of power sources, ranging from regular household ac to solar panels and batteries for portable or mobile use. We'll cover two of the most common sources: power supplies and batteries.

POWER SUPPLIES

T4A01 — What must be considered to determine the minimum current capacity needed for a transceiver power supply?

T5A06 — How much voltage does a mobile transceiver typically require?

T6D05 — What type of circuit controls the amount of voltage from a power supply?

Power supplies that operate from household ac power are the most common source of power for radios. Two types are shown in **Figure 5.12**. They convert the ac input power to dc current for the radio equipment.

A power supply has two main ratings: its output voltage and the amount of current it can supply continuously. For example, a power supply for a typical mobile radio might be rated as a "12 V, 20 Amp" supply. Radios that operate from a "12 V" supply may actually work best at the slightly higher voltage of 13.8 V typical of vehicle power systems with the engine running. Be sure your power supply can generate the correct voltage. **[T5A06]**

A supply's output voltage changes with the amount of output current. A *regulated supply* uses a *regulator* circuit to minimize the amount of voltage change. **[T6D05]** The percentage of voltage change between zero current (*no load*) and maximum current (*full load*) is the *regulation* of the supply.

The current rating of a supply must be at least as much as the sum of the maximum current needs of everything hooked up to the supply. To determine the maximum current rating needed for a transceiver, you must consider the transmitter's efficiency at full power output, how much current the receiver and control circuits require, and the power supply's regulation and ability to dissipate heat at full load. **[T4A01]** The manuals of the equipment will specify the maximum amount of current they require. A single power supply can be shared between two or more pieces of equipment if it can supply enough current.

Figure 5.12 — The traditional or "linear" power supply (top) is a reliable, if heavy and bulky, performer. The modern "switching" supply shown below uses sophisticated electronics that do not need a large iron transformer, delivering equivalent power at a fraction of the weight.

MOBILE POWER WIRING

T4A10 — What is the source of a high-pitched whine that varies with engine speed in a mobile transceiver's receive audio?

T4A11 — Where should the negative return connection of a mobile transceiver's power cable be connected?

Mobile installations have special requirements for obtaining power safely. Remember that a vehicle battery stores a lot of energy! Accidental short circuits can not only damage your radio equipment, they can start fires and do a lot of expensive damage to your car. General guidelines include:

• A fuse should be present in both the positive and negative leads of your radio near the power connection.

• Connect the radio's negative lead to the negative battery terminal or where the battery ground lead is connected to the vehicle body. **[T4A11]** Check with a dealer for the right point to attach the negative lead in vehicles that use a *battery monitoring system*.

• Use grommets or sleeves to protect wiring from chafing or rubbing on exposed metal, especially where it passes through a bulkhead or firewall.

• Don't assume all metal is connected to the battery's negative terminal — vehicle bodies are often a mix of plastic and metal.

Vehicle power wiring often carries a significant amount of noise that can affect your radio's operation. *Alternator whine* is caused by noise on the dc power system inside your own vehicle. You might hear it with the received audio but more likely it will be heard by others as a high-pitched whine on your transmitted audio that varies with your engine speed. **[T4A10]**

BATTERIES

T0A10 — What can happen if a lead-acid storage battery is charged or discharged too quickly?

T6A10 — Which of the following battery types is rechargeable?

T6A11 — Which of the following battery types is not rechargeable?

Batteries are made up of one or more *cells*. A cell is an individual package that contains chemicals to produce current from a chemical reaction. (The general term "battery" is often used to refer to single cells, as well.)

The most common types and sizes of disposable and rechargeable batteries used by hams are listed in **Table 5.3**. **[T6A10, T6A11]** The column labeled "Chemistry Type" describes the chemicals used in the battery and the "Fully-Charged Voltage" column

Table 5.3

Battery Types and Characteristics

Battery Style	Chemistry Type	Fully-Charged Voltage	Energy Rating (average)
AAA	Alkaline – Disposable	1.5 V	1100 mAh
AA	Alkaline – Disposable	1.5 V	2600 – 3200 mAh
AA	Carbon-Zinc – Disposable	1.5 V	600 mAh
AA	Nickel-Cadmium (NiCd) – Rechargeable	1.2 V	700 mAh
AA	Nickel-Metal Hydride (NiMH) – Rechargeable	1.2 V	1500 – 2200 mAh
C	Alkaline – Disposable	1.5 V	7500 mAh
D	Alkaline – Disposable	1.5 V	14000 mAh
9 V	Alkaline – Disposable	9 V	580 mAh
9 V	Nickel-Cadmium (NiCd) – Rechargeable	9 V	110 mAh
9 V	Nickel-Metal Hydride – Rechargeable	9 V	150 mAh
Coin Cells	Lithium — Disposable	3 – 3.3 V	25 – 1000 mAh
Packs	Lithium ion (Li-ion) – Rechargeable	3.3 – 3.6 V per cell	Varies
Storage	Lead-acid – Rechargeable	2 V per cell	Varies

represents the output of a fresh or recently-charged battery. The battery's *"Energy Rating"* in ampere-hours (Ah) or milliampere hours (mAh) specifies its ability to deliver current while still maintaining a steady output voltage. **Figure 5.13** shows several common types of batteries and their relative sizes.

Storage batteries, such as deep-cycle marine or RV batteries, are often used as an emergency power source in place of a power supply operating from ac power. They can store hundreds of times the energy in a small battery. Storage batteries are often left connected to a charger that can keep them fully charged with a small current, called *trickle* or *float charging*. Be sure that the charger will switch to this lower current automatically or it can overcharge and ruin these expensive batteries.

Storage batteries hold a lot of energy and must be treated with respect. They contain strong acids that can be hazardous if spilled or allowed to leak. Storage batteries can also

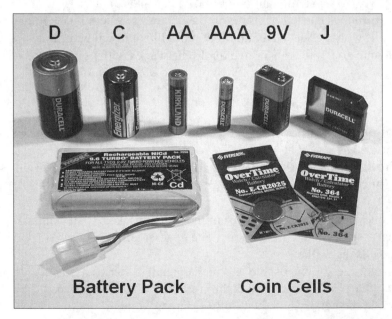

Figure 5.13 — The photo shows several common sizes of batteries. Coin cells are usually used in radios as a source of backup power for the microprocessor circuitry. Battery packs are packages of several cells in a single enclosure or case. The photo shows a battery pack used for remote control vehicles. (Courtesy Wiley Publishing, *Two-Way Radios and Scanners for Dummies*)

release or *vent* flammable hydrogen gas, that can cause an explosion. **[T0A10]** Be sure to store and charge these batteries in a well-ventilated place. Accidentally short-circuiting a storage battery with a tool or faulty wiring can easily cause a fire and damage the battery.

For More Information

A battery cell is constructed so that the chemical reaction can't occur until there is a path or circuit for electrons to flow between the cell terminals. When the chemicals are "used up" and the reaction stops, so does the current. The types of chemicals also determine the voltage of the cell.

The cells of a multiple-cell battery are connected in series so that the voltages from each cell add together. The common "9 volt" alkaline battery is actually six smaller 1.5-volt cells connected in series. An automobile's 12-volt battery is made of six cells, each a separate compartment holding the necessary chemicals to produce 2 volts.

There are many different types of batteries, but they fall into three basic groups:

• Disposable or *Primary* — the chemicals can only react once, then the battery must be discarded

• Rechargeable or *Secondary* — the chemical reaction can be reversed, recharging the battery

• *Storage* Batteries — rechargeable batteries used for long-term energy storage

To get the most energy from a battery, limit the amount of current drawn from it. A low discharge rate keeps the battery cool inside and minimizes losses due to the battery's natural internal resistance. To maximize battery life and capacity, store them in a cool, dry place. You may refrigerate batteries, but never freeze them since the resulting ice may expand enough to crack the battery. Heat accelerates the battery chemical's tendency to *self-discharge* so that they can no longer deliver as much charge. Moisture allows charge to leak slowly between the battery's external terminals. Regularly inspect batteries for damage or leakage and perform an occasional maintenance charge as part of your battery plan.

When recharging batteries, be sure to use a *charger* designed for that particular type of battery. Each different battery chemistry and size requires a certain method of charging. Too much recharging current may damage the battery. Too little current may keep the battery from reaching full charge.

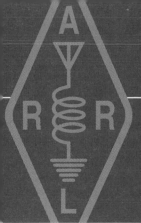

Chapter 6

Communicating With Other Hams

In this chapter, you'll learn about:

- Where and how contacts are made
- Using repeaters
- Participating in nets
- Public service communications
- Amateur emergency organizations
- Satellite operating

When you see the mouse, you'll find more information at www.arrl.org/ham-radio-license-manual

Having learned all that interesting material about rigs and electronics and radio waves, you know a lot about the technology of radio. In this section we turn to operating — how are contacts made and what does a contact consist of?

This part of the book is about "good amateur practices." There aren't many FCC rules about operating procedures, so amateurs have developed their own rules of etiquette. They work pretty well, so to be a successful and effective communicator it's a good idea to learn and practice them. The FCC (and other amateurs) expects you to follow established practices fairly closely, just as you expect other people to do in daily life. (The online supplemental material for this chapter includes a handy overview of the basic steps for casual ham radio contacts.)

We'll start by learning how the ham bands are organized so that you know where to tune. You'll then discover how ham radio is conducted using repeaters and in the organized activities called "nets," especially during emergencies. This chapter concludes with coverage of a few of ham radio's many specialty activities. Clear your throat and get ready for that first contact!

6.1 Band Plans

DEFINITIONS AND FINDING BAND PLANS

T2A10 — What is a band plan, beyond the privileges established by the FCC?

T2A11 — What term describes an amateur station that is transmitting and receiving on the same frequency?

T2B13 — Where may SSB phone be used in amateur bands above 50 MHz?

The amateur bands may not appear to be very big on a chart of the radio spectrum, but once you start tuning around, you'll find they are quite large! How can you tell where to tune for your preferred activity? What keeps the different types of operating from being spread out randomly all over the band? To answer these needs, amateurs created *band plans* that help organize the different modes and activities.

It's important to keep in mind that band plans are voluntary agreements designed for normal conditions. [T2A10] They are not regulations. Except for repeaters, whose operating frequencies are fixed, stations are expected to operate flexibly. Amateur Radio is the only service that can tune freely and use multiple modes within their allocations, so we are expected to do so. You may find that a special event or contest crowds the bands, or conditions may be unfavorable, or public service communications may be underway. Utilize ham radio's flexibility and you will be happier and more successful on the air.

The easiest place to find the band plans for US amateurs is via the ARRL's home page or on the *Ham Radio License Manual* website. You should take a few minutes to browse the band plans, particularly those for the 2 meter and 70 cm bands where many Technician licensees begin operating. **Table 6.1** shows the 2 meter band plan. Are you surprised at all the different types of activity?

On the HF bands, band plans tend to be simpler because there are no repeaters except on the 10 meter band. On the VHF and UHF bands where repeater operation is common, the band plans also show where repeaters listen as well as transmit.

Here are a few other common uses listed in band plans:

• Beacons — Automated transmissions for listeners to tell when the band is "open" to the beacon's location. The Northern California DX Foundation (**www.ncdxf.org**) operates a series of beacons around the world on the HF bands and many individual hams operate a beacon on 10 meters or the VHF/UHF bands.

• Weak signal — Modes that work better at lower signal strengths are used here, such as CW, SSB, and some digital modes. Every amateur band from 50 MHz on up has frequencies available for CW and SSB operation. [T2B13]

• Satellite uplinks and downlinks — These are segments of the bands where signals are sent to (*uplink*) and received from (*downlink*) satellites. An amateur satellite is known as an *OSCAR — Orbiting Satellite Carrying Amateur Radio*.

• Simplex — Transmitting and receiving on the same frequency [T2A11] Use these channels when no repeater is available or to avoid occupying a repeater.

• Repeater inputs and outputs — This is where the usual repeater operations are found and where nearly all FM operation occurs.

• Control links — Repeaters and other stations that are linked together or controlled by a remote operator use radio links to carry audio and control signals.

WHY BAND PLANS ARE NEEDED

You are probably beginning to understand band plans. These voluntary conventions simply make it easier for everyone to maximize their own success and share the sometimes-crowded ham bands. Sharing is particularly important because the different styles of operating are not always compatible. For example, a digital station and CW or voice station simply can't share a common frequency — they are too different. It's a lot easier for signals of the same type to operate close together than it is for a mix of modes.

Table 6.1

2 meter (144-148 MHz) Band Plan

144.00-144.05	EME (CW)
144.05-144.10	General CW and weak signals
144.10-144.20	EME and weak-signal SSB
144.200	SSB calling frequency
144.200-144.275	General SSB operation
144.275-144.300	Propagation beacons
144.30-144.50	OSCAR subband
144.50-144.60	Linear translator inputs
144.60-144.90	FM repeater inputs
144.90-145.10	Weak signal and FM simplex (145.01, 03, 05, 07,09 are widely used for packet radio)
145.10-145.20	Linear translator outputs
145.20-145.50	FM repeater outputs
145.50-145.80	Miscellaneous and experimental modes
145.80-146.00	OSCAR subband
146.01-146.37	Repeater inputs
146.40-146.58	Simplex
146.52	National Simplex Calling Frequency
146.61-147.39	Repeater outputs
147.42-147.57	Simplex
147.60-147.99	Repeater inputs

The other major reason for having band plans at VHF and above is the effective use of repeater stations. As we mentioned in the previous section, repeaters have an input and an output frequency separated by the repeater offset frequency. Having the repeater input frequencies close together and the output frequencies close together serve two purposes. It's a lot easier to tune from repeater to repeater that way, and the repeater receiver's sensitivity is improved by keeping the input frequencies separate from the powerful output signals. Everything works a lot better when the band plan is followed!

For More Information

Who makes the band plans? You might think that the ARRL created all these band plans, but that's not the case. The ARRL publishes what it understands to be the band plan based on how hams use the various frequencies. These voluntary "gentlemen's agreements" evolved over the years as the various groups of hams decided how best to coordinate their operating. The ARRL band plans simply reflect those agreements.

Repeater band plans at VHF and UHF were a bit more difficult to organize, since each region was isolated by limits to signal propagation. This often had a big impact on decisions about where to place input and output frequencies and the *channel spacing* between one repeater and the next. Fortunately, it was quickly realized that a certain amount of compatibility between the plans was needed. Hams have almost completely aligned the regional repeater band plans so that travelers can easily use repeaters anywhere.

Rules About Band Plans

As mentioned earlier, band plans are considered "good practice" by the FCC and so it expects hams to abide by them. The only time this really comes into question is when persistent interference is caused by a station operating in conflict with the band plan. For example, if someone decides to operate a repeater whose output frequency is the same as a nearby repeater's input frequency, interference will result. If the parties are unable to resolve the issue with the help of the regional *frequency coordinator*, the FCC will first look to see which repeater is operating according to the band plan.

Band plans by themselves cannot guarantee that no interference exists. For example, on 40 meters, the international RTTY calling frequency is the same as that of the QRP CW operators! The powerful RTTY and weak Morse code signals don't coexist very well. Luckily, it is relatively uncommon for interference between the two groups to last very long. Hams, being much more flexible or *frequency-agile* than any other radio service, just retune a bit and carry on.

6.2 Making Contacts

Before you transmit, be sure you are authorized to use that frequency and mode! As a Technician licensee, you will have full amateur privileges on 50 MHz and up, but there are several mode-restricted band segments. On HF, your privileges are restricted as shown in the chapter on **Licensing Regulations**.

This section covers the basic procedures you'll use for making ham radio contacts. While these "radio manners" apply to just about all contacts, repeater operation has some special aspects that are covered in the next section.

REPEATER CONTACTS

T2A04 — What is an appropriate way to call another station on a repeater if you know the other station's call sign?
T2A09 — What brief statement indicates that you are listening on a repeater and looking for a contact?
T7B10 — What might be a problem if you receive a report that your audio signal through the repeater is distorted or unintelligible?

Repeaters are frequently like social clubs; they have regular users and usually there are manners that help everyone share the facility. You can learn those manners by listening. Here are some repeater manners shared by all repeaters users:
- Listen so that you are aware of someone using the repeater
- Keep transmissions short
- Identify your station legally; identifying at the beginning of the contact is also a good idea
- Pause briefly between transmissions to listen for another station trying to break in

When using a repeater, you are responsible for operating legally. As the control operator of the originating station you are responsible, not the repeater owner, if your transmissions violate FCC rules.

Because repeaters usually have a strong signal on a known frequency, it's not necessary to make a long transmission to attract listeners tuning by. The easiest way is to just give your call sign. **[T2A09]** That announces you are listening and are available for a contact.

Many stations add a few words to make it clear that they would like to make a contact: "W1AW is monitoring." Or "W1AW is monitoring and standing by for a call." That announces to everyone listening that W1AW is available for contacts through the repeater. Customs vary from region to region and even from repeater to repeater, so listen a while first to see how others make contacts and follow their lead. (Hint — listening to learn is a sure path to success in ham radio!)

If you want to respond to a station asking for a call or want to contact a station whose call sign you already know, take advantage of the repeater's strong signal and keep it short. Just say the other station's call sign once, followed by "this is" or "from," then give your call sign. **[T2A04]** It sounds like this: "NØAX this is WA7KYI"

What if someone else is using the repeater and you accidentally interrupt them? Don't panic, just say "Sorry, W1AW clear" and wait for their contact to end or tune to a different repeater.

What if you receive a report that your signal's audio is strong, but distorted? A station that is slightly off-frequency will be strong, but distorted. This sometimes happens when a radio control knob or key gets bumped, changing frequency by a small amount. If accidentally pressing a control knob or key on your radio is a frequent problem (smaller radios are particularly prone to it), try using the LOCK feature of your radio to disable unintended key presses. You could also be causing excessive deviation by speaking too

"My name is Chris, Charlie Hotel Romeo India Sierra." Why do hams (and radio operators in general) use those strange words instead of just spelling with letters? Remember that you only hear what comes through the radio, so it's often difficult to tell the letters apart. For example, the letters E, T, B, C, D and so forth can sound a lot alike. Not only that, non-English speakers don't pronounce letters in the same way at all! The solution to both of these problems is *phonetics*.

Created in the early days of international radio, the International Telecommunication Union (ITU) developed a standardized *phonetic alphabet* that operators of all languages could use to exchange precise information. Each word was chosen because it was easy to understand over the radio. Hams should learn these standard words and use them whenever there is a need for precise, exact spelling — for example, your call sign! (A table of standard phonetics is provided in the online supplemental information for this chapter.)

You may also be familiar with the US military version of phonetics and these are used, too. Hams that specialize in DX contacts overseas sometimes use the names of countries or cities. For example, you might hear "Norway" instead of "November" or "Santiago" instead of "Sierra." There is no FCC rule about which set is required. Use the set that best suits the need.

Use caution in making up your own set of funny or cute words, such as "Wanted, One Aged Whiskey" for W1AW. Those may be fine in your local club since they're just nicknames, really, but they can be very confusing on the air, particularly to a foreign ham.

loudly into the microphone. Either lower your voice or hold the microphone farther away from your mouth. You could be transmitting from a bad location where your signal is distorted at the repeater input. Weak or *low* batteries can also cause distorted audio. **[T7B10]**

For More Information

Giving signal reports on a repeater is also part of repeater etiquette. Because the repeater is retransmitting the signal, a signal report tells the transmitting station how well the repeater hears them! You'll often hear the following terms, from strongest to weakest:

- Full quieting — your signal is strong enough that no receiver noise is heard
- White noise — not as strong as full quieting, some noise is present
- Scratchy — weaker still, noise is almost as strong as your voice
- Mobile flutter or picket fencing — rapid fading due to moving through an area of multipath propagation or shadowing
- Dropping out — mostly audible, but frequent periods of no signal
- Broken or breaking up — short periods of audibility, but mostly unreadable

These give a good description of what the signal sounds like on the repeater's output. Keep your handheld radio's antenna vertical if your signal is less than full-quieting strength.

Repeaters often add a short *courtesy beep* to the retransmitted signal when the transmitting station's signal disappears. This useful feature becomes the "over" cue to other stations to start speaking, although saying "Over" is common on repeaters as well. Some radios have the capability to add their own courtesy beep, but it is not necessary (and often confusing) on a repeater with a courtesy beep enabled already.

What if you are sure that your signal is being received by the repeater but the stations don't respond? Don't feel slighted! Remember that many hams use repeaters as a kind of on-the-air meeting place for club members or acquaintances. They may not be looking for a random contact all the time. For best success on repeaters, wait until an existing contact is finishing and then call one of the stations. This works especially well if you can discuss a topic of their just-concluded contact — a real conversation starter! Participating regularly in nets (discussed later) or other events on repeaters is also a good way to break in with a group.

SIMPLEX CHANNELS

T2A02 — What is the national calling frequency for FM simplex operations in the 2 meter band?
T2B01 — What is the most common use of the "reverse split" function of a VHF/UHF transceiver?
T2B03 — If a station is not strong enough to keep a repeater's receiver squelch open, which of the following might allow you to receive the station's signal?
T2B12 — Why are simplex channels designated in the VHF/UHF band plans?

Repeaters provide such good coverage, why would anyone not use a repeater for a contact? A repeater's wide coverage and signal strength are precisely why it's not always appropriate to use them. Since only so many repeaters can share a band in a region, hams must use them wisely. It's easy to become so used to using repeaters that direct or *simplex* communication isn't considered. In fact, it's often quite easy to make contact directly.

Many radios have a *reverse split* function that swaps your transmit and receive frequencies. This enables you to listen for the other station on the repeater's input frequency. **[T2B01]** This function is often labeled REV on FM transceivers. If you and the station you've contacted are in range of each other, why not give simplex a try? This avoids occupying or "tying up" a repeater. **[T2B12]**

Listening on the repeater's input frequency is often helpful when a weak station is trying to access the repeater, but isn't quite strong enough to hold the repeater's squelch open. **[T2B03]** If the weak station is near you, it's likely that you'll hear their signal better than the repeater does!

Here's how to move a contact to a simplex frequency:

W1AW: "NK7U this is W1AW, are you on the repeater this morning?"

NK7U: "W1AW this is NK7U. Yes, and you're strong on the input. Let's move to 146.55 simplex."

W1AW: "OK, I'll meet you on 146.55. W1AW clear."

NK7U: "NK7U clear"

Simplex channels are conveniently located between bands of repeater input and output channels. For example, the national simplex calling frequency on 2 meters is 146.52 MHz and on 70 cm it is 446.00 MHz. **[T2A02]** The antenna you use for repeater contacts will work just fine for simplex, too.

SSB, CW, AND DIGITAL CONTACTS

T2A05 — How should you respond to a station calling CQ?
T2A08 — What is the meaning of the procedural signal "CQ"?
T2A12 — Which of the following is a guideline when choosing an operating frequency for calling CQ?

Starting contacts is different on these modes than on repeaters that use fixed channels. To attract the attention of other stations, you must make a *call* long enough for someone to tune their radio to your frequency and determine your call sign. This done by *calling CQ*. CQ is a procedural signal that means "I am calling any station." **[T2A08]** The station calling CQ sends or says "CQ" several times followed by their call sign. It sounds like this:

W1AW: "CQ CQ CQ, this is W1AW Whiskey One Alfa Whiskey calling CQ and standing by."

On CW or a digital mode it looks like this:

W1AW: "CQ CQ CQ DE W1AW W1AW W1AW K"

DE means "from" and the procedural signal K means that your transmission is finished and you're ready to receive. K is used at the end of transmissions of all sorts, just as "Over" is used on phone.

Before you call CQ you should do three things [T2A12]:

• Be sure the frequency is one your license privileges authorize you to use!

• Listen to be sure the frequency is not already in use. If you don't hear any signals in five to ten seconds the frequency may be available.

• Make a short transmission asking if the frequency is in use — an ongoing contact or activity may have paused or you may not be able to hear the station currently transmitting. Simply asking "Is the frequency in use?" followed by your call sign is sufficient.

As with repeater contacts, if you accidentally interfere with or "step on" another contact, simply apologize, give your call sign and tune to another frequency or wait until the frequency is clear.

If you hear a station calling CQ, it's easy to respond. Give the CQing station's call sign once (they already know their own call!) then yours once (if they are strong and clear) or twice. Give your call clearly and distinctly so that they can understand it if there is noise or interference. [T2A05] Your response should sound like this:

N6ZFO: "W1AW this is November Six Zulu Foxtrot Oscar, November Six Zulu Foxtrot Oscar, over."

Use phonetics when using phone, so the other station gets your call sign correct.

Q-SIGNALS

T2B10 — Which Q signal indicates that you are receiving interference from other stations?

T2B11 — Which Q signal indicates that you are changing frequency?

Q-signals are a system of radio shorthand as old as wireless and developed from even older telegraphy codes. Q-signals are a set of abbreviations for common information that save time and allow communication between operators who don't speak a common language. Modern ham radio uses them extensively. **Table 6.2** lists the most common Q-signals used by hams. While Q signals were developed for use by Morse operators, their use is common on phone, as well. You will often hear, "QRZed?" as someone asks "Who is calling me?" or "I'm getting a little QRM" from an operator receiving some interference or "Let's QSY to 146.55" as two operators change from a repeater frequency to a nearby simplex communications frequency. [T2B10, T2B11]

DXING AND CONTESTING

T8C03 — What operating activity involves contacting as many stations as possible during a specified period?

T8C04 — Which of the following is good procedure when contacting another station in a radio contest?

Since the beginning of radio, even before amateurs appeared on the scene, operators strove to make contact over longer and longer distances. It's fun to see if you can be heard by stations far away and pull in signals from over the horizon.

This is called DXing, where DX stands for "distant station." Distance is a relative thing. DX means thousands of miles on HF and occasionally 6 meters. At VHF/UHF, any contact beyond the radio horizon is considered DX. Microwave operators scout out locations with unobstructed views to make contacts of many miles. Making DX contacts is best done on SSB or CW because of the efficiency of those modes.

Table 6.2
Q-Signals

These Q-signals are the ones used most often on the air. (Q abbreviations take the form of questions only when they are sent followed by a question mark.)

QRG   Your exact frequency (or that of _____) is _____kHz.
Will you tell me my exact frequency (or that of _____)?

QRL   I am busy (or I am busy with _____). Are you busy? Usually used to see if a frequency is busy.

QRM   Your transmission is being interfered with _____
(1. Nil; 2. Slightly; 3. Moderately; 4. Severely; 5. Extremely.)
Is my transmission being interfered with?

QRN   I am troubled by static _____. (1 to 5 as under QRM.)
Are you troubled by static?

QRO   Increase power. Shall I increase power?

QRP   Decrease power. Shall I decrease power?

QRQ   Send faster (_____wpm). Shall I send faster?

QRS   Send more slowly (_____wpm). Shall I send more slowly?

QRT   Stop sending. Shall I stop sending?

QRU   I have nothing for you. Have you anything for me?

QRV   I am ready. Are you ready?

QRX   I will call you again at _____hours (on _____kHz).
When will you call me again? Minutes are usually implied rather than hours.

QRZ   You are being called by _____ (on _____kHz).
Who is calling me?

QSB   Your signals are fading. Are my signals fading?

QSK   I can hear you between signals; break in on my transmission.
Can you hear me between your signals and if so can I break in on your transmission?

QSL   I am acknowledging receipt.
Can you acknowledge receipt (of a message or transmission)?

QSO   I can communicate with _____ direct (or relay through _____).
Can you communicate with _____ direct or by relay?

QSP   I will relay to _____. Will you relay to _____?

QST   General call preceding a message addressed to all amateurs and ARRL members.
This is in effect "CQ ARRL."

QSX   I am listening to _____ on _____kHz. Will you listen to _____on _____kHz?

QSY   Change to transmission on another frequency (or on _____kHz).
Shall I change to transmission on another frequency (or on _____kHz)?

QTC   I have _____messages for you (or for _____). How many messages have you to send?

QTH   My location is _____. What is your location?

QTR   The time is _____. What is the correct time?

Locations on the Grid

T8C05 — What is a grid locator?

An increasingly popular method of identifying location is the Maidenhead Locator System, better known as *grid squares*. In this system, named for the town outside London, England where the method was first created, the Earth's surface is divided into a system of rectangles based on latitude and longitude. Each rectangle is identified with a combination of letters and numbers. **[T8C05]** A four-digit code of two letters followed by two numbers identifies a unique rectangle of 1° latitude by 2° longitude. For example, ARRL Headquarters in Newington, Connecticut is located in grid square FN31. A further two letters can be added for greater precision, such as FN31pq for the precise location of the ARRL station.

Pursuing long-distance contacts really hones a ham's technical and operating skills. In the course of DXing, one learns many things about propagation, antennas, and the natural environment! To recognize the achievements of DXers there are many awards offered by the ARRL and other organizations. For contacting the numerous countries the DXCC award is popular. VHF/UHF enthusiasts contact *grid squares* (see the sidebar Locations on the Grid) for the VUCC award. Contacting all of the US states (Worked All States — WAS) is popular around the world.

If you like competitive activities, radio *contests* are held in which the competitors try to make as many short contacts as possible in a fixed period of time. **[T8C03]** Some contests, called *sprints*, are very short. Others last an entire weekend. There are contests that use just one band or mode and others that span multiple bands and multiple modes.

If you encounter a contest on the air, jump in and make a few contacts. You'll be asked for some information called an *exchange*. It may consist of your location, a signal report and a *serial number* (that's the number of contacts you've made in the contest so far). Just ask, "What do you need?" The contest station will help you provide the right information. To keep things moving, send only the minimum information needed to identify your station and complete the exchange. **[T8C04]** You'll find that it's a lot of fun for even a casual operator!

As you might imagine, pursuing operating awards and participating in contests have the potential to create a very capable operator. The excellent stations and skills of DXers and contest operators are quite applicable to emergency operating and traffic handling, discussed later in this chapter. The ARRL and other organizations sponsor contests that run the gamut from international events attracting thousands to quiet, relaxed competitions to contact lighthouses or islands. You can find the rules for these events on the ARRL's Contest Calendar web page.

VIDEO

T8D04 — What type of transmission is indicated by the term "NTSC?"

Hams have two primary means of exchanging pictures or video in real-time, aside from exchanging data files of graphic images or video. These are *image* modes and are used in the same band segments as voice signals.

You can find *amateur television* (ATV) enthusiasts on the UHF bands at 430 MHz and higher. Because of the signal's wide bandwidth (6 MHz), the mode is restricted to the wide UHF bands. Amateurs transmit both analog and digital TV signals. NTSC (National

ARRL Field Day — The Biggest Amateur Event of All!

Every year on the fourth full weekend of June, North American hams head for the hills…and the fields and the parks and the backyards. It's Field Day! This is the annual emergency preparedness exercise in which more hams participate than any other. The basic idea — set up a portable station (or several) and try to make as many contacts with other ham groups as possible on as many amateur bands as possible. If you think the bands are busy on weekends, wait until you hear them during ARRL Field Day!

Some groups focus on the emergency preparedness aspect, others get into the competitive aspect trying for the most points, and some just treat it as the annual club picnic plus radio operating. Whatever your organization prefers, Field Day is a great way to see a lot of ham radio all in one spot and all at the same time. For more information, browse to ARRL Field Day web page, read the Field Day announcement in the May issue of *QST* magazine, or enjoy the Field Day summary and results that usually appear in the December issue. CQ, Field Day!

T8C01 — Which of the following methods is used to locate sources of noise interference or jamming?
T8C02 — Which of these items would be useful for a hidden transmitter hunt?

A different and more physical type of contest is known as foxhunting. Locating a hidden transmitter (the fox) has been a popular ham activity for many years. It has its practical side, too, training hams to find downed aircraft, lost hikers, and sources of interference or jamming. **[T8C01]** You don't need much in the way of equipment. You can get started with a portable radio with a signal strength indicator and a handheld or portable directional antenna, such as a small Yagi beam. **[T8C02]** One ham hides the transmitter (hams can be very devious and inventive when it comes to hiding places) and the rest drive, walk, or bike the area taking bearings and at-tempting to be the first to locate the transmitter.

In recent years a new type of outdoor radios-port has reached US shores from Europe and Asia — radio direction finding. Held as organized events, direction finding is a hybrid of the radio fox hunt using orienteering skills to navigate outdoors with map and compass. The US Amateur Radio Direction Finding organization is just one of a number of national groups in this worldwide sport, especially popular with teens and young adults. If you are a hiker or camper, then you might be interested in applying your outdoor skills to ARDF.

Television System Committee) fast-scan color television signals are the same as analog broadcast TV signals. **[T8D04]** (NTSC analog signals are no longer used for broadcast TV, which is now all digital.) *The ARRL Operating Manual*, *The ARRL Handbook* and ATV web page provide more information on ATV.

For More Information

Slow-scan television (SSTV) was invented by hams in the 1960s in order to send still images as SSB signals in about eight seconds. Modern SSTV signals are generated by computers and inexpensive digital cameras and modern SSTV "modes" transmit images in color. You can find SSTV signals around 14.230 MHz and there is an SSTV station on the ISS, as well. Learn more about SSTV in *The ARRL Operating Manual*, *The ARRL Handbook* or through the ARRL Technical Information Service (TIS) SSTV page.

6.3 Using Repeaters

As a Technician licensee, you are likely to make contacts through a repeater. Because repeater signals can be heard by many amateurs, repeater contacts have some operating procedures that are different than for SSB, CW, and digital contacts.

FINDING REPEATERS

T4B13 — Which of the following is a use for the scanning function of an FM transceiver?

To find all of the repeaters in your area, you'll need a listing sorted by area, such as the *ARRL Repeater Directory* shown in **Figure 6.1**, or a source such as a club newsletter. Repeater frequencies are evenly spaced in *channels*, so you know exactly what frequency to use when you do find or select a repeater. You can also use the *scanning* function of your radio to listen for activity on repeater or simplex channels. **[T4B13]**

If you hear a repeater, how can you tell which one it is? Listen for a while and you may hear an automated voice announcing a call sign and possibly some other information,

Location	Mode	Call sign	Output	Input	Access	Coordinator
Sundown Town	FM	WA6TLW	920.75000	-		CARCON
	FM	W6CYX	1286.50000	-	88.5 Hz	CARCON
Susanville	FM	K6JKC	146.83500	-		
	FM	W6EXP	146.88000	-		
	FM	K6JKC	146.91000	-		
	FM	W6EXP	443.02500	+		
Tahoe City	FM	WA6FJS	444.05000	+	131.8 Hz	
Talapoosa	DMR/BM	W7TA	441.95000	+	CC1	CARCON
	FM	NK7W	145.31000	-	123.0 Hz	CARCON
Tonkin	FM	BH1KVO	438.50000	+		
Tonopah	FM	N7ARR	146.64000	-	123.0 Hz	
Topaz	FM	WW7E	442.75000			
Touplon	FM	K6ALT	445.55000	-		
Truckee	FM	WB6ALS	146.64000	-	131.8 Hz	
	FM	KJ6GM	440.27500	+		
	FM	N7PLQ	440.70000	+	100.0 Hz	
Tuscarora	FM	KD7CWA	147.30000	+	100.0 Hz	
	FM	NV7X	147.30000	+		
	FM	W7LKO	444.50000	+	100.0 Hz	CARCON
	FM	WA6TLW	444.65000	+	94.8 Hz	CARCON
Utah Hill	FM	W7KVS	146.82000	-	100.0 Hz	
Vacaville	FM	K6LNK	440.75000	+	127.3 Hz	CARCON
	FM	W6KCS	442.02500	+	156.7 Hz	CARCON
	FM	W6KCS	927.06250	902.06250	100.0 Hz	CARCON
	FM	KI6SSF	927.33750	902.33750	162.2 Hz	CARCON
Verdi-Mogul	FM	W7UIZ	145.39000	-		CARCON
	FM	WA7SIX	146.76000	-	123.0 Hz	CARCON
	FM	N7PLQ	440.07500	+	123.0 Hz	CARCON
	FM	W7NV	442.43750	+		CARCON
	FM	NV7RP	443.67500	+		
	FM	W7ENG	443.67500	+		
Walker	FM	N7TR	443.27500	+		
Warm Springs, Warm Springs Sum						
	FM	WB7WTS	146.85000	-		CARCON
Washoe Valley	FM	NH7M	145.41000	-	97.4 Hz	CARCON
	FM	W7RHC	440.55000	+	110.9 Hz	CARCON
Wedekind	FM	KA7ZAU	147.42000			CARCON
Wellington, Lobdell Peak						
	FM	KD7NHC	146.88000	-	123.0 Hz	CARCON
	FUSION	KD7NHC	440.05000	+	94.8 Hz	CARCON
Wells	FM	WA7MOC	146.79000	-	156.7 Hz	CARCON
	FM	WA7MOC	146.91000	-		
	FM	W7LKO	146.96000	-	100.0 Hz	CARCON

Figure 6.1 — Listings of repeaters, such as the ARRL's *Repeater Directory*, make it easy to find repeaters in your area or where you intend to travel. This is a typical section of a page in the *Repeater Directory*.

such as location or time. This is the repeater's *ID* and it allows you to look up the call sign online and tell for sure where it is. The repeater may also send Morse code, a *CW ID*. This is very common and is a good reason to know Morse code, even if you don't use Morse to make contacts.

Once you have located an active repeater, to access it you will need to know three things: the repeater transmitter's *output* or *transmit frequency*, the repeater receiver's *input* or *receive frequency* and the frequency of any *access control tones*.

REPEATER OFFSET OR SHIFT

T2A01 — Which of the following is a common repeater frequency offset in the 2 meter band?

T2A03 — What is a common repeater frequency offset in the 70 cm band?

T2A07 — What is meant by "repeater offset?"

Let's start with the repeater's output frequency. This is the frequency on which you hear the repeater's transmitted signal and it's the frequency by which repeaters are listed in a directory, such as the *ARRL Repeater Directory*. Hams will say, "Meet you on the 443.50 machine" or "Let's move to the 94 repeater." (*Machine* is jargon for repeater.) "94" means 146.94 MHz, a standard repeater output channel frequency. To listen to the repeater, tune to its output frequency.

To send a signal through the repeater, you must transmit on the repeater's input frequency where the repeater receiver listens. It would be chaos if every repeater owner used a different separation of input and output frequencies, so hams have decided on a standard separation between input and output frequencies. The difference between repeater input and output frequencies is called the repeater's *offset* or *shift*. [**T2A07**] The shift is the same for almost all repeaters on one band as shown in **Table 6.3**. [**T2A01, T2A03**] If the repeater's input frequency is higher than the output frequency, that is a *positive offset*. *Negative offsets* place the repeater's input frequency below the output frequency.

Instead of having to remember two frequencies, using a standard shift allows you to remember only the repeater output frequency. The SHIFT or OFFSET key or menu setting on your radio allows you to switch between positive and negative shifts, or no shift to use simplex communications. Your radio is probably already configured to use the standard shift on each band, usually referred to as *automatic repeater shift*, *auto repeater offset*, or a similar term. The instruction manual will have complete instructions on changing the direction and amount of shift.

Table 6.3
Standard Repeater Offsets by Band

Band	Offset
10 meters	–100 kHz
6 meters	Varies by region: –500 kHz, –1 MHz, –1.7 MHz
2 meters	+ or –600 kHz
1.25 meters	–1.6 MHz
70 cm	+ or –5 MHz
902 MHz	12 MHz
1296 MHz	12 MHz

LINKED REPEATER SYSTEMS

T2B14 — Which of the following describes a linked repeater network?

To extend their range and to hear signals blocked by obstacles, repeaters sometimes employ *remote receivers*. The signals from these receivers are then transmitted by an *auxiliary station* to the repeater's transmitter site for retransmission.

Repeaters can also be *linked* to other repeaters. That is, they share the signals each receives and retransmit them. [**T2B14**] This extends the coverage of any single repeater. It is also common for repeaters to retransmit signals on other bands. For example, a 2 meter repeater linked to a 70 cm repeater allows stations on either band to contact each other. If the repeaters are *co-located*, meaning located at the same site, the repeaters can be physically connected with cables. Otherwise, a *control link* is required.

REPEATER ACCESS TONES

T2B02 — What term describes the use of a sub-audible tone transmitted along with normal voice audio to open the squelch of a receiver?

T2B04 — Which of the following could be the reason you are unable to access a repeater whose output you can hear?

Most repeaters won't pass a signal from the receiver to the transmitter for retransmission unless it contains a special tone. The tone is one of 38 different frequencies, all below 300 Hz. Each repeater can have a different tone. The tone indicates to the repeater that your signal is intended for it and should be retransmitted.

Repeater access tones were invented by Motorola to allow different commercial users to share a repeater without having to listen to each other's conversations. These tones are known by various names: *Continuous Tone Coded Squelch System* (CTCSS), *PL* (for Private Line, the Motorola trade name) or *sub-audible*. FRS/GMRS radio users know these tones as *privacy codes* or *privacy tones*. **[T2B02]**

If you can hear a repeater's signal and you're sure you are using the right offset, but you can't access the repeater, then you probably don't have your radio set up to use the right type or frequency of access tone. **[T2B04]**

For More Information

Why wouldn't a signal on the proper frequency be intended for the repeater? Most repeater installations are close to other repeaters, paging transmitters and broadcast transmitters. The powerful signals from all these transmitters sometimes mix together and create false signals, called *intermod*, an abbreviation of *intermodulation*. Intermod can easily appear on a repeater's input frequency and would be retransmitted, disrupting normal communications. To prevent these signals from being retransmitted, the repeater receiver listens for the proper tone in the received signal. No tone or an improper tone indicates the signal is not intended for that repeater, so it won't be retransmitted.

Your radio will have a TONE key or menu selection that allows you to both select a tone and add it to the transmitted signal, if desired. You may also be able to set your radio's squelch to require a CTCSS tone to pass received audio to the speaker. This is called *tone squelch*. You should be aware that most repeaters filter out CTCSS tones before the received audio is retransmitted.

Picking a Tone

CTCSS tones are added to your signal to cue the repeater that it should relay your signal. Before you can transmit through a repeater that requires a CTCSS tone, you'll have to find out which of the 38 possible tones it could be. If you have an *ARRL Repeater Directory* or are using a club website or newsletter, the tone will be listed along with the output frequency of the repeater. The listing will look like this:

PODUNK VALLEY   146.94 (–)   103.5

You will hear the repeater output on 146.94 MHz and the input is 600 kHz (the standard 2 meter offset) below the output frequency, or 146.34 MHz. The (–) means that the repeater offset or shift is negative. The entry "103.5" is the frequency of the CTCSS or subaudible tone. Your radio's operating manual will explain how to select and activate the tone. There may be several tone options, such as tone squelch and *digital code squelch* (DCS). Leave them off for now.

Some radios also have the ability to determine the tone frequency from on-air signals. This is called *tone scan*. Radios with this feature can often be configured to automatically set their own CTCSS tone to the same frequency without any operator intervention. This is very handy when you are new to an area, just visiting or driving through.

Another method of squelch control is *digital code squelch* (DCS). A continuous sequence of subaudible tones must be received during a transmission to keep the output audio turned on. If the proper tone sequence is received, your receiver will open up the squelch and you can hear the calling station. Check the operating manual of your radio for information about how to configure DCS.

DIGITAL REPEATER SYSTEMS

T2B06 — What type of tones are used to control repeaters linked by the Internet Relay Linking Project (IRLP) protocol?

T2B07 — How can you join a digital repeater's "talk group"?

T2B09 — What is a "talk group" on a DMR digital repeater?

T8C06 — How is access to some IRLP nodes accomplished?

T8C07 — What is meant by Voice Over Internet Protocol (VoIP) as used in amateur radio?

T8C08 — What is the Internet Radio Linking Project (IRLP)?

T8C09 — How might you obtain a list of active nodes that use VoIP?

T8C10 — What must be done before you may use the EchoLink system to communicate using a repeater?

T8D07 — Which of the following best describes DMR (Digital Mobile Radio)?

Ham radio and the internet each have complementary advantages. Hams can roam freely, using repeaters from a vehicle, at home or on foot. The internet provides a high-speed connection between two points — nearly anywhere on Earth. It's a natural to combine the two and several systems do just that:

- IRLP (Internet Radio Linking Project)
- EchoLink
- WIRES II — a proprietary system of the Yaesu company
- D-STAR — a system based on the public D-STAR standard
- DMR — Digital Mobile Radio

The two oldest digitally-linked systems are IRLP and EchoLink. Both use VoIP (Voice over Internet Protocol) technology to link repeaters as illustrated in **Figure 6.2**. **[T8C08]** Online telephone service vendors, such as Skype, use VoIP to deliver voice communications over the internet by digital techniques. **[T8C07]** Each repeater in a VoIP repeater network is called a *node*. Nodes are listed in repeater directories, by subscribing to an online repeater listing service, or from online lists maintained by repeater coordinators. **[T8C09]**

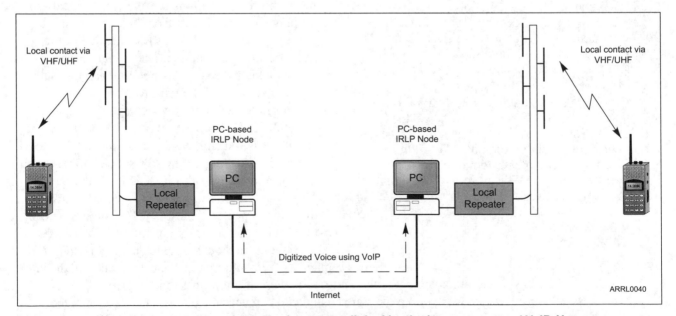

Figure 6.2 — IRLP and EchoLink are systems of repeaters linked by the internet protocol VoIP. Hams can use a local repeater and radio to make contacts worldwide by using control codes to connect to far-away repeaters.

The main difference between IRLP and EchoLink is that IRLP requires all audio to be transmitted into the system via a radio link. (IRLP does allow a PC user to *listen* to conversations.) That means you must be a licensed amateur to use repeaters linked by IRLP. EchoLink allows audio to come from a PC and microphone, so a radio is not necessary but hams are required to send a copy of their license to the EchoLink system administrators to be authorized to use the system. **[T8C10]** Much more information on internet-linked systems is available in the ARRL book *VoIP: Internet Linking for Radio Amateurs.*

WIRES II uses a proprietary voice-only standard developed by radio manufacturer Yaesu. The D-STAR system combines digital voice and data communications. The D-STAR standard was developed by the Japan Amateur Radio League (JARL) and is currently implemented in equipment manufactured by Icom and Kenwood.

The DMR system was developed for the *Land Mobile Radio* service. Over the air, DMR is a technique for time-multiplexing two digital voice signals on a single 12.5 kHz repeater channel. **[T8D07]** Your digitized voice is routed by a central network controller to other DMR repeaters through the internet. The controller organizes users of the DMR network into *talk groups*. Each talk group has an ID or code. By programming your radio with those IDs and codes, you can join the group and your audio will be shared with all other members of the group. **[T2B07]** Talk groups allow groups of users to share a channel at different times without being heard by other users on the channel. **[T2B09]**

How does an IRLP or EchoLink contact differ from a regular repeater contact? To initiate a contact, the initiating station must know the repeater control code to request an IRLP connection. The code is a sequence of DTMF (Dual-tone Multi-Frequency) tones, like dialing a phone number. **[T2B06, T8C06]** The control codes vary from repeater to repeater and obtaining them may require membership in a club.

6.4 Nets

T2C02 — What is meant by the term "NCS" used in net operation?
T2C05 — What does the term "traffic" refer to in net operation?
T2C06 — Which of the following is an accepted practice to get the immediate attention of a net control station when reporting an emergency?
T2C07 — Which of the following is an accepted practice for an amateur operator who has checked into a net?

You will encounter frequent references to *nets* in ham radio. Developed in the very early days of radio, these networks helped stations meet on the air to share news and messages. The modern network, now associated with computers, is a direct descendent of the radio net and uses many of the same terms and concepts. There are lots of nets available to the Technician licensee. This section will focus on nets that support emergency communications and public service activities. You can find more information about nets in the online supplemental information for this chapter.

Hams coordinate their emergency response activities with nets that spring into action ("activate") whenever they're needed. In areas where severe weather is common, for example, nets monitor weather conditions before a storm and assist with recovery in case damage results.

These nets usually have two purposes: they pass emergency messages and coordinate reporting and response activities. Messages following a set, formal structure are called *traffic*. **[T2C05]** The messages have built-in *routing* information to get the message to the right place. Other information and procedures insure the content is transferred correctly. Exchanging these messages is called *traffic handling*.

Between activations, emergency nets are activated for practice and to conduct training exercises. That is the time for you to learn the procedures, not after disaster strikes! Your public service team will have all the information you need to learn how to participate.

As a way to practice skills and provide service at the same time, hams also provide communications for public events, such as festivals, parades or sporting events. These public service activities are organized on the ground and on the air just as a disaster response would require. You can volunteer for one of these events. That is how many hams developed into skilled emergency response operators.

NET STRUCTURE AND PARTICIPATION

To be effective, you need to know a little bit about how a net is organized. Knowing the common procedures and signals is also important.

It is important to remember that no matter what the purpose or status of a net, a station with emergency traffic should break in at any time. If the net is operating on phone and you are reporting an emergency, break in by saying "Priority" or "Emergency," followed by your call sign. [T2C06] The *Net Control Station* (NCS) who is running the net and members of the net should always immediately suspend any lower-priority operation and respond to the emergency. [T2C02]

Once you have checked into a formal net under the direction of an NCS, it is important to not disrupt the net. Do not transmit unless you are specifically requested or authorized to do so or a request is made for capabilities or information that you can provide. [T2C07]

EXCHANGING MESSAGES

T2C03 — What should be done when using voice modes to ensure that voice messages containing unusual words are received correctly?

T2C08 — Which of the following is a characteristic of good traffic handling?

T2C10 — What information is contained in the preamble of a formal traffic message?

T2C11 — What is meant by the term "check," in reference to a formal traffic message?

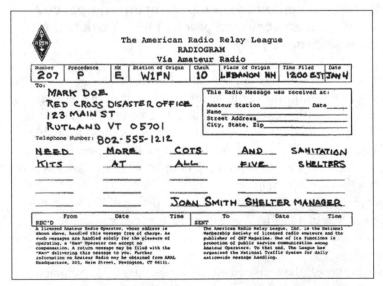

Figure 6.3 — The ARRL Radiogram form is the standard for originating and relaying messages. The preamble identifies the message and allows it to be tracked. The 25-word limit requires that the message be focused, balancing length against minimizing errors during transmission.

The most important job during emergency and disaster net operation is the ability to accurately relay or "pass" messages exactly as written, spoken or received. [T2C08] It is common for messages to be formatted as *radiograms*. Another widely used message format is the ICS-213 which is part of the Incident Command System's standard operating procedures. The exam focuses on the radiogram but similar rules and definitions apply to the ICS-213.

A typical radiogram is shown in **Figure 6.3**. A radiogram has three parts: the *preamble* (including the address), the *body* and the *signature*.

The preamble is made up of several bits of information about the message. These establish a unique identity for each message so that it can be handled and tracked appropriately as it moves through the Amateur Radio traffic handling system. **[T2C10]**

- Number — a unique number assigned by the station that creates the radiogram
- Precedence — a description of the nature of the radiogram: Routine, Priority, Emergency and Welfare
- Handling Instructions (HX) — for special instructions in how to the handle the radiogram.
- Station of Origin — the call sign of the radio station from which the radiogram was first sent by Amateur Radio. (This allows information about the message to be returned to the sending station.)
- Check — the number of words and word equivalents in the radiogram text. **[T2C11]**
- Place of Origin — the name of the town from which the radiogram started
- Time and Date — the time and date the radiogram is received at the station that first sent it
- Address — the complete name, street and number, city and state to whom the radiogram is going

Following the preamble is the text of the radiogram. Take extra care to be sure the receiving station copies the message exactly. For example, proper names (such as "John Doe") and unusual words (such as material names or model identifiers) are spelled out using standard phonetics. **[T2C03]**

For More Information

The ARRL radiogram limits the text to 25 total words. That doesn't sound like a lot, but the limit helps focus the message topic and eliminate unnecessary words. Longer messages also are more difficult to relay without errors so there must be a balance between length and accuracy. The signature follows the text and is usually the name of the person originating the message.

If you are asked to generate a radiogram, you should follow this format. If you cannot decide on what to use for some of the preamble contents, leave them blank. In an emergency, you may not always have all of the information. Another net station may be able to help you, or the message can be sent without the information. In an emergency, though, the one item that must be included is the name of the person originating the message.

If you check in to a traffic handling net, you will find that they make heavy use of the Q-signals you learned about earlier. Their clear meaning and short length greatly speed up operations. They can be found in the radiogram quick-reference card, ARRL FSD-218, which can be downloaded from the ARRL website.

6.5 Communications for Public Service

Thankfully, true emergencies and disasters are rare. Far more frequently, hams provide communications in support of public events such as parades or races. All of these are referred to as *public service* communications. Don't wait for an actual emergency or disaster to occur to participate in public service! It's a great exercise of your license privileges and provides excellent training to develop all kinds of communications skills.

This section includes a lot of supporting material not directly related to exam questions because so many new hams are interested in public service and emergency communications. It's worth reading through the section if this is your main interest.

ARES AND RACES

T1A10 — Which of the following describes the Radio Amateur Civil Emergency Service (RACES)?
T2C04 — What do RACES and ARES have in common?
T2C12 — What is the Amateur Radio Emergency Service (ARES)?

The two largest Amateur Radio emergency response organizations are ARES® (Amateur Radio Emergency Service) sponsored by the ARRL and the Radio Amateur Civil Emergency Service (RACES). Both organizations provide emergency and disaster response communications. **[T2C04]** ARES consists of licensed amateurs who have voluntarily registered their qualifications and equipment for communications duty in the public service. **[T2C12]** Its members support local and regional government and non-governmental agencies such as the Red Cross, Salvation Army, and National Weather Service. Any licensed amateur can participate in ARES.

RACES is a special part of the Amateur service created by the FCC to provide communications assistance to local, state, or federal government emergency management agencies during civil emergencies. **[T1A10]**. (See Part 97.407 of the FCC rules for more information on RACES.) Many amateurs are members of both ARES and RACES teams so that they can respond to either need.

THREATS TO LIFE AND PROPERTY

T2C01 — When do the FCC rules NOT apply to the operation of an amateur station?
T2C09 — Are amateur station control operators ever permitted to operate outside the frequency privileges of their license class?

The FCC also recognizes the need for flexibility in an emergency. For example, in defining emergency communications, Part 97.403 says:

"No provision of these rules prevents the use by an amateur station of any means of radiocommunication at its disposal to provide essential communication needs in connection with the immediate safety of human life and immediate protection of property when normal communication systems are not available."

If communications services are down and you're in the middle of a hurricane, tornado, or blizzard, and you offer your communications services to the authorities, you are permitted to do whatever you need to do to help deal with the emergency. Public safety or medical personnel can use your radio. In an emergency situation where there is immediate risk to life or property and normal forms of communication are unavailable, you may use any means possible to address that risk, including operating outside the frequency privileges of your license. **[T2C09]** You are only prohibited from transmitting information on behalf of your employer or confidential personal information of a third party, such as a disaster victim, without their consent.

Similarly, in an emergency situation you may use whatever communications means is at hand to respond — any means on any frequency. If a fire department radio or marine SSB transceiver is all that's available, by all means use it to call any station you think might hear you!

This waiver of normal rules lasts as long as the threat to life and property remains imminent *and* there are no other means of communications than Amateur Radio. Once the threat has receded or normal communications become available, you must return to normal rules, even in support of public safety agencies. You are bound by FCC rules at all times, even if using your radio in support of a public safety agency. **[T2C01]** For example, while providing post-event communications at a fire department command post, you are not permitted to use a modified ham radio on fire department frequencies.

For More Information

Many hams are regularly involved with public service communications. It may be the reason you became interested in ham radio. When providing public service communications, you must also remember to operate efficiently and strive for the highest levels of performance. Here are some good public service operating practices:

- Don't become part of the event — you are there to assist, not to participate or act as an event manager.
- Maintain your safety — you are no help if you become injured.
- Maintain radio discipline — follow established protocols and refrain from idle conversation that might impede communications.
- Never speculate or guess — strive for 100% accuracy and don't be afraid to say "I don't know." Rumors are impossible to stop, once started.
- Protect personal information — never send confidential personal information via Amateur Radio without consent.
- Don't give out unauthorized information — reporters and members of the public are often hungry for information. Direct them to the appropriate spokesperson or information source.

Tactical Communications

Tactical communications may be used to coordinate activities ("Go to the south parking lot"), report status ("The final float is leaving the staging area") or request resources ("First aid is needed at 2nd and the highway."). This type of message is rarely recorded and is not passed in radiogram format.

Tactical communication needs are usually satisfied by using VHF/UHF simplex or repeater channels. Mobile, portable, and handheld radios are particularly useful when working with public safety and government agencies.

To increase efficiency and smooth coordination, stations engaged in tactical communications should use *tactical call signs*, such as "Command Post Three" or "School Kitchen" or "Judges Stand." These describe a function, location or organization. This allows operators to change without changing the call sign of the stations and frees non-amateur personnel from having to use amateur call signs. Tactical call signs do not, however, satisfy the FCC regulations for station identification, which must still be followed. Identify with your call sign every 10 minutes and at the end of the communication.

Emergencies and Disaster Relief

Providing communications assistance during an emergency or in response to a natural disaster is one of the Amateur Service's most important reasons for existing at all. The FCC places its highest priority on emergency communications which have priority over all other types of Amateur Radio communications on any frequency.

In a serious, widespread emergency, the FCC may declare a *temporary state of communications emergency*. The declaration will contain any special conditions or rules that are to be observed during the emergency. The declaration is in force until the FCC lifts it. Communications emergency declarations are distributed by the FCC through its website, via ARRL bulletins on headquarters station W1AW and the ARRL website, and through the National Traffic System and Official Relay Stations. Amateur websites and e-mail lists pick up the declarations and relay them throughout the amateur community.

The only exception to the "no one owns a frequency" rule is during a natural disaster or other communications emergency when you should avoid operating on or near frequencies used to provide disaster relief.

Distress Calls

If you are in immediate danger or require immediate emergency help, you may make a distress call on any frequency on which you have a chance of being heard. In these circumstances, here's what to do:

• On a voice mode, say "Mayday Mayday Mayday" or on CW send "$\overline{SOS}$ $\overline{SOS}$ $\overline{SOS}$" (Mayday should not be confused with the Pan-Pan urgency call) followed by "any station come in please"
• Identify the transmission with your call sign
• Give your location with enough detail to be located
• State the nature of the situation
• Describe the type of assistance required
• Give any other pertinent information

Then pause for any station to answer. Repeat the procedure as long as possible or until you get an answer. The reason for giving all of the information during each call is so that if you can't hear responding stations, they'll still learn where you are and what help you need. Under no circumstances make a false distress call or allow others to do so using your equipment. Your amateur license could be revoked and you could be subject to a substantial penalty or even imprisonment.

If you hear a distress call — on any frequency — you may respond. Outside the amateur bands, such as on the international marine distress calling frequency of 2182 kHz, be sure that no other station or vessel is responding before you call the station. Inside the amateur bands, suspend any other ongoing communications immediately. Record everything the station sends and then respond. If they hear you, let them know that you have copied their information, clarify any information as required and immediately contact the proper authorities. Stay on frequency with the station in distress until authorities are either on frequency or arrive at the scene.

Emergency Communications Training

To be truly effective when responding to an emergency, you need some training and even better, some practice opportunities! Doesn't music sound a lot better when the musicians have learned the music and practiced it before the show? Don't let your license gather dust while you wait for the "Big One" — by getting on the air you can continuously improve your skills and have fun doing it.

Start by joining a local amateur emergency preparedness team. Your local radio club, ARES team, RACES team, county Search-and-Rescue or Salvation Army chapter (just to name a few) are all organizations to investigate. Choose the one that suits your interests.

Take advantage of any training the group might provide or recommend. For example, the ARRL offers a basic emergency communications online training class. The Federal Emergency Management Agency (FEMA) offers free emergency preparedness training courses on their website. The courses on the National Incident Management System (NIMS) are very helpful to learn how public safety agencies will be organized in a disaster.

When your group has a drill or exercise, try to participate, even if just in the planning and organization stage. The experience will serve you well when a real activation occurs. The ARRL sponsors an annual Simulated Emergency Test (SET) in October of every year. If your club participates in ARRL Field Day, be sure to participate. Almost every town has at least one public event with communications needs that ham radio could fill. Help plan to put an amateur team on the job!

Finally, test your own preparedness! Check your go-kit and emergency equipment every six months to be sure it's all together and working. Double check your power sources, especially batteries that might grow weak over time. You're only as effective as your equipment will let you be.

Emergency Communications and Your Employer

When you are providing public service communications, remember that you are not allowed to receive payment for your services except for reimbursement of actual out-of-pocket expenses, including mileage. You may not charge an hourly fee or arrange a trade of your services for something else of value to you or your organization. Avoid providing communications when there is no benefit to the public, such as a private event.

If you are confused about what is and is not permitted, review the guidelines published in *The Commercialization of Amateur Radio: The Rules, The Risks, The Issues* and available on the ARRL website. If you are interested in getting involved with emergency communications in your area and have questions, your instructor can help you contact your local ARES emergency leadership, such as an ARES team Emergency Coordinator (EC).

Many emergency and public safety personnel have obtained an Amateur Radio license, attracted by our service's flexibility and adaptability. Many employers have also taken note of the service's capabilities. This has the potential to conflict with part 97.113(a)(3) that forbids amateurs from having a financial interest in their communications:

"No amateur shall transmit...Communications in which the station licensee or control operator has a pecuniary interest, including communications on behalf of an employer."

There are only two exceptions to this rule. They are part 97.113(c) and (d) — teachers who use ham radio as part of their instruction and operators employed to operate a club station that transmits bulletins and code practice at least 40 hours per week on at least six amateur bands.

Many radio clubs are made up of employees of a particular employer. This is permitted, as is communications while you are at work as long as it is not on behalf of your employer (and your employer permits it).

Participating in training exercises and drills organized by your employer is allowed but only according to the restrictions spelled out in 97.113(a)(i). The drills are limited in number and duration as a balance between readiness and keeping Amateur Radio free of commercial operating. If you have any questions about this type of drill, ask your ARES Emergency Coordinator.

It is important to preserve the "bright line" between the strictly-volunteer foundation of Amateur Radio and the many commercial and government uses of radio — worthy though they may be. Communications on a regular basis that could reasonably be furnished through other radio services are not permitted.

It is also important to note that news messages and reports are not considered emergency communications by the FCC. You are not allowed to relay such information on behalf of broadcasters via Amateur Radio. Inform reporters who ask you to relay reports that you can't do that under FCC rules.

6.6 Satellite Operating

T1E02 — Who may be the control operator of a station communicating through an amateur satellite or space station?

Amateurs have built more than 50 satellites since 1961, launching them when extra space is available in a rocket payload. Amateur satellites are nicknamed *OSCAR* for *Orbiting Satellite Carrying Amateur Radio*.

Communicating through an amateur satellite sounds like a very complicated, high-tech effort, but it can be quite simple. What you need is a radio that can transmit on one band and listen on another (most can, even handhelds). Satellite contacts, including contacts with the amateur station on the International Space Station can be made by any amateur licensed to transmit on the *uplink* frequency. **[T1E02]** For example, a Technician licensee could communicate through a satellite that is listening for uplink signals on 2 meters and transmitting on a 10 meter *downlink* frequency even though a Technician is not permitted to transmit on 10 meters.

Satellite uplink and downlink frequencies are restricted to the special satellite *sub-bands* listed in **Table 6.4**, segments of frequencies set aside for Earth-to-space communications.

Amateur satellites relay signal between bands, usually on VHF and UHF, or act as FM repeaters that can be accessed with regular FM transceivers. The ionosphere is usually transparent to signals at these frequencies, so the signals can pass between Earth and space easily. If two stations both have the satellite in view at the same time as shown in **Figure 6.4**, they can make contact via line-of-sight propagation to and from the satellite.

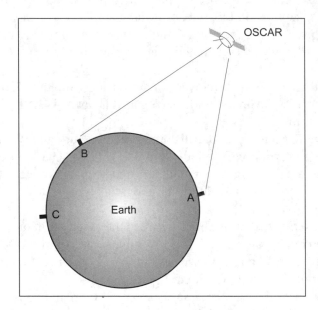

Figure 6.4 — Amateur satellites (OSCARs) can relay VHF and UHF signals between any two stations that both have the satellite in view at the same time. Contacts through the satellite are possible between station A and B, but not with station C.

Table 6.4

Selected Satellite Sub-bands

29.300 — 29.510 MHz
145.80 — 146.00 MHz
435.00 — 438.00 MHz
1260 — 1270 MHz
2400 — 2410 and 2430 — 2438 MHz

SATELLITE DEFINITIONS

T1A07 — What is the FCC Part 97 definition of a "space station"?
T8B05 — What is a satellite beacon?
T8B07 — With regard to satellite communications, what is Doppler shift?
T8B09 — What causes spin fading of satellite signals?
T8B10 — What do the initials LEO tell you about an amateur satellite?

- Apogee — The point of a satellite's orbit that is farthest from Earth
- Beacon — A signal from the satellite containing information about a satellite **[T8B05]**

Working the International Space Station

T1B02 — Which amateur radio stations may make contact with an amateur radio station on the International Space Station (ISS) using 2 meter and 70 cm band frequencies?

It is a pleasant surprise to learn that Amateur Radio has a place on the International Space Station (ISS)! Not only that, but nearly all of the astronauts hold Amateur Radio licenses. Depending on their workload, astronauts can be active from their orbiting home on the ISS. Any amateur licensed to use the 2 meter and 70 cm bands can join in the fun. **[T1B02]**

The astronauts frequently operate using FM voice. A packet bulletin board system (BBS) and a voice FM system are both on-board. One or the other is active at all times — you can check the mode of the station on the AMSAT website. The ISS also carries an APRS digipeater and an SSTV station! (Packet radio and APRS were discussed in the **Amateur Radio Equipment** chapter.)

When the ISS is in view, you can connect to the packet BBS with a regular packet station using a TNC and your 2 meter radio. If you prefer, you can also just listen to 145.800 MHz in hopes of hearing one of the astronauts on voice. To call the space station, call sign NA1SS, set your radio to transmit on 145.990 MHz and listen on 145.800 MHz.

- Doppler shift — A shift in a signal's frequency due to relative motion between the satellite and the Earth station **[T8B07]**
- Elliptical orbit — An orbit with a large difference between apogee and perigee
- LEO — A satellite in Low Earth Orbit **[T8B10]**
- Perigee — The point of a satellite's orbit that is nearest the Earth
- Space station — Defined by the FCC as an amateur station located more than 50 km above the Earth's surface **[T1A07]**
- Spin fading — Signal fading caused by rotation of the satellite and its antennas **[T8B09]**

TRACKING A SATELLITE

T8B03 — Which of the following are provided by satellite tracking programs?

T8B06 — Which of the following are inputs to a satellite tracking program?

To find out when a satellite will make a *pass* above the horizon at your location and can be accessed, you'll need a *satellite tracking program*. The tracking program will need you to enter certain bits of data about the satellite's orbit called the *Keplerian elements*. **[T8B06]** "Keps" as they are often called are available online and the program may be able to download them automatically. Using those values, the software can provide real-time maps of the satellite's location, the trajectory the satellite will follow across the sky, and even the amount of Doppler shift the signals will experience. **[T8B03]** It is good practice to enter the elements for the International Space Station (ISS) and then find it visually in the sky, watching it pass overhead at sunset or dawn.

OPERATING VIA SATELLITES

T8B01 — What telemetry information is typically transmitted by satellite beacons?

T8B02 — What is the impact of using too much effective radiated power on a satellite uplink?

T8B04 — What mode of transmission is used by amateur radio satellites?

T8B08 — What is meant by the statement that a satellite is operating in mode U/V?

T8B11 — Who may receive telemetry from a space station?

T8B12 — Which of the following is a good way to judge whether your uplink power is neither too low nor too high?

You'll need to determine the satellite's operational *mode* — the bands on which it is transmitting and receiving. Most satellites only have one mode, but some have several that can be controlled by ground stations. Mode is specified as two letters separated by a slash. The first letter indicates the uplink band and the second letter indicates the downlink band. For example, the uplink for a satellite in U/V mode is in the UHF band (70 cm) and a downlink is in the VHF band (2 meters). **[T8B08]** Satellites can use any amateur mode. The most common are SSB, FM, CW, and data. **[T8B04]**

When you are ready to try a satellite contact, known as "squirting the bird," you'll get best results with a beam antenna that you can aim at the satellite as directed by your tracking program. A small beam is best for starting because it will not have to be pointed very precisely. Some satellites can be contacted with simple vertical antennas when they are directly overhead and the distance to them is low. As you get better at pointing the antenna, you can use a more powerful beam and contact the satellite closer and closer to the horizon, increasing the number of stations on Earth that are in view of the satellite at the same time as your station.

You can tell when the satellite is within range by listening for the beacon. Satellite beacons may transmit telemetry using CW (the most common) as well as RTTY and packet radio. The telemetry data from the satellite contains information on the health and status of the satellite. **[T8B01]** Unless you need to copy the telemetry, it is useful to just listen to tell when the satellite is close enough for a contact. Even if you don't have an amateur license, you can still tune in to the stream of telemetry data from a space station. Anyone can receive satellite telemetry! **[T8B11]**

Always use the minimum amount of transmitter power to contact satellites, since their relay transmitter power is limited by their solar panels and batteries. **[T8B02]** If your signal on the satellite downlink is about the same strength as that of the satellite's beacon, you're using the right amount of power. **[T8B12]**

For more information on amateur satellites, investigate the website of AMSAT. AMSAT is the organization that coordinates the building and launch of most amateur satellites. You'll find a lot of information about how satellites work and how to find them on the air and in the sky. There are also bulletins that you can receive to update you on satellite status and news about amateur satellites. Choose one of the active satellites listed on the website and start your quest for a satellite QSO!

Chapter 7

Licensing Regulations

In this chapter, you'll learn about:

- **How FCC rules are organized**
- **Amateur Radio's "mission"**
- **Types of licenses**
- **Licensing exams and Volunteer Examiners**
- **Responsibilities of licensees**
- **Frequency and emission privileges**
- **International radio rules**
- **Amateur call signs**

When you see the mouse, you'll find more information at **www.arrl.org/ham-radio-license-manual**

It's time for the rules of the road, ham radio style! In the preceding chapters, you've learned the technology and customs of Amateur Radio. Now you have the background to understand what the rules and regulations are intended to accomplish. In turn, that will make it a lot easier for you to learn (and remember!) the rules.

There are two chapters of the book that deal with the rules and regulations. This section deals with licensing regulations — bands and frequencies, call signs, international rules, how the licensing process works, and so forth. These are administrative rules. The next chapter will deal with rules about operating.

7.1 Licensing Terms

In dealing with rules and regulations, it's very important everyone uses the same words to mean the same things, so we'll begin with a series of definitions. They are, after all, what the rules are made of! In case you want to look up a specific rule or definition, they're all online at the ARRL: **www.arrl.org/part-97-amateur-radio**. The ARRL's *FCC Rules and Regulations for the Amateur Radio Service* contains the latest rules along with some explanation. It is a useful reference for you.

PART 97

T1A02 — Which agency regulates and enforces the rules for the Amateur Radio Service in the United States?

Each of the radio services administered by the FCC has its own section of rules and regulations. The amateur service is defined by and operates according to the rules in Part 97 of the FCC's rules. (The FCC rules are one part of Title 47 of the Code of Federal Regulations (CFR) which is the section on Telecommunications.) Each rule is defined separately and is assigned a number beginning with 97, such as Part 97.101, a set of General Standards. Within each rule, individual parts get additional designators, for example Part 97.101(a) that specifies good practices be used. This looks complicated at first, but the numbering system actually helps you find the exact rule quickly.

These rules are where it all begins: the service, the operator, and the station. There are many other definitions, of course. Some will be familiar words that may be used in unfamiliar ways. If you are in doubt about the meaning of any word in the rules, it's likely that a precise definition is already waiting for you in Part 97.3, including technical terms.

Let's start with the question, "Who makes and enforces the rules for the Amateur Radio service in the United States?" This is a pretty important thing to know! The answer, of course, is the *Federal Communications Commission* or *FCC*. **[T1A02]** No matter what you're doing on the air, the FCC rules must be followed, even if you are operating on behalf of another government agency! The FCC is also the agency that grants your Amateur Radio license.

Basis and Purpose
T1A01 — Which of the following is a purpose of the Amateur Radio Service as stated in the FCC rules and regulations?

Part 97.1 is the most important rule of all — it's the *Basis and Purpose* of Amateur Radio. This explains the "mission" of Amateur Radio, why we are allocated precious RF spectrum, and what Amateur Radio is intended to accomplish. Here's what Part 97.1 says, with a little explanation added:

"The rules and regulations in this Part are designed to provide an amateur radio service having a fundamental purpose as expressed in the following principles:

(a) Recognition and enhancement of the value of the amateur service to the public as a voluntary noncommercial communication service, particularly with respect to providing emergency communications."

An important word to remember is "noncommercial." Hams aren't allowed to be paid for their services (with a few exceptions) and must operate on a voluntary basis. That includes conducting or promoting one's business activities over the air. Hams are extremely valuable when they respond to emergencies and disasters to provide temporary communications, especially because they are volunteers. In fact, responding to emergencies may be the most important reason that the amateur service exists today — it is, after all, the very first reason given!

"(b) Continuation and extension of the amateur's proven ability to contribute to the advancement of the radio art."

Hams have a history of discovering and inventing that continues today. After World War I, hams were given all of the "worthless" shortwave bands, but soon discovered that they were perfect for long-distance communications. Even with all the communications research going on around the world, hams still invent useful systems and antennas. Ham radio's famous creativity pays back the public's investment of spectrum many times over.

"(c) Encouragement and improvement of the amateur service through rules which provide for advancing skills in both the communications and technical phases of the art."

Not only do hams tinker with radios, but they train to operate them in useful ways. Events such as ARRL Field Day and the myriad exercises held all around the world are ways in which amateurs keep their emergency response skills sharp. Competitive operating events, chasing awards, and station-building continually develop the ham's communications skills. **[T1A01]**

"(d) Expansion of the existing reservoir within the amateur radio service of trained operators, technicians, and electronics experts."

Having a bunch of folks around who are handy with radios has turned out to be a great idea over the years! There is a long list of ways in which hams have shown their communications skills to be a valuable resource to the public, to the military, and to private industry.

"(e) Continuation and extension of the amateur's unique ability to enhance international goodwill."

It has been said that ham radio is an international "Passport to Friendship." There is nothing like a live connection with someone far away, whether by Morse code on the HF bands or an IRLP chat between two hams holding handheld radios. Hams are almost unique in their ability to "make contact" with people around the world every day, from all walks of life with little or no intervening systems or bureaucracy.

Through ham radio, you will encounter many different activities and events, from conducting radio experiments to simply communicating with other licensed hams around the world. As long as they satisfy one or more of these criteria, then, yes, they are "real" ham radio. We have by no means exhausted the possibilities!

TYPE AND CLASSES OF LICENSES

T1A04 — How many operator/primary station license grants may be held by any one person?

T1C01 — For which license classes are new licenses currently available from the FCC?

T1F11 — Which of the following is a requirement for the issuance of a club station license grant?

An Amateur Radio license actually consists of two parts — an *operator license* and a *station license*. In most other services, they are granted separately, such as for broadcast stations where employees actually operate the equipment. The operator license gives you permission to operate an amateur station according to the rules of the amateur service. The station license authorizes you to have an amateur station. The combined license is an amateur *operator/primary station license*. Each person can have only one such license. **[T1A04]**

Figure 7.1 shows an actual Amateur Radio license of the type you can print out from the FCC website or receive in the mail if you request one from the FCC. (For details and options, see **www.arrl.org/obtain-license-copy**.) You are supposed to have your license available for inspection at any time. Making a laminated copy of the business card-sized section allows you to have a copy of your license with you wherever you are.

There are three classes of Amateur Radio licenses being granted today: Technician, General, and Amateur Extra. **[T1C01]** Each carries a different set of *frequency and operating privileges* that expand from Technician to General to Extra along with the comprehensiveness of the exams. As you pass harder exams, you get more privileges. There are other license classes — the Novice, Technician Plus, and Advanced. No new licenses being granted being granted for these classes. There are still people who hold these licenses — you'll meet them on the air.

Clubs can also be license holders. Each club must have a licensed *trustee* who actually holds the club license and is designated by a club officer. Clubs must have at least four members and be organized as in rule 97.5 (b). **[T1F11]** (There is more information about call signs for clubs and special event stations in this chapter's supplemental information.)

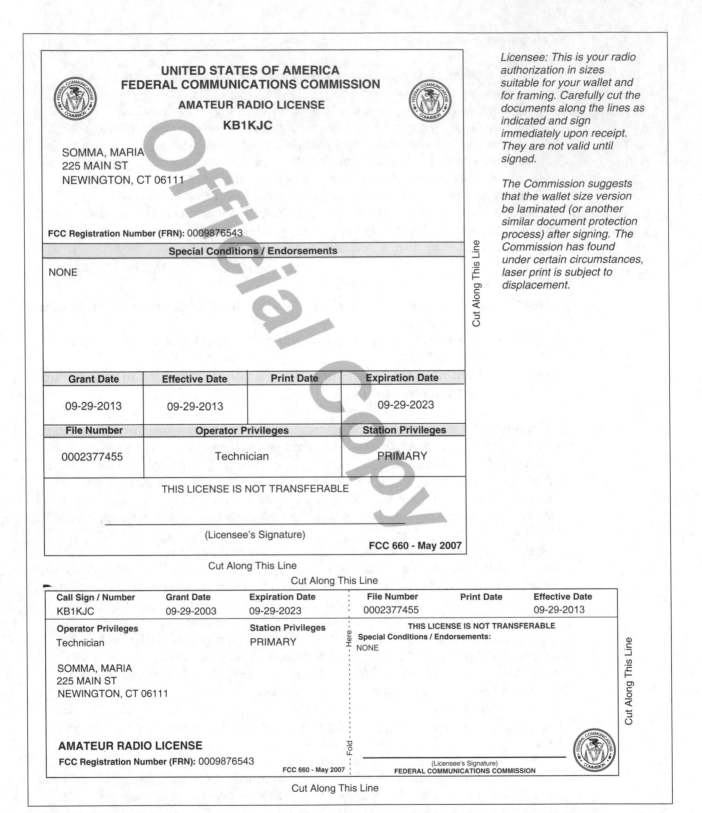

Figure 7.1 — An FCC Amateur Radio license is both an operator and a station license. The printed license shown here has two sections: one for posting in your station and one to carry with you. For information on obtaining a copy of your license, see www.arrl.org/obtain-license-copy.

Table 7.1

Amateur License Class Examinations

License Class	Exam Element	Number of Questions
Technician	2 (Written)	35 (passing is 26 correct)
General	3 (Written)	35 (passing is 26 correct)
Amateur Extra	4 (Written)	50 (passing is 37 correct)

EXAMINATIONS

T1A05 — What is proof of possession of an FCC-Issued operator/primary license grant?

T1C10 — How soon after passing the examination for your first amateur radio license may you operate a transmitter on an Amateur Radio Service frequency?

Unique among the various radio services, amateurs give their own exams, even making up the *question pool* used on the exams! This is part of ham radio's self-policing, self-regulating history. How amateur exams are given is discussed later in this chapter. Amateur volunteers run their own exam sessions and the results have been very good, with thousands and thousands of successful exam sessions.

The exams themselves are referred to as *elements*. A Technician license requires that you pass Element 2. Higher license classes require that you pass a specific element and all lower-class elements. For example, to obtain the General class license, you must pass Elements 2 and 3 in order. **Table 7.1** shows the elements that must be passed for each license class.

Once you pass your exam, your forms are filed with the FCC by the VEC responsible for your exam session. You can't begin operating, though, until you are notified of your call sign. Once your information shows up in the FCC ULS consolidated database, that's proof you have been granted an operator/station license and are fully authorized to go on the air! **[T1A05, T1C10]**

TERM OF LICENSE AND RENEWAL

T1C08 — What is the normal term for an FCC-issued primary station/operator amateur radio license grant?

T1C09 — What is the grace period following the expiration of an amateur license within which the license may be renewed?

T1C11 — If your license has expired and is still within the allowable grace period, may you continue to operate a transmitter on Amateur Radio Service frequencies?

Amateur licenses are good for a 10-year term. **[T1C08]** You can renew them indefinitely without ever taking another exam. You can renew online by using the FCC's Universal Licensing System (ULS). Up until 90 days before your license expires, you can also fill out a paper FCC Form 605 and mail it to the FCC. (After that time, the paperwork may not be processed in time to prevent expiration.)

What if your license does expire? People do forget! If your license expires, you are supposed to stop transmitting because your license is not valid after it expires. **[T1C11]** Nevertheless, you have a two-year grace period to apply for a new license without taking the exam again. **[T1C09]**

For More Information
Volunteer Examiners

An amateur who actually gives the exams and runs the *exam sessions* is a *Volunteer Examiner* (VE). A Volunteer Examiner is accredited by one or more of the Volunteer Examiner Coordinators (VECs) to administer amateur license exams. Each exam session requires at least three VEs be present that hold an amateur license with a class higher than those of the prospective licensees. For example, to give a Technician exam (Element 2), the VEs must hold a General class license or higher. The exception is that VEs holding Amateur Extra licenses may give Amateur Extra class exams.

Although Technicians can't be counted as part of the three required VEs, they can help process paperwork and assist with running the session, except for grading and handling General or Extra exams. This is a great way to help others get their license.

Taking the Exam

The first step is to find a exam session by contacting the VECs in your area or checking their websites. You can find exam sessions registered with the ARRL/VEC on the ARRL's licensing web page. Some exam sessions are held on a regular basis and are open to the public. Others are held at events such as conventions and hamfests (an Amateur Radio flea market). Others are hosted by individuals or clubs at a private residence or facility.

Once you've selected a session, be sure to register or check if they accept *walk-ins*, or unregistered attendees. (They might not have extra exam materials.) Then show up on time and ready to take the exam. Take a check or cash for the exam fee — most exam sessions cannot process credit cards.

The VEs will register you, check your ID (bring at least two forms of identification, one being a photo ID), and set you up with the necessary exam papers. The exam is in multiple-question format. There will be 35 questions on the Technician exam and you have to answer 26 correctly to pass. Take your time and be sure you're happy with your answers before you turn in the exam — there are no extra points given for speed!

CSCE and Form 605

Once you've turned in your answer sheet, the VEs will grade it while you relax a bit! Did you pass? Congratulations! If not, don't despair — check with the VEs running the exam session about taking another version of the exam for that element. Lots of hams took the exam a couple of times before passing!

Those who pass will be given two forms to fill out: a *Certificate of Successful Completion of Examination* (CSCE) and a *NCVEC Quick Form 605* (**Figure 7.2**). The CSCE is your "receipt" of successfully passing the exam for an element and what class of license you have earned. You should keep the CSCE until the FCC database has been updated with all of your new information. The CSCE is good for 365 days as proof that you have successfully passed one or more elements.

The NCVEC Quick Form 605 that you fill out as shown in Figure 7.2 will be filed with the FCC. It records your personal information and will be used to link your identity with a specific call sign. The exam session VEs will help you fill out the form correctly. Then all you have to do is wait until your information (and a call sign!) appear in the FCC database.

Obtaining Form 605

If you decide to "do the paperwork" on real paper instead of online, you'll need to get a blank FCC 605 Main Form. This is not difficult! You can get FCC 605 Main Form with detailed instructions from the FCC Forms web page — **www.fcc.gov/licensing-databases/forms**.

The ARRL VEC offers an overview of the various FCC and VEC forms and their uses online at **www.arrl.org/fcc-forms**.

Figure 7.2 — The NCVEC Form 605 that you fill out will be filed with the FCC. The CSCE (Certificate of Successful Completion of Examination) is your exam session receipt that serves as proof that you have completed one or more exam elements. It can be used at other exam sessions for 365 days.

NCVEC QUICK-FORM 605 APPLICATION
AMATEUR OPERATOR/PRIMARY STATION LICENSE

SECTION 1 - TO BE COMPLETED BY APPLICANT

PRINT LAST NAME: Somma SUFFIX (Jr., Sr.): FIRST NAME: MARIA M.I.: STATION CALL SIGN (IF LICENSED): KB1KJC

MAILING ADDRESS (Number and Street or P.O. Box): 225 MAIN ST.

FEDERAL REGISTRATION NUMBER (FRN) - IF NONE, THEN SOCIAL SECURITY NUMBER (SSN): 0009876543

CITY: NEWINGTON STATE CODE: CT ZIP CODE (5 or 9 Numbers): 06111 DAYTIME TELEPHONE NUMBER (Include Area Code):

E-MAIL ADDRESS (MANDATORY TO RECEIVE LICENSE NOTIFICATION EMAIL FROM FCC): KB1KJC@arrl.org

Basic Qualification Question:
Has the Applicant or any party to this application, or any party directly or indirectly controlling the Applicant, ever been convicted of a felony by any state or federal court? ☐YES ☒NO

If "YES", see "FCC BASIC QUALIFICATION QUESTION INSTRUCTIONS AND PROCEDURES" on the back of this form.

I HEREBY APPLY FOR (Make an X in the appropriate box(es)):

☐ EXAMINATION for a new license grant

☒ EXAMINATION for **upgrade** of my license class

☐ CHANGE my **name** on my license to my new name

Former Name: _____
(Last name) (Suffix) (First name) (MI)

☐ CHANGE my mailing address to **above** address

☐ CHANGE my station **call sign** systematically
Applicant's Initials: To Confirm _____

☐ RENEWAL of my license grant
Exp. Date: _____

Do you have another license application on file with the FCC which has not been acted upon? PURPOSE OF OTHER APPLICATION PENDING FILE NUMBER (FOR VEC USE ONLY)

I certify that:
- I waive any claim to the use of any particular frequency regardless of prior use by license or otherwise;
- All statements and attachments are true, complete and correct to the best of my knowledge and belief and are made in good faith;
- I am not a representative of a foreign government;
- I am not subject to a denial of Federal benefits pursuant to Section 5301 of the Anti-Drug Abuse Act of 1988, 21 U.S.C. § 862.
- The construction of my station will NOT be an action which is likely to have a significant environmental effect (See 47 CFR Sections 1.1301-1.1319 and Section 97.13(a));
- I have read and WILL COMPLY with Section 97.13(c) of the Commission's Rules regarding RADIOFREQUENCY (RF) RADIATION SAFETY and the amateur service section of OST/OET Bulletin Number 65.

Signature of Applicant:
X _Maria Somma_ Date Signed: 03-13-2018

SECTION 2 - TO BE COMPLETED BY ALL ADMINISTERING VEs

Applicant is qualified for operator license class:

☐ NO NEW LICENSE OR UPGRADE WAS EARNED

☐ TECHNICIAN Element 2

☒ GENERAL Elements 2 and 3

☐ AMATEUR EXTRA Elements 2, 3 and 4

DATE OF EXAMINATION SESSION: 03-13-2018

EXAMINATION SESSION LOCATION: NEWINGTON CT

VEC ORGANIZATION: ARRL

VEC RECEIPT DATE:

I CERTIFY THAT I HAVE COMPLIED WITH THE ADMINISTERING VE REQUIRMENTS IN PART 97 OF THE COMMISSION'S RULES AND WITH THE INSTRUCTIONS PROVIDED BY THE COORDINATING VEC AND THE FCC.

	VEs NAME (Print First, MI, Last, Suffix)	VEs STATION CALL SIGN	VEs SIGNATURE (Must match name)	DATE SIGNED
1st	Kenny Harts	N1NAG	Kenny Harts	3/19/18
2nd	Rose-Ann Lawrence	KB1DMW	Rose-Ann Lawrence	03-13-18
3rd	Perry Green	WY1O	Perry Green	03/13/18

DO NOT SEND THIS FORM TO FCC – THIS IS NOT AN FCC FORM.
IF THIS FORM IS SENT TO FCC, FCC WILL RETURN IT TO YOU WITHOUT ACTION.

NCVEC FORM 605 - September 2017
FOR VE/VEC USE ONLY - Page 1

American Radio Relay League VEC
Certificate of Successful Completion of Examination ARRL The national association for AMATEUR RADIO

Test Site (City/State): NEWINGTON, CT Test Date: 03-13-18

CREDIT for ELEMENTS PASSED VALID FOR 365 DAYS
You have passed the written element(s) indicated at right. Your will be given credit for the appropriate examination element(s), for up to 365 days from the date shown at the top of this certificate.

LICENSE UPGRADE NOTICE
If you also hold a valid FCC-issued Amateur radio license grant, this Certificate validates temporary operation with the operating privileges of your new operator class (see Section 97.9[b] of the FCC's Rules) until you are granted the license for your new operator class, or for a period of 365 days from the test date stated above on this certificate, whichever comes first.

LICENSE STATUS INQUIRIES
You can find out if a new license or upgrade has been "granted" by the FCC. For on-line inquiries see the FCC Web at http://wireless.fcc.gov/uls/ ("Click on Search Licenses" button), or see the ARRL Web at http://www.arrl.org/fcc/search; or by calling FCC toll free at 888-225-5322; or by calling the ARRL at 1-860-594-0300 during business hours. Allow 15 days from the test date before calling.

THIS CERTIFICATE IS NOT A LICENSE, PERMIT, OR ANY OTHER KIND OF OPERATING AUTHORITY IN AND OF ITSELF. THE ELEMENT CREDITS AND/OR OPERATING PRIVILEGES THAT MAY BE INDICATED IN THE LICENSE UPGRADE NOTICE ARE VALID FOR 365 DAYS FROM THE TEST DATE. THE HOLDER NAMED HEREON MUST ALSO HAVE BEEN GRANTED AN AMATEUR RADIO LICENSE ISSUED BY THE FCC TO OPERATE ON THE AIR.

Candidate's Signature: Maria Somma Call Sign: KB1KJC (If none, write none)

Candidate's Name: MARIA SOMMA

Address: 225 MAIN ST.

City: NEWINGTON State: CT ZIP: 06111

NOTE TO VE TEAM:
COMPLETELY CROSS OUT ALL BOXES BELOW THAT DO NOT APPLY TO THIS CANDIDATE.

The applicant named herein has presented valid proof for the exam element credit(s) indicated below:
Element 3 credit
Element 4 credit

EXAM ELEMENTS EARNED
~~Passed written Element 2~~
(Passed written Element 3)
~~Passed written Element 4~~

NEW LICENSE CLASS EARNED
~~TECHNICIAN~~
(GENERAL)
~~EXTRA~~
~~NONE~~

VE #1: Kenny Harts Signature Call Sign: N1NAG

VE #2: Rose-Ann Lawrence Signature Call Sign: KB1DMW

VE #3: Perry Green Signature Call Sign: WY1O

COPIES: WHITE–Candidate, YELLOW–VE Team, PINK–ARRL VEC
MVE 07/2015

YOUR RESPONSIBILITIES

Congratulations on a job well done, Amateur Radio licensee! You are ready to join the ranks of other US hams! Remember your primary responsibility as the holder of an Amateur Radio license — your station must be operated in accordance with the FCC rules.

Personal Information

T1C07 — What may result when correspondence from the FCC is returned as undeliverable because the grantee failed to provide and maintain a correct mailing address with the FCC?

The FCC requires you to provide and maintain a valid current mailing address in their database at all times. This is so you can be contacted by mail, if needed. If you move or even change P.O. boxes, be sure to update your information using the FCC ULS online system. If mail to you is returned to the FCC as undeliverable, your license can be suspended or revoked and removed from the database. [T1C07]

The other piece of information that might be unfamiliar is the FRN (Federal Registration Number). This is an identification number assigned to you as a licensee. You can use your Social Security Number as the Taxpayer ID Number. Registering with the FCC is covered in the online supplemental information for this chapter.

Station Inspection

T1F01 — When must the station licensee make the station and its records available for FCC inspection?

As a federal licensee, you are obligated to make your station available for inspection upon request by an FCC representative. By accepting the FCC rules and regulations for the amateur service, you agree that your station could be inspected any time. These visits are very rare and only occur when there is reason to believe that your station has been operated improperly. Remember to keep your original license available for inspection, too! [T1F01]

7.2 Bands and Privileges

The frequencies and modes and methods that hams are allowed to use are all known to the rules and regulations as *privileges*. What gives the FCC authority to grant privileges is the Communications Act of 1934. What then grants these privileges to you is your license. By signing Form 605 and applying for a license, you agree to be bound by the FCC rules and that means staying within the privileges of your license.

FREQUENCY PRIVILEGES

T1B03 — Which frequency is within the 6 meter amateur band?

T1B04 — Which amateur band are you using when your station is transmitting on 146.52 MHz?

T1B06 — On which HF bands does a Technician class operator have phone privileges?

T1B10 — Which of the following HF bands have frequencies available to the Technician class operator for RTTY and data transmissions?

The most important privileges are *frequency privileges*. There are literally hundreds of bands and dozens of different types of radio spectrum users. The frequency privileges granted to the various services are called *allocations*. For example, amateurs are allocated 144 – 148 MHz, the 2 meter band. **Figure 7.3** is a grand overview of the radio spectrum showing amateur frequency privileges.

You can see that amateur allocations are sprinkled throughout the radio spectrum. As you recall from our discussion on propagation, radio signals of different frequencies propagate differently. We are fortunate that spectrum planning has resulted in amateurs having access to a wide range of frequencies for experimenting and communicating in different ways.

Table 7.2 shows the most commonly used Technician VHF/UHF frequency privileges. Remember that a band can be referred to by frequency ("50 MHz") or by wavelength ("6 meters"). Use the formula:

f (in MHz) = 300 / wavelength (in meters) or wavelength (in meters) = 300 / f (in MHz)

to convert between frequency and wavelength. **[T1B03, T1B04]**

You should memorize the frequencies for the most common bands used by Technicians: 6 meters (50 – 54 MHz), 2 meters (144 – 148 MHz) and 70 cm (420 – 450 MHz).

Table 7.2

Most Popular VHF and UHF Technician Amateur Bands

ITU Region 2

Band (Wavelength)	Frequency Limits
VHF Range	
6 meters	50 – 54 MHz
2 meters	144 – 148 MHz
1.25 meters	219 – 220 MHz
1.25 meters	222 – 225 MHz
UHF Range	
70 centimeters	420 — 450 MHz
33 centimeters	902 — 928 MHz
23 centimeters	1240 – 1300 MHz
13 centimeters	2300 – 2310 MHz
13 centimeters	2390 – 2450 MHz

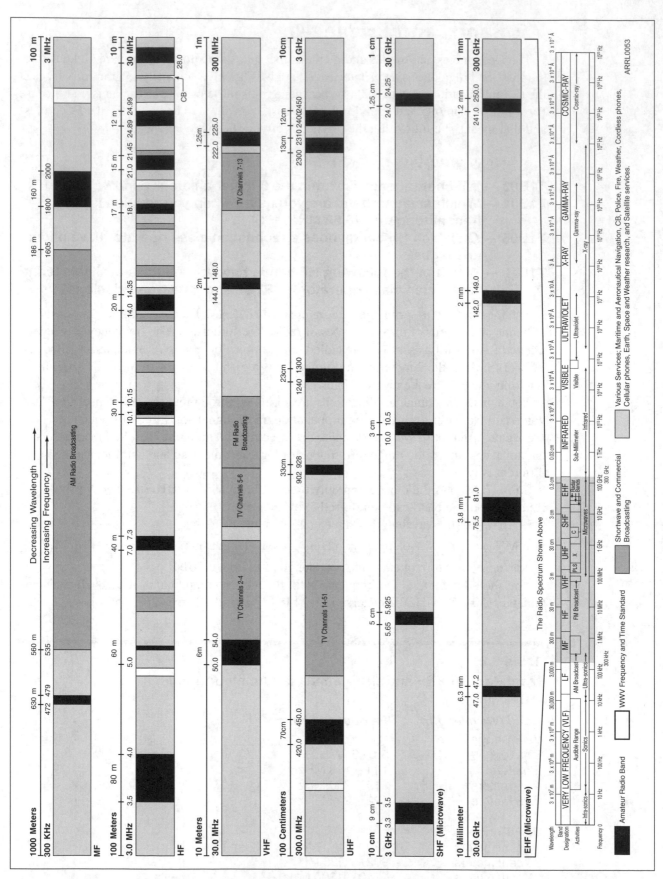

Figure 7.3 — Amateur allocations, the black rectangles in the chart, are distributed relatively evenly throughout the radio spectrum. The variations in propagation at these different frequencies give hams a lot of opportunities to experiment with different types of communications systems and methods.

Table 7.3

Technician HF Privileges

200 watts PEP maximum output

Band (Wavelength)	Frequency (MHz)
80 meters	3.525 – 3.600 (CW only)
40 meters	7.025 – 7.125 (CW only)
15 meters	21.025 – 21.200 (CW only)
10 meters	28.000 – 28.300 (CW, RTTY and data)
	28.300 – 28.500 (CW and SSB)

Emission Type Designators

As you read about amateur rules and regulations, you will occasionally encounter *emission mode designators*, such as A1A for amplitude-modulated CW for aural reception or J3E for single-sideband, suppressed-carrier telephony. It is not necessary to memorize them, but it is a good idea to know where to look them up if you need to. A table of designators for the most common amateur emission types can be found on this book's website and a complete discussion of emission types is contained in *The ARRL Handbook*.

Hams keep a chart of their privileges handy — not many of us have every one of them memorized. To help you remember, copy the information onto a piece of paper and tape it in your car or near your computer or on the refrigerator. Take every opportunity to recite the information, reinforcing it time after time. You'll find that it's not nearly as hard as it seems at first!

The HF privileges for Technicians in **Table 7.3** are useful and interesting. (A full-page chart of Technician privileges is provided on this book's website and in Chapter 1.) Depending on solar activity, the 10 meter band can provide contacts worldwide. Along with phone, you can also try out RTTY and other HF data modes. [**T1B06, T1B10**] The CW-only privileges on other bands will acquaint you with "classic" ham radio on the shortwave bands.

Within the amateur HF bands, access to frequencies is determined by license class. From the Technician class, as higher class licenses are obtained, more and more frequency privileges are granted until all amateur privileges are granted to Amateur Extra licensees. For example, on the 80 meter band, Technicians may use CW from 3.525 to 3.600 MHz.

EMISSION PRIVILEGES

T1A06 — What is the FCC Part 97 definition of a "beacon"?

T1B05 — What is the limitation for emissions on the frequencies between 219 and 220 MHz?

T1B07 — Which of the following VHF/UHF frequency ranges are limited to CW only?

Within most of the ham bands, additional restrictions are made by mode or *emission type*. (Emission is the formal name for any radio signal from a transmitter.) Just as a frequency privilege is permission to use a specific frequency, an *emission privilege* is permission to communicate using a particular mode, such as phone, CW, data, or image. **Table 7.4** lists the modes that can be used by amateurs — as a Technician class licensee, you can use all of them.

The amateur bands are divided into combinations of frequency, license class, and emission privileges. These subdivisions are called *sub-bands*. Parts of the ham bands in which only certain modes can be used are called *mode-restricted*. As a Technician licensee, your situation is very simple: There is a small CW-only sub-band occupying

Table 7.4
Amateur Emission Types

Emission	Description
CW	Morse code telegraphy
Data	Computer-to-computer communication modes, usually called digital modes
Image	Television (fast-scan and slow-scan) and facsimile or fax
MCW	Tone-modulated CW, Morse code generated by keying an audio tone
Phone	Speech or voice communications, including digital voice modes
Pulse	Communications using a sequence of pulses whose characteristics are modulated in order to carry information
RTTY	Narrow-band, direct-printing telegraphy received by automatic equipment, such as a computer or teleprinter
SS	Spread-spectrum communications in which the signal is spread out over a wide band of frequencies
Test	Transmissions containing no information

the bottom 100 kHz of the 6 and 2 meter bands. [T1B07] The segment of the 1.25 meter band from 219 – 220 MHz is restricted to digital message forwarding by fixed stations and systems. [T1B05] For all amateur allocations above 222 MHz, there are no other sub-bands! See the Technician privilege chart in Chapter 1 or online.

Beacons are another type of station restricted to certain sub-bands. These stations make transmissions for the purpose of observing propagation or other experiments. [T1A06] You will find them on 10 meters between 28.2 and 28.3 MHz and in the lower segments of the VHF, UHF, and microwave bands. (See rule 97.203.) Most send a grid locator or other location information so you know if there is propagation to that area, a very handy tool on these bands.

Why have mode-restricted sub-bands? Because the methods of operating for the different modes are sometimes not compatible. CW and phone operation, for example, are conducted quite differently and the signals interfere with each other. Hams solve this problem by using narrow-bandwidth modes, such as CW, at the low-frequency end of the bands and wider-bandwidth signals, from data through voice, higher in the band. That is the price of flexibility to experiment and use all the different modes!

POWER LIMITS

T1B11 — What is the maximum peak envelope power output for Technician class operators using their assigned portions of the HF bands?

T1B12 — Except for some specific restrictions, what is the maximum peak envelope power output for Technician class operators using frequencies above 30 MHz?

Output power from a transmitter or amplifier is defined in terms of *peak envelope power* (PEP). PEP is the average power during one RF cycle of the radio signal at the very peak of a modulating waveform, such as for speech. For a CW signal, PEP is measured during the *key-down period* in which the transmitter is *on*. FM and most digital modes have a constant power whether voice or data is being transmitted or not.

With a few specific restrictions (see the privileges chart) amateurs are allowed the full legal limit of 1500 watts PEP output. This applies to Technician operators above 30 MHz. [T1B12] Below 30 MHz, Novice and Technician licensees are limited to 200 watts PEP on HF bands. [T1B11]

PRIMARY AND SECONDARY ALLOCATIONS

T1B08 — Which of the following is a result of the fact that the Amateur Radio Service is secondary in all or portions of some amateur bands (such as portions of the 70 cm band)?

It would be nice if every type of radio user had exclusive access to their allocations. Many amateur bands are exclusively allocated to hams, worldwide. Because spectrum is scarce and many services have valid needs for radio communications, occasionally two services receive *shared allocations,* including some of the amateur bands. When this happens, one group is generally given priority and these are called *primary allocations.* Groups that have access to spectrum on a lower priority receive *secondary allocations.* The groups that receive the allocations are *primary and secondary services.*

The primary service is *protected* from harmful interference by signals from secondary services. The secondary service gains access to the frequencies in the allocation with the understanding that it must not cause harmful interference to primary service users and it must accept interference from primary users. For example, amateurs have a secondary allocation in the 70 cm band and must avoid interfering with radiolocation stations that have primary status. **[T1B08]**

By sharing the bands in this way, more frequencies are available for more users than if every frequency were exclusively allocated to one service alone. Hams share several of our bands and enjoy wider access to frequencies than would otherwise be the case.

Part 97.303 lists all of the frequency-sharing requirements for US hams and is available on the ARRL website. It is worth familiarizing yourself with sharing requirements to avoid interference either to or from your station.

REPEATER COORDINATION

T1A08 — Which of the following entities recommends transmit/receive channels and other parameters for auxiliary and repeater stations?
T1A09 — Who selects a Frequency Coordinator?

It's a natural question, "Who decides what repeater can use a specific pair of frequencies?" You may be surprised to learn that hams themselves decide, and the FCC has nothing to do with it. This is part of the Amateur Radio tradition of self-policing and self-administration. Hams developed a system of regional *frequency coordination* to ensure that repeaters use the amateur bands wisely and avoid interference to the greatest degree possible.

Repeaters and their auxiliary stations are grouped together into one or two segments of a band. Their input and output *frequency pairs* are fixed and have a common offset in each region. This enables the maximum number of repeaters to use the limited amount of spectrum. To keep order, a committee of volunteers known as a *frequency coordinator* recommends transmit and receive frequencies. **[T1A08]** Where regions overlap, the coordinators work together to minimize interference and keep the coordination process orderly. A list of frequency coordinators is available on the website of the National Frequency Coordinators' Council.

Because repeaters cover wide areas, it is also necessary for the frequency coordinator to consider other operating parameters such as transmit power, the height of antennas, and whether a repeater should employ access tones. The frequency coordinator representatives are selected by the local or regional amateurs whose stations are eligible to be auxiliary or repeater stations. **[T1A09]**

A *coordinated* repeater uses frequencies approved by a regional coordinator. *Uncoordinated* repeaters are strongly discouraged because they often cause interference.

Before putting their repeater on the air, repeater owners apply to their region's coordinator for an available pair of frequencies. The coordinators determine what frequencies are best suited for the repeater's location. Once the frequency pair is assigned, the repeater owner can then turn on the repeater's transmitter.

7.3 International Rules

ITU (INTERNATIONAL TELECOMMUNICATION UNION)

T1B01 — What is the International Telecommunications Union (ITU)?

FCC doesn't have authority in other countries — every country has its equivalent agency. How do they coordinate? It would be chaos if every country made up their own allocations, since radio waves don't stop at international borders! Realizing the need for international coordination, the *International Telecommunication Union* (ITU) was formed as an agency of the United Nations (UN) in 1949. The ITU is an administrative forum for working out international telecommunications treaties and laws, including frequency allocations. The ITU also maintains international radio laws that all UN countries agree to abide by. **[T1B01]**

The ITU divides the world into the three regions shown in **Figure 7.4** and organizes frequency allocations accordingly. North and South America, including Alaska and Hawaii, form Region 2. Some US possessions and territories in the Pacific are located in Region 3.

Because VHF and UHF signals frequently do not travel far beyond the radio horizon, it was decided that allocations in these frequency ranges did not have to align precisely. As a result, the amateur allocations vary between regions. Table 7.2 shows some of the allocations for Amateur Radio above 50 MHz in Region 2. Allocations on those bands are different for amateurs in Regions 1 and 3.

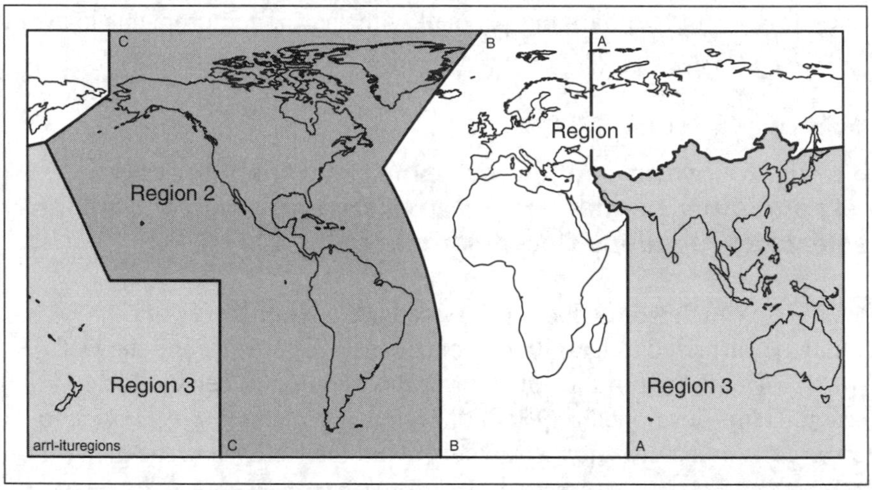

Figure 7.4 — The map shows the world divided into the three administrative regions of the International Telecommunication Union. This helps the ITU and member nations manage frequency allocations around the world.

International Amateur Radio Union (IARU)

Just as the countries of the world support the ITU, so do the amateur "countries" support the IARU. Each country with a national society, such as the ARRL in the US, is part of the IARU, which is organized in three regions, just like the ITU. Formed in 1925 as national governments began forming radio law, the IARU acts as the worldwide amateur voice to government and international rules making bodies, such as the ITU.

PERMITTED CONTACTS AND COMMUNICATIONS

T1C03 — What types of international communications is an FCC-licensed amateur radio station permitted to make?
T1D01 — With which countries are FCC-licensed amateur radio stations prohibited from exchanging communications?

Unless specifically prohibited by the government of either country, any ham can talk to any other ham. International communications must be limited to the purposes of the amateur service or remarks of a personal nature. **[T1C03]** Some countries do not recognize Amateur Radio, although the number is very small. The FCC can prohibit contacts between US citizens and those of specific other countries by notifying the ITU of its objections. **[T1D01]** This is very uncommon. Remember that in a communications emergency, you can still talk to any ham anywhere if needed to prevent loss of life or property.

INTERNATIONAL OPERATING

T1C04 — When are you allowed to operate your amateur station in a foreign country?
T1C06 — From which of the following locations may an FCC-licensed amateur station transmit?

Operating in a foreign country can be a lot of fun! You can meet local hams, and if you are licensed for HF operation you can become "DX" and attract a crowd on the air. To operate at all, the foreign country must permit amateur operation. **[T1C04]** In addition, you must have permission and when you are inside a country's national boundaries, including territorial waters, you are required to operate according to their rules. You may also operate from any vessel or craft that is documented or registered in the United States. **[T1C06]** If the vessel is in territorial waters, regulations of the host country and those of the vessel's registry both apply.

To operate using your US amateur license, there must be a reciprocal operating agreement between the countries. There are three ways of getting operating permission: reciprocal operating authority, an International Amateur Radio Permit (IARP), and the European Conference of Postal and Telecommunications Administrations (CEPT) license agreement. For more information on these agreements, information is available on the ARRL's website in the Licensing, Education, & Training section. (More information on reciprocal operating agreements is available in the online supplemental information for this chapter.)

Regardless of which avenue is available, don't forget the final part of the amateur service's basis and purpose — to foster goodwill. You are a ham radio ambassador while on the air!

7.4 Call Signs

Call signs are our "radio names" and each amateur's is unique. Call signs all have a common structure and once you learn it, figuring out the nationality of call sign (or *call*) is easy.

PREFIX AND SUFFIX

Every amateur call sign has a *prefix* and a *suffix*. In the US, an amateur call sign prefix consists of one or two letters and one numeral. The suffix consists of one to three letters. For example, W3ABC is a valid US amateur call sign, while KDKA and KMA3505 are call signs from other US radio services.

Every country is assigned at least one unique *block* of prefixes. For example, US amateur call signs begin with K, N, W, or the two-letter combination AA through AL. No matter what, if you hear a call sign beginning with those letters, you know it's a US call sign. Most Canadian hams use VA through VG, French hams use F, Japanese amateur call signs begin with a J, and hams from Singapore have calls beginning with 9V.

The suffix of a call sign is the unique part that identifies the particular station and consists of only letters. In the call W1AW, "AW" is unique among all other calls beginning with "W1" (known as "W1 calls"). Suffixes are one, two, or three letters. The combination of prefix and suffix uniquely identify a station anywhere on Earth. Within a country, the call signs can be assigned to indicate license class or location or other special characteristics.

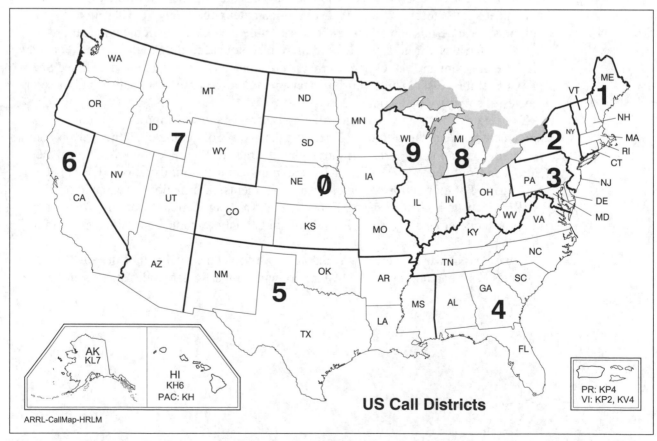

Figure 7.5 — There are 10 US call districts in the continental United States. When an amateur passes their initial license exam, the numeral of the district in which he or she resides becomes part of their assigned call sign. Alaska and the US possessions in the Pacific and Caribbean form three more districts and have calls with unique prefixes.

Table 7.5

US Amateur Call Signs in Districts 0 – 9

Group	License Class	Format
Group A	Amateur Extra	Prefix K, N or W with two-letter suffix (1×2), or two-letter prefix beginning with A, N, K or W and one-letter suffix (2×1), or two-letter prefix beginning with A and a two-letter suffix (2×2)
Group B	Advanced	Two-letter prefix beginning with K, N or W and a two-letter suffix (2×2)
Group C	General	One-letter prefix beginning with K, N or W and a three-letter suffix (1×3)
Group D	Technician, Novice, and Club	Two-letter prefix beginning with K or W and a three-letter suffix (2×3)

US Call Districts and Call Signs

In the US, the number in the call sign's prefix indicate in which one of the 10 districts shown in **Figure 7.5** the call was originally assigned. The call sign is permanently assigned to the individual operator in the US and remains the same, no matter where the operator moves in the country. W3IZ, for example, originally got his call in the third district but now lives in Connecticut.

A US call sign is further classified by the number of letters in the prefix and suffix. A call such as AA5BT with a two-letter prefix, "AA", and a two-letter suffix, "BT", is called a *2-by-2 or 2×2*. WA1ZMS is a 2×3. W1A is a 1×1. Regular US call signs have only one numeral in the prefix. The FCC grants these calls by license class as shown in **Table 7.5**. When you receive your Technician license, you will receive the next sequential call sign available to Technicians. Calls are always assigned in sequential order — you get the next one on the stack, just like vehicle license plates.

CHOOSING A CALL SIGN

T1C02 — Who may select a desired call sign under the vanity call sign rules?

T1C05 — Which of the following is a valid call sign for a Technician class amateur radio station?

You can also choose your own call sign! You can have almost as much fun choosing a call from the *vanity call* program as in choosing a vanity license plate for your car. Many hams pick a call with their initials in the suffix or one that forms a short word. Licensed hams can pick any available call authorized for their license class as shown in Table 7.5. There are lots of available calls for Technician licensees to choose from in Group C (1 × 3) and Group D (2 × 3). **[T1C02, T1C05]**

The Slashed Zero — Ø

You will notice right away that hams from the "zero" or tenth district write their calls with a forward slash through the zero — Ø. (The tenth district was created in the late 1930s when the ninth district's ham population got too big!) The slash was needed because the typewriters of those days made it hard to distinguish between 0 (zero) and O (capital letter O). It's still hard today in many fonts. Commercial and military operators adopted the custom of backspacing one space and typing a slash over the zero. Not in the usual set of characters used by word processing programs, the slashed zero is assigned the sequence of keyboard keys ALT-0216 in many character sets.

Chapter 8

Operating Regulations

In this chapter, you'll learn about:

- Control operators and control points
- Guest operating and privileges
- Identification on the air
- Tactical call signs
- Rules about interference
- Third-party communications
- Remote and automatic control
- Prohibited communications
- Broadcasting

When you see the mouse, you'll find more information at www.arrl.org/ham-radio-license-manual

8.1 Control Operators

T1E01 — When is an amateur station permitted to transmit without a control operator?
T1E03 — Who must designate the station control operator?
T1E05 — What is an amateur station control point?

Reading the rules themselves can be a bit confusing, so let's be sure to clearly define the terms. Operating rules are based on two ideas: a *control operator* and the *control point*. The control operator is a licensed operator who is responsible for making sure all FCC rules are followed. The control point is wherever the control operator operates the transmitter. That can be at the controls of the radio or by using some kind of connecting link from some other location.

• A control operator is the licensed amateur designated to be responsible for making sure that transmissions comply with FCC rules. That doesn't have to be the same person as the station owner. The station licensee is responsible for designating the control operator. **[T1E03]** Any licensed amateur can be a control operator.

• A control operator must be named in the FCC amateur license database or be an alien with reciprocal operating authorization. (An alien is a citizen of another country.) This is a simple requirement — the FCC has to know who you are, that you are licensed, and where you can be contacted.

• All transmissions must be made under the supervision of a control operator. **[T1E01]** There is only one control operator for a station at a time.

• The control point is where the station's control function is performed. Usually, the control point is at the transmitter and the control operator physically manipulates the controls of the transmitter. The control point can be remotely located and connected by phone lines, the internet or a radio link. **[T1E05]**

T1E04 — What determines the transmitting privileges of an amateur station?

T1E06 — When, under normal circumstances, may a Technician class licensee be the control operator of a station operating in an exclusive Amateur Extra class operator segment of the amateur bands?

T1E07 — When the control operator is not the station licensee, who is responsible for the proper operation of the station?

T1E11 — Who does the FCC presume to be the control operator of an amateur station, unless documentation to the contrary is in the station records?

As the control operator, you may operate the station in any way permitted by the privileges of your license class. **[T1E04]** It doesn't matter what the station owner's privileges are, only the privileges of the control operator. When the station owner and the control operator are the same person, responsibilities are easy to understand.

Being a guest operator is very common — you may allow another amateur to use your station or you may be the guest. Either way, it's important to understand what sets the control operator's privileges. A guest operator hosted by a higher-class licensee can operate using the host's privileges only if the host is the control operator. If the host is not the control operator, the guest is restricted to the privileges of their license.

Here's an example — you, a Technician class licensee, are invited to spend the afternoon at the station of a friend, who holds an Extra class license. While your friend is supervising and acting as control operator, you can operate the station on any amateur band and mode. This is very common and is a good way to learn about the HF bands and styles of operating not used on VHF/UHF. However, if your friend decides to step out of the station or run an errand, you are restricted to your Technician privileges. **[T1E06]**

What if you are the guest and have a higher-class license than the host? A guest operator hosted by a lower-class licensee can use their higher-class privileges as the control operator whether the host is present or not. In this case, there are special identification rules described in the section on Guest Operators in the online supplemental information for this chapter.

Regardless of license class, though, both the guest operator and station owner are responsible for proper operation of the station. **[T1E07]** The control operator is responsible for the station's transmissions. The station owner is responsible for limiting access to the station only to responsible licensees who will follow the FCC rules. The FCC will presume the station licensee to be the control operator unless there is a written record to the contrary. **[T1E11]**

Rebecca, KS4RX (left, an Extra class licensee), acts as control operator for Amanda, KG4NBF (a Technician class licensee), during Field Day. Rebecca is responsible for making sure all FCC rules are followed when the station is operating on bands and modes not available to Technicians.

8.2 Identification

In most contacts the other party can't see you — they have no other way of identifying your signals other than your call sign. It's also important that other stations be able to determine who is transmitting. Your call sign is your identity on the air and "to identify" or "identification" means to send or speak your call sign over the air.

Identification rules apply at all times. Proper identification is important so the FCC knows who's transmitting and for any other station that wants to contact you or to know where your signal is coming from. This is why identification is one of the few areas in which the FCC tells you how to operate. The online supplemental information for this chapter includes more information on special rules for identification, as well.

NORMAL IDENTIFICATION

T1A03 — What are the FCC rules regarding the use of a phonetic alphabet for station identification in the Amateur Radio Service?

T1D11 — When may an amateur station transmit without on-the-air identification?

T1F03 — When is an amateur station required to transmit its assigned call sign?

T1F04 — Which of the following is an acceptable language to use for station identification when operating in a phone sub-band?

T1F05 — What method of call sign identification is required for a station transmitting phone signals?

The first rule of identification is that unidentified transmissions are not allowed. Unidentified means that no call sign was associated with a transmission. The only exception is when your signals are controlling a model craft. **[T1D11]** Remote control signals are weak and don't travel long distances, so a call sign is not of much use.

If you need to make a short transmission to test an antenna or make adjustments to your radio, just stating or sending your call sign will suffice. For example, to see if you are in reach of a distant repeater, don't just key the microphone and listen for the repeater's signal — that's called *kerchunking* because of the sound that everyone monitoring will have to listen to. Just state your call sign once as you transmit.

The identification rules are simple — give your call sign at least once every 10 minutes during a contact and when the communication is finished. **[T1F03]** Why don't you have to give your call sign at the beginning of the contact? You generally need to give your call to establish contact so that is almost always done anyway. What if

Bob Raymond, WA1Z, is an active contester. He knows and practices all the FCC rules that govern Amateur Radio, including the need to identify your station. The purpose of identification is to identify the source of your signal, not those of other stations. Giving the other station's call sign is for convenience and is considered good practice.

the contact is shorter than 10 minutes? Just give your call sign as you end the contact.

You don't have to give the other station's call sign, either. The purpose of identification is to identify the source of *your* signal, not those of other stations. Giving the other station's call sign is for convenience and is considered good practice. Here's a tip: It's not necessary to say, "For ID," since whenever you give your call sign, you ID!

Your call can be given in Morse code, by voice, in an image, or as part of a digital transmission. Video and digital call signs will need to be transmitted in a standard protocol or format so that anyone can receive it. If you are using phone, you are required to identify in English, even if you are communicating in a language other than English. **[T1F04]** The FCC recommends the use of phonetics when you identify by voice — that avoids confusing letters that sound alike. **[T1A03]** The standard phonetics are words in the English language, as well. You may also identify by CW even if using phone. **[T1F05]**

Tactical Calls

T1F02 — When using tactical identifiers such as "Race Headquarters" during a community service net operation, how often must your station transmit the station's FCC-assigned call sign?

Tactical call signs (or tactical IDs) are used to help identify where a station is and what it is doing. Examples of tactical calls include "Waypoint 5," "First Aid Station," "Hollywood and Vine" and "Fire Watch on Coldwater Ridge." Tactical calls can be used at any time, but are usually used in emergency and public service operation when providing communications. Tactical calls allow consistent identification that streamlines communication based on function.

Tactical calls don't replace regular call signs and the regular identification rules apply — give your FCC-assigned call sign every 10 minutes and at the end of the communication. **[T1F02]** It would be really confusing if everyone had to remember which individual call sign was performing which function. It's common, for example, for a station to have different operators at different times. When a new operator takes over, he or she simply gives their FCC-assigned call sign along with a tactical call, such as "This is N1OJS at Race Headquarters." They use "Race Headquarters" as the tactical call from then on, giving the FCC-assigned call sign (N1OJS) once every 10 minutes.

Self-Assigned Indicators

T1F06 — Which of the following formats of a self-assigned indicator is acceptable when identifying using a phone transmission?

Licensee or Trustee?

There can be confusion about whether the person whose name is on the license for a repeater or a remote base is the "licensee" or the "trustee" of the station. The answer depends upon the type of license for the station.

If the repeater or remote base is operating using the call sign of an individual amateur's personal station license, then the operator is the "licensee" of the station.

If it is operating using an FCC-issued club station license and call sign, then the person whose name appears on the license is the "trustee."

When operating away from your home station, you should add information to your call sign so that other stations are aware of your location. For example, an Alaskan station would add some extra information when operating in the lower 48 contiguous states. Otherwise, the special Alaskan prefixes (AL7, KL7, NL7, WL7) would cause confusion about the location of the station. For example, if KL7CC is operating from a location in the 3rd district, he could give his call sign as "KL7CC/W3." The added "/W3" is called a *self-assigned indicator*.

FCC Part 97.119(c) says, "*One or more indicators may be included with the call sign. Each indicator must be separated from the call sign by the slant mark (/) or by any suitable word that denotes the slant mark. If an indicator is self-assigned, it must be included before, after, or both before and after, the call sign.*" For example, on phone, KL7CC could identify as W3/KL7CC or KL7CC/W3, using "stroke," "slash" or "portable" between the indicator and the call sign. **[T1F06]**

Note that the indicator is not allowed to conflict with some other indicator specified in the FCC rules, such as /KT, /AG and /AE which indicate an upgraded license class. It may not conflict with a prefix assigned to some other country.

Test Transmissions

T2A06 — Which of the following is required when making on-the-air test transmissions?

Identification rules apply to on-the-air test transmissions, as well, no matter how brief. The call sign must be given once every 10 minutes and at the end of transmissions. **[T2A06]** Test transmissions must be kept brief to avoid causing interference or to keep from occupying an otherwise useful frequency. The usual method of identifying during a test transmission is to say "W1AW testing" or send "W1AW VVV", where "V" is usually used as a Morse code test signal.

8.3 Interference

Interference, otherwise known as *QRM*, causes severe distortion to this image sent by "slow scan" TV. While harmful interference can be irritating, accidental interference is common, as is the case here.

Interference is caused by "noise" and by "signals." Noise interference is caused by natural sources, such as thunderstorms (atmospheric static is referred to as *QRN*), or by signals unintentionally radiated by appliances, industrial equipment, and computing equipment. The type of interference discussed in this section is caused by signals from other transmitters.

Interference from nearby signals, or *QRM*, is part of the price of frequency flexibility. If hams operated on assigned and evenly-spaced channels, there would be much less interference. The channels would also be frequently overloaded! Interference is not necessarily illegal, just inconvenient. Most interference is manageable. Hams have learned various ways of dealing with QRM starting with the following:

• Common sense and courtesy help avoid many problems
• Be sure to equip your radio with good filters to reject interference
• Develop your operating skills to withstand interference
• Remember that no one owns a frequency — be flexible and plan ahead
• Be aware of other activities, such as special events, DXpeditions, and contests

HARMFUL AND WILLFULL INTERFERENCE

T1A11 — When is willful interference to other amateur radio stations permitted?

T2B08 — Which of the following applies when two stations transmitting on the same frequency interfere with each other?

If a transmission seriously degrades, obstructs, or repeatedly interrupts the communications of a regulated service, that's considered harmful interference. What should you do if harmful interference occurs to your contact? Can you change frequency a little bit or change antenna direction? Common courtesy should prevail but remember that no one has an absolute right to any frequency. **[T2B08]** Be flexible — it's one of ham radio's greatest strengths! What should you do when you cause harmful interference? If it's your fault, apologize, identify and take the necessary steps to reduce interference — change frequency, reduce power, or re-aim your antenna.

Intentionally creating harmful interference is called *willful interference* and is never allowed. **[T1A11]** The interference doesn't have to be aimed at one specific contact or group. Any time communications are deliberately disrupted, that's willful interference. For example, intentionally transmitting spurious signals by overmodulating is willful interference. Luckily, willful interference is pretty rare on the ham bands since most people have the good sense and maturity to not do it.

For More Information

Every ham should make sure to both transmit and receive in a way that minimizes the possibility of causing harmful interference. Reports of interference such as transmitting

---

Don't Be Too Sensitive!

Harmful interference is not necessarily intentional; it may simply be due to an overloaded receiver! Modern receivers are tremendously sensitive, but it's expecting too much of them to run at full sensitivity while rejecting strong signals nearby. Signal processing features such as noise blankers and preamplifiers can create problems where there are none. What is perceived as harmful interference can often be reduced or eliminated with good receiver operating technique

A frequent source of problems is the noise blanker. Most noise blankers operate by sensing short, sharp noise pulses. They look at an entire band, not just what is coming through the narrow signal filters. A strong nearby signal can confuse a noise blanker to the point of nearly shutting down a receiver or causing what sounds like severe splatter over many kilohertz. Unless you have really strong local line or ignition noise, turn off your noise blanker. If the band is full of strong signals, noise blankers are useless or worse.

The RF attenuator can be your biggest friend when dealing with strong nearby signals. It's surprisingly easy for a strong signal to overload a receiver. Overload causes the receiver to create spurious signals and noise up and down the band. Switching on the attenuator cures a surprising number of ailments because your receiver is no longer being overloaded. Remember that the goal is to maximize understandability by increasing the ratio of signal to noise. Try out your attenuator and you may be surprised at how much it cleans up a band!

The RF gain control can make your receiver very sensitive but also susceptible to overloading. Experiment with reducing RF gain to see if it improves your receiver's performance on a busy band. Even during casual operating, turning down the RF gain can dramatically reduce background noise.

Does your receiver have passband tuning, IF shift, variable bandwidth, or similar controls? All those new digital signal processing (DSP) features you paid for can also clean up noise and attenuate low-frequency or high-frequency audio. Read the receiver's manual and learn what these controls do. By effectively using the capabilities of a modern receiver, you will surely find that the band is quieter and nearby signals less disruptive. In fact, you will find yourself making better use of your receiver's controls every day!

off-frequency or generating spurious signals (called splatter and buckshot) should be checked out. When testing or tuning a transmitter, use a dummy load and always keep your test transmissions short.

While harmful interference can be vexing, accidental interference is common. For example, propagation on a band can change due to ionospheric or atmospheric conditions. A signal that wasn't audible a few minutes ago might suddenly become strong enough to disrupt your contact. Changing an antenna direction can allow a previously rejected signal to be heard, or the new heading might transmit a signal toward other stations. Sometimes, an operator will begin listening during a pause in activity and start transmitting thinking the frequency is available. These things happen — you shouldn't expect a perfectly clear frequency!

8.4 Third-Party Communications

T1F07 — Which of the following restrictions apply when a non-licensed person is allowed to speak to a foreign station using a station under the control of a Technician class control operator?

T1F08 — What is meant by the term "Third Party Communications"?

Third party communication can be fun! In this photo, Neil Foster, N4FN, is assisting an unlicensed student during the School Club Roundup contest.

Ham radio is frequently used to send messages, written or not, on behalf of unlicensed persons or organizations. One of the ham radio's oldest activities is relaying messages from station to station until a ham is able to deliver the message to the addressee. This is *third-party communication*. The exact definition of third-party communication is a message from an amateur station control operator to another amateur station control operator on behalf of another person. That "other person" is the "third party." **[T1F08]**

Simplifying the definition, any time that you send or receive information via ham radio on behalf of any unlicensed person or an organization, even if the person is right there in the station with you — that's third-party communications.

Because third-party communications bypass the usual commercial systems, the FCC and other governments do not want the amateur service to become a non-commercial messaging system. So, we have some rules specifically governing third-party communications.

DEFINITIONS AND RULES

Let's start by defining the important aspects of third-party communications:

• The entity on whose behalf the message is sent is the "third party" and the control operators that make the radio contact are the first and second parties. A third party can also be the recipient of a message generated by a ham.

• A licensed amateur capable of being a control operator at either station is not considered a third party.

• The third party need not be present in either station. A message can be taken to a ham station or a ham can transmit speech from a third-party's telephone call over the ham radio — this is called a *phone patch*.

Table 8.1
Third-Party Agreements
The United States has third-party agreements with the following nations.

V2	Antigua/Barbuda
LO-LW	Argentina
VK	Australia
V3	Belize
CP	Bolivia
E7	Bosnia-Herzegovina
PP-PY	Brazil
VE, VO, VY	Canada
CA-CE	Chile
HJ-HK	Colombia
D6	Comoros (Federal Islamic Republic of)
TI, TE	Costa Rica
CM, CO	Cuba
HI	Dominican Republic
J7	Dominica
HC-HD	Ecuador
YS	El Salvador
C5	Gambia, The
9G	Ghana
J3	Grenada
TG	Guatemala
8R	Guyana
HH	Haiti
HQ-HR	Honduras
4X, 4Z	Israel
6Y	Jamaica
JY	Jordan
EL	Liberia
V7	Marshall Islands
XA-XI	Mexico
V6	Micronesia, Federated States of
YN	Nicaragua
HO-HP	Panama
ZP	Paraguay
OA-OC	Peru
DU-DZ	Philippines
VR6	Pitcairn Island
V4	St. Kitts/Nevis
J6	St. Lucia
J8	St. Vincent and the Grenadines
9L	Sierra Leone
ZR-ZU	South Africa
3DA	Swaziland
9Y-9Z	Trinidad/Tobago
TA-TC	Turkey
GB	United Kingdom
CV-CX	Uruguay
YV-YY	Venezuela
4U1ITU	ITU — Geneva
4U1VIC	VIC — Vienna

• The communications transmitted on behalf of the third party need not be written. Spoken words, data, or images can all be third-party communications.

• The third party may participate in transmitting or receiving the message at either station. An unlicensed person in your station sends third-party communications when they speak into the microphone, send Morse code, or type on a keyboard.

• An organization, such as a church or school, can also be a third party.

Here are some examples to help you understand what is and isn't third-party communications:

• A message from one ham to another ham is not third-party communications, whether directly transmitted or relayed by other stations.

• Letting an unlicensed neighbor make a contact under your supervision is third-party communications, even if the contact is short and for demonstration or training purposes.

• Handing the microphone to an unlicensed police operator to talk to a coordinator at the Emergency Operations Center is third-party traffic.

When signals cross borders, the rules change. International third-party communications are restricted to those countries that specifically allow third-party communications with US hams. **Table 8.1** shows which countries have *third-party agreements* with the United States. If the other country isn't on this list, third-party communication with that country is not permitted. **[T1F07]** The ARRL maintains a current Third-Party Agreement List online, as well.

• If you contact a DX station that asks you to pass a message to a family member in your state, doing so would be third-party communications. Check to be sure the DX station's country has a third-party agreement with the US before accepting the message.

• Making a contact to allow a visiting student to talk to his family in South America is third-party communications even if both the student and the family are present at the stations involved. Be sure there is a third-party agreement in place.

8.5 Remote and Automatic Operation

T1E08 — Which of the following is an example of automatic control?
T1E09 — Which of the following is true of remote control operation?
T1E10 — Which of the following is an example of remote control as defined in Part 97?

Many stations, such as repeaters and beacons, operate without a human control operator present to perform control functions. It is also becoming common to operate a station via a link over the internet or phone lines. These two types of operation are specially defined in the rules, but the requirement remains the same — the station must be operated in compliance with FCC rules, no matter where the control point is located.

DEFINITIONS

Local control — a control operator is physically present at the transmitter. This is the situation for nearly all amateur stations, including mobile operation. Any type of station can be locally controlled.

Remote operation — the control point is located away from the transmitter and the control operator adjusts or operates the transmitter indirectly via some kind of *control link*. The control operator must be present at the control point during all transmission. Many stations operate under remote control over an internet link. **[T1E09, T1E10]** Any station can be remotely controlled.

Automatic operation — the station operates completely under the control of devices and procedures that ensure compliance with FCC rules. A control operator is still required, but need not be at the control point when the station is transmitting. Repeaters, beacons and space stations are allowed to be automatically controlled. Digipeaters that relay messages, such as for the APRS network, are also automatically controlled. **[T1E08]**

RESPONSIBILITIES

T1F10 — Who is accountable should a repeater inadvertently retransmit communications that violate the FCC rules?

No matter what type of control is asserted — local, remote, or automatic — the station must operate in compliance with FCC rules at all times. No excuses! Automatic stations might not have a control operator controlling the station at all times, but a control operator must be responsible for the station's operation.

Repeater owners must install the necessary equipment and procedures for automatic control that ensures the repeater operates in compliance with FCC rules. If automatic control results in rule violations, the FCC can require a repeater to be placed on remote control (meaning that a control operator must be present when the repeater is operating). Repeater users are responsible for proper operation via the repeater, however. **[T1F10]**

Because digital protocols are designed to operate automatically, there are special rules for automatic control when using them. Stations using a data mode (including RTTY) may operate under automatic control in certain segments of the HF bands and above 50 MHz as listed in Part 97.221(b). Data stations are the only type of automatically-controlled station allowed to forward third-party communications. (Note that it is okay to pass third-party messages using a repeater.)

8.6 Prohibited Transmissions

T1D06 — What, if any, are the restrictions concerning transmission of language that may be considered indecent or obscene?

Not many types of transmissions are specifically prohibited because amateurs are given wide latitude to communicate within the technical and procedural rules. While other services are very tightly regulated, hams are encouraged to experiment and be flexible. There are limits — here are four types of communications prohibited for reasons that are hopefully obvious:

- Unidentified transmissions — any transmission without an identifying call sign during the required time period.
- False or deceptive signals — transmissions intended to deceive the listener, such as using someone else's call sign.
- False distress or emergency signals — because of the legal requirement to respond, these are taken very seriously by the FCC and other authorities.
- Obscene or indecent speech — avoid controversial topics and expletives. **[T1D06]**

Generally speaking, regular communications that could reasonably be performed through some other radio service are also prohibited. For example, regularly directing boat traffic on a lake should be done on marine VHF channels, not ham radio. Communications in return for some kind of compensation is also prohibited as we discuss below. None of these prohibitions are unreasonable and help keep Amateur Radio a useful and rewarding activity free of commercial intrusion.

BUSINESS COMMUNICATIONS

T1D05 — When may amateur radio operators use their stations to notify other amateurs of the availability of equipment for sale or trade?
T1D08 — In which of the following circumstances may the control operator of an amateur station receive compensation for operating that station?

No transmissions related to conducting your business or employer's activities are permitted. This is, after all, *amateur* radio, and there are plenty of radio services available for commercial activities. However, one's own personal activities don't count as "business" communications. For example, it's perfectly okay for you to use ham radio to talk to your spouse about doing some shopping or to confer about what to pick up at the store. You can order things over the air, as long as you don't do it regularly or as part of your normal income-making activities. It is also okay to advertise equipment for sale as long as it pertains to Amateur Radio and it's not your regular business. **[T1D05]** Here are some examples of acceptable and non-acceptable activities:

OK

- Using a repeater's autopatch to make or change a doctor's appointment
- Advertising a radio on a swap-and-shop net
- Describing your business as part of a casual conversation

NOT OK

- Using a repeater's autopatch to call a business client and change an appointment
- Selling household or sporting goods on a swap-and-shop net
- Regularly selling radio equipment at a profit over the air
- Advertising your professional services over the air

Another broad prohibition is being paid for operating an amateur station. Your employer can set up an emergency amateur station, and even pay you to build it, but you can't be paid for time you spend operating it. This is also true for employees of public safety and medical organizations as you learned when reading about emergency communications.

One exception to the profession or business prohibition is that teachers may use ham radio as part of their classroom instruction. In that case, they can be a control operator of a ham station, but it must be incidental to their job and can't be the majority of their duties. **[T1D08]**

ENCRYPTED TRANSMISSIONS

T1D03 — When is it permissible to transmit messages encoded to hide their meaning?

Amateur Radio is a public form of communication. That is part of the agreement we make in trade for our operating privileges. As a consequence, it is not okay to transmit secret codes or to obscure the content of the transmission if the intent is to prevent others from receiving the information.

Translating information into data for transmission is called *encoding*. Recovering the encoded information is called *decoding*. Reducing the size of a message to transmit it more efficiently is called *compression*. Most forms of encoding and compression are okay because they are done according to a published protocol. Any ham can look up the protocol and develop the appropriate capabilities to receive and decode data sent with that protocol.

Encoding that uses codes or ciphers to hide the meaning of the transmitted message is called *encryption*. Recovering the encrypted information is called *decryption*. Amateurs may not use encryption techniques except for radio control and control transmissions to space stations where interception or unauthorized transmissions could have serious consequences. **[T1D03]**

The difference between encoding and encryption are sometimes not always clear-cut. If a transmission is encoded according to an obscure and little-used protocol, for most hams it might as well be encrypted. But as long as the protocol is published and available to the public, that transmission is acceptable. The general rule to remember is that no ham should be prevented from receiving the communications of another ham because the necessary information has been withheld.

BROADCASTING AND RETRANSMISSION

T1D02 — Under which of the following circumstances may an amateur radio station make one-way transmissions?

T1D04 — Under what conditions is an amateur station authorized to transmit music using a phone emission?

T1D07 — What types of amateur stations can automatically retransmit the signals of other amateur stations?

T1D09 — Under which of the following circumstances are amateur stations authorized to transmit signals related to broadcasting, program production, or news gathering, assuming no other means is available?

T1D10 — What is the meaning of the term "broadcasting" in the FCC rules for the Amateur Radio Service?

Non-hams often refer to ham transmissions as "broadcasting" but that is inaccurate. Broadcasting consists of *one-way transmissions* intended for reception by the general public. **[T1D10]** Hams are not permitted to make this type of transmission except for the purposes of transmitting code practice, information bulletins for other amateurs, or when necessary for emergency communications. **[T1D02]**

The prohibition on broadcasting includes repeating and relaying transmissions from other communications services. Hams are also specifically prohibited from assisting and participating in news gathering by broadcasting organizations. **[T1D09]**

The prohibition against transmission of music (and other entertainment-type material in video and image transmissions) extends to incidental retransmission of music from a nearby radio. This means that you should turn down the car radio or music player when you're using the ham radio! Music can only be rebroadcast as part of an authorized rebroadcast of space station transmissions — a rather unusual circumstance. **[T1D04]**

Retransmitting the signals of another station is also generally prohibited, except when you are relaying messages or digital data from another station. Some types of stations (repeaters, auxiliary stations, and space stations) are allowed to automatically retransmit signals on different frequencies or channels. **[T1D07]**

Chapter 9

Safety

In this chapter, you'll learn about:

- **Working safely with electricity**
- **AC safety grounding and lightning protection**
- **Managing RF current**
- **RF interference (RFI)**
- **RF exposure rules and evaluating your station**
- **Reducing exposure to RF**
- **Tower and antenna installation safety**

When you see the mouse, you'll find more information at www.arrl.org/ham-radio-license-manual

Safety is important enough that you'll encounter questions about it on your exam. We'll begin with basic electrical safety information before moving on to radio. Safety coverage concludes by reviewing some of the mechanical aspects of your radio activities. Depending on your background, some of this material might be a review — nothing wrong with learning about safety from a new perspective!

Remember, this information is not here to frighten you. Radio and electricity are not automatically unsafe. As you learn about radio technology it's a good idea to learn the appropriate safety techniques at the same time.

9.1 Electrical Safety

There is nothing particularly risky about working with electricity, even though you can't see it. Compared to many activities, radio is one of the safest hobbies for people of all ages. Most hams go through an entire lifetime of ham radio without having a serious safety incident. This is because they educate themselves about safety and follow simple rules.

Safety is just as important for radio as it is for house wiring or working on an engine or using power tools. The key to safety is understanding the potential hazards, taking steps to *mitigate* (avoid or eliminate) them, and being able to respond to an injury in the unlikely event that one occurs. By being informed and prepared, your exposure to electrical hazards is greatly reduced.

Working safely with electricity mostly means avoiding contact with it! Most modern ham radio equipment is solid-state and uses low voltage dc power, but the ac line voltage that powers most equipment is dangerous. You may also encounter vacuum tubes and the high voltages they use. Treat electricity with respect.

This section only touches on a few important points about electrical safety. You can learn a lot more by visiting the ARRL's "Safety" page at **www.arrl.org/safety**. There are many articles and resources that will help you build your station with safety in mind.

ELECTRICAL INJURIES

T0A02 — What health hazard is presented by electrical current flowing through the body?

Electrical current through the body can disrupt the electrical function of cells. Currents of more than a few milliamps can also cause involuntary muscle contractions which leads to the jerking and jumping image on TV and in the movies. No joking matter, muscle spasms can cause falls and sudden large movements. The sudden pulling back of an outstretched hand or finger that comes in contact with an energized conductor is a result of arm muscles contracting. Large currents can burn the skin and heat tissue. **Table 9.1** lists some of the effects of current in the body. **[T0A02]**

Avoiding Electrical Hazards

T0A01 — Which of the following is a safety hazard of a 12-volt storage battery?

T0A11 — What kind of hazard might exist in a power supply when it is turned off and disconnected?

If you need to work on equipment with the power on — sometimes there's no way around it — follow these simple safety steps:

• Keep one hand in your pocket while probing or testing energized equipment and wear insulating shoes. This gives current nowhere to flow in or along your body.

• It's also easy to fall into bad habits after working with low-voltage or battery-powered equipment that poses few hazards. Be extra careful when changing to work around higher voltages.

• Never bypass a safety interlock during testing unless specifically instructed to do so. Safety interlocks remove power when access panels, covers, or doors are opened to hazardous areas in equipment. They are intended to prevent unintentionally opening a cabinet or enclosure where dangerous voltages or intense RF may be present.

• Capacitors in a power supply can store charge after a charging circuit is turned off, presenting a hazardous voltage for a long time. This includes small-value capacitors charged to a high voltage! Make sure capacitors are discharged by testing them with a meter or use a *grounding stick* to shunt their charge to ground. **[T0A11]**

• Storage batteries release a lot of energy if shorted, leading to burns, fire, or an explosion. Keep metal objects such as tools and sheet metal clear of battery terminals and avoid working on equipment with the bat-

Table 9.1

Effects of Electric Current in the Human Body

Current	Reaction
Below 1 milliampere	Generally not perceptible
1 milliampere	Faint tingle
5 milliamperes	Slight shock felt; not painful but disturbing. Average individual can let go. Strong involuntary reactions can lead to other injuries.
6-25 milliamperes (women) 9-30 milliamperes (men)	Painful shock, loss of muscular control*; the freezing current or "can't let-go" range.
50-150 milliamperes	Extreme pain, respiratory arrest, severe muscular contractions. Death is possible.
1000-4300 milliamperes	Rhythmic pumping action of the heart ceases. Muscular contraction and nerve damage occur; death likely.
10,000 milliamperes	Cardiac arrest, severe burns; death probable

* If the extensor muscles are excited by the shock, the person may be thrown away from the power source.

Source: W.B. Kouwenhoven, "Human Safety and Electric Shock," Electrical Safety Practices, Monograph, 112, Instrument Society of America, p 93. November 1968.

tery connected. **[T0A01]**

- Remove unnecessary jewelry from your hands because metal is an excellent conductor. Rings can also absorb RF energy and get quite hot in a strong RF field, such as inside an amplifier, filter, or antenna tuner.
- Avoid working alone around energized equipment.
- Remember that electricity moves a *lot* faster than you! Even your briefest touch is plenty long enough for electricity to flow.

For More Information

Electrical hazards can result in two types of injury: shocks and burns. Whenever electricity can flow through any part of your body, both can occur. Shocks and burns can be caused by ac or dc current flowing through the body.

Depending on the voltages present, shocks and burns can range from insignificant to deadly. Voltage is what causes the current to flow but doesn't shock all by itself. Just like in a regular resistor, as the voltage applied across your body varies so does current. While parts of the body such as hair and fingernails are not good conductors, the interior of the body conducts electricity quite well, being mostly salty water.

While any shock can be painful, the most dangerous currents are those that travel through the heart, such as from hand-to-hand or hand-to-foot. Electrical currents of 100 mA or more can disrupt normal heart rhythm. Depending on the resistance of the path taken by the current, voltages as low as 30 volts can cause enough current flow to be dangerous.

Burns caused by dc current or low-frequency ac current are a result of resistance to current in the skin, either through it to the body's interior or along it from point to point. The current creates heat and that's what results in the burn.

Shocks and burns are completely preventable if there is no way for you to come in contact with an energized conductor — simply prevent current flow through the body! Start by never working on "live" equipment unless it is necessary for troubleshooting or testing. Remove, insulate, or otherwise secure loose wires and cables before testing or repairing equipment. Never assume equipment is off or de-energized before beginning your work. Check with a meter or tester first.

The *ARRL Handbook* has an excellent discussion of workbench and station safety. You can also follow the links on the *Ham Radio License Manual* web page and the ARRL's Technical Information Service web page to more articles on all kinds of radio and electrical safety, including first aid for electrical injuries.

Responding to Electrical Injury

If you received a shock while in your station, would others be able to help? The first step in any first aid response to electrical injury is to remove power. Install a clearly-labeled master ON/OFF switch for ac power to your station and workbench. It should be located away from the electrically-powered equipment where you are likely to be. Show your family and friends how to turn off power at the master switch and at your home's circuit-breaker box.

It's also a good idea for all sorts of reasons for you and your family to get CPR training and to learn how to administer first aid for electrical injuries. To learn more about responding to electrical injuries browse the online WebMD first aid section on "electric shock treatment."

Grounding and Bonding for the Radio Amateur

Electrical safety, lightning protection, and managing RF in your station cover more topics than this license study guide can provide. The ARRL book *Grounding and Bonding for the Radio Amateur* will help you understand what you need to do in your station.

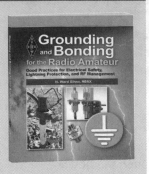

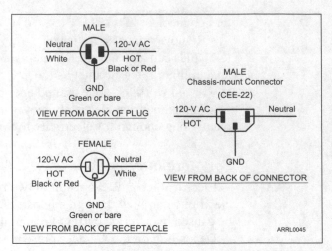

Figure 9.1 — The correct wiring technique for 120 V ac power cords and receptacles in the US. The white wire is neutral and the green wire is the safety ground. The hot wire can be either black or red. These connectors are shown from the back, or wiring side.

AC SAFETY GROUNDING

T0A03 — In the United States, what is connected to the green wire in a three-wire electrical AC plug?

T0A06 — What is a good way to guard against electrical shock at your station?

T0A08 — What safety equipment should always be included in home-built equipment that is powered from 120V AC power circuits?

A large part of electrical safety is to not create hazards in the first place! This is why the National Electrical Code and your local building codes were created — to prevent common electrical hazards. A home wired "to code" has properly sized outlets and wiring and a *safety ground* to help prevent shocks.

The safety ground (also known as *equipment ground* and *green-wire ground*) is a connection to the power system's ground reference connection in your main electrical service box. It provides a safe path for current in case of an accidental short-circuit between either the hot or neutral wires and an appliance's metal enclosure or *chassis*. The ground connection causes a fuse or circuit breaker to remove power from the equipment.

Most ham stations don't require new wiring and can operate with complete safety when powered from your home's ac wiring. That is, as long as you follow simple guidelines: **[T0A06]**

• Use three-wire power cords and plugs for all ac-powered equipment.

• Make sure all of your equipment has a connection to the ac safety ground.

• Use ground fault circuit interrupter (GFCI) circuit breakers or circuit breaker outlets.

• Verify ac wiring is done properly by using an ac circuit tester.

Table 9.2
Current-Carrying Capability of Some Common Wire Sizes

Copper Wire Size (AWG)	Allowable Current (A)	Max Fuse or Circuit Breaker (A)
6	55	50
8	40	40
10	30	30
12	25 (20)[1]	20
14	20 (15)[1]	15

[1]The National Electrical Code limits the fuse or circuit breaker size (and as such, the maximum allowable circuit load current) to 15 A for #14 AWG copper wire and to 20 A for #12 AWG copper wire conductors.

- Never replace a fuse or circuit breaker with one of a larger size.
- Don't overload single outlets.

If you do decide to run new wiring for your station as it grows, either have a licensed electrician do the wiring or inspect it. Be sure to follow the US standard of hot — black wire (occasionally red); neutral — white wire; safety or equipment ground — green or bare wire shown in **Figure 9.1**. **[T0A03]** Use cable and wire sufficiently rated for the expected current load as shown in **Table 9.2**. Use the proper size fuses and circuit breakers. If you build your own equipment and power it from the 120 V or 240 V ac lines, be sure fuses or circuit breakers are installed in series with the hot conductor or conductors. **[T0A08]**

LIGHTNING PROTECTION

T0A07 — Which of these precautions should be taken when installing devices for lightning protection in a coaxial cable feed line?

T0A09 — What should be done to all external ground rods or earth connections?

T0B10 — Which of the following is true when installing grounding conductors used for lightning protection?

T0B11 — Which of the following establishes grounding requirements for an amateur radio tower or antenna?

T0B12 — Which of the following is good practice when installing ground wires on a tower for lightning protection?

Even though amateur antennas and towers are generally struck by lightning no more frequently than tall trees or other nearby structures, it is wise to take some precautionary steps. This is especially true for stations in areas with frequent severe weather and lightning. Lightning protection is intended to provide fire protection for your home, since most of the damage to a home resulting from a lightning strike is from fire.

Starting at your antennas, all towers, masts, and antenna mounts should be grounded according to your local building and electrical codes. **[T0B11]** These connections are made at the tower base, or in the case of roof mounts, though a large-diameter wire to a ground rod. Ground connections should be as short and direct as possible — avoid sharp bends. **[T0B10, T0B12]** Where cables and feed lines enter the house, use lightning arrestors grounded to a common plate that is in turn connected to a nearby external ground such as a ground rod. **[T0A07]** All ground rods and earth connections must be bonded together with heavy wire, as well. **[T0A09]** *The ARRL Ham Radio License Manual's* web page lists links to resources on lightning protection.

For More Information

When lightning is anticipated, the best protection is to disconnect all cables outside the house and unplug equipment power cords inside the house. This interrupts the lightning's path to get to ground. In fact, it's not a bad idea to disconnect both power and phone cords to household appliances and long network and signal cables to your computing equipment. If you think you will unplug your equipment frequently, it might be a good idea to use or make power strips so that you can unplug many pieces of equipment with a single cable. Don't just turn them off — lightning jumps across switches quite easily. Physically unplug the power cable.

Determine whether your renter's or homeowner's insurance will cover you for damage from a lightning strike and whether the presence of antennas modifies that coverage. Your insurance agent will be able to help you determine the exact coverage and whether any special riders or amendments are needed. You may want to investigate the equipment insurance available to ARRL members, as well.

Regardless of how much protection you install on your antenna system, operating during a thunderstorm is a bad idea. Even a nearby strike can create a voltage surge of thousands of volts in a power or phone line, causing equipment damage or setting the house on fire!

9.2 Managing RF in Your Station

T4A08 — Which of the following conductors provides the lowest impedance to RF signals?
T7B11 — What is a symptom of RF feedback in a transmitter or transceiver?

Your amateur station is close to the transmitting antenna. As a result, the station wiring, feed lines, power connections, and other cables all pick up RF from your transmitted signal. The feed lines and cables are in turn connected to your equipment enclosures and the connections between them. The resulting current is called *common-mode* because it flows on all wires and enclosures.

It is not practical to "ground" this RF current in the same way as for ac power and lightning protection. Instead of trying to create a "zero volts" point, the best approach for amateurs is to *bond* all of the equipment together. This keeps all of your equipment at the same voltage so that RF current does not flow between the different pieces.

RF current on cables and enclosures can cause audio distortion, erratic operation of computer equipment, and occasionally RF "burns" where the RF voltage happens to be high. (RF burns rarely cause injury.) It is far more likely for RF current flowing in sensitive audio cables or data cables to interfere with your station's normal function, just as your strong transmitter signal might be picked up and detected by a neighbor's telephone or audio system. "RF feedback" via a microphone cable can cause distorted transmitted audio, for example. **[T7B11]**

Each station is a little different, so you will have to come up with a solution that works for you. Low-power VHF/UHF stations usually have few RF problems. **Figure 9.2** shows the general idea. Here are some guidelines for managing RF:

• Bond all metal equipment enclosures to a common RF ground bus such as piece of copper pipe, heavy wire, or a sheet of flashing.

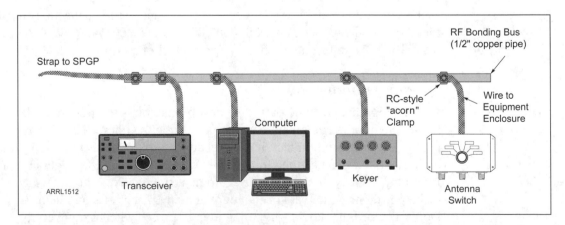

Figure 9.2 — An effective station RF ground bus keeps all equipment bonded together electrically with short, low-impedance connections. The bus is made of material such as copper pipe, flashing, or even heavy copper wire. The bus is then connected to a nearby ground rod with strap or wire. (SPGP in the drawing stands for *single-point ground panel*. This is the point at which all antenna system feed lines and control lines are brought together to share a common ground connection.)

• Use short, wide conductors such as copper flashing or strap or heavy solid wire (#8 AWG or larger). Solid strap is best because it presents the lowest impedance to RF. **[T4A08]**

• Keep all connections, straps and wires as short and direct as possible.

• Connect the ground bus to your ac safety ground and any earth connections for lightning protection.

9.3 RF Interference (RFI)

As more and more electronic devices and electrical appliances are put in use, interference between them and ham radio, called *radio frequency interference* (RFI), becomes more commonplace. RFI can occur in either direction — to or from the Amateur Radio equipment. Interference becomes more severe with higher power or closer spacing to the interference's source. The ARRL's Technical Information Service website (**www. arrl.org/radio-frequency-interference-rfi**) and *The ARRL RFI Book* provide information on all kinds of RFI and the means to correct it.

FILTERS

T4A09 — Which of the following could you use to cure distorted audio caused by RF current on the shield of a microphone cable?

T7B04 — Which of the following is a way to reduce or eliminate interference from an amateur transmitter to a nearby telephone?

Filters are an important part of radio and nowhere are they as important as in preventing and eliminating RFI. Filters are used both to prevent unwanted signals from being radiated in the first place and to keep unwanted signals from being received. To select the correct type of filter, you have to know the nature of the interfering signals. **Figure 9.3** shows how filters are applied for several common types of RFI.

AC power line filters keep RF signals from passing into or out of equipment via the hot

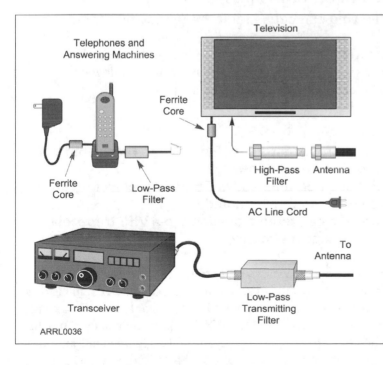

Figure 9.3 — Filters are used in a number of different ways to reduce interference. Telephone or answering machine interference is often cured with a ferrite core placed on the power supply cable and a low-pass filter on the phone line. Both prevent RF signals from getting to the phone's electronics. A high-pass filter in the antenna feed line often prevents strong amateur signals from entering the TV receiver and causing overload. Ferrite cores on the power cable keep RF from entering the TV by that route. A low-pass filter on the output of a transceiver prevents weak harmonics from being picked up by a radio or TV as interference. In difficult cases you may need a notch filter (not shown) tuned to the offending signal's frequency.

ARRL0036

Ferrite — The RFI Buster

One of the most useful materials in dealing with RFI is the *ferrite core*. Ferrite is a ceramic magnetic material — you may have used ferrite magnets. The type of ferrite used for RFI suppression is specially designed to absorb RF energy over a broad frequency range, such as HF or VHF. Ferrite is available in many different *mixes* of slightly different composition that absorbs best in a particular range.

One popular form of ferrite is the snap-core shown in the figure. The actual ferrite is a rectangular block with a large hole in it, sawn in half. A plastic case with a snap holds the two pieces together. This allows cords or cables to be wound on the core even if they already have connectors attached, such as power cords or video cables.

Ferrite is available as round *cores* (toroids), rods and beads shown in **Figure 9.4**. Wires or cables are then wound on or passed through the ferrite forms. Beads are made large enough that they can be slipped over coaxial cables and secured with tape or a locking wire-tie. A wire or cable wound on such a ferrite core forms an RF choke.

Figure 9.4 — Ferrite is a ceramic magnetic material used to make choke filters for RFI suppression. It is available in many different forms: rings (toroids), rods, and beads. Cables can be passed through or wound on these cores to prevent RF signals from flowing along their outside surfaces.

and neutral conductors of the ac power connection. They reject all signals with frequencies greater than a few kHz. *Low-pass* and *high-pass filters* are installed in antenna feed lines to reject interfering RF signals. Low-pass RF filters connected at the modular jack are the best way to reduce RFI to telephones. **[T7B04]**

RF choke or *common-mode* filters made of *ferrite* material are used to reduce RF currents flowing on unshielded wires such as speaker cables, ac power cords, and telephone modular cords. *Ferrite chokes* are also used to reduce RF current on the outside of shielded audio, microphone, and computer cables. **[T4A09]**

INTERFERENCE FROM AMATEUR TRANSMISSIONS

T7B03 — Which of the following can cause radio frequency interference?

The most common causes of RFI from your transmissions are *fundamental overload*, *harmonics*, and *spurious emissions*. **[T7B03]** They are discussed in the following sections. Each has a different effect and is eliminated by different techniques.

Fundamental Overload

T7B02 — What would cause a broadcast AM or FM radio to receive an amateur radio transmission unintentionally?

T7B05 — How can overload of a non-amateur radio or TV receiver by an amateur signal be reduced or eliminated?

T7B07 — Which of the following can reduce overload to a VHF transceiver from a nearby FM broadcast station?

Very strong signals may overwhelm a receiver's ability to reject them. This is called *fundamental overload*. Overload usually results in severe interference to all channels of a broadcast TV, AM, or FM receiver. Consumer equipment is often unable to reject strong signals outside the bands it is intended to receive. **[T7B02]** Similarly, an amateur may hear noise across an entire band when the strong signal is present. If adding attenuation (either by turning on a receiver's attenuator or removing an antenna) causes the interference to disappear, it's probably caused by overload.

A *high-pass filter* can be connected at the antenna input of FM and TV receivers as shown in Figure 9.3 to reject strong lower-frequency signals from amateur HF signals. [T7B05] (Do not use feed line filters of any sort in a cable TV feed line.) A *band-reject* or *notch filter* can be used to reduce interference from amateur VHF or UHF signals. [T7B07] A filter at the amateur's transmitter will not solve overload problems — the problem lies within the receiver.

Both consumer and amateur receivers can experience overload from nearby broadcast stations. *Broadcast-reject* filters attenuate signals from nearby AM, FM, or TV broadcast stations. The type of signal to be rejected must be specified when purchasing the filter since those stations transmit on different frequencies.

HARMONICS, SPURIOUS EMISSIONS, AND LEAKAGE

T7B12 — What should be the first step to resolve cable TV interference from your ham radio transmission?

Due to minor imperfections, every transmitter's RF output signal contains weak *harmonics* of the desired output signal (see the chapter on Radio Signals and Fundamentals) and other *spurious emissions* that can cause interference to nearby equipment. In extreme cases, a misadjusted or defective transmitter can generate strong interfering signals. To prevent harmonics from being radiated by your station, a low-pass or band-pass filter must be installed at the transmitter's connection to the antenna feed line as shown in Figure 9.3.

Another possible source of interference, both to hams and to cable TV customers, is *leakage*. Leakage refers to signals from inside the cable TV feed line getting out. This can cause interference to amateur signals, usually in the 2 meter band. Leakage also refers to external signals getting into the cable TV feed line. An amateur transmission on a frequency used by the cable system can cause interference if it gets into the feed line. The most common cause of leakage in either direction is faulty coaxial connectors on the cable feed line. They might be improperly installed or simply loose. Be sure the connectors are installed correctly and attached tightly. [T7B12]

GOOD PRACTICES IN YOUR STATION

T6D12 — Which of the following is a common reason to use shielded wire?
T7B06 — Which of the following actions should you take if a neighbor tells you that your station's transmissions are interfering with their radio or TV reception?

Regardless of the source, you can reduce or eliminate much interference by making sure your own station follows good amateur practices for grounding and filtering.

• Start by making sure your station is in good working order with appropriate grounding, filtering, and good quality connections, especially for the RF signals.

• Use shielded wire and shielded cables to prevent coupling with unwanted signals and undesired radiation. [T6D12] Be sure to connect the shield properly, such as to the outside of metal equipment enclosures.

• Eliminate interference to your own home appliances and televisions first. Demonstrating that you aren't interfering with your own devices is a good start. Eliminating interference at home is considered good practice! [T7B06]

• Eliminate sources of interference in your own home, such as worn out motors, poorly filtered power supplies, and so forth. Not only will it make operating more pleasant, it will be much easier to determine whether noise is caused elsewhere.

RFI AND NEIGHBORS

T7B08 — What should you do if something in a neighbor's home is causing harmful interference to your amateur station?

You may eventually encounter a situation where your signals are causing interference to a neighbor, or a device the neighbor owns is causing interference to you. Diplomacy is often required, even though your transmissions may not be at fault. Techniques for dealing with RFI to or from others is discussed on the ARRL's RFI Resources website listed previously.

Remember these simple suggestions:

• Start by making sure it's really your transmissions that are causing the problem. It's not unknown for the mere presence of an antenna to generate a report of interference, deserved or not!

• Offer to help determine the nature of interference — detection, overload, or harmonics. Knowing the cause leads to solutions.

On other occasions, you may be receiving harmful interference from equipment in the neighbor's home. Start with the following steps: **[T7B08]**

• Make sure your station meets the standards of good amateur practices.

• You can offer to help determine the source of interference. Severe noise often indicates defective equipment that could be a safety or fire hazard.

• You may have to politely explain to the neighbor that FCC rules prohibit them from using a device that causes harmful interference.

Be diplomatic in dealing with your neighbors, even though it may be their responsibility to deal with interference to or from their devices. They are probably unaware of FCC rules!

PART 15 RULES

T7B09 — What is a Part 15 device?

Part 15 of the FCC's rules governs the responsibilities of owners of unlicensed devices that use low-power RF communications or radiate low-power signals on frequencies used by licensed services, such as Amateur Radio. Examples include cordless phones or wireless data transceivers and power lines, electric fences or computers. These are called *Part 15 devices*. **[T7B09]**

Reducing Part 15 to its basic principles:

• An unlicensed device permitted under Part 15 or an unintentional radiator may not cause interference to a licensed communications station, such as to an Amateur Radio station. Its owner must prevent it from causing such interference or stop operating it.

• An unlicensed device permitted under Part 15 must accept interference caused by a properly operating licensed communications station, such as from an Amateur Radio station.

What this means is that as long as your station is operating properly under the FCC's rules, then your operation is protected against interference by and complaints of interference to unlicensed equipment. If your signals are interfering with a television or telephone, it is the TV or telephone owner's responsibility to eliminate it, even though you may offer to assist them. Similarly, it is the owner's responsibility to eliminate interference caused by their device, even with assistance from you. In such cases, you can see the advantages of being federally licensed! These rules are printed in the owner's manual for all unlicensed devices and are available on the FCC website.

Remember that the FCC is a last resort for everyone. Before getting involved, the FCC will require that all parties to take all reasonable steps to identify and mitigate the effects of the interference.

9.4 RF Exposure

T0C01 — What type of radiation are VHF and UHF radio signals?
T0C05 — Why do exposure limits vary with frequency?
T0C07 — What could happen if a person accidentally touched your antenna while you were transmitting?
T0C12 — How does RF radiation differ from ionizing radiation (radioactivity)?

In recent years, there has been a lot of discussion about whether there are health and safety hazards from exposure to electromagnetic radiation (EMR). Many studies have been done at both power line frequencies (50 and 60 Hz) and RF (both shortwave and mobile phone frequencies). No link has been established between exposure to low-level EMR and health risks, including those frequencies used by amateurs.

RF radiation is not the same as *ionizing radiation* from radioactivity because the energy in signals at radio frequencies is far too low to cause an electron to leave an atom (ionize) and therefore cannot cause genetic damage. **[T0C12]** With its relatively low frequency, RF energy is *non-ionizing radiation*. **[T0C01]**

Nevertheless, high levels of RF can cause heating of the body. It is prudent to avoid unnecessary exposure to high levels of RF. The FCC regulations set limits on the *Maximum Permissible Exposure* (MPE) from radio transmitters of any sort. To abide by these rules without requiring expensive testing, hams are expected to evaluate their stations to see if their operation has the potential to exceed MPE levels. The evaluation process is covered later in this section. The ARRL's *RF Exposure and You* contains a detailed treatment of RF exposure rules and safety techniques. Additional resources are available on the ARRL website (**www.arrl.org/rf-exposure**).

The only demonstrated hazards from exposure to RF energy are *thermal effects* (heating). *Biological* (athermal) effects have not been demonstrated at amateur frequencies and power levels. RF energy can only cause injury to the human body if the combination of frequency and power causes excessive energy to be absorbed. Measurable heating occurs only for very strong fields or in fields that originate very close to the body.

RF safety techniques involve making sure that persons are not exposed to high-strength fields in one of two ways:

• Preventing access to locations where strong fields are present, such as near antennas.

• Making sure strong fields are not created in or directed to areas where people might be present.

Heating as a result of exposure to RF fields is caused by the body absorbing RF energy. Absorption occurs because the RF energy causes the molecules to vibrate at the same frequency. The energy of the vibrations is dissipated within the body as heat. The stronger the field, the more the molecules vibrate and the more heating of the body's tissues results. Absorption also varies with frequency because the body absorbs more RF energy at some frequencies than others. **[T0C05]** The total amount of heating then depends on both the RF field's intensity and frequency and is called the *specific absorption rate* or SAR.

RF burns caused by touching or coming close to conducting surfaces with a high RF voltage present are also an effect of heating. While these are sometimes painful, they are rarely hazardous. RF burns can be eliminated by proper bonding techniques or by preventing access to an antenna. **[T0C07]**

Power Density

The intensity of an RF field is called *power density*. Power density is the amount of energy per unit of area. The most common way of stating power density is in milliwatts per square centimeter (mW/cm²). The power density of an RF field is highest near antennas and in the directions where antennas have the most gain. Power density can also be very high inside transmitting equipment.

Increasing transmitter power increases power density everywhere around an antenna to the same degree that transmitter power increased. Increasing distance from an antenna lowers power density in proportion to the square of the distance from the antenna. For example, at twice the distance from an antenna, power density is divided by four. Controlling these two factors, power and distance, forms the basis for amateur RF safety.

EXPOSURE LIMITS

T0C02 — Which of the following frequencies has the lowest value for Maximum Permissible Exposure limit?

Table 9.3

Maximum Permissible Exposure (MPE) Limits

Controlled Exposure (6-Minute Average)

Frequency Range (MHz)	Power Density (mW/cm²)
0.3-3.0	(100)*
3.0-30	(900/f²)*
30-300	1.0
300-1500	f/300
1500-100,000	5

Uncontrolled Exposure (30-Minute Average)

Frequency Range (MHz)	Magnetic Field Power Density (mW/cm²)
0.3-1.34	(100)*
1.34-30	(180/f²)*
30-300	0.2
300-1500	f/1500
1500-100,000	1.0

f = frequency in MHz
* = Plane-wave equivalent power density

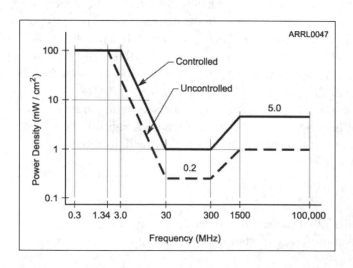

Safe levels of exposure based on demonstrated hazards have been established by the FCC. These are the *Maximum Permissible Exposure* (MPE) levels. Because the *specific absorption rate* (SAR) varies with frequency, so does the MPE as shown in **Figure 9.5** and **Table 9.3**. Where SAR is high, MPE is low.

SAR depends on the size of the body or body part affected and is highest where the body and body parts are naturally resonant. An adult-size body is resonant at about 35 MHz if the person is grounded and 70 MHz if they are not grounded. Body parts are resonant at higher frequencies (smaller wavelengths). For example, an adult's head is resonant at the much higher frequency of 400 MHz.

Above and below the ranges of highest absorption, the body responds less and less to the RF energy, just like an antenna responds poorly to signals away from its natural resonant frequency. Frequencies at which the body has the highest SAR are from 30 to 1500 MHz. These are the regions on the MPE graph where the limits for exposure are the lowest. For example, when comparing MPE for amateur bands at 3.5, 50, 440 and 1296 MHz, you can see that MPE is lowest at 50 MHz and highest at 3.5 MHz. **[T0C02]**

Controlled and Uncontrolled Environments

You'll notice in Figure 9.5 that there are two sets of lines, one called *controlled* and the other *uncontrolled*. These refer to the type of

Figure 9.5 — Maximum Permissible Exposure (MPE) limits vary with frequency because the body responds differently to energy at different frequencies. The controlled and uncontrolled limits refer to the environment in which people are exposed to the RF energy.

environments in which the exposure to RF fields takes place.

• People in controlled environments are aware of their exposure and can take the necessary steps to minimize it.

• People in uncontrolled environments are not aware of their exposure, such as in areas open to the general public or your neighbor's property.

The FCC has determined that the higher controlled-environment limits generally apply to amateur operators and members and guests in their immediate households, provided that they are aware of RF fields being used. If this is the case, the controlled-environment limits apply to your home and property — wherever you control physical access.

AVERAGING AND DUTY CYCLE

T0C10 — Why is duty cycle one of the factors used to determine safe RF radiation exposure levels?

T0C11 — What is the definition of duty cycle during the averaging time for RF exposure?

T0C13 — If the averaging time for exposure is 6 minutes, how much power density is permitted if the signal is present for 3 minutes and absent for 3 minutes rather than being present for the entire 6 minutes?

Since the effects from RF exposure are related to heating and take place over many seconds, the MPE limits are based on *averages*, not *peak* exposure. This allows exposure to be averaged over fixed time intervals.

• The averaging period is 6 minutes for controlled environments.

• The averaging period is 30 minutes for uncontrolled environments.

The difference in averaging periods reflects the difference in how long people are expected to be present and exposed. People are assumed less likely to stay in an uncontrolled environment receiving continuous exposure, so the averaging period is much longer.

During the averaging period, a transmitter may only be generating RF for a fraction of the time. For most amateur contacts, the transmitter output is no more than 50% of the time and usually much less. This pattern lowers the *duty cycle* of the emissions. Duty cycle is the ratio of the transmitted signal's on-the-air time to the total operating time during the measurement period and has a maximum of 100%. Stated simply, duty cycle is the percentage of time a transmitter is transmitting. **[T0C11]** (*Duty factor* is the same as duty cycle expressed as a fraction, instead of percent, for example 0.25 instead of 25%.)

Since duty cycle affects the average power level of transmissions, it must be considered when evaluating exposure. **[T0C10]** The lower the duty cycle (less transmitting), the higher the transmitter output can be and still have an average value within the exposure limits. For example, what is the result if a transmitted signal in a controlled environment is present for 3 minutes and then absent for the remaining 3 minutes of the averaging period? Because the signal is only present for ½ of the time (50% duty cycle), the signal power can be twice as high and still have the same average power as it would if transmitted continuously with a duty cycle of 100%. **[T0C13]**

EVALUATING EXPOSURE

T0C03 — What is the maximum power level that an amateur radio station may use at VHF frequencies before an RF exposure evaluation is required?

T0C04 — What factors affect the RF exposure of people near an amateur station antenna?

T0C06 — Which of the following is an acceptable method to determine that your station complies with FCC RF exposure regulations?

T0C09 — How can you make sure your station stays in compliance with RF safety regulations?

Table 9.4

Power Thresholds for RF Exposure Evaluation

Band	Power (W)
160 meters	500
80	500
40	500
30	425
20	225
17	125
15	100
12	75
10	50
6	50
2	50
1.25	50
70 cm	70
33	150
23	200
13	250
SHF (all bands)	250
EHF (all bands)	250

According to FCC rules, all fixed stations must perform an exposure evaluation. (Mobile and handheld transceivers are exempt.) There are three ways of making this evaluation. By far the most common evaluation uses the techniques outlined in the FCC's OET Bulletin 65 (OET stands for *Office of Engineering Technology*). **[T0C06]** This method uses tables and simple formulas to evaluate whether your station has the potential of causing an exposure hazard.

You could also obtain RF power density instrumentation and actually measure the power density of your transmissions. It is also acceptable to make computer models of your station and use those results. Both of these methods are rarely used due to the expense or effort required.

Once you've done an evaluation, you don't need to re-evaluate unless you change equipment in your station that affects average output power, such as increasing transmitter power or antenna gain. You'll also need to re-evaluate if you add a new frequency band. **[T0C09]**

Before you start, check to see if your station is exempt from the evaluation requirement. If the transmitter power (using PEP) to the antenna is less than the levels shown in **Table 9.4** on the frequencies at which you operate, then no evaluation is required! **[T0C03]** The FCC has determined that the risk of exposure from these power levels is too small to create an exposure risk. So, if you have a 25-watt VHF/UHF mobile rig or a 5-watt handheld transceiver, there's no need for an evaluation of any sort.

If you do need to do an evaluation, don't despair. It's not as complicated as it seems. The *Ham Radio License Manual* web page lists resources that make the job a lot easier, such as on-line exposure calculators and pre-calculated tables you can use for common antennas. You'll need information on the RF signal's frequency and power level, distance from the antenna and the antenna's radiation pattern. **[T0C04]**

EXPOSURE SAFETY MEASURES

T0C08 — Which of the following actions might amateur operators take to prevent exposure to RF radiation in excess of FCC-supplied limits?

What if you do find a potential hazard? What if you are just beginning to build a station and want to avoid creating a hazard? You have plenty of options as shown in **Figure 9.6**:

• Locate antennas away from where people can get close to them and away from property lines. This is always a good idea since touching an antenna energized with even low-power signals can result in an RF burn. **[T0C08]**

• Raise the antenna. This is another good idea because it usually improves your signal in distant locations, as well.

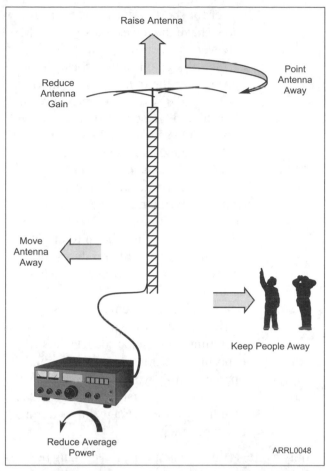

Figure 9.6 — There are many ways to reduce RF exposure to nearby people. Whatever lowers the power density in areas where people are will work. Raising the antenna will even benefit your signal strength to other stations as it lowers power density on the ground!

• If you have a beam antenna, avoid pointing the antenna where people are likely to be.

• Use a lower gain antenna to reduce radiated power density or reduce transmitter power. You may find that you're able to make contacts just as well with less power or gain.

• Limit the average power of your transmissions by transmitting for shorter periods or even using a mode with a lower duty cycle.

Any of these techniques will reduce RF exposure to you and your neighbors. You'll likely be able to find a combination that has a minimum effect on your operations yet still makes sure you are within the MPE limits.

Even though emissions from mobile and handheld transmitters are exempt from evaluation, there are some good ways to minimize unnecessary RF exposure:

• Place mobile antennas on the roof or trunk of the car to maximize shielding of the passengers.

• Use a remote microphone to hold a handheld transceiver away from your head while transmitting.

RF exposure safety measures are easy to apply and part of good amateur practices. By understanding the reason for exposure limits and how to mitigate RF exposure hazards, you will be able to make more informed choices about designing, building and operating your station.

For More Information

Some modes have lower average power than others as illustrated in **Figure 9.7**. For example, while sending Morse code (CW), the transmitter is off between the individual dots and dashes. SSB signals only reach peak

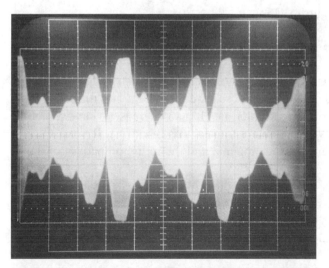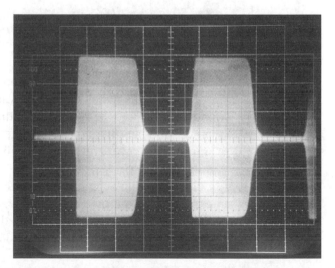

Figure 9.7 — The SSB signal on the left and the Morse code signal on the right both have the same peak power, but the average power of the SSB signal is lower.

Table 9.5
Operating Duty Cycle of Modes Commonly Used by Amateurs

Mode	Duty Cycle	Notes
Conversational SSB	20%	1
Conversational SSB	40%	2
SSB AFSK	100%	
SSB SSTV	100%	
Voice AM, 50% modulation	50%	3
Voice AM, 100% modulation	25%	
Voice AM, no modulation	100%	
Voice FM	100%	
Digital FM	100%	
Analog ATV, video image	60%	
Analog ATV, video black screen	80%	
Digital ATV	100%	
Conversational CW	40%	
Carrier	100%	4
Digital (PSK31, RTTY)	100%	

Note 1: Includes voice characteristics and syllabic duty cycle. No speech processing.

Note 2: Includes voice characteristics and syllabic duty cycle. Heavy speech processor employed.

Note 3: Full-carrier, double-sideband modulation, referenced to PEP. Typical for voice speech. Can range from 25% to 100%, depending on modulation.

Note 4: A full carrier is commonly used for tune-up purposes.

power for short periods at voice peaks and so have the lowest duty cycle. FM, however, is a constant-power mode and so the signal is continuously at full power when the transmitter is on. The *operating duty cycle* for typical uses of each mode (also called the *emission duty cycle*) is shown in **Table 9.5**.

Because most amateur operation is intermittent, the time spent transmitting on the air is low. For example, during a roundtable contact among three stations, each is likely to be transmitting only one-third or 33% of the time. This further reduces average exposure, regardless of the mode being used.

For a given peak envelope power (PEP), an emission with a lower operating duty cycle produces less RF exposure. PEP multiplied by the mode's operating duty cycle and the fraction of the time spent transmitting gives the resulting overall average power during the exposure period.

Average power = PEP × operating duty cycle × (time transmitting / averaging period)

For example, let's say that your 100-watt transmitter is generating conversational SSB without speech processing. Table 9.5 shows an operating duty cycle of 20% for that mode. During your operating period you transmit for 1 minute out of every 3. Your average power during the evaluation period is:

100 watts × 20% for conversational SSB × (1 min / 3 min) = 100 × 0.2 × 0.33 = 6.6 watts

During a 2 meter net as net control, using your 50-watt VHF FM transmitter, you transmit and listen for equal periods. Your average power is:

50 watts × 100% for FM × 50% on/off = 25 watts

Effect of Antenna Gain

There is one additional effect that has to be taken into account. As you've learned, beam antennas focus radiated power toward one direction, creating gain. Gain has the effect of increasing your average power in the preferred direction. (It also decreases your average power in other directions.) This means that there are four factors that affect RF exposure: transmitter power and frequency, distance to the antenna, and the radiation pattern of the antenna.

If you use an antenna with gain, you will need to include the effect of gain in your exposure evaluations. For example, if your antenna has 6 dBi of gain, corresponding to a four-fold increase in power radiated in the preferred direction, you would multiply your average power by four when calculating RF exposure in the antenna's forward direction.

RF Exposure Evaluation

The general procedure consists of several steps:

• Start with the average power from each transmitter on each band. Use the same process discussed above, starting with full PEP and then applying the various corrections for mode and patterns of use.

• If you have long coaxial feed lines, you may want to subtract feed line losses, particularly in the 30 to 1500 MHz frequency range.

• Then use the ARRL tables to include the effects of antenna gain and height.

• Finally, use the tables to determine the distance required from the antenna to comply with MPE limits.

The process is the same whether you do it manually using tables or online with a web page calculator. Both require the same information from you about your station and use the same tables.

Don't forget to do the evaluation for each frequency band and antenna used on that band. You can save yourself some work by performing the evaluation for the highest average power, mode, and usage on each antenna. That will show the minimum or worst-case separation requirements under all circumstances for that frequency and antenna.

Once the evaluation is complete, compare the minimum separation with your actual installation. Chances are, you'll find no hazard exists — most stations are simply not capable of causing a health hazard.

9.5 Mechanical Safety

Just as workshop safety is important, there are plenty of mechanical aspects to Amateur Radio that generate their own safety concerns. Amateurs have been building and installing radios and antennas for more than 100 years, developing a large body of knowledge about the safe way to do things. The following sections provide some guidelines as you build and maintain your radio equipment.

Most importantly, follow the manufacturer's directions and recommendations. For example, how tight should guy wires be? The tower manufacturer will tell you — do what they say to do. This holds true for all types of installation, antenna, and tower work.

PUTTING UP ANTENNAS AND SUPPORTS

T0B04 — Which of the following is an important safety precaution to observe when putting up an antenna tower?

T0B06 — What is the minimum safe distance from a power line to allow when installing an antenna?

T0B08 — What is considered to be a proper grounding method for a tower?

T0B09 — Why should you avoid attaching an antenna to a utility pole?

T0B13 — What is the purpose of a safety wire through a turnbuckle used to tension guy lines?

Before you can start, you should be sure your plans satisfy any local zoning codes or covenants or restrictions in your deed or lease. If you are putting up a very tall tower (200 feet or higher) or the antenna will be near an airport, check the rules about maximum height of structures near an airport. The Federal Aviation Administration (FAA) and FCC have specific regulations about towers in these locations.

Above all, follow the manufacturer's directions — they want you to have a successful experience with their product and often provide useful information in product manuals and on their websites. If you haven't put up an antenna before, enlist the help of a more experienced ham.

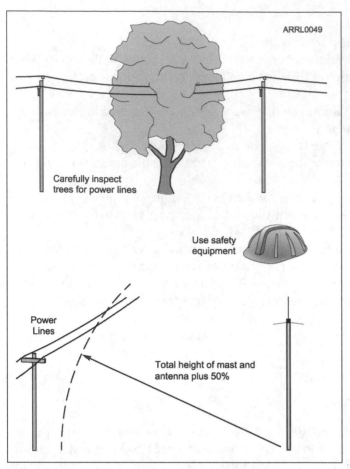

Figure 9.8 — Antennas or supports falling onto a power line can result in electrocution. Take extra care in locating and erecting your antenna to avoid a deadly accident!

When you're ready to put up the antenna, look carefully at the area around your antenna and any supporting structures it requires. Of course, people should not be able to come in contact with the antenna accidentally. If an antenna is to be mounted at ground level, consider surrounding it with a wooden or plastic fence. If you're installing a wire antenna, make sure the feed line does not sag below head height to snag an unwary passerby. If you're in a rural area, be sure that deer or other antlered animals won't catch the feed line with their headgear.

Power lines are the enemy of antenna installers. Place all antennas and feed lines well clear of power lines, including the utility service drop to your home. **[T0B04] Figure 9.8** illustrates the idea. Be sure that if the any part of the antenna or support structure falls, it cannot fall onto power lines. A good guideline is to separate the antenna from the nearest power line by 150% of total height of tower or mast plus antenna — a minimum of 10 feet of clearance during a fall is a must. **[T0B06]** Never attach an antenna or guy wire to a utility pole, since a mechanical failure could result in contact with high-voltage power lines. **[T0B09]**

Trees are often used as wire supports. If you decide to throw or shoot a supporting line through or over trees, be sure the projected flight path is completely safe and clear of people and power lines. A line that breaks or snags can whip or rebound, often with a lot of energy, so wear protective gloves and goggles.

Once your antenna is in place, secure the feed line with tape or plastic wire ties. Keep all supporting guy lines above head height, if possible. Where someone can walk into guy wires, surround the guy anchor point with a fence or flag the wires with colored warning or survey tape.

Grounding rules for antennas and supports must be followed according to your local electrical code. Towers should be grounded with separate 8-foot long ground rods for each tower leg, bonded to the tower and each other. **[T0B08]** A smaller antenna mast should be grounded with a heavy wire and ground rod.

Guy wires must be installed according to the tower manufacturer's instructions. Place a safety wire through any turnbuckles used to tension guy lines. This prevents them from loosening due to vibration and twisting. **[T0B13]**

Tower Work and Climbing Safety

T0B01 — When should members of a tower work team wear a hard hat and safety glasses?

T0B02 — What is a good precaution to observe before climbing an antenna tower?

T0B03 — Under what circumstances is it safe to climb a tower without a helper or observer?

T0B05 — What is the purpose of a gin pole?

T0B07 — Which of the following is an important safety rule to remember when using a crank-up tower?

While you may not immediately decide to put up a tower yourself, it is common for amateurs to help each other with antenna projects that involve tower work. Whether you decide to work on the tower itself or as part of the ground crew, safety is absolutely critical. The following safety guidelines will help you safely contribute to tower projects of your own or of others. For more information about working safely on and around towers, *The ARRL Handbook* and *The ARRL Antenna Book* cover the subject in some detail.

Starting with personal preparation, both climbers and ground crew should wear appropriate protective gear any time work is under way on the tower. Each member of the crew should wear a hard hat, goggles or safety glasses and heavy duty gloves suitable for working with ropes. **[T0B01]** If you are the climber, use an inspected and approved climbing harness (fall arrester) and work boots to protect the arches of your feet. **[T0B02]** Don't use a leather "lineman's belt" as they are unsafe and no longer approved for tower work. Many climbers prefer footwear with a steel shank that supports the foot while standing on a narrow rung. **Figure 9.9** shows a properly equipped climber ready for tower work.

Before climbing or starting work, perform a thorough inspection of all equipment and installed hardware. Surprises during tower work are rarely a good thing!

• Inspect all tower guying and support hardware. Repair or tighten as necessary before anyone goes up!

• Crank-up towers must be fully retracted or mechanical safety locking devices must have been installed. Never

Figure 9.9 — The well-dressed tower climber. Note the waist D-rings for positioning lanyard attachment as well as the suspenders and leg loops. The photo on the right shows an adjustable positioning lanyard. Be sure to wear protective gear — hard hat, goggles and gloves — whether you are working on the tower or as part of the ground crew. [Steve Morris, K7LXC, photos]

climb a crank-up tower supported only by the cable that supports the sections. **[T0B07]**

• Double-check all climbing belts and lanyards before climbing. Make sure clips and carabineers work smoothly without sticking open or closed. Replace or discard frayed straps and slings.

• Make sure all ropes and load-bearing hardware are in good condition before placing them in service.

• Use a gin pole (a temporary mast used to lift materials such as antennas or tower sections) so that you do not have to hoist things directly. **[T0B05]**

• Double-check the latest weather report, since you don't want to get caught on the tower in a storm.

• It's a good idea to visit the bathroom before starting your climb and don't forget the sunblock lotion!

Having a ground crew is important; avoid climbing alone whenever possible because it's never safe. **[T0B03]** If you do climb alone, take along a handheld radio. A ground crew should have enough members to do the job safely, including rendering aid if necessary. While everyone is on the ground, review the job in detail and agree on who gives instructions. If hand signals will be used, make sure everyone understands them! It also helps to rehearse the steps so that everyone knows the sequence. Does everyone know the proper knots and rope-handling technique? If not, make sure those who do are the ones who will be responsible for handling the lines.

During the job, keep distracting chatter to a minimum. One member of the crew should always be watching the climber or climbers. Stay clear of the tower base unless you need to be there because that's where dropped objects are likely to land. *Never* remove your hard hat while work is proceeding on the tower — an object dropped from 60 feet will be traveling a bit over 40 mph when it lands!

By participating as part of a team, you'll learn how to perform tower work safely. Even if you never set foot on a tower yourself, knowing how to help can make a contribution to these significant projects.

For More Information - Mobile Installations

Putting a radio in a vehicle sounds pretty straightforward and it can be. However, there are a few common safety hazards that are often overlooked by a first-time installer. The most important consideration, even beyond good RF performance, is to preserve the safety of you and your passengers.

Anything loose in a passenger compartment can become a deadly projectile in an accident — imagine being knocked on the head by a loose radio traveling at 30 miles per hour or more! Secure *all* equipment in a vehicle, including accessories such as diplexers, switches, and microphones. If possible, use *control heads* (detachable front panels) that connect to the radio with a long cable. Mount the heavier radio under a seat or in the trunk where it can't move.

Don't install the radio where it diverts your attention from the road. Don't block your vision by placing equipment on dashboards or in your field of view. (It's also a good idea to keep radios out of direct sunlight.) Place the radio or control head where the controls can be easily seen without taking your attention away from the road for prolonged periods.

Even with your radio properly mounted you still need to be a safe driver! Follow safe operating practices by adhering to these simple rules:

• Don't operate in heavy traffic. Hang up the microphone and resume the contact later.

• Pull over to make complicated adjustments to the radio. Fumbling through a radio's menu or trying to press two buttons at once is a sure way to risk an accident.

Know the traffic laws in your state that concern operation of two-way radios while driving. State legislatures have been making laws in response to careless mobile phone use. While Amateur Radio operations are usually exempt, certain types of operating may be restricted. It may be illegal to use headphones while driving or have a speaker on too loud to hear emergency vehicles. Scanners and radio equipment that can receive public safety transmissions may be illegal in vehicles, even though amateur transceivers are often exempted. It is a good idea to carry your amateur license and a copy of the state regulations exempting Amateur Radio with you whenever you are operating from your car.

Chapter 10

Glossary

Words in definitions that are *italicized* have a separate glossary entry.
A word in **bold** is defined in that entry.

The ARRL website also provides a glossary with broader coverage of ham radio terms.

73 — Ham abbreviation for "best regards." Generally expressed at the end of a contact.

Active filter — See *filter*.

Adapters — *Connectors* that convert one type to another.

Allocations — Frequencies authorized for a particular FCC telecommunications *service*.

Alternating current or voltage (ac) — Electrical *current* or *voltage* with a direction or polarity, respectively, that reverses at regular intervals.

Amateur operator — A person named in an amateur operator/primary license station grant on the ULS consolidated licensee database to be the control operator of an amateur station.

Amateur Radio Emergency Service (ARES®) — An organization of amateur volunteers that is sponsored by the ARRL and provides emergency communication services to groups such as the American Red Cross and local Emergency Operations Centers (EOC).

Amateur service — A radio communication service for the purpose of self-training, intercommunication and technical investigations carried out by amateurs, that is, duly authorized persons interested in radio technique solely with a personal aim and without *pecuniary* interest.

Amateur station — A station licensed in the amateur service, including necessary equipment, used for amateur communication.

Amateur television (ATV) — Analog fast-scan television using commercial transmission standards (NTSC in North America).

American Radio Relay League (ARRL) — The national association for Amateur Radio.

Ammeter — A test instrument that measures *current*.

Ampere (A) — The basic unit of electrical *current*, also abbreviated amps. One ampere is the flow of one *coulomb* of charge per second.

Amplifier — A device or piece of equipment used to *amplify* a signal.

Amplify — Increasing the strength or *amplitude* of a signal.

Amplitude — The strength or magnitude of a signal.

Amplitude modulation (AM) — The process of adding information to a signal or *carrier* by varying its amplitude. Transmissions referred to as **AM phone** are usually composed of two sidebands and a carrier. Shortwave broadcast stations use this type of AM, as do stations in the Standard Broadcast Band (535-1710 kHz). AM in which only one sideband is transmitted is called *single-sideband* or *SSB* and is the most popular voice mode on the *high frequency (HF)* bands

AMSAT (Radio Amateur Satellite Corporation) — Organization that manages many of the amateur satellite programs.

Analog (linear) signal — A signal (usually electrical) that can have any amplitude (voltage or current) value, and whose amplitude can vary smoothly over time. Also see *digital signal*.

Antenna — A device that radiates or receives radio frequency energy.

Antenna matching network — see *impedance matching network*.

Antenna switch — A switch used to connect one transmitter, receiver or transceiver to several different antennas.

Antenna tuner — See *impedance matching network*.

Apogee — The point in a satellite's orbit at which it is farthest from the Earth. See *perigee*.

AGC — See *automatic gain control*.

ALC — See *automatic level control*.

Automatic Packet Reporting System (APRS) — A system by which amateurs report their position automatically by radio to central servers from which their locations can be observed.

Amateur Radio Direction Finding (ARDF) — Competitions in which amateurs combine orienteering with *radio direction finding*.

Anode — The more positively charged *electrode* of a *diode* or *vacuum tube*.

Antenna analyzer — A portable instrument that combines a low-power signal source, a frequency counter and an *SWR meter*. Also known as an **SWR analyzer**.

Array — An antenna with more than one *element*. In a **driven array** all elements are *driven elements*. In a **parasitic array** some elements are *parasitic elements*.

Attenuate — To reduce the strength of a signal. An **attenuator** is a device that attenuates a signal.

Audio frequency (AF) signal — An ac electrical signal in the range of 20 hertz to 20 kilohertz (20,000 hertz). This is called an audio signal because human hearing responds to sound waves in the same frequency range.

Automatic control — A station operating under the control of devices or procedures that ensure compliance with FCC rules.

Automatic gain control (AGC) — A circuit that automatically adjusts RF Gain in a receiver to maintain a relatively constant output volume.

Automatic level control (ALC) — A circuit that automatically controls transmitter power to reduce distortion of the output signal that can cause interference to other stations.

Automatic Repeat Request (ARQ) — The method of requesting a retransmission of data if the data is received with errors. Also known as **Automatic Repeat Query**.

Autopatch — A device that allows users to make telephone calls through a *repeater*.

Auxiliary station — A station that operates in support of another station, such as a *repeater*, by transmitting control information or relaying audio.

Balanced line — *Transmission line* in which none of the conductors is connected directly to *ground*. See *open-wire line*.

Balun — Contraction of "balanced to unbalanced" and pronounced "BAHL-un." A device to transfer power between a balanced load and an unbalanced feed line or device, or vice versa.

Band — A range of frequencies. An **amateur band** is a range of frequencies on which amateurs are allowed to transmit.

Band-pass filter (BPF) —A *filter* designed to pass signals within a range of frequencies called the **pass-band**, while attenuating signals outside the pass-band.

Band plan — Voluntary organization of activity on an amateur band under normal circumstances.

Band-stop filter — See *notch filter*.

Bandwidth — (1) Bandwidth is the range of frequencies occupied by a radio signal. (2) FCC Part 97 defines bandwidth for regulatory purposes as "The width of a frequency band outside of which the mean power is attenuated at least 26 dB below the mean power of the transmitted signal within the band." [Part 97.3 (8)]

Base — (1) A station at a fixed location. (2) See *transistor*.

Battery — A package of one or more *cells*.

Battery pack — A package of several individual *cells* connected together (usually in series to provide higher voltages) and treated as a single battery.

Baud — The rate at which symbols are transmitted in a *digital mode*.

Baudot — The code used for *radioteletype* (RTTY) characters.

Beacon station — An amateur station transmitting communications for the purposes of observation of propagation and reception or other related experimental activities.

Beam antenna — See *directional antenna*.

Bit error rate (BER) — The rate at which bit-level errors occur in a stream of digital data.

BJT — See *transistor*.

Block diagram — A drawing using boxes to represent sections of a complicated device or process. The block diagram shows the connections between sections. A block diagram shows the internal functions of a complex piece of equipment without the detail of a *schematic diagram*.

BNC — A type of *RF connector*.

Bonding — Connecting equipment or circuits together to keep them at the same voltage.

Break-in — Switching between transmit and receive during CW operation so that you can listen to the operating frequency between Morse *elements* (full break-in) or during short pauses in your transmissions (semi-break-in).

Breaking in — The term for joining an ongoing contact by transmitting your *call sign* during a pause in the contact.

Broadband Hamnet — Amateur system that uses reprogrammed commercial network equipment in shared bands to create self-organizing (ad hoc) data networks.

Broadcasting — One-way transmissions intended to be received by the general public, either direct or relayed.

Bug — A mechanical Morse *key* that uses a spring to send dots automatically.

Bus — An electrical conductor for distributing power or to provide a common connection.

Call — (1) Abbreviated form of *call sign*. (2) Attempt to make contact.

Call district — The ten administrative areas established by the FCC.

Call sign — The letters and numbers that identify a specific amateur and the country in which the license was granted.

Calling frequency — A frequency on which amateurs establish contact before moving to a different frequency. Usually used by hams with a common interest or activity.

Capacitance — A measure of the ability to store energy in an *electric field*. Capacitance is measured in *farads*.

Capacitor — An electrical *component* that stores energy in an *electric field*. Capacitors are made from a pair of conductive surfaces called *electrodes* that are separated by an *insulator* called the *dielectric*.

Carrier — The unmodulated RF signal to which information is added during *modulation*. Also see *modulate*.

Cathode — The more negatively charged *electrode* of a *diode* or *vacuum tube*.

Cell (electrochemical cell) — A combination of chemicals and *electrodes* that converts chemical energy into electrical energy. See *battery*.

Centi (c) — The metric prefix for 10^{-2} or division by 100.

Certificate of Successful Completion of Examination (CSCE) — A document that verifies that an individual has passes one or more exam *elements*. A CSCE is good for 365 days and may be used as evidence of having passed an element at any other amateur license exam session.

Channel — (1) A range of *frequencies* used for one radio or communications signal. (2) The structure connecting the *source* and *drain* of an *FET* and through which *current* flows.

Channel spacing — The difference in frequency between *channels*.

Characteristic impedance — The ratio of RF *voltage* to *current* in a *transmission line* that is *matched*.

Charge — Store energy in a *battery* by reversing the chemical reaction in its *cells*.

Chassis ground — The common connection for all parts of a *circuit* that connect to the metal enclosure or chassis (pronounced *"CHAA-see"*) of the circuit.

Check in — Register your station's presence on a *net* with the *net control station.*

Checksum — A method of detecting errors in digital data by including a calculated value with the data.

Choke balun — A type of *balun* made by forming a coaxial feed line into a coil or placing ferrite cores on the feed line, creating an *RF choke.*

Circuit — A conductive path through which *current* can flow.

Circuit breaker — A protective component that "breaks" or opens a *circuit* or *trips* when an excessive *current* flow occurs.

Citizen's Band (CB) —An unlicensed radio service operating near 27 MHz intended for use by individuals and businesses over ranges of a few miles.

Closed repeater — A *repeater* that restricts access to members of a certain group of amateurs. See *open repeater.*

Closed circuit — An electrical circuit with an uninterrupted path for the current to follow. Turning a switch on, for example, closes or completes the circuit, allowing current to flow. Also called a **complete circuit**.

Coaxial cable — Coax (pronounced *KOH-aks*). A type of *transmission line* with a single center conductor inside an outer shield made from braid or solid metal and both sharing a concentric central axis. The outer conductor is covered by a plastic **jacket**.

Color code — A system in which numerical values are assigned to various colors. Colored stripes or dots are painted on the body of *resistors* and other *components* to represent their value.

Collector — See *transistor.*

Common — Term for the shared reference for all voltages in a circuit. Also referred to as *circuit* common. See *ground* and *bonding.*

Common-mode — Currents that flow equally on all conductors of a multiconductor cable, such as speaker wires or telephone cables, or on the outer surface of shielded cables.

Common-mode choke — see *Choke balun*

Communications emergency — A situation in which communication is required for immediate safety of human life or protection of property.

Component — (1) A device having a specific quantity of an electrical property (such as *resistance*) or that has a specific electrical function. (2) One signal of a group that makes up a *composite* signal.

Composite signal — A signal with information encoded by a group of *component* signals. For example, an AM signal is a composite signal that consists of three components: the carrier and the upper and lower sidebands.

Compression — See *speech compression.*

Conductor — A material in which *electrons* move freely in response to an applied *voltage.*

Connector — A *component* used to connect and disconnect electrical circuits and equipment.

Continuous wave (CW) — Radio communications transmitted by on/off *keying* of a continuous radio-frequency signal. Another name for international *Morse code*.

Control code — Information in the form of data or tones used to adjust a station under *remote control*.

Control link — The means by which a control operator can make adjustments to a station operating under *remote control*.

Control operator — The person designated by the licensee of a station to be responsible for the transmissions of an amateur station.

Control point — The location at which the control functions of the station are performed.

Controlled environment — Any area in which an RF signal may cause radiation exposure to people who are aware of the radiated electric and magnetic fields and who can exercise some control over their exposure to these fields. The FCC generally considers amateur operators and their families to be in a controlled RF exposure environment to determine the *maximum permissible exposure* levels. See *uncontrolled environment*.

Conventional current — See *current*.

Core — In an *inductor*, the core is the material or space the wire is wound around or passed through.

CORES — Commission Registration System of the *FCC*.

Coulomb (C) — The basic unit of electrical charge. One coulomb is 6.25×10^{18} *electrons*. 1 *ampere* equals the flow of 1 coulomb of electrons per second.

Courtesy tone (beep) — A short burst of audio transmitted by a *repeater* to indicate that the previous station has stopped transmitting. It can also be used to indicate that the *time-out timer* has been reset.

CQ — "Calling any station," the general method of requesting a contact with any station.

Crossband — Able to receive and transmit on different amateur frequency bands. For example, a *repeater* might receive a signal on 70 cm and retransmit it at 2 meters.

CTCSS — Continuous Tone Coded Squelch System. A low frequency tone (also called subaudible tone) required to access many *repeaters*. See *PL*.

Current (electrical) — The movement of electrons in response to an electromotive force, also called *electronic current*. *Conventional current* is the flow of positive charge that moves in the opposite direction of electronic current.

Cutoff frequency — The frequency at which a *filter's* output *power* is reduced to one-half the input power.

Cycle — One complete repetition of a repeating waveform, such as a *sine wave*

CW (Morse code) — See *continuous wave*.

D region — The lowest region of the *ionosphere*. The D region (or layer) acts mainly to absorb energy from radio waves as they pass through it.

Data (digital) mode — Computer-to-computer communication, such as by *packet radio* or *radioteletype* (*RTTY*), in which information is exchanged as data characters or digital information.

DC voltage — A voltage with a constant *polarity*. See *direct current*.

Deceptive (or false) signals — Transmissions that are intended to mislead or confuse those who may receive the transmissions. For example, distress calls transmitted when there is no actual emergency are false or deceptive signals.

Decibel (dB) — In electronics decibels are used to express ratios of *power*, *voltage*, or *current*. 1 dB = 10 $\log_{10}$ (power ratio) or 20 $\log_{10}$ (voltage or current ratio).

Deci (or lower case d) — The metric prefix for 10^{-1} or division by 10.

Delta loop — A loop antenna in the shape of a triangle.

Degree — A measure of angle or phase. There are 360 degrees in a circle or *cycle*.

Demodulate — To recover the information from a modulated signal by reversing the process of *modulation*. See *modulate*.

Designator — Letters and numbers used to identify a specific electronic *component*.

Detect — (1) To determine the presence of a signal. (2) To recover the information directly from a modulated signal.

Detector — The stage in a receiver in which the *modulation* (voice or other information) is recovered from a *modulated* RF signal.

Deviation — The change in *frequency* of an FM *carrier* due to a *modulating* signal. Also called **carrier deviation.**

Dielectric — The *insulating* material in which a *capacitor* stores electrical energy.

Diffraction — To alter the direction of a radio wave as it passes by edges of or through openings in obstructions such as buildings or hills. **Knife-edge diffraction** results if the dimensions of the edge are small in terms of the wave's wavelength.

Digipeater — A type of *repeater* station that retransmits or forwards digital messages.

Digital mode — See *data mode*.

Digital signal — (1) A signal (usually electrical) that can only have certain specific amplitude values, or steps — usually two; 0 and 1 or ON and OFF. (2) See *data mode*.

Digital signal processing (DSP) — The process of converting an *analog signal* to *digital* form and using a microprocessor to process the signal in some way such as filtering or reducing noise.

Diode — An electronic *component* that allows electric *current* to flow in only one direction.

Diplexer — A device that allows radios on two different bands to share a single antenna. Diplexers are used to allow a dual-band radio to use a single dual-band antenna. See *duplexer*.

Dipole — As used in Amateur Radio, the term usually refers to a *half-wave dipole* antenna.

Direct conversion — A type of receiver that recovers the modulating signal directly from the modulated RF signal.

Direct current (dc) — Electrical *current* that flows in only one direction.

Direct detection — A device acting as an unintentional receiver by converting a strong RF signal directly to voltages and currents internally, usually resulting in *radio frequency interference* to the receiving device.

Directional antenna — An antenna with an ability to receive and transmit that is enhanced in a specific (forward) direction and attenuated in one or more directions. See *front-to-back ratio* and *front-to-side ratio*.

Directional wattmeter — See *wattmeter*.

Director — A parasitic element of a *Yagi antenna* that focuses the radiated signal in the desired direction. See *reflector*.

Discharge — Extract energy from a *battery* or *cell*. **Self-discharge** refers to the internal loss of energy without an external *circuit*.

Discriminator — See *frequency discriminator*.

Dish — A curved *directional antenna* that uses a *reflector* to focus radio waves.

Distress call — A transmission made in order to attract attention in an emergency. (See *MAYDAY* and *SOS*)

Doping — Adding impurities to *semiconductor* material to change its conductive properties. **N-type** material is created if adding the impurity results in more *electrons* being available to flow as *current*. **P-type** material results if fewer *electrons* are available.

Doppler shift — A change in observed frequency of a signal caused by relative motion between the transmitter and receiver. Also called the **Doppler effect**.

Doubling — Two or more operators transmitting at the same time on the same frequency.

Downlink — Transmitted signals or the range of frequencies for transmissions from a satellite to Earth. See *uplink*.

Drain — See *transistor*.

Driven element — An antenna *element* supplied directly with power from the transmitter.

Driver — The *amplifier* stage immediately preceding a *power amplifier* in a transmitter.

Dual-band antenna — An antenna designed for use on two different amateur bands.

Dummy antenna or **dummy load** — A station accessory that dissipates a transmitted signal as heat to allow testing or adjustment of transmitting equipment without radiating a signal on the air.

Duplex — (1) Transmitting on one frequency and receiving on another, such as for *repeater* operation. (2) A mode of communications (also known as **full duplex**) in which a user transmits on one frequency and receives on another frequency simultaneously. This is in contrast to **half duplex** in which the user transmits at one time and receives at other times.

Duplexer — A device that allows bidirectional communication on closely spaced frequencies or *channels*. In a *repeater*, the duplexer also allows the transmitter and receiver to share a single antenna. See *diplexer*.

Duty cycle — The percentage of time that a signal or device, such as a transmitter, is active. **Duty factor** is the same as duty cycle, but expressed as a fraction instead of percent.

DX — Distance, distant stations, foreign countries.

DXpedition — An expedition for the purpose of making contacts from a rare or unusual location.

E region — The second lowest *ionospheric* region, the E region (or layer) exists only during the day. Under certain conditions, it may refract radio waves enough to return them to Earth.

Earth connection — An electrical connection to the Earth for electrical safety purposes. See also *ground*.

Earth station — An amateur station located on or within 50 km of the Earth's surface, intended for communications with space stations or with other Earth stations by means of one or more other objects in space.

Earth-Moon-Earth (EME) or **moonbounce** — A method of communicating with other stations by reflecting radio signals off the Moon's surface.

Echolink — A system of linking repeaters and computer-based users by using the Voice-Over-Internet Protocol.

Electric field — A region of space in which electrical energy is stored and in which a stationary electrically charged object will feel a force. The **electric potential** between two points in the electric field is the amount of energy required to move a single electron between those two points.

Electrode — The general term for an electrical contact or connection point.

Electromagnetic wave — Energy composed of a continuously varying *electric field* and *magnetic field* moving through space or a *transmission line*.

Electromotive force (EMF) — The force that causes *electrons* or other charged objects to move.

Electron — A negatively charged atomic particle. Moving electrons make up an electrical *current*.

Electronic current — See *current*.

Element — (1) The conducting part or parts of an antenna designed to radiate or receive *radio waves*. (2) An examination for an FCC license in the amateur service. (3) A dot or dash in the *Morse code*.

Elmer — A ham radio mentor or teacher.

Emcomm — An abbreviation for *emergency communications*

Emergency — A situation where there is an immediate threat to the safety of human life or property.

Emergency communications — Communications conducted under adverse conditions where normal channels of communications are not available.

Emergency traffic — Messages with life and death urgency or requests for medical help and supplies that leave an area shortly after an emergency.

Emission — The transmitted signal from an *amateur station*.

Emission privilege — Permission to use a particular *emission type* (such as Morse code or voice).

Emission types — Term for the different modes authorized for use on the Amateur Radio bands. Examples are CW, SSB, RTTY and FM.

Emitter — See *transistor*.

Encoding — Changing the form of a signal into one suitable for storage or transmission. **Decoding** is the process of returning the signal to its original form.

Encryption — Changing the form of a signal into a privately-known format intended to obscure the meaning of the signal. **Decryption** is the process of reversing the encryption.

Energy — The ability to do work; the ability to exert a force to move some object.

Envelope — The outline of an RF signal formed by the peaks of the individual RF cycles.

Extended-coverage receiver — A receiver that tunes frequencies from around 30 MHz to several hundred MHz or into the GHz range. Also known as a **wide-range receiver**.

F region — A combination of the two highest *ionospheric* regions (or layers), the F1 and F2 regions. The F region refracts radio waves and returns them to Earth. Its height varies greatly depending on the time of day, season of the year and amount of sunspot activity.

Farad (F) — The basic unit of *capacitance*.

Federal Communications Commission (FCC) — Federal agency in the United States that regulates use and allocation of the frequency spectrum among many different services, including Amateur Radio.

Federal Registration Number (FRN) — An identification number assigned to an individual by the FCC to use when performing license modification or renewal.

Feed line — See *transmission line*.

Feed line loss — The fraction of power dissipated as heat as it travels through a feed line.

Feed point — The point at which a *transmission line* is electrically connected to an antenna.

Feed point impedance — The ratio of RF voltage to current at the *feed point* of an antenna.

Ferrite — A ceramic material with magnetic properties used in *inductors*. Ferrite is often formed into beads or cores so that it may be placed on cables, forming an *RF choke*.

FET — See *transistor*.

Filter — A circuit or system whose effect on a signal depends on its frequency or other characteristics. A **passive filter** is constructed entirely from unpowered devices such as *resistors*, *capacitors* and *inductors*. An **active filter** also uses powered devices such as *amplifiers* or *transistors*. A **digital filter** performs the filtering functions by operating on digital data that represents a signal.

Form 605 — An FCC form that serves as the application for your Amateur Radio license, or for modifications to an existing license.

Forward power — Power in a *transmission line* traveling from a transmitter toward a *load* or *antenna*.

Fox hunting — Exercises in which participants look for a hidden transmitter (the fox) to test *radio direction-finding* skills. Also called a **bunny hunt**.

Frequency — The number of complete cycles per second of an *ac current* or *ac voltage*.

Frequency band — A continuous range of frequencies in which one type of communications is authorized. See *band*.

Frequency coordination — Allocating *repeater* input and output frequencies to minimize interference between repeaters and to other users of the band.

Frequency coordinator — An elected individual or group that recommends repeater frequencies to reduce or eliminate interference between *repeaters* operating on or near the same frequency in the same geographical area.

Frequency discriminator — A *detector* used for FM signals.

Frequency modulation (FM) — The process of adding information to an RF signal or *carrier* by varying its frequency. FM broadcast stations and most professional communications (police, fire, taxi) use FM. **FM phone** is used on most *repeaters*.

Frequency privilege — Authorization to use a particular group of frequencies.

Frequency-shift keying (FSK) — A method of digital *modulation* that shifts the transmitter frequency to represent the bits of digital data.

Front-end overload — Interference to a receiver caused by a strong signal that causes the receiver's sensitive input circuitry ("front end") to be overloaded. Front-end overload results in distortion of the desired signal and the generation of unwanted spurious signals within the receiver. See **receiver overload**.

Front-to-back ratio (F/B) — The ratio of an antenna's *gain* in the forward direction to that in the opposite or rear direction.

Front-to-side ratio (F/S) — The ratio of an antenna's *gain* in the forward direction to that at right angles to the forward direction.

FRS — Family Radio Service. An unlicensed radio service that uses low-power radios operating near 460 MHz and intended for short-range communications by family members.

Fundamental — The frequency of which all *harmonics* are integer multiples.

Fundamental overload — *Radio frequency interference (RFI)* caused when a strong RF signal exceeds a receiver's ability to reject it.

Fuse — A thin metal strip mounted in a holder. When excessive *current* passes through the fuse, the metal strip melts and opens the *circuit* to protect it against further current overload.

Gain — (1) Enhancing an antenna's ability to receive or radiate signals in a specific direction. (2) The ability of a component, circuit, or piece of equipment to *amplify* a signal. (3) **Mic Gain** — sensitivity of the microphone amplifier circuit. (4) **RF Gain** — sensitivity of the receiver to incoming RF signals. (5) **AF Gain** — receiver audio output volume.

Gate — See *transistor*.

Gateway — A station that serves to connect one network of stations with the Internet or another network of stations.

General-coverage receiver — A receiver used to listen to a wide range of frequencies, not just specific bands. Most general-coverage receivers tune from frequencies below the AM broadcast band (550 – 1700 kHz) to around 30 MHz. (See *extended-coverage receiver*.)

Generator — A device that uses a motor to convert mechanical energy into ac or dc electrical energy. See also *signal generator*.

GFI (also **GFCI**) — Ground-fault interrupting *circuit breaker* that opens a circuit when an imbalance of current flow is detected between the hot and neutral wires of an ac power circuit. An **AFCI** or arc-fault circuit interrupter opens a circuit when an arc is detected.

Giga (or lower case G) — The metric prefix for 10^9 or multiplication by 1,000,000,000.

GMRS — General Mobile Radio Service. A licensed radio service operating 460 MHz intended for family businesses and members to communicate within a city or region.

Go-kit — A pre-packaged collection of equipment or supplies kept at hand to allow an operator to quickly report where needed in time of need.

Grace period — The time allowed by the FCC following the expiration of an amateur license to renew that license without having to retake an examination. Those who hold an expired license may not operate an *amateur station* until the license is reinstated.

Grant — Authorization given by the FCC

Grid square — A locator in the Maidenhead Locator System.

Ground — (1) An electrical connection to the Earth (*Earth connection*) for the purposes of electrical safety. (2) A reference voltage point or surface (see *ground plane*) in a circuit or system of equipment. (3) To connect a circuit to a ground.

Ground loss — RF energy that is converted to heat while reflecting from or traveling through or along the Earth's surface.

Ground rod — A metallic rod driven into the Earth to make a **ground connection** or *Earth connection*. Also known as a **ground electrode** or **earth electrode**.

Ground plane — A conducting surface of continuous metal or discrete wires that acts to create an electrical image of an antenna. **Ground-plane antennas** require a ground-plane in order to operate properly.

Ground-wave propagation — *Propagation* in which radio waves travel along the Earth's surface.

Ham-band receiver — A receiver designed to receive only frequencies in the amateur bands.

Hamfest — A flea-market for ham radio, electronic and computer equipment and accessories.

Half-wave dipole — A popular antenna that is ½-wavelength long at the desired operating frequency. Dipoles usually consist of a single length of wire or tubing with a feed point at the center. See *dipole*.

Harmful interference — Interference that seriously degrades, obstructs or repeatedly interrupts a radio communication service operating in accordance with the Radio Regulations. [Part 97.3 (a) (22)]

Harmonic — A signal that is an integer multiple (2×, 3×, 4×, etc) of a *fundamental* frequency.

Hand-held radio — A VHF or UHF transceiver that can be carried in the hand or pocket. Also known as an **HT**.

Header — The first part of a digital message containing routing and control information about the message. See *preamble*.

Headphones — A pair of speakers held against or inserted into each ear. A **headset** or **boomset** combines headphones with a microphone for additional convenience.

Health and Welfare traffic — Messages about the well-being of individuals in a disaster area. Such messages must wait for **Emergency** and **Priority traffic** to clear, and results in advisories to those outside the disaster area awaiting news from family and friends.

Henry (H) — The basic unit of *inductance*.

Hertz (Hz) —The basic unit of frequency. 1 Hz = 1 cycle per second.

High frequency (HF) — The term used for the frequency range from 3 MHz to 30 MHz.

High-pass filter (HPF) — A filter designed to pass signals above a specified *cutoff frequency*, while attenuating lower-frequency signals.

High-speed Multimedia (HSMM) — see *Broadband Hamnet*.

Hop — See *sky-wave propagation*.

ICS (Incident Command System) — method of organizing a response to emergencies and disasters used in the United States. (see also *National Incident Management System*)

Impedance — The ratio of ac voltage to ac current, including *phase*. The combination of *reactance* and *resistance* that constitutes opposition to *ac current*. Impedance is measured in *ohms*.

Impedance match — To adjust *impedances* to be equal or the case in which two impedances are equal. Usually refers to the point at which a feed line is connected to an antenna or to transmitting equipment. If the impedances are different, that is a **mismatch**. See *matched*.

Impedance matching network — A device that transforms one impedance to another, such as an antenna system input *impedance* to match that of a transmitter or receiver. Also called an *antenna-matching network* or **transmatch**.

Indicator — (1) A device used to signal status audibly or visually. (2) Characters added before or after a call sign signifying a change in license class or that the station or operator is transmitting away from the registered location.

Inductance — A measure of the ability to store energy in a *magnetic field*. Inductance is measured in *henries*.

Inductor — An electrical *component* that stores energy in a *magnetic field*. An inductor is usually composed of a coil of wire wound around a central core.

Input frequency — A *repeater's* receiving frequency.

Insulator — A material in which *electrons* do not move easily in response to an applied *voltage*. Insulation is used to prevent *current* flow between points at different voltages.

Integrated circuit (IC or chip) — An electronic *component* made up of many individual components in a single package.

Intermediate frequency (IF) — The stages in a *superheterodyne* receiver that follow a *mixer* circuit and that operate at a fixed frequency. Most of the receiver's *gain* and *selectivity* are achieved in the IF stages.

Intermodulation (intermod or **IMD)** — Spurious signals created by the combination of other signals. Usually related to the overload of circuits by strong signals.

International Amateur Radio Union (IARU) — The international organization of national Amateur Radio societies.

International Telecommunication Union (ITU) — The organization of the United Nations responsible for coordinating international telecommunications agreements.

Internet Radio Linking Project (IRLP) — A system of linking repeaters by using the Voice-Over-Internet Protocol.

Inverted V — A *dipole* antenna supported in the middle with each half sloping downward.

Inverter — A circuit that converts dc power into ac power.

Ion — An electrically-charged atom or molecule.

Ionosphere — A region of electrically charged (ionized) gases high in the atmosphere that affects the *propagation* of radio waves through it. See *sky-wave propagation.*

Isotropic antenna — An *antenna* that radiates and receives equally in all directions, both vertical and horizontal.

Jack (receptacle) — A *connector* designed to have a mating assembly inserted into it, usually mounted on a piece of equipment.

Keplerian elements — Numeric parameters describing a satellite's orbit that can be used to compute the position of the satellite at any point in time.

Kerchunk — The sound made when a brief transmission activates a repeater.

Key — A manually operated switch that turns a transmitter on and off to send *Morse code.*

Key click — Spurious signals generated as a transmitter is turned on and off that are heard as clicks by stations on nearby frequencies.

Keyboard-to-keyboard — A *digital mode* intended for operators to exchange text messages as the characters are entered.

Keyer or **electronic keyer** —A device that makes it easier to send well-formed Morse code. It sends a continuous string of either dots or dashes, depending on which lever of a connected *paddle* is pressed.

Kilo (k) — The metric prefix for 10^3 or multiplication by 1000.

Knife-edge — See *diffraction.*

Ladder line — See *open-wire line.*

Lag — In comparing two *waveforms,* refers to the waveform in which positive change occurs last.

Lead — (pronounced "*leed*") (1) Refers to the wires or connection points on an electrical *component* or the probes and cables that are used to connect test instruments to the devices being measured. (2) In comparing two *waveforms,* refers to the waveform in which change in the positive direction occurs first.

Light-emitting diode (LED) — A *diode* that emits light when current flows through it.

Lightning protection — Methods to prevent lightning damage to your equipment (and your house), such as unplugging equipment, disconnecting antenna *feed lines* and using a **lightning arrestor.**

Line-of-sight propagation — The term used to describe VHF and UHF *propagation* within the radio horizon in a straight line directly from one station to another.

Linear — (1) To act on a signal such that the result is a replica of the original signal at a different scale. (2) Equipment that amplifies the output of a transmitter, often to the full legal amateur power limit of 1500 W *peak envelope power* (*PEP*).

Liquid-crystal display (LCD) — A device for displaying graphics or characters by passing light through a liquid crystal between patterns of *electrodes*.

Local control — Operation of a station with a *control operator* physically present at the transmitter.

Load — A device or system to which electrical *power* is delivered, such as a heating element or *antenna*. Also the amount of power consumed or that can be safely dissipated, such as a "50-watt load."

Loading — (1) Attaching or increasing an electrical load. (2) Increasing an antenna's apparent electrical length by inserting inductance or capacitance.

Lobe — A direction of maximum reception or transmission in an antenna's *radiation pattern*. The **main lobe** has the greatest strength for the entire pattern. A **side lobe** is a maximum located at an angle to the main lobe.

Log — The documents of a station that detail operation of the station. They can be used as supporting evidence and for troubleshooting interference-related problems or complaints.

Log periodic — a type of frequency independent antenna

Loop — (1) An antenna with *element(s)* constructed as continuous lengths of wire or tubing. (2) A point of maximum voltage or current on an antenna.

Low Frequency (LF) — 30 to 300 kHz. A reference to the 2200 meter band.

Lower sideband (LSB) — (1) In an *AM* or *single sideband* signal, the *sideband* located below the *carrier* frequency. (2) The common single sideband operating mode on the 40, 80 and 160 meter amateur bands.

Lowest usable frequency (LUF) — The lowest frequency that can be used for communication using *sky-wave propagation* along a specific path.

Low-pass filter (LPF) — A filter designed to pass signals below a specified *cutoff frequency*, while attenuating higher-frequency signals.

Machine — Slang for *repeater*.

Magnetic field — A region of space in which magnetic energy is stored and in which a moving electrically charged object will feel a force.

Matched — A transmission or feed line that is terminated by a load that has the same *impedance* as the feed line's *characteristic impedance*.

Maximum usable frequency (MUF) — The highest frequency that can be used for communication via *sky-wave propagation* along a specific path.

Maximum permissible exposure (MPE) — The maximum intensity of RF radiation to which a human being may safely be exposed. FCC Rules establish maximum permissible exposure values for humans to RF radiation. [Part 1.1310 and Part 97.13 (c)]

MAYDAY — From the French *m'aidez* (help me), MAYDAY is used when calling for emergency assistance in voice modes.

Medium Frequency (MF) — 300 kHz to 3 MHz. A reference to the 630 meter or 160 meter bands.

Mega (M) — The metric prefix for 10^6 or multiplication by 1,000,000.

Memory channel — Frequency and mode information stored by a radio and referenced by a number or alphanumeric designator.

Meteor scatter — Communication by signals reflected by the ionized meteor trails in the upper atmosphere.

Meter (instrument) — A device that displays a numeric value as a number or as the position of an indicator on a numeric scale.

Metric prefixes — A series of terms used in the *metric system* of measurement.

Metric system — A system of measurement that uses a set of prefixes to indicate multiples of 10 of a basic unit.

Medium frequency (MF) — The term used for the frequency range from 300 kHz to 3 MHz.

Micro (μ) — The metric prefix for 10^{-6} or division by 1,000,000.

Microphone (mic or mike) — A device that converts sound waves into electrical energy.

Microwave — The conventional term for frequencies greater than 1000 MHz (1 GHz).

Milli (m) — The metric prefix for 10^{-3} or division by 1000.

Mixer — (1) A circuit that combines two RF signals and generates **products** at both the signal's sum and difference frequencies. (2) An **audio mixer** adds multiple signals together into a single signal.

Mobile station — Any station that can be operated while in motion, typically in a car, but also on a boat, a motorcycle or bicycle, truck or RV.

Mobile flutter — Rapid amplitude variation of a signal from a moving vehicle experiencing *multipath interference*. Also called **picket fencing**.

Mode — (1) The combination of a type of information and a method of transmission. For example, FM radiotelephony or *FM phone* consists of using FM modulation to carry voice information. (2) The combination of a satellite's *uplink* and *downlink* bands.

Mode-restricted — Portions of the amateur bands in which only certain *emission types* are allowed.

Modem — Short for **mo**dulator/**dem**odulator. A modem changes data into audio signals that can be transmitted by radio and *demodulates* a received signal to recover transmitted data.

Modulate — The process of adding information to an RF signal or *carrier* by varying its *amplitude*, *frequency*, or *phase*.

Moonbounce — see *Earth-Moon-Earth*.

Morse code — The system of encoding characters as dots and dashes invented by Samuel Morse. See *continuous wave*.

MUF — See *maximum usable frequency*.

Multiband antenna — An antenna capable of operating on more than one amateur band, usually using a single *transmission line*.

Multi-hop— Long-distance radio *propagation* using several skips or hops between the Earth and the *ionosphere*. See *sky-wave propagation*.

Multimeter — An electronic test instrument used to measure *current*, *voltage* and *resistance*. Alternate names are **volt-ohm-milliammeter (VOM)** and **vacuum-tube voltmeter (VTVM)**. If the numeric display is digital, the instrument may also be called a **digital multimeter (DMM)** or **digital voltmeter (DVM)**.

Multimode radio — Transceiver capable of SSB, CW and FM operation.

Multipath propagation — *Propagation* by means of multiple reflections. When the reflected signals partially cancel, it is referred to as **multipath interference**.

Multiple Protocol Controller (MPC) — A piece of equipment that can act as a *modem* or *TNC* for several *protocols*.

N or type N connector — A type of *RF connector* that can be used through *microwave* frequencies.

N-type — See *doping*.

Nano (n) — The metric prefix for 10^{-9} or division by 1,000,000,000.

National Electrical Code (NEC) — A set of guidelines governing electrical safety, including antennas.

National Incident Management System (NIMS) — The method by which emergency situations are managed by US public safety agencies.

Net — A formal system of operation in order to exchange or manage information.

Net control station (NCS) — The station in charge of a *net*.

Network — (1) A term used to describe several digital stations linked together to relay data over long distances. (2) A general term for electrical circuits.

Node — (1) One station in a digital network. (2) A point of minimum voltage or current on an *antenna*.

Noise blanker — A circuit or function that mutes the receiver output during noise pulses.

Noise reduction — Removing random noise from a receiver's audio output.

Notch filter — A *filter* that removes a very narrow range of frequencies, usually from a receiver's audio output audio. Also known as a *band-stop filter*.

Null — (1) Tune or adjust for a minimum response (2) A direction of minimum reception or transmission in an antenna's *radiation pattern*.

Offset frequency — The difference between a *repeater's* transmitter and receiver frequencies. Also known as the repeater's **split** or **offset**.

Ohm — The basic unit of electrical *resistance* and represented by the symbol Ω.

Ohm's Law — A basic electrical law stating that the *current* (I) through a *circuit* is directly proportional to the *voltage* (E) across the circuit and inversely proportional to the *resistance* (R) of the circuit: I = E / R. Ohm's Law is equivalently stated as E = I × R or R = E / I.

Ohmmeter — A device used to measure *resistance*.

Omnidirectional — An *antenna* that radiates and receives equally in all horizontal directions.

One-way communications — Radio signals not directed to a specific station, or for which no reply is expected. The FCC Rules provide for limited types of one-way communications on the amateur bands. [Part 97.111 (b)]

Open circuit — A break in an electrical *circuit* that prevents *current* from flowing.

Open repeater — A *repeater* available for use by all hams.

Open-wire line — A *transmission line* made from two parallel wires separated by insulation. Also known as **ladder line**, **parallel-conductor feed line**, **twin-lead**, or **window line**.

Operator/primary station license — An amateur license actually consists of two licenses. The **operator license** is that portion of an Amateur Radio license that gives permission to operate an *amateur station*. The **primary station license** is that portion of an Amateur Radio license that authorizes an *amateur station* at a specific location. The station license also lists the *call sign* of that station.

OSCAR — Orbiting Satellite Carrying Amateur Radio

Oscillate — To vibrate continuously at a single *frequency*. An **oscillator** is a device or circuit that generates a signal at a single frequency.

Output frequency — A *repeater's* transmitting frequency.

P-type — See *doping*.

Packet radio — A system of digital communication using the AX.25 protocol whereby information is broken into data groups called **packets** that also contain addressing and error-detection information.

Paddle —A pair of contacts operated by one or two levers used to control an electronic *keyer* that generates *Morse code* automatically.

Panadapter — Similar to the display of a spectrum analyzer, a panadapter centers the operating frequency in the middle of the display with signals on adjacent frequencies to the left and right.

Parallel circuit — An electrical *circuit* in which *current* may follow more than one path.

Parallel-conductor line — See *open-wire line*.

Parasitic element — An antenna *element* that affects the antenna performance by receiving and re-radiating energy from a *driven element* without being connected directly to the feed line.

Parity — An error detection method for *digital data* that counts the number of 1 bits in each data character. One bit added to each character — the parity bit — is used to indicate whether the correct number of 1 bits is odd or even.

Part 15 — The section of the FCC's rules that deal with unlicensed devices likely to transmit or receive RF signals.

Part 97 — The section of the FCC's rules that regulate Amateur Radio.

Passive filter — See *filter*.

Peak envelope power (PEP) — The average *power* during one RF cycle of a radio signal at the crest of the modulated *waveform*

Pecuniary — Payment of any type, whether money or other goods or services.

Perigee — The point in a satellite's orbit at which it is closest to the Earth. See *apogee*.

Period — The time it takes for one complete cycle of a repeating *waveform*. The reciprocal of *frequency*.

Phase — A measure of position in time within a repeating *waveform*, such as a *sine wave*. Phase is measured in *degrees* or *radians*.

Phase modulation (PM) — The process of adding information to a signal by varying its *phase*. Phase modulation is very similar to FM. PM signals can be received by FM receivers.

Phase-shift keying (PSK) — A method of digital *modulation* that shifts the transmitted signal's *phase* to represent the bits of digital data.

Phone — Another name for voice communications. An abbreviation for *radiotelephone*.

Phone emission — The FCC's name for voice transmissions.

Phone patch — Conducting a telephone call via radio communications.

Phonetic alphabet — A standardized list of words used on voice modes to make it easier to understand letters of the alphabet, such as those in call signs. The call sign KA6LMN stated phonetically is *Kilo Alfa Six Lima Mike November*.

Pico (p) — The metric prefix for 10^{-12} or division by 1,000,000,000,000.

PL (see **CTCSS**) — An abbreviation for Private Line, a trademark of Motorola.

Plug — An electrical *connector* designed to be inserted into a *jack* or *receptacle*.

PN junction — The interface between *N-type* and *P-type* material.

Polarity — The orientation or direction of a *voltage* or *current* with respect to a convention that assigns positive and negative.

Polarization — The orientation of the *electric field* of a *radio wave*. A radio wave can be horizontally, vertically, or circularly polarized.

Pole — In a *switch*, refers to a controlled *current* path or *circuit*.

Portable designator — Additional identifying information added to a *call sign* specifying the station's location.

Portable device — Generally considered to be a radio transmitting device designed to be transported easily and set up for operation independently of normal infrastructure. For purposes of RF exposure regulations, a portable device is one designed to have a transmitting antenna that is generally within 20 centimeters of a human body.

Potential — see *voltage*.

Potentiometer — (pronounced *po-ten-chee-AH-me-ter*) Another name for a variable *resistor* in which the resistance value can be changed without removing it from a circuit. Also called a **pot**.

Power — The rate of energy consumption or expenditure. To calculate power in an electrical *circuit* multiply the *voltage* applied to the circuit by the *current* through the circuit ($P = I \times E$).

Power amplifier — See *linear*.

Power density — The strength of a *radio wave* measured as power per unit of area.

Power supply — A device that converts ac power from a utility or other service to ac or dc power used by equipment.

Preamble — The information at the beginning of a *radiogram* that contains routing and other information about the message. See *header*.

Preamplifier — An amplifier used to increase the strength of a received signal. Preamplifier circuits are often included in a receiver and may be turned on or off.

Prefix — The leading letters and numbers of a call sign that indicate the country in which the *call sign* was assigned.

Primary service — When a frequency band is shared among two or more different radio services, the primary service is preferred. Stations in a **secondary service** must not cause harmful interference to, and must accept interference from stations in the primary service. [Part 97.303]

Primary station license — See *operator/primary station license*.

Priority traffic — Emergency-related messages, but not as important as *emergency traffic*.

Privileges — The frequencies and modes of communication that are permitted in an FCC telecommunications service

Procedural signals (prosign) — For *Morse code* communications, one or two letters sent as a single character, such as $\overline{AR}$ or $\overline{SK}$, to indicate the operator's intention or to control the communication. For *phone* communications, prosigns consist of single words, such as "Break" or "Over."

Propagation — The method by which *radio waves* travel.

Protocol — A method of *encoding*, packaging, and exchanging digital data.

Push to talk (PTT) — Turning a transmitter on and off manually with a switch, usually thumb- or foot-activated.

Q signals — Three-letter symbols beginning with Q used in *Morse code* to save time and to improve communication. Some examples are QRS (send slower) and QTH (location).

Q system — A method of providing signal quality reports on a scale of 1 ("Q1") to 5 ("Q5").

QSL card — A postcard that serves as a confirmation of communication between two hams. QSL is a *Q-signal* meaning "received and understood."

QSO — A conversation between two radio amateurs. QSO is a *Q signal* meaning "I am in contact."

Quad antenna — A *directional antenna* with *elements* in the shape of four-sided loops, one *wavelength* in circumference.

Quarter-wave vertical — A *ground-plane* antenna constructed of a ¼-wavelength radiating *element*, usually oriented perpendicularly to the Earth or ground-plane.

Question pool — The set of questions from which an amateur license exam is constructed. There is one pool for each license class.

Radial — A wire forming part of a *ground plane*, attached at an antenna's base and running radially away from the antenna.

Radian — A measure of angle or *phase*. Each radian equals $360/2\pi$ or 57.3 degrees.

Radiation — To emit or give off energy, such as a radio wave. **Ionizing radiation** has sufficient energy to cause an electron to escape from an atom, creating a charged *ion*. RF energy used for radio communication is much less energetic and is called **non-ionizing radiation**.

Radiation pattern — A graph showing how an *antenna* radiates and receives in different directions. An **azimuthal pattern** shows radiation in horizontal directions. An **elevation pattern** shows radiation at different vertical angles.

Radio Amateur Civil Emergency Service (RACES) — A part of the Amateur Service that provides radio communications for civil defense organizations during local, regional or national civil emergencies.

Radio direction finding (RDF) — The method of locating a transmitter by determining the bearings of received signals.

Radio frequency (RF) exposure — FCC Rules establish *maximum permissible exposure* (MPE) values for humans to RF radiation. [Part 1.1310 and Part 97.13 (c)]

Radio frequency (RF) signals — RF or **radio signals** are generally considered to be any electrical signals with a frequency higher than 20,000 Hz, up to 300 GHz.

Radio-frequency interference (RFI) — Disturbance to electronic equipment or to radio communication caused by radio-frequency signals.

Radiogram — A formal message exchanged via radio.

Radio horizon — The most distant point on the Earth to which radio signals can travel without *ionospheric* or *tropospheric propagation*. See *sky-wave propagation*.

Radioteletype (RTTY) — A *data mode* that used the Baudot code to encode characters.

Radio wave — An *electromagnetic wave* with a frequency greater than 20 kHz.

Ragchew — An informal conversation.

Range — The distance over which radio signals are exchanged.

Reactance — The property of opposition to ac current. Capacitors exhibit **capacitive reactance** and inductors exhibit **inductive reactance**. Reactance is measured in *ohms*.

Receiver (RVCR) — A device that converts radio waves into signals we can hear, see, or be read by a computer.

Receiver overload — Interference to a receiver caused by a RF signal too strong for the receiver input circuits. A signal that overloads the receiver RF input causes *front-end overload*. Receiver overload is sometimes called **RF overload**.

Receiver incremental tuning (RIT) — A transceiver control to adjust the receive frequency without affecting the transmit frequency. See also *transmitter incremental tuning*.

Receiving converter — A device that shifts the frequency of incoming signals so that a receiver can be used on another band.

Recharge — See *charge*.

Reciprocal operating authority — Permission for amateur radio operators from another country to operate in the US using their home license. This permission is based on various treaties between the US government and the governments of other countries.

Rectifier — A diode intended for use in *power supplies* and power conversion circuits.

Rectify — Convert *ac* to *dc*.

Reflected power — Power in a *transmission line* returning to the transmitter from the load or antenna.

Reflector — (1) A parasitic element of a *Yagi antenna* that cancels the radiated signal in the undesired direction. (2) A conducting surface that acts as an electrical mirror to reflect radio waves.

Refract — Bending of an *electromagnetic wave* as it travels through materials with different properties. Radio waves are refracted as they travel through the *ionosphere*.

Region — Administrative areas defined by the *International Telecommunication Union (ITU)*.

Regulation — The ability of a *power supply* to control output voltage.

Relay — A *switch* operated by an electromagnet.

Remote control — Operation of a station in which the control functions of the station are operated by a *control operator* over a *control link*.

Remote receiver — A receiver at a separate location from a transmitter. Used by *repeater* systems to extend listening range or by individual stations to improve reception capabilities.

Repeater — A station that retransmits the signals of other stations to give them greater range.

Resistance — The property of opposing an electric *current*. Resistance is measured in *ohms*.

Resistor — An electronic *component* with a specific value of *resistance*, used to oppose or control current through a *circuit*. Resistors can be either fixed or variable. (See *potentiometer*.)

Resonance — The condition in an electrical circuit or antenna in which *reactance* is zero.

Resonant circuit — A circuit that exhibits *resonance* at one or more frequencies.

Resonant frequency — The frequency at which a circuit or antenna is resonant. See *tuned circuit*.

RF burn — A burn produced by contact with high RF voltages.

RF choke — An *inductor* or other impedance used to prevent or reduce the flow of RF current.

RF connector — A type of electrical *connector* designed specifically for use with RF signals.

RF feedback — Distortion of transmitted speech caused by RF signals being picked up by the microphone input circuits.

RF ground — The technique of maintaining the enclosures of radio equipment at a common RF voltage. See *bonding*.

RF overload — See *receiver overload*.

RF safety — Preventing injury or illness to humans from the effects of radio-frequency energy.

Rig — The radio amateur's term for a transmitter, receiver or transceiver.

Round-table — A contact in which several station take turns transmitting.

RST — A system of numbers used for signal reports: R is readability, S is strength and T is tone. (On phone, only R and S reports are used.)

Rubber duck antenna — A flexible rubber-coated antenna used mainly with hand-held VHF or UHF transceivers.

S meter — A meter that provides an indication of the relative strength of received signals in **S-units**.

Safety interlock — A switch that automatically turns off power to a piece of equipment when the enclosure is opened.

Safety ground — A *ground* connection intended to prevent shock hazards.

Scanning — Rapidly switching between frequencies to listen for an active *channel*.

Tone scanning determines what CTCSS access tones are present in specific signal.

Scattering — Radio wave *propagation* by means of multiple reflections in the layers of the atmosphere or from an obstruction.

Schematic diagram — A drawing that describes the electrical connections in a piece of electric or electronic equipment by using symbols to represent the electrical *components*.

Schematic symbol — A standardized symbol used to represent an electrical or electronic *component* on a *schematic diagram*.

SDR (Software Defined Radio) — Radio in which signal processing functions are performed by software that can be reconfigured automatically or under operator control.

Secondary service — See *primary service*.

Selectivity — The ability of a receiver to distinguish between signals.

Semiconductor — (1) A material with conductivity between that of a *conductor* and an *insulator*. (2) An electrical *component* constructed from semiconductor material.

Sensitivity — The ability of a receiver to detect signals.

Series circuit — An electrical *circuit* in which there is only one path for the *current* to follow.

Service — A set of regulations by the FCC that defines a certain type of telecommunications activity.

Shack — The room or location in which an *amateur station* is constructed.

Shield — (1) A cable's metallic layer or coating intended to prevent external signals from being picked up by an internal conductor or to prevent signals from being radiated from the internal conductor. (2) A metal wall or case that blocks RF signals.

Shielding — Surrounding an electronic circuit with conductive material to block RF signals from being radiated or received.

Short circuit — An electrical connection that causes *current* to bypass the intended path. Short-circuit often refers to an accidental connection that results in improper operation of equipment or circuits.

Sideband — An RF signal that results from modulating the amplitude or frequency of a *carrier*. An AM sideband can be either higher in frequency (**upper sideband** or **USB**) or lower in frequency (**lower sideband** or **LSB**) than the carrier. FM sidebands are produced on both sides of the carrier frequency.

Signal generator — A device that produces a low-level signal that can be set to a desired frequency.

Signal report — An evaluation of the transmitting station's signal and reception quality. See *Q system* and *RST*.

Simplex — Receiving and transmitting on the same frequency. See *duplex* and *half-duplex*.

Sine wave — A *waveform* with an amplitude equal to the sine of frequency × time.

Single sideband (SSB) — SSB is a form of *amplitude modulation* in which one *sideband* and the *carrier* are removed.

Skip — See *sky-wave propagation*.

Skip zone — An area of poor radio communication, too distant for *ground-wave propagation* and too close for *sky-wave propagation*.

Skyhook — Slang for antenna.

Sky-wave propagation — The method of *propagation* by which radio waves travel through the *ionosphere* and back to Earth. Also referred to as *skip*. Travel from the Earth's surface to the ionosphere and back is called a *hop*.

Slow-scan television (SSTV) — A television system used by amateurs to transmit pictures within the *bandwidth* required for a voice signal.

SMA — A type of RF connector used at *microwave* frequencies.

Software Defined Radio — see *SDR*.

SOS — A *Morse code* call for emergency assistance.

Source — See *transistor*.

Space station — An *amateur station* located more than 50 km above the Earth's surface.

Speaker — A device that turns an *audio frequency* electrical signal into sound.

Specific absorption rate (SAR) — A term that describes the rate at which RF energy is absorbed by the human body. *Maximum permissible exposure* (*MPE*) limits are based on whole-body SAR values.

Spectrum — The range of electromagnetic signals. The radio spectrum includes signals between audio frequencies and infrared light.

Speech compression or **processing** — Increasing the average *power* of a voice signal by amplifying low-level *components* of the signal more than high-level *components*.

Splatter — A type of interference to stations on nearby frequencies that occurs when a transmitter is *overmodulated*.

Sporadic E (Es or **E-skip)** — A form of *propagation* that occurs when radio signals are reflected from small, densely ionized regions in the *E region* of the *ionosphere*. Sporadic E has been observed from the 15 meter through 1.25 meter bands.

Spurious emissions — Signals from a transmitter on frequencies other than the operating frequency.

Squelch — Circuitry that mutes the audio output of a receiver when no signal is received. **Carrier squelch** operates only on the presence of a signal carrier. **Tone squelch** requires a specific *CTCSS* tone to be present before allowing receiver audio to be heard. **Digital Code Squelch (DCS)** requires a continuous sequence of tones.

Squelch tail — The burst of noise heard from an FM receiver between when a station stops transmitting and when the receiver's *squelch* circuit mutes the receiver.

Stage — One of several circuits or devices that act on a signal in sequence.

Standard offset — The standard transmitter/receiver frequency offset used by a *repeater* on a particular *amateur band*. For example, the standard offset on 2 meters is 600 kHz. Also see *offset frequency*.

Standing-wave ratio (SWR) — A measure of the impedance match between the transmission line's *characteristic impedance* and that of the *load* (usually an *antenna* or *antenna system*). **VSWR** is the ratio of maximum voltage to minimum voltage along the transmission line formed by the standing waves that result from power being reflected by the antenna or load. SWR is also the ratio of feed point impedance or load impedance to the feed line's *characteristic impedance*.

Station license — See *operator/primary station license*.

Stratosphere — The part of the Earth's *atmosphere* between the troposphere and ionosphere, extending from about 7 miles to 30 miles above the Earth.

Sub-audible tone — See *CTCSS*.

Suffix — The letters that follow a *call sign* prefix identifying a specific amateur.

Sunspot cycle — The number of sunspots increases and decreases in a predictable cycle that lasts about 11 years.

Sunspots — Dark spots on the surface of the Sun where magnetic fields create regions of cooler (darker) temperatures.

Superheterodyne — A type of receiver that shifts signals to a fixed *intermediate frequency (IF)* for *amplification* and *demodulation*. Each frequency shift is termed a **conversion** and the superheterodyne is described as being a single-, double-, or triple-conversion.

Surge protector — A device that is used to prevent temporary or *transient* excessive voltages from damaging sensitive electronic equipment.

Switch — A *component* used by an operator to connect or disconnect electrical *circuits*.

SWR meter — A measuring instrument that can indicate when an antenna system is working well. A device used to measure SWR. See *standing wave ratio*.

Tactical call signs — Names used to identify a station's location or function during emergency communications.

Tactical communications — Communications to coordinate actions or logistics during an emergency, disaster, or public service operation.

Telecommand — A one-way radio transmission to start, change or end functions of a device at a distance.

Telemetry — Information about a device sent to a receiving station by radio.

Television interference (TVI) — Disruption of television reception caused by another signal.

Temporary state of communications emergency — When a disaster disrupts normal communications in a particular area, the FCC can declare this type of emergency. Certain rules may apply for the duration of the emergency.

Terminal Node Controller (TNC) — A device that acts as an interface between a computer and a radio for implementing a *data mode*.

Termination — A load or antenna connected to a *transmission line*.

Third-party — An unlicensed person on whose behalf communications is passed by amateur radio.

Third-party communications — Messages passed from one amateur to another on behalf of a third person.

Third-party communications agreement — An official agreement between the United States and another country that allows amateurs in both countries to participate in third-party communications.

Third-party participation — An unlicensed person participating in amateur communications. A *control operator* must ensure compliance with FCC rules.

Throw — In a *switch*, refers to the number of alternative *current* paths for a controlled *circuit*.

Ticket — Slang for an Amateur Radio license.

Time-out timer — A device that limits the amount of time a *repeater* can transmit without a pause by the input signal.

Tolerance — The allowed variation in the dimensions or value of an electrical or mechanical *component*, usually expressed in percent or as a range of values.

Track — To follow a satellite as it travels around the Earth. **Tracking software** uses the satellite's *Keplerian elements* to determine its location and when it is visible from a specific location.

Traffic — Formal messages exchanged via radio. *Traffic handling* is the process of exchanging traffic. A *traffic net* is a net specially created and managed to handle traffic.

Transformer — An electrical *component* that transfers ac power from one circuit to another by means of a magnetic field shared by two or more *inductors*.

Transient — A short pulse of electrical energy.

Transceiver (XCVR) — A radio transmitter and receiver combined in one unit.

Transistor — A *semiconductor* device used as a *switch* or *amplifier*. A **bipolar junction transistor (BJT)** is made from a pair of back-to-back *PN junctions*, and is controlled by a *current*. A BJT has three *electrodes*: **base**, **collector**, and **emitter**. A **field-effect transistor (FET)** uses an *electric field* to control *current* flow through a conducting *channel*. An FET has three electrodes: **gate**, **drain**, and **source**.

Transmatch — see *impedance matching network*.

Transmission line — Cable used to connect a transmitter, receiver or transceiver to an *antenna* or *load*.

Transmit-receive (TR) switch — A circuit or device that switches an *antenna* between *transmitter* and *receiver* circuits or equipment.

Transmitter (XMTR) — A device that produces radio frequency signals with sufficient power to be useful for communications.

Transmitter Incremental Tuning (XIT) — A transceiver control to adjust the transmit frequency without affecting the receive frequency. Also see *receiver incremental tuning*.

Transponder — A device usually used on satellites that retransmit all signals in a range of frequencies.

Transverter — A device that converts signals so that a transceiver can operate on another band.

Trip — Activate when a threshold is exceeded or an event is detected. A *circuit breaker* trips, opening a circuit, when excessive *current* flow occurs, for example.

Troposphere — The region in Earth's atmosphere between the Earth's surface and the *stratosphere*.

Tropospheric bending — When radio waves are bent or *refracted* in the *troposphere*, they return to Earth farther away than the visible horizon.

Tropospheric ducting — A type of VHF propagation that can occur when warm air overruns cold air (a **temperature inversion**).

Tropospheric propagation (tropo) — Any method of propagation by means of atmospheric phenomena in the *troposphere*.

Tuned circuit — A circuit with a *resonant frequency* that can be adjusted, usually through the use of adjustable *capacitors* or *inductors*.

Tuning — Adjusting a radio or *circuit* that is frequency-sensitive.

Twin-lead — See *open-wire line*.

UHF connector — A type of *RF connector* usually used below 500 MHz.

Ultra high frequency (UHF) — The term used for the frequency range from 300 MHz to 3000 MHz (3 GHz).

Ultraviolet (UV) — *Electromagnetic waves* with frequencies greater than visible light. Literally, "above violet," which is the high-frequency end of the visible range.

Unbalanced line — *Transmission line* with one conductor connected to *ground*, such as *coaxial cable*.

Uncontrolled environment — Any area in which an RF signal may cause radiation exposure to people who may not be aware of the radiated electric and magnetic fields. The FCC generally considers members of the general public and an amateur's neighbors to be in an uncontrolled RF radiation exposure environment to determine the *maximum permissible exposure* levels. See *controlled environment*.

Unidentified communications or signals — Signals or radio communications in which the transmitting station's *call sign* is not transmitted.

Unintentional radiator — A device that radiates RF signals not required for its normal operation.

Universal Licensing System (ULS) — FCC database for all FCC radio services and licensees.

Uplink — Transmitted signals or the range of frequencies for transmissions from Earth to a satellite. See *downlink*.

Upper sideband (USB) — (1) In an AM signal, the *sideband* located above the carrier frequency. (2) The common single-sideband operating mode on the 60, 20, 17, 15, 12 and 10 meter HF amateur bands, and all the VHF and UHF bands.

Vacuum tube — An electronic *component* that operates by controlling *electron* flow between two or more *electrodes* in a vacuum.

Vanity call — A *call sign* selected by the amateur instead of one sequentially assigned by the FCC.

Variable-frequency oscillator (VFO) — An *oscillator* with an adjustable frequency. A VFO is used in receivers and transmitters to control the operating frequency.

Vertical antenna — An antenna with a single vertical radiating *element*. See *ground-plane antenna*.

Very high frequency (VHF) — The term used for the frequency range from 30 MHz to 300 MHz.

Visible horizon — The most distant point one can see visually.

Voice mode (communications) — Any of the several methods used by amateurs to transmit speech that is listened to as it is received. Voice modes include analog modes such as FM and SSB as well as digital modes such as D-STAR and DMR.

Voice Over Internet Protocol (VOIP) — A method of sending voice and other audio over the Internet as digital data.

Volt (V) — The basic unit of electric potential or *electromotive force*.

Voltage — A measure of *electric potential* between two points.

Voltmeter — A test instrument used to measure *voltage*.

Volunteer Examiner (VE) — A licensed amateur who is accredited by a Volunteer Examiner Coordinator (VEC) to administer amateur license examinations.

Volunteer Examiner Coordinator (VEC) — An organization that has entered into an agreement with the FCC to coordinate amateur license examinations.

Voice-Operated Transmission (VOX) — Turning a transmitter on and off under control of the operator's voice.

Waterfall display — Used with digital modes, this type of display consists of a sequence of horizontal lines showing signal strength as a change of brightness with frequency represented by position on the line. Older lines move down the display so that the history of the signal's strength and frequency form a "waterfall-like" picture.

Watt (W) — The unit of *power* in the metric system.

Wattmeter — Also called a *power meter*, a test instrument used to measure the power output (in watts) of a transmitter. A **directional wattmeter** can measure power flowing in either direction in a feed line.

Waveform — The amplitude of an ac signal over time.

Wavelength —The distance a *radio wave* travels during one *cycle*. The wavelength relates to frequency in that higher frequency waves have shorter wavelengths. Represented by the symbol λ.

Weak-signal — (1) Refers to the use of SSB, digital, or CW on the VHF and UHF bands because they provide better communications at low signal levels than FM signals. (2) Any mode of operation that involves very low signal levels, such as *Earth-Moon-Earth*.

Whip antenna — An antenna with an *element* made of a single, flexible rod or tube.

Willful interference — Intentional, deliberate obstruction of radio communications.

Window line — See *open-wire line*.

Winlink — A system of email transmission and distribution using Amateur Radio for the connection between individual amateurs and mailbox stations known as **Radio Message Servers (RMS)**.

WSJT — A suite of software programs for *weak signal* and *scatter mode* communications.

WWV/WWVH — Radio stations run by the National Institute of Standards and Technology (NIST) to provide accurate time and frequencies.

XCVR — Transceiver

XIT — see *transmitter incremental tuning*.

XMTR — Transmitter

Yagi antenna — The most popular type of *directional antenna* or *beam*. It has one *driven element* and one or more *parasitic elements*.

Chapter 11

Question Pool

Technician Class Syllabus
Effective July 1, 2018 to June 30, 2022

SUBELEMENT T1 — FCC Rules, descriptions, and definitions for the Amateur Radio Service, operator and station license responsibilities

[6 Exam Questions — 6 Groups]

T1A   Amateur Radio Service: purpose and permissible use of the Amateur Radio Service, operator/primary station license grant; Meanings of basic terms used in FCC rules; Interference; RACES rules; Phonetics; Frequency Coordinator

T1B   Authorized frequencies: frequency allocations; ITU; emission modes; restricted sub-bands; spectrum sharing; transmissions near band edges; contacting the International Space Station; power output

T1C   Operator licensing: operator classes; sequential and vanity call sign systems; international communications; reciprocal operation; places where the Amateur Radio Service is regulated by the FCC; name and address on FCC license database; license term; renewal; grace period

T1D   Authorized and prohibited transmission: communications with other countries; music; exchange of information with other services; indecent language; compensation for use of station; retransmission of other amateur signals; codes and ciphers; sale of equipment; unidentified transmissions; one-way transmission

T1E   Control operator and control types: control operator required; eligibility; designation of control operator; privileges and duties; control point; local, automatic and remote control; location of control operator

T1F   Station identification; repeaters; third-party communications; club stations; FCC inspection

SUBELEMENT T2 — Operating Procedures

[3 Exam Questions — 3 Groups]

T2A   Station operation: choosing an operating frequency; calling another station; test transmissions; procedural signs; use of minimum power; choosing an operating frequency; band plans; calling frequencies; repeater offsets

T2B   VHF/UHF operating practices: SSB phone; FM repeater; simplex; splits and shifts; CTCSS; DTMF; tone squelch; carrier squelch; phonetics; operational problem resolution; Q signals

T2C   Public service: emergency and non-emergency operations; applicability of FCC rules; RACES and ARES; net and traffic procedures; operating restrictions during emergencies

SUBELEMENT T3 — Radio wave characteristics: properties of radio waves; propagation modes

[3 Exam Questions — 3 Groups]

T3A   Radio wave characteristics: how a radio signal travels; fading; multipath; polarization; wavelength vs absorption; antenna orientation

T3B   Radio and electromagnetic wave properties: the electromagnetic spectrum; wavelength vs frequency; nature and velocity of electromagnetic waves; definition of UHF, VHF, HF bands; calculating wavelength

T3C   Propagation modes: line of sight; sporadic E; meteor and auroral scatter and reflections; tropospheric ducting; F layer skip; radio horizon

SUBELEMENT T4 — Amateur radio practices and station set-up

[2 Exam Questions — 2 Groups]

T4A   Station setup: connecting microphones; reducing unwanted emissions; power source; connecting a computer; RF grounding; connecting digital equipment; connecting an SWR meter

T4B   Operating controls: tuning; use of filters; squelch function; AGC; transceiver operation; memory channels

SUBELEMENT T5 — Electrical principles: math for electronics; electronic principles; Ohm's Law

[4 Exam Questions — 4 Groups]

T5A   Electrical principles, units, and terms: current and voltage; conductors and insulators; alternating and direct current; series and parallel circuits

T5B   Math for electronics: conversion of electrical units; decibels; the metric system

T5C   Electronic principles: capacitance; inductance; current flow in circuits; alternating current; definition of RF; definition of polarity; DC power calculations; impedance

T5D   Ohm's Law: formulas and usage; components in series and parallel

SUBELEMENT T6 — Electrical components; circuit diagrams; component functions

[4 Exam Questions — 4 Groups]

T6A   Electrical components: fixed and variable resistors; capacitors and inductors; fuses; switches; batteries

T6B   Semiconductors: basic principles and applications of solid state devices; diodes and transistors

T6C   Circuit diagrams; schematic symbols

T6D   Component functions: rectification; switches; indicators; power supply components; resonant circuit; shielding; power transformers; integrated circuits

SUBELEMENT T7 — Station equipment: common transmitter and receiver problems; antenna measurements; troubleshooting; basic repair and testing

[4 Exam Questions — 4 Groups]

T7A   Station equipment: receivers; transmitters; transceivers; modulation; transverters; transmit and receive amplifiers

T7B   Common transmitter and receiver problems: symptoms of overload and overdrive; distortion; causes of interference; interference and consumer electronics; part 15 devices; over-modulation; RF feedback; off frequency signals

T7C   Antenna measurements and troubleshooting: measuring SWR; dummy loads; coaxial cables; causes of feed line failures

T7D   Basic repair and testing: soldering; using basic test instruments; connecting a voltmeter, ammeter, or ohmmeter

SUBELEMENT T8 — Modulation modes: amateur satellite operation; operating activities; non-voice and digital communications

[4 Exam Questions — 4 Groups]

T8A   Modulation modes: bandwidth of various signals; choice of emission type

T8B   Amateur satellite operation; Doppler shift; basic orbits; operating protocols; transmitter power considerations; telemetry and telecommand; satellite tracking

T8C   Operating activities: radio direction finding; radio control; contests; linking over the internet; grid locators

T8D   Non-voice and digital communications: image signals; digital modes; CW; packet radio; PSK31; APRS; error detection and correction; NTSC; amateur radio networking; Digital Mobile/Migration Radio

SUBELEMENT T9 — Antennas and feed lines

[2 Exam Questions — 2 Groups]

T9A   Antennas: vertical and horizontal polarization; concept of gain; common portable and mobile antennas; relationships between resonant length and frequency; concept of dipole antennas

T9B   Feed lines: types, attenuation vs frequency, selecting; SWR concepts; Antenna tuners (couplers); RF Connectors: selecting, weather protection

SUBELEMENT T0 — Electrical safety: AC and DC power circuits; antenna installation; RF hazards

[3 Exam Questions — 3 Groups]

T0A   Power circuits and hazards: hazardous voltages; fuses and circuit breakers; grounding; lightning protection; battery safety; electrical code compliance

T0B   Antenna safety: tower safety and grounding; erecting an antenna support; safely installing an antenna

T0C   RF hazards: radiation exposure; proximity to antennas; recognized safe power levels; exposure to others; radiation types; duty cycle

SUBELEMENT T1
FCC Rules, descriptions, and definitions for the Amateur Radio Service, operator and station license responsibilities
[6 Exam Questions — 6 Groups]

T1A — Amateur Radio Service: purpose and permissible use of the Amateur Radio Service, operator/primary station license grant; Meanings of basic terms used in FCC rules; Interference; RACES rules; Phonetics; Frequency Coordinator

T1A01
Which of the following is a purpose of the Amateur Radio Service as stated in the FCC rules and regulations?
    A. Providing personal radio communications for as many citizens as possible
    B. Providing communications for international non-profit organizations
    C. Advancing skills in the technical and communication phases of the radio art
    D. All of these choices are correct

T1A01
(C)
[97.1]
Page 7-2

T1A02
Which agency regulates and enforces the rules for the Amateur Radio Service in the United States?
    A. FEMA
    B. Homeland Security
    C. The FCC
    D. All of these choices are correct

T1A02
(C)
[97.1]
Page 7-2

T1A03
What are the FCC rules regarding the use of a phonetic alphabet for station identification in the Amateur Radio Service?
    A. It is required when transmitting emergency messages
    B. It is prohibited
    C. It is required when in contact with foreign stations
    D. It is encouraged

T1A03
(D)
[97.119(b)(2)]
Page 8-4

T1A04
How many operator/primary station license grants may be held by any one person?
    A. One
    B. No more than two
    C. One for each band on which the person plans to operate
    D. One for each permanent station location from which the person plans to operate

T1A04
(A)
[97.5(b)(1)]
Page 7-3

T1A05
(C)
[97.7]
Page 7-5

T1A05
What is proof of possession of an FCC-issued operator/primary license grant?
    A. A printed operator/primary station license issued by the FCC must be displayed at the transmitter site
    B. The control operator must have an operator/primary station license in his or her possession when in control of a transmitter
    C. The control operator's operator/primary station license must appear in the FCC ULS consolidated licensee database
    D. All of these choices are correct

T1A06
(C)
[97.3(a)(9)]
Page 7-12

T1A06
What is the FCC Part 97 definition of a beacon?
    A. A government transmitter marking the amateur radio band edges
    B. A bulletin sent by the FCC to announce a national emergency
    C. An amateur station transmitting communications for the purposes of observing propagation or related experimental activities
    D. A continuous transmission of weather information authorized in the amateur bands by the National Weather Service

T1A07
(C)
[97.3(a)(41)]
Page 6-23

T1A07
What is the FCC Part 97 definition of a space station?
    A. Any satellite orbiting the earth
    B. A manned satellite orbiting the earth
    C. An amateur station located more than 50 km above the Earth's surface
    D. An amateur station using amateur radio satellites for relay of signals

T1A08
(B)
[97.3(a)(22)]
Page 7-13

T1A08
Which of the following entities recommends transmit/receive channels and other parameters for auxiliary and repeater stations?
    A. Frequency Spectrum Manager appointed by the FCC
    B. Volunteer Frequency Coordinator recognized by local amateurs
    C. FCC Regional Field Office
    D. International Telecommunications Union

T1A09
(C)
[97.3(a)(22)]
Page 7-13

T1A09
Who selects a Frequency Coordinator?
    A. The FCC Office of Spectrum Management and Coordination Policy
    B. The local chapter of the Office of National Council of Independent Frequency Coordinators
    C. Amateur operators in a local or regional area whose stations are eligible to be repeater or auxiliary stations
    D. FCC Regional Field Office

T1A10
(D)
[97.3(a)(38),
97.407]
Page 6-18

T1A10
Which of the following describes the Radio Amateur Civil Emergency Service (RACES)?
    A. A radio service using amateur frequencies for emergency management or civil defense communications
    B. A radio service using amateur stations for emergency management or civil defense communications
    C. An emergency service using amateur operators certified by a civil defense organization as being enrolled in that organization
    D. All of these choices are correct

T1A11

When is willful interference to other amateur radio stations permitted?

A. To stop another amateur station which is breaking the FCC rules
B. At no time
C. When making short test transmissions
D. At any time, stations in the Amateur Radio Service are not protected from willful interference

T1B — Authorized frequencies: frequency allocations; ITU; emission modes; restricted sub-bands; spectrum sharing; transmissions near band edges; contacting the International Space Station; power output

T1B01

What is the International Telecommunications Union (ITU)?

A. An agency of the United States Department of Telecommunications Management
B. A United Nations agency for information and communication technology issues
C. An independent frequency coordination agency
D. A department of the FCC

T1B02

Which amateur radio stations may make contact with an amateur radio station on the International Space Station (ISS) using 2 meter and 70 cm band frequencies?

A. Only members of amateur radio clubs at NASA facilities
B. Any amateur holding a Technician or higher-class license
C. Only the astronaut's family members who are hams
D. Contacts with the ISS are not permitted on amateur radio frequencies

T1B03

Which frequency is within the 6 meter amateur band?

A. 49.00 MHz
B. 52.525 MHz
C. 28.50 MHz
D. 222.15 MHz

T1B04

Which amateur band are you using when your station is transmitting on 146.52 MHz?

A. 2 meter band
B. 20 meter band
C. 14 meter band
D. 6 meter band

T1B05

What is the limitation for emissions on the frequencies between 219 and 220 MHz?

A. Spread spectrum only
B. Fixed digital message forwarding systems only
C. Emergency traffic only
D. Fast-scan television only

T1B06

On which HF bands does a Technician class operator have phone privileges?

A. None
B. 10 meter band only
C. 80 meter, 40 meter, 15 meter and 10 meter bands
D. 30 meter band only

T1A11
(B)
[97.101
(D)]
Page 8-6

T1B01
(B)
Page 7-14

T1B02
(B)
[97.301,
97.207(c)]
Page 6-23

T1B03
(B)
[97.301(a)]
Page 7-9

T1B04
(A)
[97.301(a)]
Page 7-9

T1B05
(B)
[97.305(c)]
Page 7-12

T1B06
(B)
[97.301(e),
97.305]
Page 7-11

T1B07
(A)
[97.305(a),
(c)]
Page 7-12

T1B07
Which of the following VHF/UHF frequency ranges are limited to CW only?
A. 50.0 MHz to 50.1 MHz and 144.0 MHz to 144.1 MHz
B. 219 MHz to 220 MHz and 420.0 MHz to 420.1 MHz
C. 902.0 MHz to 902.1 MHZ
D. All of these choices are correct

T1B08
(A)
[97.303]
Page 7-13

T1B08
Which of the following is a result of the fact that the Amateur Radio Service is secondary in all or portions of some amateur bands (such as portions of the 70 cm band)?
A. U.S. amateurs may find non-amateur stations in those portions, and must avoid interfering with them
B. U.S. amateurs must give foreign amateur stations priority in those portions
C. International communications are not permitted in those portions
D. Digital transmissions are not permitted in those portions

T1B09
(D)
[97.101(a),
97.301(a-e)]
Page 5-7

T1B09
Why should you not set your transmit frequency to be exactly at the edge of an amateur band or sub-band?
A. To allow for calibration error in the transmitter frequency display
B. So that modulation sidebands do not extend beyond the band edge
C. To allow for transmitter frequency drift
D. All of these choices are correct

T1B10
(D)
[97.301(e),
97.305(c)]
Page 7-11

T1B10
Which of the following HF bands have frequencies available to the Technician class operator for RTTY and data transmissions?
A. 10 meter, 12 meter, 17 meter, and 40 meter bands
B. 10 meter, 15 meter, 40 meter, and 80 meter bands
C. 30 meter band only
D. 10 meter band only

T1B11
(A)
[97.313]
Page 7-12

T1B11
What is the maximum peak envelope power output for Technician class operators using their assigned portions of the HF bands?
A. 200 watts
B. 100 watts
C. 50 watts
D. 10 watts

T1B12
(D)
[97.313(b)]
Page 7-12

T1B12
Except for some specific restrictions, what is the maximum peak envelope power output for Technician class operators using frequencies above 30 MHz?
A. 50 watts
B. 100 watts
C. 500 watts
D. 1500 watts

T1C — Operator licensing: operator classes; sequential and vanity call sign systems; international communications; reciprocal operation; places where the Amateur Radio Service is regulated by the FCC; name and address on FCC license database; license term; renewal; grace period

T1C01

For which license classes are new licenses currently available from the FCC?
- A. Novice, Technician, General, Advanced
- B. Technician, Technician Plus, General, Advanced
- C. Novice, Technician Plus, General, Advanced
- D. Technician, General, Amateur Extra

T1C02

Who may select a desired call sign under the vanity call sign rules?
- A. Only a licensed amateur with a General or Amateur Extra class license
- B. Only a licensed amateur with an Amateur Extra class license
- C. Only a licensed amateur who has been licensed continuously for more than 10 years
- D. Any licensed amateur

T1C03

What types of international communications is an FCC-licensed amateur radio station permitted to make?
- A. Communications incidental to the purposes of the Amateur Radio Service and remarks of a personal character
- B. Communications incidental to conducting business or remarks of a personal nature
- C. Only communications incidental to contest exchanges, all other communications are prohibited
- D. Any communications that would be permitted by an international broadcast station

T1C04

When are you allowed to operate your amateur station in a foreign country?
- A. When the foreign country authorizes it
- B. When there is a mutual agreement allowing third party communications
- C. When authorization permits amateur communications in a foreign language
- D. When you are communicating with non-licensed individuals in another country

T1C05

Which of the following is a valid call sign for a Technician class amateur radio station?
- A. K1XXX
- B. KA1X
- C. W1XX
- D. All of these choices are correct

T1C06

From which of the following locations may an FCC-licensed amateur station transmit?
- A. From within any country that belongs to the International Telecommunications Union
- B. From within any country that is a member of the United Nations
- C. From anywhere within International Telecommunications Union (ITU) Regions 2 and 3
- D. From any vessel or craft located in international waters and documented or registered in the United States

T1C01	(D) [97.9(a), 97.17(a)] Page 7-3
T1C02	(D) [97.19] Page 7-17
T1C03	(A) [97.117] Page 7-15
T1C04	(A) [97.107] Page 7-15
T1C05	(A) Page 7-17
T1C06	(D) [97.5(a)(2)] Page 7-15

T1C07
(B)
[97.23]
Page 7-8

T1C07
What may result when correspondence from the FCC is returned as undeliverable because the grantee failed to provide and maintain a correct mailing address with the FCC?
    A. Fine or imprisonment
    B. Revocation of the station license or suspension of the operator license
    C. Require the licensee to be re-examined
    D. A reduction of one rank in operator class

T1C08
(C)
[97.25]
Page 7-5

T1C08
What is the normal term for an FCC-issued primary station/operator amateur radio license grant?
    A. Five years
    B. Life
    C. Ten years
    D. Twenty years

T1C09
(A)
[97.21(a)
(b)]
Page 7-5

T1C09
What is the grace period following the expiration of an amateur license within which the license may be renewed?
    A. Two years
    B. Three years
    C. Five years
    D. Ten years

T1C10
(C)
[97.5a]
Page 7-5

T1C10
How soon after passing the examination for your first amateur radio license may you operate a transmitter on an Amateur Radio Service frequency?
    A. Immediately
    B. 30 days after the test date
    C. As soon as your operator/station license grant appears in the FCC's license database
    D. You must wait until you receive your license in the mail from the FCC

T1C11
(A)
[97.21(b)]
Page 7-5

T1C11
If your license has expired and is still within the allowable grace period, may you continue to operate a transmitter on Amateur Radio Service frequencies?
    A. No, transmitting is not allowed until the FCC license database shows that the license has been renewed
    B. Yes, but only if you identify using the suffix GP
    C. Yes, but only during authorized nets
    D. Yes, for up to two years

T1D — Authorized and prohibited transmission: communications with other countries; music; exchange of information with other services; indecent language; compensation for use of station; retransmission of other amateur signals; codes and ciphers; sale of equipment; unidentified transmissions; one-way transmission

T1D01
(A)
[97.111(a)(1)]
Page 7-15

T1D01
With which countries are FCC-licensed amateur radio stations prohibited from exchanging communications?
    A. Any country whose administration has notified the International Telecommunications Union (ITU) that it objects to such communications
    B. Any country whose administration has notified the American Radio Relay League (ARRL) that it objects to such communications
    C. Any country engaged in hostilities with another country
    D. Any country in violation of the War Powers Act of 1934

T1D02

Under which of the following circumstances may an amateur radio station make one-way transmissions?

A. Under no circumstances

B. When transmitting code practice, information bulletins, or transmissions necessary to provide emergency communications

C. At any time, as long as no music is transmitted

D. At any time, as long as the material being transmitted did not originate from a commercial broadcast station

T1D02
(B)
[97.113(b),
97.111(b)]
Page 8-12

T1D03

When is it permissible to transmit messages encoded to hide their meaning?

A. Only during contests

B. Only when operating mobile

C. Only when transmitting control commands to space stations or radio control craft

D. Only when frequencies above 1280 MHz are used

T1D03
(C)
[97.211(b),
97.215(b),
97.114(a)(4)]
Page 8-11

T1D04

Under what conditions is an amateur station authorized to transmit music using a phone emission?

A. When incidental to an authorized retransmission of manned spacecraft communications

B. When the music produces no spurious emissions

C. When the purpose is to interfere with an illegal transmission

D. When the music is transmitted above 1280 MHz

T1D04
(A)
[97.113(a)(4),
97.113(c)]
Page 8-12

T1D05

When may amateur radio operators use their stations to notify other amateurs of the availability of equipment for sale or trade?

A. When the equipment is normally used in an amateur station and such activity is not conducted on a regular basis

B. When the asking price is $100.00 or less

C. When the asking price is less than its appraised value

D. When the equipment is not the personal property of either the station licensee or the control operator or their close relatives

T1D05
(A)
[97.113(a)(3)(ii)]
Page 8-10

T1D06

What, if any, are the restrictions concerning transmission of language that may be considered indecent or obscene?

A. The FCC maintains a list of words that are not permitted to be used on amateur frequencies

B. Any such language is prohibited

C. The ITU maintains a list of words that are not permitted to be used on amateur frequencies

D. There is no such prohibition

T1D06
(B)
[97.113(a)(4)]
Page 8-10

T1D07

What types of amateur stations can automatically retransmit the signals of other amateur stations?

A. Auxiliary, beacon, or Earth stations

B. Repeater, auxiliary, or space stations

C. Beacon, repeater, or space stations

D. Earth, repeater, or space stations

T1D07
(B)
[97.113(d)]
Page 8-12

T1D08
(B)
[97.113(a)(3)(iii)]
Page 8-11

T1D08

In which of the following circumstances may the control operator of an amateur station receive compensation for operating that station?
- A. When the communication is related to the sale of amateur equipment by the control operator's employer
- B. When the communication is incidental to classroom instruction at an educational institution
- C. When the communication is made to obtain emergency information for a local broadcast station
- D. All of these choices are correct

T1D09
(A)
[97.113(5)(b)]
Page 8-12

T1D09

Under which of the following circumstances are amateur stations authorized to transmit signals related to broadcasting, program production, or news gathering, assuming no other means is available?
- A. Only where such communications directly relate to the immediate safety of human life or protection of property
- B. Only when broadcasting communications to or from the space shuttle
- C. Only where noncommercial programming is gathered and supplied exclusively to the National Public Radio network
- D. Only when using amateur repeaters linked to the internet

T1D10
(D)
[97.3(a)(10)]
Page 8-12

T1D10

What is the meaning of the term broadcasting in the FCC rules for the Amateur Radio Service?
- A. Two-way transmissions by amateur stations
- B. Transmission of music
- C. Transmission of messages directed only to amateur operators
- D. Transmissions intended for reception by the general public

T1D11
(D)
[97.119(a)]
Page 8-3

T1D11

When may an amateur station transmit without on-the-air identification?
- A. When the transmissions are of a brief nature to make station adjustments
- B. When the transmissions are unmodulated
- C. When the transmitted power level is below 1 watt
- D. When transmitting signals to control model craft

T1E — Control operator and control types: control operator required; eligibility; designation of control operator; privileges and duties; control point; local, automatic and remote control; location of control operator

T1E01
(D)
[97.7(a)]
Page 8-1

T1E01

When is an amateur station permitted to transmit without a control operator?
- A. When using automatic control, such as in the case of a repeater
- B. When the station licensee is away and another licensed amateur is using the station
- C. When the transmitting station is an auxiliary station
- D. Never

T1E02
(D)
[97.301, 97.207(c)]
Page 6-22

T1E02

Who may be the control operator of a station communicating through an amateur satellite or space station?
- A. Only an Amateur Extra Class operator
- B. A General class or higher licensee who has a satellite operator certification
- C. Only an Amateur Extra Class operator who is also an AMSAT member
- D. Any amateur whose license privileges allow them to transmit on the satellite uplink frequency

T1E03

Who must designate the station control operator?

A. The station licensee
B. The FCC
C. The frequency coordinator
D. The ITU

T1E03
(A)
[97.103(b)]
Page 8-1

T1E04

What determines the transmitting privileges of an amateur station?

A. The frequency authorized by the frequency coordinator
B. The frequencies printed on the license grant
C. The highest class of operator license held by anyone on the premises
D. The class of operator license held by the control operator

T1E04
(D)
[97.103(b)]
Page 8-2

T1E05

What is an amateur station control point?

A. The location of the station's transmitting antenna
B. The location of the station transmitting apparatus
C. The location at which the control operator function is performed
D. The mailing address of the station licensee

T1E05
(C)
[97.3(a)(14)]
Page 8-1

T1E06

When, under normal circumstances, may a Technician class licensee be the control operator of a station operating in an exclusive Amateur Extra class operator segment of the amateur bands?

A. At no time
B. When operating a special event station
C. As part of a multi-operator contest team
D. When using a club station whose trustee is an Amateur Extra class operator licensee

T1E06
(A)
[97.301]
Page 8-2

T1E07

When the control operator is not the station licensee, who is responsible for the proper operation of the station?

A. All licensed amateurs who are present at the operation
B. Only the station licensee
C. Only the control operator
D. The control operator and the station licensee are equally responsible

T1E07
(D)
[97.103(a)]
Page 8-2

T1E08

Which of the following is an example of automatic control?

A. Repeater operation
B. Controlling the station over the internet
C. Using a computer or other device to send CW automatically
D. Using a computer or other device to identify automatically

T1E08
(A)
[97.3(a)(6),
97.205(d)]
Page 8-9

T1E09

Which of the following is true of remote control operation?

A. The control operator must be at the control point
B. A control operator is required at all times
C. The control operator indirectly manipulates the controls
D. All of these choices are correct

T1E09
(D)
[97.109(c)]
Page 8-9

T1E10
(B)
[97.3(a)(39)]
Page 8-9

T1E10
Which of the following is an example of remote control as defined in Part 97?
- A. Repeater operation
- B. Operating the station over the internet
- C. Controlling a model aircraft, boat, or car by amateur radio
- D. All of these choices are correct

T1E11
(D)
[97.103(a)]
Page 8-2

T1E11
Who does the FCC presume to be the control operator of an amateur station, unless documentation to the contrary is in the station records?
- A. The station custodian
- B. The third-party participant
- C. The person operating the station equipment
- D. The station licensee

T1F — Station identification; repeaters; third-party communications; club stations; FCC inspection

T1F01
(B)
[97.103(c)]
Page 7-8

T1F01
When must the station licensee make the station and its records available for FCC inspection?
- A. At any time ten days after notification by the FCC of such an inspection
- B. At any time upon request by an FCC representative
- C. Only after failing to comply with an FCC notice of violation
- D. Only when presented with a valid warrant by an FCC official or government agent

T1F02
(C)
[97.119(a)]
Page 8-4

T1F02
When using tactical identifiers such as "Race Headquarters" during a community service net operation, how often must your station transmit the station's FCC-assigned call sign?
- A. Never, the tactical call is sufficient
- B. Once during every hour
- C. At the end of each communication and every ten minutes during a communication
- D. At the end of every transmission

T1F03
(D)
[97.119(a)]
Page 8-3

T1F03
When is an amateur station required to transmit its assigned call sign?
- A. At the beginning of each contact, and every 10 minutes thereafter
- B. At least once during each transmission
- C. At least every 15 minutes during and at the end of a communication
- D. At least every 10 minutes during and at the end of a communication

T1F04
(C)
[97.119(b)(2)]
Page 8-4

T1F04
Which of the following is an acceptable language to use for station identification when operating in a phone sub-band?
- A. Any language recognized by the United Nations
- B. Any language recognized by the ITU
- C. The English language
- D. English, French, or Spanish

T1F05
(B)
[97.119(b)(2)]
Page 8-4

T1F05
What method of call sign identification is required for a station transmitting phone signals?
- A. Send the call sign followed by the indicator RPT
- B. Send the call sign using a CW or phone emission
- C. Send the call sign followed by the indicator R
- D. Send the call sign using only a phone emission

T1F06

Which of the following formats of a self-assigned indicator is acceptable when identifying using a phone transmission?
- A. KL7CC stroke W3
- B. KL7CC slant W3
- C. KL7CC slash W3
- D. All of these choices are correct

T1F07

Which of the following restrictions apply when a non-licensed person is allowed to speak to a foreign station using a station under the control of a Technician class control operator?
- A. The person must be a U.S. citizen
- B. The foreign station must be one with which the U.S. has a third-party agreement
- C. The licensed control operator must do the station identification
- D. All of these choices are correct

T1F08

What is meant by the term Third Party Communications?
- A. A message from a control operator to another amateur station control operator on behalf of another person
- B. Amateur radio communications where three stations are in communications with one another
- C. Operation when the transmitting equipment is licensed to a person other than the control operator
- D. Temporary authorization for an unlicensed person to transmit on the amateur bands for technical experiments

T1F09

What type of amateur station simultaneously retransmits the signal of another amateur station on a different channel or channels?
- A. Beacon station
- B. Earth station
- C. Repeater station
- D. Message forwarding station

T1F10

Who is accountable should a repeater inadvertently retransmit communications that violate the FCC rules?
- A. The control operator of the originating station
- B. The control operator of the repeater
- C. The owner of the repeater
- D. Both the originating station and the repeater owner

T1F11

Which of the following is a requirement for the issuance of a club station license grant?
- A. The trustee must have an Amateur Extra class operator license grant
- B. The club must have at least four members
- C. The club must be registered with the American Radio Relay League
- D. All of these choices are correct

T1F06
(D)
[97.119(c)]
Page 8-5

T1F07
(B)
[97.115(a)(2)]
Page 8-8

T1F08
(A)
[97.3(a)(47)]
Page 8-7

T1F09
(C)
[97.3(a)(40)]
Page 2-8

T1F10
(A)
[97.205(g)]
Page 8-9

T1F11
(B)
[97.5(b)(2)]
Page 7-3

SUBELEMENT T2
Operating Procedures
[3 Exam Questions — 3 Groups]

T2A — Station operation: choosing an operating frequency; calling another station; test transmissions; procedural signs; use of minimum power; choosing an operating frequency; band plans; calling frequencies; repeater offsets

T2A01
(B)
Page 6-12

T2A01

Which of the following is a common repeater frequency offset in the 2 meter band?
- A. Plus or minus 5 MHz
- B. Plus or minus 600 kHz
- C. Plus or minus 500 kHz
- D. Plus or minus 1 MHz

T2A02
(A)
Page 6-6

T2A02

What is the national calling frequency for FM simplex operations in the 2 meter band?
- A. 146.520 MHz
- B. 145.000 MHz
- C. 432.100 MHz
- D. 446.000 MHz

T2A03
(A)
Page 6-12

T2A03

What is a common repeater frequency offset in the 70 cm band?
- A. Plus or minus 5 MHz
- B. Plus or minus 600 kHz
- C. Plus or minus 500 kHz
- D. Plus or minus 1 MHz

T2A04
(B)
Page 6-4

T2A04

What is an appropriate way to call another station on a repeater if you know the other station's call sign?
- A. Say "break, break," then say the station's call sign
- B. Say the station's call sign, then identify with your call sign
- C. Say "CQ" three times, then the other station's call sign
- D. Wait for the station to call CQ, then answer it

T2A05
(C)
Page 6-7

T2A05

How should you respond to a station calling CQ?
- A. Transmit "CQ" followed by the other station's call sign
- B. Transmit your call sign followed by the other station's call sign
- C. Transmit the other station's call sign followed by your call sign
- D. Transmit a signal report followed by your call sign

T2A06
(A)
Page 8-5

T2A06

Which of the following is required when making on-the-air test transmissions?
- A. Identify the transmitting station
- B. Conduct tests only between 10 p.m. and 6 a.m. local time
- C. Notify the FCC of the transmissions
- D. All of these choices are correct

T2A07
What is meant by "repeater offset?"
  A. The difference between a repeater's transmit frequency and its receive frequency
  B. The repeater has a time delay to prevent interference
  C. The repeater station identification is done on a separate frequency
  D. The number of simultaneous transmit frequencies used by a repeater

T2A07
(A)
Page 6-12

T2A08
What is the meaning of the procedural signal "CQ"?
  A. Call on the quarter hour
  B. A new antenna is being tested (no station should answer)
  C. Only the called station should transmit
  D. Calling any station

T2A08
(D)
Page 6-6

T2A09
What brief statement indicates that you are listening on a repeater and looking for a contact?
  A. The words "Hello test" followed by your call sign
  B. Your call sign
  C. The repeater call sign followed by your call sign
  D. The letters "QSY" followed by your call sign

T2A09
(B)
Page 6-4

T2A10
What is a band plan, beyond the privileges established by the FCC?
  A. A voluntary guideline for using different modes or activities within an amateur band
  B. A mandated list of operating schedules
  C. A list of scheduled net frequencies
  D. A plan devised by a club to indicate frequency band usage

T2A10
(A)
Page 6-2

T2A11
What term describes an amateur station that is transmitting and receiving on the same frequency?
  A. Full duplex
  B. Diplex
  C. Simplex
  D. Multiplex

T2A11
(C)
Page 6-2

T2A12
Which of the following is a guideline when choosing an operating frequency for calling CQ?
  A. Listen first to be sure that no one else is using the frequency
  B. Ask if the frequency is in use
  C. Make sure you are in your assigned band
  D. All of these choices are correct

T2A12
(D)
Page 6-7

T2B — VHF/UHF operating practices: SSB phone; FM repeater; simplex; splits and shifts; CTCSS; DTMF; tone squelch; carrier squelch; phonetics; operational problem resolution; Q signals

T2B01
What is the most common use of the "reverse split" function of a VHF/UHF transceiver?
  A. Reduce power output
  B. Increase power output
  C. Listen on a repeater's input frequency
  D. Listen on a repeater's output frequency

T2B01
(C)
Page 6-6

T2B02
(D)
Page 6-13

T2B02

What term describes the use of a sub-audible tone transmitted along with normal voice audio to open the squelch of a receiver?

    A. Carrier squelch
    B. Tone burst
    C. DTMF
    D. CTCSS

T2B03
(B)
Page 6-6

T2B03

If a station is not strong enough to keep a repeater's receiver squelch open, which of the following might allow you to receive the station's signal?

    A. Open the squelch on your radio
    B. Listen on the repeater input frequency
    C. Listen on the repeater output frequency
    D. Increase your transmit power

T2B04
(D)
Page 6-13

T2B04

Which of the following could be the reason you are unable to access a repeater whose output you can hear?

    A. Improper transceiver offset
    B. The repeater may require a proper CTCSS tone from your transceiver
    C. The repeater may require a proper DCS tone from your transceiver
    D. All of these choices are correct

T2B05
(C)
Page 5-8

T2B05

What might be the problem if a repeater user says your transmissions are breaking up on voice peaks?

    A. You have the incorrect offset
    B. You need to talk louder
    C. You are talking too loudly
    D. Your transmit power is too high

T2B06
(A)
Page 6-15

T2B06

What type of tones are used to control repeaters linked by the Internet Relay Linking Project (IRLP) protocol?

    A. DTMF
    B. CTCSS
    C. EchoLink
    D. Sub-audible

T2B07
(C)
Page 6-15

T2B07

How can you join a digital repeater's "talk group"?

    A. Register your radio with the local FCC office
    B. Join the repeater owner's club
    C. Program your radio with the group's ID or code
    D. Sign your call after the courtesy tone

T2B08

Which of the following applies when two stations transmitting on the same frequency interfere with each other?
- A. Common courtesy should prevail, but no one has absolute right to an amateur frequency
- B. Whoever has the strongest signal has priority on the frequency
- C. Whoever has been on the frequency the longest has priority on the frequency
- D. The station that has the weakest signal has priority on the frequency

T2B08
(A)
Page 8-6

T2B09

What is a "talk group" on a DMR digital repeater?
- A. A group of operators sharing common interests
- B. A way for groups of users to share a channel at different times without being heard by other users on the channel
- C. A protocol that increases the signal-to-noise ratio when multiple repeaters are linked together
- D. A net that meets at a particular time

T2B09
(B)
Page 6-15

T2B10

Which Q signal indicates that you are receiving interference from other stations?
- A. QRM
- B. QRN
- C. QTH
- D. QSB

T2B10
(A)
Page 6-7

T2B11

Which Q signal indicates that you are changing frequency?
- A. QRU
- B. QSY
- C. QSL
- D. QRZ

T2B11
(B)
Page 6-7

T2B12

Why are simplex channels designated in the VHF/UHF band plans?
- A. So that stations within mutual communications range can communicate without tying up a repeater
- B. For contest operation
- C. For working DX only
- D. So that stations with simple transmitters can access the repeater without automated offset

T2B12
(A)
Page 6-6

T2B13

Where may SSB phone be used in amateur bands above 50 MHz?
- A. Only in sub-bands allocated to General class or higher licensees
- B. Only on repeaters
- C. In at least some portion of all these bands
- D. On any band as long as power is limited to 25 watts

T2B13
(C)
Page 6-2

T2B14

Which of the following describes a linked repeater network?
- A. A network of repeaters where signals received by one repeater are repeated by all the repeaters
- B. A repeater with more than one receiver
- C. Multiple repeaters with the same owner
- D. A system of repeaters linked by APRS

T2B14
(A)
Page 6-12

T2C — Public service: emergency and non-emergency operations; applicability of FCC rules; RACES and ARES; net and traffic procedures; operating restrictions during emergencies

T2C01
(D)
[97.103(a)]
Page 6-18

T2C01

When do the FCC rules NOT apply to the operation of an amateur station?
   A. When operating a RACES station
   B. When operating under special FEMA rules
   C. When operating under special ARES rules
   D. Never, FCC rules always apply

T2C02
(B)
Page 6-16

T2C02

What is meant by the term "NCS" used in net operation?
   A. Nominal Control System
   B. Net Control Station
   C. National Communications Standard
   D. Normal Communications Syntax

T2C03
(C)
Page 6-17

T2C03

What should be done when using voice modes to ensure that voice messages containing unusual words are received correctly?
   A. Send the words by voice and Morse code
   B. Speak very loudly into the microphone
   C. Spell the words using a standard phonetic alphabet
   D. All of these choices are correct

T2C04
(D)
Page 6-18

T2C04

What do RACES and ARES have in common?
   A. They represent the two largest ham clubs in the United States
   B. Both organizations broadcast road and weather information
   C. Neither may handle emergency traffic supporting public service agencies
   D. Both organizations may provide communications during emergencies

T2C05
(A)
Page 6-15

T2C05

What does the term "traffic" refer to in net operation?
   A. Formal messages exchanged by net stations
   B. The number of stations checking in and out of a net
   C. Operation by mobile or portable stations
   D. Requests to activate the net by a served agency

T2C06
(C)
Page 6-16

T2C06

Which of the following is an accepted practice to get the immediate attention of a net control station when reporting an emergency?
   A. Repeat "SOS" three times followed by the call sign of the reporting station
   B. Press the push-to-talk button three times
   C. Begin your transmission by saying "Priority" or "Emergency" followed by your call sign
   D. Play a pre-recorded emergency alert tone followed by your call sign

T2C07

Which of the following is an accepted practice for an amateur operator who has checked into a net?

    A. Provided that the frequency is quiet, announce the station call sign and location every 5 minutes

    B. Move 5 kHz away from the net's frequency and use high power to ask other hams to keep clear of the net frequency

    C. Remain on frequency without transmitting until asked to do so by the net control station

    D. All of these choices are correct

T2C08

Which of the following is a characteristic of good traffic handling?

    A. Passing messages exactly as received

    B. Making decisions as to whether messages are worthy of relay or delivery

    C. Ensuring that any newsworthy messages are relayed to the news media

    D. All of these choices are correct

T2C09

Are amateur station control operators ever permitted to operate outside the frequency privileges of their license class?

    A. No

    B. Yes, but only when part of a FEMA emergency plan

    C. Yes, but only when part of a RACES emergency plan

    D. Yes, but only if necessary in situations involving the immediate safety of human life or protection of property

T2C10

What information is contained in the preamble of a formal traffic message?

    A. The email address of the originating station

    B. The address of the intended recipient

    C. The telephone number of the addressee

    D. The information needed to track the message

T2C11

What is meant by the term "check," in reference to a formal traffic message?

    A. The number of words or word equivalents in the text portion of the message

    B. The value of a money order attached to the message

    C. A list of stations that have relayed the message

    D. A box on the message form that indicates that the message was received and/or relayed

T2C12

What is the Amateur Radio Emergency Service (ARES)?

    A. Licensed amateurs who have voluntarily registered their qualifications and equipment for communications duty in the public service

    B. Licensed amateurs who are members of the military and who voluntarily agreed to provide message handling services in the case of an emergency

    C. A training program that provides licensing courses for those interested in obtaining an amateur license to use during emergencies

    D. A training program that certifies amateur operators for membership in the Radio Amateur Civil Emergency Service

T2C07
(C)
Page 6-16

T2C08
(A)
Page 6-16

T2C09
(D)
Page 6-18

T2C10
(D)
Page 6-17

T2C11
(A)
Page 6-17

T2C12
(A)
Page 6-18

SUBELEMENT T3

Radio wave characteristics: properties of radio waves; propagation modes

[3 Exam Questions — 3 Groups]

T3A — Radio wave characteristics: how a radio signal travels; fading; multipath; polarization; wavelength vs absorption; antenna orientation

T3A01
(D)
Page 4-2

T3A01
What should you do if another operator reports that your station's 2 meter signals were strong just a moment ago, but now they are weak or distorted?
- A. Change the batteries in your radio to a different type
- B. Turn on the CTCSS tone
- C. Ask the other operator to adjust his squelch control
- D. Try moving a few feet or changing the direction of your antenna if possible, as reflections may be causing multi-path distortion

T3A02
(B)
Page 4-2

T3A02
Why might the range of VHF and UHF signals be greater in the winter?
- A. Less ionospheric absorption
- B. Less absorption by vegetation
- C. Less solar activity
- D. Less tropospheric absorption

T3A03
(C)
Page 4-16

T3A03
What antenna polarization is normally used for long-distance weak-signal CW and SSB contacts using the VHF and UHF bands?
- A. Right-hand circular
- B. Left-hand circular
- C. Horizontal
- D. Vertical

T3A04
(B)
Page 4-6

T3A04
What can happen if the antennas at opposite ends of a VHF or UHF line of sight radio link are not using the same polarization?
- A. The modulation sidebands might become inverted
- B. Signals could be significantly weaker
- C. Signals have an echo effect on voices
- D. Nothing significant will happen

T3A05
(B)
Page 4-16

T3A05
When using a directional antenna, how might your station be able to access a distant repeater if buildings or obstructions are blocking the direct line of sight path?
- A. Change from vertical to horizontal polarization
- B. Try to find a path that reflects signals to the repeater
- C. Try the long path
- D. Increase the antenna SWR

T3A06
What term is commonly used to describe the rapid fluttering sound sometimes heard from mobile stations that are moving while transmitting?

A. Flip-flopping
B. Picket fencing
C. Frequency shifting
D. Pulsing

T3A06
(B)
Page 4-3

T3A07
What type of wave carries radio signals between transmitting and receiving stations?

A. Electromagnetic
B. Electrostatic
C. Surface acoustic
D. Ferromagnetic

T3A07
(A)
Page 4-6

T3A08
Which of the following is a likely cause of irregular fading of signals received by ionospheric reflection?

A. Frequency shift due to Faraday rotation
B. Interference from thunderstorms
C. Random combining of signals arriving via different paths
D. Intermodulation distortion

T3A08
(C)
Page 4-2

T3A09
Which of the following results from the fact that skip signals refracted from the ionosphere are elliptically polarized?

A. Digital modes are unusable
B. Either vertically or horizontally polarized antennas may be used for transmission or reception
C. FM voice is unusable
D. Both the transmitting and receiving antennas must be of the same polarization

T3A09
(B)
Page 4-7

T3A10
What may occur if data signals arrive via multiple paths?

A. Transmission rates can be increased by a factor equal to the number of separate paths observed
B. Transmission rates must be decreased by a factor equal to the number of separate paths observed
C. No significant changes will occur if the signals are transmitted using FM
D. Error rates are likely to increase

T3A10
(D)
Page 4-3

T3A11
Which part of the atmosphere enables the propagation of radio signals around the world?

A. The stratosphere
B. The troposphere
C. The ionosphere
D. The magnetosphere

T3A11
(C)
Page 4-3

T3A12
How might fog and light rain affect radio range on the 10 meter and 6 meter bands?

A. Fog and rain absorb these wavelength bands
B. Fog and light rain will have little effect on these bands
C. Fog and rain will deflect these signals
D. Fog and rain will increase radio range

T3A12
(B)
Page 4-2

T3A13

What weather condition would decrease range at microwave frequencies?
- A. High winds
- B. Low barometric pressure
- C. Precipitation
- D. Colder temperatures

T3B — Radio and electromagnetic wave properties: the electromagnetic spectrum; wavelength vs frequency; nature and velocity of electromagnetic waves; definition of UHF, VHF, HF bands; calculating wavelength

T3B01

What is the name for the distance a radio wave travels during one complete cycle?
- A. Wave speed
- B. Waveform
- C. Wavelength
- D. Wave spread

T3B02

What property of a radio wave is used to describe its polarization?
- A. The orientation of the electric field
- B. The orientation of the magnetic field
- C. The ratio of the energy in the magnetic field to the energy in the electric field
- D. The ratio of the velocity to the wavelength

T3B03

What are the two components of a radio wave?
- A. AC and DC
- B. Voltage and current
- C. Electric and magnetic fields
- D. Ionizing and non-ionizing radiation

T3B04

How fast does a radio wave travel through free space?
- A. At the speed of light
- B. At the speed of sound
- C. Its speed is inversely proportional to its wavelength
- D. Its speed increases as the frequency increases

T3B05

How does the wavelength of a radio wave relate to its frequency?
- A. The wavelength gets longer as the frequency increases
- B. The wavelength gets shorter as the frequency increases
- C. There is no relationship between wavelength and frequency
- D. The wavelength depends on the bandwidth of the signal

T3B06

What is the formula for converting frequency to approximate wavelength in meters?
- A. Wavelength in meters equals frequency in hertz multiplied by 300
- B. Wavelength in meters equals frequency in hertz divided by 300
- C. Wavelength in meters equals frequency in megahertz divided by 300
- D. Wavelength in meters equals 300 divided by frequency in megahertz

T3B07
What property of radio waves is often used to identify the different frequency bands?
A. The approximate wavelength
B. The magnetic intensity of waves
C. The time it takes for waves to travel one mile
D. The voltage standing wave ratio of waves

T3B08
What are the frequency limits of the VHF spectrum?
A. 30 to 300 kHz
B. 30 to 300 MHz
C. 300 to 3000 kHz
D. 300 to 3000 MHz

T3B09
What are the frequency limits of the UHF spectrum?
A. 30 to 300 kHz
B. 30 to 300 MHz
C. 300 to 3000 kHz
D. 300 to 3000 MHz

T3B10
What frequency range is referred to as HF?
A. 300 to 3000 MHz
B. 30 to 300 MHz
C. 3 to 30 MHz
D. 300 to 3000 kHz

T3B11
What is the approximate velocity of a radio wave as it travels through free space?
A. 150,000 kilometers per second
B. 300,000,000 meters per second
C. 300,000,000 miles per hour
D. 150,000 miles per hour

T3C — Propagation modes: line of sight; sporadic E; meteor and auroral scatter and reflections; tropospheric ducting; F layer skip; radio horizon

T3C01
Why are direct (not via a repeater) UHF signals rarely heard from stations outside your local coverage area?
A. They are too weak to go very far
B. FCC regulations prohibit them from going more than 50 miles
C. UHF signals are usually not reflected by the ionosphere
D. UHF signals are absorbed by the ionospheric D layer

T3C02
Which of the following is an advantage of HF vs VHF and higher frequencies?
A. HF antennas are generally smaller
B. HF accommodates wider bandwidth signals
C. Long distance ionospheric propagation is far more common on HF
D. There is less atmospheric interference (static) on HF

T3B07
(A)
Page 2-6

T3B08
(B)
Page 2-4

T3B09
(D)
Page 2-4

T3B10
(C)
Page 2-4

T3B11
(B)
Page 2-5

T3C01
(C)
Page 4-4

T3C02
(C)
Page 4-4

Question Pool 11-23

T3C03

What is a characteristic of VHF signals received via auroral reflection?
  A. Signals from distances of 10,000 or more miles are common
  B. The signals exhibit rapid fluctuations of strength and often sound distorted
  C. These types of signals occur only during winter nighttime hours
  D. These types of signals are generally strongest when your antenna is aimed west

T3C04

Which of the following propagation types is most commonly associated with occasional strong over-the-horizon signals on the 10, 6, and 2 meter bands?
  A. Backscatter
  B. Sporadic E
  C. D layer absorption
  D. Gray-line propagation

T3C05

Which of the following effects might cause radio signals to be heard despite obstructions between the transmitting and receiving stations?
  A. Knife-edge diffraction
  B. Faraday rotation
  C. Quantum tunneling
  D. Doppler shift

T3C06

What mode is responsible for allowing over-the-horizon VHF and UHF communications to ranges of approximately 300 miles on a regular basis?
  A. Tropospheric ducting
  B. D layer refraction
  C. F2 layer refraction
  D. Faraday rotation

T3C07

What band is best suited for communicating via meteor scatter?
  A. 10 meter band
  B. 6 meter band
  C. 2 meter band
  D. 70 centimeter band

T3C08

What causes tropospheric ducting?
  A. Discharges of lightning during electrical storms
  B. Sunspots and solar flares
  C. Updrafts from hurricanes and tornadoes
  D. Temperature inversions in the atmosphere

T3C09

What is generally the best time for long-distance 10 meter band propagation via the F layer?
  A. From dawn to shortly after sunset during periods of high sunspot activity
  B. From shortly after sunset to dawn during periods of high sunspot activity
  C. From dawn to shortly after sunset during periods of low sunspot activity
  D. From shortly after sunset to dawn during periods of low sunspot activity

T3C10
Which of the following bands may provide long distance communications during the peak of the sunspot cycle?
    A. 6 or 10 meter bands
    B. 23 centimeter band
    C. 70 centimeter or 1.25 meter bands
    D. All of these choices are correct

T3C10
(A)
Page 4-4

T3C11
Why do VHF and UHF radio signals usually travel somewhat farther than the visual line of sight distance between two stations?
    A. Radio signals move somewhat faster than the speed of light
    B. Radio waves are not blocked by dust particles
    C. The Earth seems less curved to radio waves than to light
    D. Radio waves are blocked by dust particles

T3C11
(C)
Page 4-2

SUBELEMENT T4

Amateur radio practices and station set-up
[2 Exam Questions — 2 Groups]

T4A — Station setup: connecting microphones; reducing unwanted emissions; power source; connecting a computer; RF grounding; connecting digital equipment; connecting an SWR meter

T4A01
(D)
Page 5-16

T4A01

What must be considered to determine the minimum current capacity needed for a transceiver power supply?
- A. Efficiency of the transmitter at full power output
- B. Receiver and control circuit power
- C. Power supply regulation and heat dissipation
- D. All of these choices are correct

T4A02
(D)
Page 5-11

T4A02

How might a computer be used as part of an amateur radio station?
- A. For logging contacts and contact information
- B. For sending and/or receiving CW
- C. For generating and decoding digital signals
- D. All of these choices are correct

T4A03
(A)
Page 5-17

T4A03

Why should wiring between the power source and radio be heavy-gauge wire and kept as short as possible?
- A. To avoid voltage falling below that needed for proper operation
- B. To provide a good counterpoise for the antenna
- C. To avoid RF interference
- D. All of these choices are correct

T4A04
(C)
Page 5-15

T4A04

Which computer sound card port is connected to a transceiver's headphone or speaker output for operating digital modes?
- A. Headphone output
- B. Mute
- C. Microphone or line input
- D. PCI or SDI

T4A05
(A)
Page 4-18

T4A05

What is the proper location for an external SWR meter?
- A. In series with the feed line, between the transmitter and antenna
- B. In series with the station's ground
- C. In parallel with the push-to-talk line and the antenna
- D. In series with the power supply cable, as close as possible to the radio

T4A06
(C)
Page 5-15

T4A06

Which of the following connections might be used between a voice transceiver and a computer for digital operation?
- A. Receive and transmit mode, status, and location
- B. Antenna and RF power
- C. Receive audio, transmit audio, and push-to-talk (PTT)
- D. NMEA GPS location and DC power

T4A07

How is a computer's sound card used when conducting digital communications?
- A. The sound card communicates between the computer CPU and the video display
- B. The sound card records the audio frequency for video display
- C. The sound card provides audio to the radio's microphone input and converts received audio to digital form
- D. All of these choices are correct

T4A07
(C)
Page 5-15

T4A08

Which of the following conductors provides the lowest impedance to RF signals?
- A. Round stranded wire
- B. Round copper-clad steel wire
- C. Twisted-pair cable
- D. Flat strap

T4A08
(D)
Page 9-7

T4A09

Which of the following could you use to cure distorted audio caused by RF current on the shield of a microphone cable?
- A. Band-pass filter
- B. Low-pass filter
- C. Preamplifier
- D. Ferrite choke

T4A09
(D)
Page 9-8

T4A10

What is the source of a high-pitched whine that varies with engine speed in a mobile transceiver's receive audio?
- A. The ignition system
- B. The alternator
- C. The electric fuel pump
- D. Anti-lock braking system controllers

T4A10
(B)
Page 5-17

T4A11

Where should the negative return connection of a mobile transceiver's power cable be connected?
- A. At the battery or engine block ground strap
- B. At the antenna mount
- C. To any metal part of the vehicle
- D. Through the transceiver's mounting bracket

T4A11
(A)
Page 5-17

T4B — Operating controls: tuning; use of filters; squelch function; AGC; transceiver operation; memory channels

T4B01

What may happen if a transmitter is operated with the microphone gain set too high?
- A. The output power might be too high
- B. The output signal might become distorted
- C. The frequency might vary
- D. The SWR might increase

T4B01
(B)
Page 5-8

T4B02
(A)
Page 5-6

T4B02
Which of the following can be used to enter the operating frequency on a modern transceiver?
- A. The keypad or VFO knob
- B. The CTCSS or DTMF encoder
- C. The Automatic Frequency Control
- D. All of these choices are correct

T4B03
(D)
Page 5-9

T4B03
What is the purpose of the squelch control on a transceiver?
- A. To set the highest level of volume desired
- B. To set the transmitter power level
- C. To adjust the automatic gain control
- D. To mute receiver output noise when no signal is being received

T4B04
(B)
Page 5-7

T4B04
What is a way to enable quick access to a favorite frequency on your transceiver?
- A. Enable the CTCSS tones
- B. Store the frequency in a memory channel
- C. Disable the CTCSS tones
- D. Use the scan mode to select the desired frequency

T4B05
(C)
Page 5-10

T4B05
Which of the following would reduce ignition interference to a receiver?
- A. Change frequency slightly
- B. Decrease the squelch setting
- C. Turn on the noise blanker
- D. Use the RIT control

T4B06
(D)
Page 5-10

T4B06
Which of the following controls could be used if the voice pitch of a single-sideband signal seems too high or low?
- A. The AGC or limiter
- B. The bandwidth selection
- C. The tone squelch
- D. The receiver RIT or clarifier

T4B07
(B)
Page 5-10

T4B07
What does the term "RIT" mean?
- A. Receiver Input Tone
- B. Receiver Incremental Tuning
- C. Rectifier Inverter Test
- D. Remote Input Transmitter

T4B08
(B)
Page 5-9

T4B08
What is the advantage of having multiple receive bandwidth choices on a multimode transceiver?
- A. Permits monitoring several modes at once
- B. Permits noise or interference reduction by selecting a bandwidth matching the mode
- C. Increases the number of frequencies that can be stored in memory
- D. Increases the amount of offset between receive and transmit frequencies

T4B09

Which of the following is an appropriate receive filter bandwidth for minimizing noise and interference for SSB reception?

- A. 500 Hz
- B. 1000 Hz
- C. 2400 Hz
- D. 5000 Hz

T4B10

Which of the following is an appropriate receive filter bandwidth for minimizing noise and interference for CW reception?

- A. 500 Hz
- B. 1000 Hz
- C. 2400 Hz
- D. 5000 Hz

T4B11

What is the function of automatic gain control, or AGC?

- A. To keep received audio relatively constant
- B. To protect an antenna from lightning
- C. To eliminate RF on the station cabling
- D. An asymmetric goniometer control used for antenna matching

T4B12

Which of the following could be used to remove power line noise or ignition noise?

- A. Squelch
- B. Noise blanker
- C. Notch filter
- D. All of these choices are correct

T4B13

Which of the following is a use for the scanning function of an FM transceiver?

- A. To check incoming signal deviation
- B. To prevent interference to nearby repeaters
- C. To scan through a range of frequencies to check for activity
- D. To check for messages left on a digital bulletin board

T4B09
(C)
Page 5-9

T4B10
(A)
Page 5-9

T4B11
(A)
Page 5-9

T4B12
(B)
Page 5-10

T4B13
(C)
Page 6-10

SUBELEMENT T5
Electrical principles: math for electronics; electronic principles; Ohm's Law
[4 Exam Questions — 4 Groups]

T5A — Electrical principles, units, and terms: current and voltage; conductors and insulators; alternating and direct current; series and parallel circuits

T5A01
(D)
Page 3-1

T5A01
Electrical current is measured in which of the following units?
- A. Volts
- B. Watts
- C. Ohms
- D. Amperes

T5A02
(B)
Page 3-7

T5A02
Electrical power is measured in which of the following units?
- A. Volts
- B. Watts
- C. Ohms
- D. Amperes

T5A03
(D)
Page 3-1

T5A03
What is the name for the flow of electrons in an electric circuit?
- A. Voltage
- B. Resistance
- C. Capacitance
- D. Current

T5A04
(B)
Page 3-2

T5A04
What is the name for a current that flows only in one direction?
- A. Alternating current
- B. Direct current
- C. Normal current
- D. Smooth current

T5A05
(A)
Page 3-1

T5A05
What is the electrical term for the electromotive force (EMF) that causes electron flow?
- A. Voltage
- B. Ampere-hours
- C. Capacitance
- D. Inductance

T5A06
(A)
Page 5-16

T5A06
How much voltage does a mobile transceiver typically require?
- A. About 12 volts
- B. About 30 volts
- C. About 120 volts
- D. About 240 volts

T5A07
Which of the following is a good electrical conductor?
  A. Glass
  B. Wood
  C. Copper
  D. Rubber

T5A08
Which of the following is a good electrical insulator?
  A. Copper
  B. Glass
  C. Aluminum
  D. Mercury

T5A09
What is the name for a current that reverses direction on a regular basis?
  A. Alternating current
  B. Direct current
  C. Circular current
  D. Vertical current

T5A10
Which term describes the rate at which electrical energy is used?
  A. Resistance
  B. Current
  C. Power
  D. Voltage

T5A11
What is the unit of electromotive force?
  A. The volt
  B. The watt
  C. The ampere
  D. The ohm

T5A12
What describes the number of times per second that an alternating current makes a complete cycle?
  A. Pulse rate
  B. Speed
  C. Wavelength
  D. Frequency

T5A13
In which type of circuit is current the same through all components?
  A. Series
  B. Parallel
  C. Resonant
  D. Branch

T5A14
In which type of circuit is voltage the same across all components?
  A. Series
  B. Parallel
  C. Resonant
  D. Branch

T5A07
(C)
Page 3-5

T5A08
(B)
Page 3-5

T5A09
(A)
Page 3-2

T5A10
(C)
Page 3-7

T5A11
(A)
Page 3-2

T5A12
(D)
Page 2-3

T5A13
(A)
Page 3-2

T5A14
(B)
Page 3-2

T5B01
(C)
Page 2-2

T5B01
How many milliamperes is 1.5 amperes?
    A. 15 milliamperes
    B. 150 milliamperes
    C. 1500 milliamperes
    D. 15,000 milliamperes

T5B02
(A)
Page 2-2

T5B02
What is another way to specify a radio signal frequency of 1,500,000 hertz?
    A. 1500 kHz
    B. 1500 MHz
    C. 15 GHz
    D. 150 kHz

T5B03
(C)
Page 2-2

T5B03
How many volts are equal to one kilovolt?
    A. One one-thousandth of a volt
    B. One hundred volts
    C. One thousand volts
    D. One million volts

T5B04
(A)
Page 2-2

T5B04
How many volts are equal to one microvolt?
    A. One one-millionth of a volt
    B. One million volts
    C. One thousand kilovolts
    D. One one-thousandth of a volt

T5B05
(B)
Page 2-2

T5B05
Which of the following is equal to 500 milliwatts?
    A. 0.02 watts
    B. 0.5 watts
    C. 5 watts
    D. 50 watts

T5B06
(C)
Page 2-2

T5B06
If an ammeter calibrated in amperes is used to measure a 3000-milliampere current, what reading would it show?
    A. 0.003 amperes
    B. 0.3 amperes
    C. 3 amperes
    D. 3,000,000 amperes

T5B07
(C)
Page 2-2

T5B07
If a frequency display calibrated in megahertz shows a reading of 3.525 MHz, what would it show if it were calibrated in kilohertz?
    A. 0.003525 kHz
    B. 35.25 kHz
    C. 3525 kHz
    D. 3,525,000 kHz

T5B08

How many microfarads are equal to 1,000,000 picofarads?

- A. 0.001 microfarads
- B. 1 microfarad
- C. 1000 microfarads
- D. 1,000,000,000 microfarads

T5B09

What is the approximate amount of change, measured in decibels (dB), of a power increase from 5 watts to 10 watts?

- A. 2 dB
- B. 3 dB
- C. 5 dB
- D. 10 dB

T5B10

What is the approximate amount of change, measured in decibels (dB), of a power decrease from 12 watts to 3 watts?

- A. −1 dB
- B. −3 dB
- C. −6 dB
- D. −9 dB

T5B11

What is the amount of change, measured in decibels (dB), of a power increase from 20 watts to 200 watts?

- A. 10 dB
- B. 12 dB
- C. 18 dB
- D. 28 dB

T5B12

Which of the following frequencies is equal to 28,400 kHz?

- A. 28.400 MHz
- B. 2.800 MHz
- C. 284.00 MHz
- D. 28.400 kHz

T5B13

If a frequency display shows a reading of 2425 MHz, what frequency is that in GHz?

- A. 0.002425 GHz
- B. 24.25 GHz
- C. 2.425 GHz
- D. 2425 GHz

T5C — Electronic principles: capacitance; inductance; current flow in circuits; alternating current; definition of RF; definition of polarity; DC power calculations; impedance

T5C01

What is the ability to store energy in an electric field called?

- A. Inductance
- B. Resistance
- C. Tolerance
- D. Capacitance

T5B08
(B)
Page 2-2

T5B09
(B)
Page 4-8

T5B10
(C)
Page 4-8

T5B11
(A)
Page 4-8

T5B12
(A)
Page 2-2

T5B13
(C)
Page 2-2

T5C01
(D)
Page 3-9

T5C02
(A)
Page 3-9

T5C02
What is the basic unit of capacitance?
  A. The farad
  B. The ohm
  C. The volt
  D. The henry

T5C03
(D)
Page 3-9

T5C03
What is the ability to store energy in a magnetic field called?
  A. Admittance
  B. Capacitance
  C. Resistance
  D. Inductance

T5C04
(C)
Page 3-9

T5C04
What is the basic unit of inductance?
  A. The coulomb
  B. The farad
  C. The henry
  D. The ohm

T5C05
(A)
Page 2-3

T5C05
.What is the unit of frequency?
  A. Hertz
  B. Henry
  C. Farad
  D. Tesla

T5C06
(A)
Page 2-4

T5C06
What does the abbreviation "RF" refer to?
  A. Radio frequency signals of all types
  B. The resonant frequency of a tuned circuit
  C. The real frequency transmitted as opposed to the apparent frequency
  D. Reflective force in antenna transmission lines

T5C07
(B)
Page 4-6

T5C07
A radio wave is made up of what type of energy?
  A. Pressure
  B. Electromagnetic
  C. Gravity
  D. Thermal

T5C08
(A)
Page 3-7

T5C08
What is the formula used to calculate electrical power in a DC circuit?
  A. Power (P) equals voltage (E) multiplied by current (I)
  B. Power (P) equals voltage (E) divided by current (I)
  C. Power (P) equals voltage (E) minus current (I)
  D. Power (P) equals voltage (E) plus current (I)

T5C09
How much power is being used in a circuit when the applied voltage is 13.8 volts DC and the current is 10 amperes?
    A. 138 watts
    B. 0.7 watts
    C. 23.8 watts
    D. 3.8 watts

T5C10
How much power is being used in a circuit when the applied voltage is 12 volts DC and the current is 2.5 amperes?
    A. 4.8 watts
    B. 30 watts
    C. 14.5 watts
    D. 0.208 watts

T5C11
How many amperes are flowing in a circuit when the applied voltage is 12 volts DC and the load is 120 watts?
    A. 0.1 amperes
    B. 10 amperes
    C. 12 amperes
    D. 132 amperes

T5C12
What is impedance?
    A. A measure of the opposition to AC current flow in a circuit
    B. The inverse of resistance
    C. The Q or Quality Factor of a component
    D. The power handling capability of a component

T5C13
What is a unit of impedance?
    A. Volts
    B. Amperes
    C. Coulombs
    D. Ohms

T5C14
What is the proper abbreviation for megahertz?
    A. mHz
    B. mhZ
    C. Mhz
    D. MHz

T5D — Ohm's Law: formulas and usage; components in series and parallel

T5D01
What formula is used to calculate current in a circuit?
    A. Current (I) equals voltage (E) multiplied by resistance (R)
    B. Current (I) equals voltage (E) divided by resistance (R)
    C. Current (I) equals voltage (E) added to resistance (R)
    D. Current (I) equals voltage (E) minus resistance (R)

T5C09
(A)
Page 3-7

T5C10
(B)
Page 3-7

T5C11
(B)
Page 3-7

T5C12
(A)
Page 3-10

T5C13
(D)
Page 3-10

T5C14
(D)
Page 2-3

T5D01
(B)
Page 3-5

T5D02
What formula is used to calculate voltage in a circuit?
- A. Voltage (E) equals current (I) multiplied by resistance (R)
- B. Voltage (E) equals current (I) divided by resistance (R)
- C. Voltage (E) equals current (I) added to resistance (R)
- D. Voltage (E) equals current (I) minus resistance (R)

T5D03
What formula is used to calculate resistance in a circuit?
- A. Resistance (R) equals voltage (E) multiplied by current (I)
- B. Resistance (R) equals voltage (E) divided by current (I)
- C. Resistance (R) equals voltage (E) added to current (I)
- D. Resistance (R) equals voltage (E) minus current (I)

T5D04
What is the resistance of a circuit in which a current of 3 amperes flows through a resistor connected to 90 volts?
- A. 3 ohms
- B. 30 ohms
- C. 93 ohms
- D. 270 ohms

T5D05
What is the resistance in a circuit for which the applied voltage is 12 volts and the current flow is 1.5 amperes?
- A. 18 ohms
- B. 0.125 ohms
- C. 8 ohms
- D. 13.5 ohms

T5D06
What is the resistance of a circuit that draws 4 amperes from a 12-volt source?
- A. 3 ohms
- B. 16 ohms
- C. 48 ohms
- D. 8 ohms

T5D07
What is the current in a circuit with an applied voltage of 120 volts and a resistance of 80 ohms?
- A. 9600 amperes
- B. 200 amperes
- C. 0.667 amperes
- D. 1.5 amperes

T5D08
What is the current through a 100-ohm resistor connected across 200 volts?
- A. 20,000 amperes
- B. 0.5 amperes
- C. 2 amperes
- D. 100 amperes

T5D09

What is the current through a 24-ohm resistor connected across 240 volts?
- A. 24,000 amperes
- B. 0.1 amperes
- C. 10 amperes
- D. 216 amperes

T5D09
(C)
Page 3-6

T5D10

What is the voltage across a 2-ohm resistor if a current of 0.5 amperes flows through it?
- A. 1 volt
- B. 0.25 volts
- C. 2.5 volts
- D. 1.5 volts

T5D10
(A)
Page 3-6

T5D11

What is the voltage across a 10-ohm resistor if a current of 1 ampere flows through it?
- A. 1 volt
- B. 10 volts
- C. 11 volts
- D. 9 volts

T5D11
(B)
Page 3-7

T5D12

What is the voltage across a 10-ohm resistor if a current of 2 amperes flows through it?
- A. 8 volts
- B. 0.2 volts
- C. 12 volts
- D. 20 volts

T5D12
(D)
Page 3-7

T5D13

What happens to current at the junction of two components in series?
- A. It divides equally between them
- B. It is unchanged
- C. It divides based on the on the value of the components
- D. The current in the second component is zero

T5D13
(B)
Page 3-2

T5D14

What happens to current at the junction of two components in parallel?
- A. It divides between them dependent on the value of the components
- B. It is the same in both components
- C. Its value doubles
- D. Its value is halved

T5D14
(A)
Page 3-2

T5D15

What is the voltage across each of two components in series with a voltage source?
- A. The same voltage as the source
- B. Half the source voltage
- C. It is determined by the type and value of the components
- D. Twice the source voltage

T5D15
(C)
Page 3-2

T5D16

What is the voltage across each of two components in parallel with a voltage source?
- A. It is determined by the type and value of the components
- B. Half the source voltage
- C. Twice the source voltage
- D. The same voltage as the source

T5D16
(D)
Page 3-3

SUBELEMENT T6

Electrical components; circuit diagrams; component functions
[4 Exam Questions — 4 Groups]

T6A — Electrical components: fixed and variable resistors; capacitors and inductors; fuses; switches; batteries

T6A01
(B)
Page 3-9

T6A01
What electrical component opposes the flow of current in a DC circuit?
  A. Inductor
  B. Resistor
  C. Voltmeter
  D. Transformer

T6A02
(C)
Page 3-9

T6A02
What type of component is often used as an adjustable volume control?
  A. Fixed resistor
  B. Power resistor
  C. Potentiometer
  D. Transformer

T6A03
(B)
Page 3-9

T6A03
What electrical parameter is controlled by a potentiometer?
  A. Inductance
  B. Resistance
  C. Capacitance
  D. Field strength

T6A04
(B)
Page 3-9

T6A04
What electrical component stores energy in an electric field?
  A. Resistor
  B. Capacitor
  C. Inductor
  D. Diode

T6A05
(D)
Page 3-9

T6A05
What type of electrical component consists of two or more conductive surfaces separated by an insulator?
  A. Resistor
  B. Potentiometer
  C. Oscillator
  D. Capacitor

T6A06
(C)
Page 3-9

T6A06
What type of electrical component stores energy in a magnetic field?
  A. Resistor
  B. Capacitor
  C. Inductor
  D. Diode

T6A07

What electrical component usually is constructed as a coil of wire?
- A. Switch
- B. Capacitor
- C. Diode
- D. Inductor

T6A08

What electrical component is used to connect or disconnect electrical circuits?
- A. Magnetron
- B. Switch
- C. Thermistor
- D. All of these choices are correct

T6A09

What electrical component is used to protect other circuit components from current overloads?
- A. Fuse
- B. Capacitor
- C. Inductor
- D. All of these choices are correct

T6A10

Which of the following battery types is rechargeable?
- A. Nickel-metal hydride
- B. Lithium-ion
- C. Lead-acid gel-cell
- D. All of these choices are correct

T6A11

Which of the following battery types is not rechargeable?
- A. Nickel-cadmium
- B. Carbon-zinc
- C. Lead-acid
- D. Lithium-ion

T6B — Semiconductors: basic principles and applications of solid state devices; diodes and transistors

T6B01

What class of electronic components uses a voltage or current signal to control current flow?
- A. Capacitors
- B. Inductors
- C. Resistors
- D. Transistors

T6B02

What electronic component allows current to flow in only one direction?
- A. Resistor
- B. Fuse
- C. Diode
- D. Driven element

T6A07
(D)
Page 3-9

T6A08
(B)
Page 3-13

T6A09
(A)
Page 3-12

T6A10
(D)
Page 5-17

T6A11
(B)
Page 5-17

T6B01
(D)
Page 3-12

T6B02
(C)
Page 3-12

T6B03
(C)
Page 3-12

T6B03
Which of these components can be used as an electronic switch or amplifier?
- A. Oscillator
- B. Potentiometer
- C. Transistor
- D. Voltmeter

T6B04
(B)
Page 3-12

T6B04
Which of the following components can consist of three layers of semiconductor material?
- A. Alternator
- B. Transistor
- C. Triode
- D. Pentagrid converter

T6B05
(A)
Page 3-12

T6B05
Which of the following electronic components can amplify signals?
- A. Transistor
- B. Variable resistor
- C. Electrolytic capacitor
- D. Multi-cell battery

T6B06
(B)
Page 3-12

T6B06
How is the cathode lead of a semiconductor diode often marked on the package?
- A. With the word "cathode"
- B. With a stripe
- C. With the letter C
- D. With the letter K

T6B07
(B)
Page 3-12

T6B07
What does the abbreviation LED stand for?
- A. Low Emission Diode
- B. Light Emitting Diode
- C. Liquid Emission Detector
- D. Long Echo Delay

T6B08
(A)
Page 3-12

T6B08
What does the abbreviation FET stand for?
- A. Field Effect Transistor
- B. Fast Electron Transistor
- C. Free Electron Transmitter
- D. Frequency Emission Transmitter

T6B09
(C)
Page 3-12

T6B09
What are the names of the two electrodes of a diode?
- A. Plus and minus
- B. Source and drain
- C. Anode and cathode
- D. Gate and base

T6B10

Which of the following could be the primary gain-producing component in an RF power amplifier?
- A. Transformer
- B. Transistor
- C. Reactor
- D. Resistor

T6B10
(B)
Page 3-12

T6B11

What is the term that describes a device's ability to amplify a signal?
- A. Gain
- B. Forward resistance
- C. Forward voltage drop
- D. On resistance

T6B11
(A)
Page 3-12

T6C — Circuit diagrams; schematic symbols

T6C01

What is the name of an electrical wiring diagram that uses standard component symbols?
- A. Bill of materials
- B. Connector pinout
- C. Schematic
- D. Flow chart

T6C01
(C)
Page 3-14

T6C02

What is component 1 in figure T1?
- A. Resistor
- B. Transistor
- C. Battery
- D. Connector

T6C02
(A)
Page 3-16

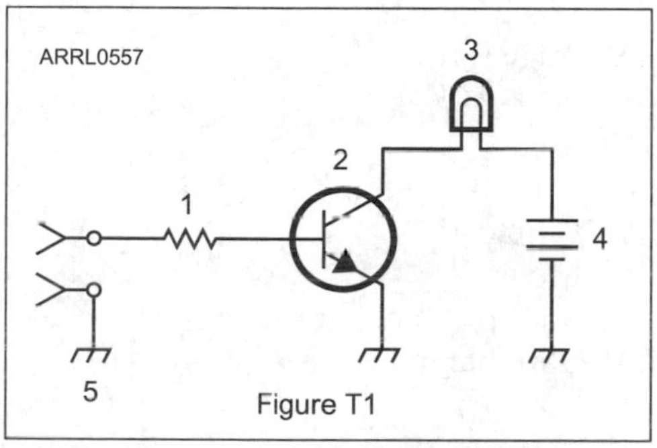

Figure T1 — Refer to this figure for questions T6C02 through T6C05 and T6D10.

T6C03

What is component 2 in figure T1?
- A. Resistor
- B. Transistor
- C. Indicator lamp
- D. Connector

T6C03
(B)
Page 3-16

T6C04

What is component 3 in figure T1?
- A. Resistor
- B. Transistor
- C. Lamp
- D. Ground symbol

T6C04
(C)
Page 3-16

T6C05

What is component 4 in figure T1?
- A. Resistor
- D. Transistor
- C. Battery
- D. Ground symbol

T6C05
(C)
Page 3-16

T6C06
(B)
Page 3-16

T6C06

What is component 6 in figure T2?
- A. Resistor
- B. Capacitor
- C. Regulator IC
- D. Transistor

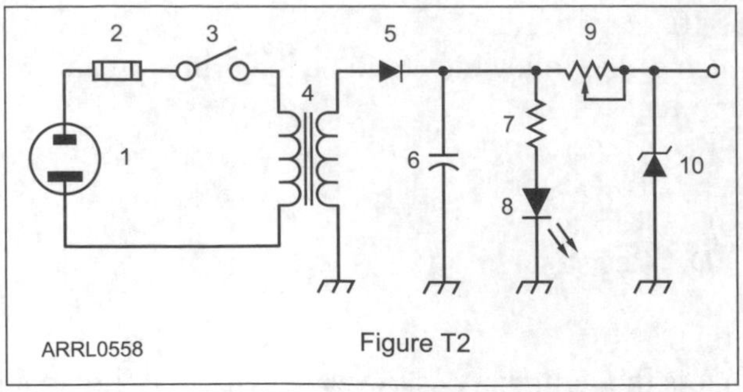

Figure T2

ARRL0558

Figure T2 — Refer to this figure for questions T6C06 through T6C09 and T6D03.

T6C07
(D)
Page 3-16

T6C07

What is component 8 in figure T2?
- A. Resistor
- B. Inductor
- C. Regulator IC
- D. Light emitting diode

T6C08
(C)
Page 3-16

T6C08

What is component 9 in figure T2?
- A. Variable capacitor
- B. Variable inductor
- C. Variable resistor
- D. Variable transformer

T6C09
(D)
Page 3-16

T6C09

What is component 4 in figure T2?
- A. Variable inductor
- B. Double-pole switch
- C. Potentiometer
- D. Transformer

T6C10
(D)
Page 3-16

T6C10

What is component 3 in figure T3?
- A. Connector
- B. Meter
- C. Variable capacitor
- D. Variable inductor

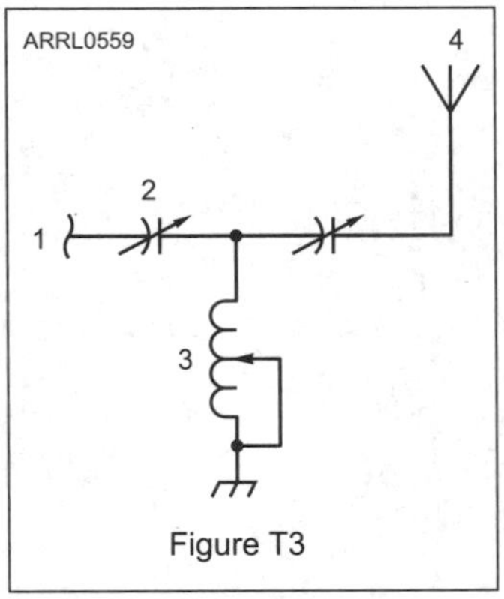

ARRL0559

Figure T3

Figure T3 — Refer to this figure for questions T6C10 and T6C11.

T6C11
(A)
Page 3-16

T6C11

What is component 4 in figure T3?
- A. Antenna
- B. Transmitter
- C. Dummy load
- D. Ground

T6C12
(A)
Page 3-14

T6C12

What do the symbols on an electrical schematic represent?
- A. Electrical components
- B. Logic states
- C. Digital codes
- D. Traffic nodes

T6C13
(C)
Page 3-14

T6C13

Which of the following is accurately represented in electrical schematics?
- A. Wire lengths
- B. Physical appearance of components
- C. The way components are interconnected
- D. All of these choices are correct

**T6D — Component functions: rectification; switches; indicators; power supply
 components; resonant circuit; shielding; power transformers; integrated circuits**

T6D01
Which of the following devices or circuits changes an alternating current into a varying
direct current signal?
   A. Transformer
   B. Rectifier
   C. Amplifier
   D. Reflector

T6D01
(B)
Page 3-12

T6D02
What is a relay?
   A. An electrically-controlled switch
   B. A current controlled amplifier
   C. An optical sensor
   D. A pass transistor

T6D02
(A)
Page 3-13

T6D03
What type of switch is represented by component 3 in figure T2?
   A. Single-pole single-throw
   B. Single-pole double-throw
   C. Double-pole single-throw
   D. Double-pole double-throw

T6D03
(A)
Page 3-14

T6D04
Which of the following displays an electrical quantity as a numeric value?
   A. Potentiometer
   B. Transistor
   C. Meter
   D. Relay

T6D04
(C)
Page 3-14

T6D05
What type of circuit controls the amount of voltage from a power supply?
   A. Regulator
   B. Oscillator
   C. Filter
   D. Phase inverter

T6D05
(A)
Page 5-16

T6D06
What component is commonly used to change 120V AC house current to a lower AC
voltage for other uses?
   A. Variable capacitor
   B. Transformer
   C. Transistor
   D. Diode

T6D06
(B)
Page 3-9

T6D07
Which of the following is commonly used as a visual indicator?
   A. LED
   B. FET
   C. Zener diode
   D. Bipolar transistor

T6D07
(A)
Page 3-12

T6D08
Which of the following is combined with an inductor to make a tuned circuit?
    A. Resistor
    B. Zener diode
    C. Potentiometer
    D. Capacitor

T6D09
What is the name of a device that combines several semiconductors and other components into one package?
    A. Transducer
    B. Multi-pole relay
    C. Integrated circuit
    D. Transformer

T6D10
What is the function of component 2 in Figure T1?
    A. Give off light when current flows through it
    B. Supply electrical energy
    C. Control the flow of current
    D. Convert electrical energy into radio waves

T6D11
Which of the following is a resonant or tuned circuit?
    A. An inductor and a capacitor connected in series or parallel to form a filter
    B. A type of voltage regulator
    C. A resistor circuit used for reducing standing wave ratio
    D. A circuit designed to provide high-fidelity audio

T6D12
Which of the following is a common reason to use shielded wire?
    A. To decrease the resistance of DC power connections
    B. To increase the current carrying capability of the wire
    C. To prevent coupling of unwanted signals to or from the wire
    D. To couple the wire to other signals

SUBELEMENT T7

Station equipment: common transmitter and receiver problems; antenna measurements; troubleshooting; basic repair and testing
[4 Exam Questions — 4 Groups]

T7A — Station equipment: receivers; transmitters; transceivers; modulation; transverters; transmit and receive amplifiers

T7A01
Which term describes the ability of a receiver to detect the presence of a signal?
  A. Linearity
  B. Sensitivity
  C. Selectivity
  D. Total Harmonic Distortion

T7A02
What is a transceiver?
  A. A type of antenna switch
  B. A unit combining the functions of a transmitter and a receiver
  C. A component in a repeater that filters out unwanted interference
  D. A type of antenna matching network

T7A03
Which of the following is used to convert a radio signal from one frequency to another?
  A. Phase splitter
  B. Mixer
  C. Inverter
  D. Amplifier

T7A04
Which term describes the ability of a receiver to discriminate between multiple signals?
  A. Discrimination ratio
  B. Sensitivity
  C. Selectivity
  D. Harmonic distortion

T7A05
What is the name of a circuit that generates a signal at a specific frequency?
  A. Reactance modulator
  B. Product detector
  C. Low-pass filter
  D. Oscillator

T7A06
What device converts the RF input and output of a transceiver to another band?
  A. High-pass filter
  B. Low-pass filter
  C. Transverter
  D. Phase converter

T7A01
(B)
Page 5-9

T7A02
(B)
Page 2-7

T7A03
(B)
Page 3-18

T7A04
(C)
Page 5-9

T7A05
(D)
Page 3-17

T7A06
(C)
Page 5-11

T7A07
(D)
Page 5-7

T7A07
What is meant by "PTT"?
    A. Pre-transmission tuning to reduce transmitter harmonic emission
    B. Precise tone transmissions used to limit repeater access to only certain signals
    C. A primary transformer tuner use to match antennas
    D. The push-to-talk function that switches between receive and transmit

T7A08
(C)
Page 3-17

T7A08
Which of the following describes combining speech with an RF carrier signal?
    A. Impedance matching
    B. Oscillation
    C. Modulation
    D. Low-pass filtering

T7A09
(B)
Page 5-10

T7A09
What is the function of the SSB/CW-FM switch on a VHF power amplifier?
    A. Change the mode of the transmitted signal
    B. Set the amplifier for proper operation in the selected mode
    C. Change the frequency range of the amplifier to operate in the proper portion of the band
    D. Reduce the received signal noise

T7A10
(B)
Page 5-10

T7A10
What device increases the low-power output from a handheld transceiver?
    A. A voltage divider
    B. An RF power amplifier
    C. An impedance network
    D. All of these choices are correct

T7A11
(A)
Page 5-9

T7A11
Where is an RF preamplifier installed?
    A. Between the antenna and receiver
    B. At the output of the transmitter's power amplifier
    C. Between a transmitter and antenna tuner
    D. At the receiver's audio output

T7B — Common transmitter and receiver problems: symptoms of overload and overdrive; distortion; causes of interference; interference and consumer electronics; part 15 devices; over-modulation; RF feedback; off frequency signals

T7B01
(D)
Page 5-8

T7B01
What can you do if you are told your FM handheld or mobile transceiver is over-deviating?
    A. Talk louder into the microphone
    B. Let the transceiver cool off
    C. Change to a higher power level
    D. Talk farther away from the microphone

T7B02
(A)
Page 9-8

T7B02
What would cause a broadcast AM or FM radio to receive an amateur radio transmission unintentionally?
    A. The receiver is unable to reject strong signals outside the AM or FM band
    B. The microphone gain of the transmitter is turned up too high
    C. The audio amplifier of the transmitter is overloaded
    D. The deviation of an FM transmitter is set too low

T7B03

Which of the following can cause radio frequency interference?

A. Fundamental overload
B. Harmonics
C. Spurious emissions
D. All of these choices are correct

T7B03
(D)
Page 9-8

T7B04

Which of the following is a way to reduce or eliminate interference from an amateur transmitter to a nearby telephone?

A. Put a filter on the amateur transmitter
B. Reduce the microphone gain
C. Reduce the SWR on the transmitter transmission line
D. Put an RF filter on the telephone

T7B04
(D)
Page 9-8

T7B05

How can overload of a non-amateur radio or TV receiver by an amateur signal be reduced or eliminated?

A. Block the amateur signal with a filter at the antenna input of the affected receiver
B. Block the interfering signal with a filter on the amateur transmitter
C. Switch the transmitter from FM to SSB
D. Switch the transmitter to a narrow-band mode

T7B05
(A)
Page 9-9

T7B06

Which of the following actions should you take if a neighbor tells you that your station's transmissions are interfering with their radio or TV reception?

A. Make sure that your station is functioning properly and that it does not cause interference to your own radio or television when it is tuned to the same channel
B. Immediately turn off your transmitter and contact the nearest FCC office for assistance
C. Tell them that your license gives you the right to transmit and nothing can be done to reduce the interference
D. Install a harmonic doubler on the output of your transmitter and tune it until the interference is eliminated

T7B06
(A)
Page 9-9

T7B07

Which of the following can reduce overload to a VHF transceiver from a nearby FM broadcast station?

A. RF preamplifier
B. Double-shielded coaxial cable
C. Using headphones instead of the speaker
D. Band-reject filter

T7B07
(D)
Page 9-9

T7B08

What should you do if something in a neighbor's home is causing harmful interference to your amateur station?

A. Work with your neighbor to identify the offending device
B. Politely inform your neighbor about the rules that prohibit the use of devices that cause interference
C. Check your station and make sure it meets the standards of good amateur practice
D. All of these choices are correct

T7B08
(D)
Page 9-10

T7B09

What is a Part 15 device?
  A. An unlicensed device that may emit low-powered radio signals on frequencies used by a licensed service
  B. An amplifier that has been type-certified for amateur radio
  C. A device for long-distance communications using special codes sanctioned by the International Amateur Radio Union
  D. A type of test set used to determine whether a transmitter complies with FCC regulation 91.15

T7B10

What might be a problem if you receive a report that your audio signal through the repeater is distorted or unintelligible?
  A. Your transmitter is slightly off frequency
  B. Your batteries are running low
  C. You are in a bad location
  D. All of these choices are correct

T7B11

What is a symptom of RF feedback in a transmitter or transceiver?
  A. Excessive SWR at the antenna connection
  B. The transmitter will not stay on the desired frequency
  C. Reports of garbled, distorted, or unintelligible voice transmissions
  D. Frequent blowing of power supply fuses

T7B12

What should be the first step to resolve cable TV interference from your ham radio transmission?
  A. Add a low-pass filter to the TV antenna input
  B. Add a high-pass filter to the TV antenna input
  C. Add a preamplifier to the TV antenna input
  D. Be sure all TV coaxial connectors are installed properly

T7C — Antenna measurements and troubleshooting: measuring SWR; dummy loads; coaxial cables; causes of feed line failures

T7C01

What is the primary purpose of a dummy load?
  A. To prevent transmitting signals over the air when making tests
  B. To prevent over-modulation of a transmitter
  C. To improve the efficiency of an antenna
  D. To improve the signal-to-noise ratio of a receiver

T7C02

Which of the following instruments can be used to determine if an antenna is resonant at the desired operating frequency?
  A. A VTVM
  B. An antenna analyzer
  C. A Q meter
  D. A frequency counter

T7C03

What, in general terms, is standing wave ratio (SWR)?
- A. A measure of how well a load is matched to a transmission line
- B. The ratio of high to low impedance in a feed line
- C. The transmitter efficiency ratio
- D. An indication of the quality of your station's ground connection

T7C03 (A) Page 4-11

T7C04

What reading on an SWR meter indicates a perfect impedance match between the antenna and the feed line?
- A. 2 to 1
- B. 1 to 3
- C. 1 to 1
- D. 10 to 1

T7C04 (C) Page 4-11

T7C05

Why do most solid-state amateur radio transmitters reduce output power as SWR increases?
- A. To protect the output amplifier transistors
- B. To comply with FCC rules on spectral purity
- C. Because power supplies cannot supply enough current at high SWR
- D. To improve the impedance match to the feed line

T7C05 (A) Page 4-11

T7C06

What does an SWR reading of 4:1 indicate?
- A. Loss of -4 dB
- B. Good impedance match
- C. Gain of +4 dB
- D. Impedance mismatch

T7C06 (D) Page 4-11

T7C07

What happens to power lost in a feed line?
- A. It increases the SWR
- B. It comes back into your transmitter and could cause damage
- C. It is converted into heat
- D. It can cause distortion of your signal

T7C07 (C) Page 4-9

T7C08

What instrument other than an SWR meter could you use to determine if a feed line and antenna are properly matched?
- A. Voltmeter
- B. Ohmmeter
- C. Iambic pentameter
- D. Directional wattmeter

T7C08 (D) Page 4-19

T7C09

Which of the following is the most common cause for failure of coaxial cables?
- A. Moisture contamination
- B. Gamma rays
- C. The velocity factor exceeds 1.0
- D. Overloading

T7C09 (A) Page 4-17

T7C10

Why should the outer jacket of coaxial cable be resistant to ultraviolet light?
- A. Ultraviolet resistant jackets prevent harmonic radiation
- B. Ultraviolet light can increase losses in the cable's jacket
- C. Ultraviolet and RF signals can mix, causing interference
- D. Ultraviolet light can damage the jacket and allow water to enter the cable

T7C10 (D) Page 4-17

T7C11
(C)
Page 4-18

T7C11
What is a disadvantage of air core coaxial cable when compared to foam or solid dielectric types?
- A. It has more loss per foot
- B. It cannot be used for VHF or UHF antennas
- C. It requires special techniques to prevent water absorption
- D. It cannot be used at below freezing temperatures

T7C12
(B)
Page 5-7

T7C12
What does a dummy load consist of?
- A. A high-gain amplifier and a TR switch
- B. A non-inductive resistor and a heat sink
- C. A low-voltage power supply and a DC relay
- D. A 50 ohm reactance used to terminate a transmission line

T7D — Basic repair and testing: soldering; using basic test instruments; connecting a voltmeter, ammeter, or ohmmeter

T7D01
(B)
Page 3-2

T7D01
Which instrument would you use to measure electric potential or electromotive force?
- A. An ammeter
- B. A voltmeter
- C. A wavemeter
- D. An ohmmeter

T7D02
(B)
Page 3-3

T7D02
What is the correct way to connect a voltmeter to a circuit?
- A. In series with the circuit
- B. In parallel with the circuit
- C. In quadrature with the circuit
- D. In phase with the circuit

T7D03
(A)
Page 3-3

T7D03
How is a simple ammeter connected to a circuit?
- A. In series with the circuit
- B. In parallel with the circuit
- C. In quadrature with the circuit
- D. In phase with the circuit

T7D04
(D)
Page 3-1

T7D04
Which instrument is used to measure electric current?
- A. An ohmmeter
- B. A wavemeter
- C. A voltmeter
- D. An ammeter

T7D05
(D)
Page 3-5

T7D05
What instrument is used to measure resistance?
- A. An oscilloscope
- B. A spectrum analyzer
- C. A noise bridge
- D. An ohmmeter

T7D06

Which of the following might damage a multimeter?
A. Measuring a voltage too small for the chosen scale
B. Leaving the meter in the milliamps position overnight
C. Attempting to measure voltage when using the resistance setting
D. Not allowing it to warm up properly

T7D06
(C)
Page 3-4

T7D07

Which of the following measurements are commonly made using a multimeter?
A. SWR and RF power
B. Signal strength and noise
C. Impedance and reactance
D. Voltage and resistance

T7D07
(D)
Page 3-4

T7D08

Which of the following types of solder is best for radio and electronic use?
A. Acid-core solder
B. Silver solder
C. Rosin-core solder
D. Aluminum solder

T7D08
(C)
Page 4-18

T7D09

What is the characteristic appearance of a cold solder joint?
A. Dark black spots
B. A bright or shiny surface
C. A grainy or dull surface
D. A greenish tint

T7D09
(C)
Page 4-18

T7D10

What is probably happening when an ohmmeter, connected across an unpowered circuit, initially indicates a low resistance and then shows increasing resistance with time?
A. The ohmmeter is defective
B. The circuit contains a large capacitor
C. The circuit contains a large inductor
D. The circuit is a relaxation oscillator

T7D10
(B)
Page 3-4

T7D11

Which of the following precautions should be taken when measuring circuit resistance with an ohmmeter?
A. Ensure that the applied voltages are correct
B. Ensure that the circuit is not powered
C. Ensure that the circuit is grounded
D. Ensure that the circuit is operating at the correct frequency

T7D11
(B)
Page 3-4

T7D12

Which of the following precautions should be taken when measuring high voltages with a voltmeter?
A. Ensure that the voltmeter has very low impedance
B. Ensure that the voltmeter and leads are rated for use at the voltages to be measured
C. Ensure that the circuit is grounded through the voltmeter
D. Ensure that the voltmeter is set to the correct frequency

T7D12
(B)
Page 3-4

Modulation modes: amateur satellite operation; operating activities; non-voice and digital communications
[4 Exam Questions — 4 Groups]

T8A — Modulation modes: bandwidth of various signals; choice of emission type

T8A01
(C)
Page 5-3

T8A01

Which of the following is a form of amplitude modulation?
- A. Spread spectrum
- B. Packet radio
- C. Single sideband
- D. Phase shift keying (PSK)

T8A02
(A)
Page 5-4

T8A02

What type of modulation is most commonly used for VHF packet radio transmissions?
- A. FM
- B. SSB
- C. AM
- D. PSK

T8A03
(C)
Page 5-4

T8A03

Which type of voice mode is most often used for long-distance (weak signal) contacts on the VHF and UHF bands?
- A. FM
- B. DRM
- C. SSB
- D. PM

T8A04
(D)
Page 5-4

T8A04

Which type of modulation is most commonly used for VHF and UHF voice repeaters?
- A. AM
- B. SSB
- C. PSK
- D. FM

T8A05
(C)
Page 5-5

T8A05

Which of the following types of emission has the narrowest bandwidth?
- A. FM voice
- B. SSB voice
- C. CW
- D. Slow-scan TV

T8A06
(A)
Page 5-5

T8A06

Which sideband is normally used for 10 meter HF, VHF, and UHF single-sideband communications?
- A. Upper sideband
- B. Lower sideband
- C. Suppressed sideband
- D. Inverted sideband

T8A07
What is an advantage of single sideband (SSB) over FM for voice transmissions?
  A. SSB signals are easier to tune
  B. SSB signals are less susceptible to interference
  C. SSB signals have narrower bandwidth
  D. All of these choices are correct

T8A07
(C)
Page 5-4

T8A08
What is the approximate bandwidth of a single sideband (SSB) voice signal?
  A. 1 kHz
  B. 3 kHz
  C. 6 kHz
  D. 15 kHz

T8A08
(B)
Page 5-5

T8A09
What is the approximate bandwidth of a VHF repeater FM phone signal?
  A. Less than 500 Hz
  B. About 150 kHz
  C. Between 10 and 15 kHz
  D. Between 50 and 125 kHz

T8A09
(C)
Page 5-5

T8A10
What is the typical bandwidth of analog fast-scan TV transmissions on the 70 centimeter band?
  A. More than 10 MHz
  B. About 6 MHz
  C. About 3 MHz
  D. About 1 MHz

T8A10
(B)
Page 5-5

T8A11
What is the approximate maximum bandwidth required to transmit a CW signal?
  A. 2.4 kHz
  B. 150 Hz
  C. 1000 Hz
  D. 15 kHz

T8A11
(B)
Page 5-5

T8B — Amateur satellite operation; Doppler shift; basic orbits; operating protocols; transmitter power considerations; telemetry and telecommand; satellite tracking

T8B01
What telemetry information is typically transmitted by satellite beacons?
  A. The signal strength of received signals
  B. Time of day accurate to plus or minus 1/10 second
  C. Health and status of the satellite
  D. All of these choices are correct

T8B01
(C)
Page 6-24

T8B02
What is the impact of using too much effective radiated power on a satellite uplink?
  A. Possibility of commanding the satellite to an improper mode
  B. Blocking access by other users
  C. Overloading the satellite batteries
  D. Possibility of rebooting the satellite control computer

T8B02
(B)
Page 6-24

T8B03

Which of the following are provided by satellite tracking programs?
- A. Maps showing the real-time position of the satellite track over the earth
- B. The time, azimuth, and elevation of the start, maximum altitude, and end of a pass
- C. The apparent frequency of the satellite transmission, including effects of Doppler shift
- D. All of these choices are correct

T8B04

What mode of transmission is commonly used by amateur radio satellites?
- A. SSB
- B. FM
- C. CW/data
- D. All of these choices are correct

T8B05

What is a satellite beacon?
- A. The primary transmit antenna on the satellite
- B. An indicator light that shows where to point your antenna
- C. A reflective surface on the satellite
- D. A transmission from a satellite that contains status information

T8B06

Which of the following are inputs to a satellite tracking program?
- A. The weight of the satellite
- B. The Keplerian elements
- C. The last observed time of zero Doppler shift
- D. All of these choices are correct

T8B07

With regard to satellite communications, what is Doppler shift?
- A. A change in the satellite orbit
- B. A mode where the satellite receives signals on one band and transmits on another
- C. An observed change in signal frequency caused by relative motion between the satellite and the earth station
- D. A special digital communications mode for some satellites

T8B08

What is meant by the statement that a satellite is operating in mode U/V?
- A. The satellite uplink is in the 15 meter band and the downlink is in the 10 meter band
- B. The satellite uplink is in the 70 centimeter band and the downlink is in the 2 meter band
- C. The satellite operates using ultraviolet frequencies
- D. The satellite frequencies are usually variable

T8B09

What causes spin fading of satellite signals?
- A. Circular polarized noise interference radiated from the sun
- B. Rotation of the satellite and its antennas
- C. Doppler shift of the received signal
- D. Interfering signals within the satellite uplink band

T8B10

What do the initials LEO tell you about an amateur satellite?

A. The satellite battery is in Low Energy Operation mode
B. The satellite is performing a Lunar Ejection Orbit maneuver
C. The satellite is in a Low Earth Orbit
D. The satellite uses Light Emitting Optics

T8B10
(C)
Page 6-23

T8B11

Who may receive telemetry from a space station?

A. Anyone who can receive the telemetry signal
B. A licensed radio amateur with a transmitter equipped for interrogating the satellite
C. A licensed radio amateur who has been certified by the protocol developer
D. A licensed radio amateur who has registered for an access code from AMSAT

T8B11
(A)
Page 6-24

T8B12

Which of the following is a good way to judge whether your uplink power is neither too low nor too high?

A. Check your signal strength report in the telemetry data
B. Listen for distortion on your downlink signal
C. Your signal strength on the downlink should be about the same as the beacon
D. All of these choices are correct

T8B12
(C)
Page 6-24

T8C — Operating activities: radio direction finding; radio control; contests; linking over the internet; grid locators

T8C01

Which of the following methods is used to locate sources of noise interference or jamming?

A. Echolocation
B. Doppler radar
C. Radio direction finding
D. Phase locking

T8C01
(C)
Page 6-10

T8C02

Which of these items would be useful for a hidden transmitter hunt?

A. Calibrated SWR meter
B. A directional antenna
C. A calibrated noise bridge
D. All of these choices are correct

T8C02
(B)
Page 6-10

T8C03

What operating activity involves contacting as many stations as possible during a specified period?

A. Contesting
B. Net operations
C. Public service events
D. Simulated emergency exercises

T8C03
(A)
Page 6-9

T8C04

Which of the following is good procedure when contacting another station in a radio contest?

A. Sign only the last two letters of your call if there are many other stations calling
B. Contact the station twice to be sure that you are in his log
C. Send only the minimum information needed for proper identification and the contest exchange
D. All of these choices are correct

T8C04
(C)
Page 6-9

T8C05

What is a grid locator?
- A. A letter-number designator assigned to a geographic location
- B. A letter-number designator assigned to an azimuth and elevation
- C. An instrument for neutralizing a final amplifier
- D. An instrument for radio direction finding

T8C06

How is access to some IRLP nodes accomplished?
- A. By obtaining a password that is sent via voice to the node
- B. By using DTMF signals
- C. By entering the proper internet password
- D. By using CTCSS tone codes

T8C07

What is meant by Voice Over Internet Protocol (VoIP) as used in amateur radio?
- A. A set of rules specifying how to identify your station when linked over the internet to another station
- B. A set of guidelines for contacting DX stations during contests using internet access
- C. A technique for measuring the modulation quality of a transmitter using remote sites monitored via the internet
- D. A method of delivering voice communications over the internet using digital techniques

T8C08

What is the Internet Radio Linking Project (IRLP)?
- A. A technique to connect amateur radio systems, such as repeaters, via the internet using Voice Over Internet Protocol (VoIP)
- B. A system for providing access to websites via amateur radio
- C. A system for informing amateurs in real time of the frequency of active DX stations
- D. A technique for measuring signal strength of an amateur transmitter via the internet

T8C09

How might you obtain a list of active nodes that use VoIP?
- A. By subscribing to an on line service
- B. From on line repeater lists maintained by the local repeater frequency coordinator
- C. From a repeater directory
- D. All of these choices are correct

T8C10

What must be done before you may use the EchoLink system to communicate using a repeater?
- A. You must complete the required EchoLink training
- B. You must have purchased a license to use the EchoLink software
- C. You must be sponsored by a current EchoLink user
- D. You must register your call sign and provide proof of license

T8C11

What name is given to an amateur radio station that is used to connect other amateur stations to the internet?

- A. A gateway
- B. A repeater
- C. A digipeater
- D. A beacon

T8D — Non-voice and digital communications: image signals; digital modes; CW; packet radio; PSK31; APRS; error detection and correction; NTSC; amateur radio networking; Digital Mobile/Migration Radio

T8D01

Which of the following is a digital communications mode?

- A. Packet radio
- B. IEEE 802.11
- C. JT65
- D. All of these choices are correct

T8D02

What does the term "APRS" mean?

- A. Automatic Packet Reporting System
- B. Associated Public Radio Station
- C. Auto Planning Radio Set-up
- D. Advanced Polar Radio System

T8D03

Which of the following devices is used to provide data to the transmitter when sending automatic position reports from a mobile amateur radio station?

- A. The vehicle speedometer
- B. A WWV receiver
- C. A connection to a broadcast FM sub-carrier receiver
- D. A Global Positioning System receiver

T8D04

What type of transmission is indicated by the term "NTSC?"

- A. A Normal Transmission mode in Static Circuit
- B. A special mode for earth satellite uplink
- C. An analog fast scan color TV signal
- D. A frame compression scheme for TV signals

T8D05

Which of the following is an application of APRS (Automatic Packet Reporting System)?

- A. Providing real-time tactical digital communications in conjunction with a map showing the locations of stations
- B. Showing automatically the number of packets transmitted via PACTOR during a specific time interval
- C. Providing voice over internet connection between repeaters
- D. Providing information on the number of stations signed into a repeater

T8C11
(A)
Page 5-15

T8D01
(D)
Page 5-12

T8D02
(A)
Page 5-13

T8D03
(D)
Page 5-13

T8D04
(C)
Page 6-10

T8D05
(A)
Page 5-14

T8D06
(B)
Page 5-13

T8D06

What does the abbreviation "PSK" mean?
- A. Pulse Shift Keying
- B. Phase Shift Keying
- C. Packet Short Keying
- D. Phased Slide Keying

T8D07
(A)
Page 6-15

T8D07

Which of the following best describes DMR (Digital Mobile Radio)?
- A. A technique for time-multiplexing two digital voice signals on a single 12.5 kHz repeater channel
- B. An automatic position tracking mode for FM mobiles communicating through repeaters
- C. An automatic computer logging technique for hands-off logging when communicating while operating a vehicle
- D. A digital technique for transmitting on two repeater inputs simultaneously for automatic error correction

T8D08
(D)
Page 5-13

T8D08

Which of the following may be included in packet transmissions?
- A. A check sum that permits error detection
- B. A header that contains the call sign of the station to which the information is being sent
- C. Automatic repeat request in case of error
- D. All of these choices are correct

T8D09
(C)
Page 5-11

T8D09

What code is used when sending CW in the amateur bands?
- A. Baudot
- B. Hamming
- C. International Morse
- D. All of these choices are correct

T8D10
(D)
Page 5-12

T8D10

Which of the following operating activities is supported by digital mode software in the WSJT suite?
- A. Moonbounce or Earth-Moon-Earth
- B. Weak-signal propagation beacons
- C. Meteor scatter
- D. All of these choices are correct

T8D11
(C)
Page 5-13

T8D11

What is an ARQ transmission system?
- A. A special transmission format limited to video signals
- B. A system used to encrypt command signals to an amateur radio satellite
- C. A digital scheme whereby the receiving station detects errors and sends a request to the sending station to retransmit the information
- D. A method of compressing the data in a message so more information can be sent in a shorter time

T8D12

Which of the following best describes Broadband-Hamnet(TM), also referred to as a high-speed multi-media network?
- A. An amateur-radio-based data network using commercial Wi-Fi gear with modified firmware
- B. A wide-bandwidth digital voice mode employing DRM protocols
- C. A satellite communications network using modified commercial satellite TV hardware
- D. An internet linking protocol used to network repeaters

T8D13

What is FT8?
- A. A wideband FM voice mode
- B. A digital mode capable of operating in low signal-to-noise conditions that transmits on 15-second intervals
- C. An eight channel multiplex mode for FM repeaters
- D. A digital slow scan TV mode with forward error correction and automatic color compensation

T8D14

What is an electronic keyer?
- A. A device for switching antennas from transmit to receive
- B. A device for voice activated switching from receive to transmit
- C. A device that assists in manual sending of Morse code
- D. An interlock to prevent unauthorized use of a radio

T8D12
(A)
Page 5-12

T8D13
(B)
Page 5-12

T8D14
(C)
Page 5-7

SUBELEMENT T9
Antennas and feed lines
[2 Exam Questions — 2 Groups]

T9A — Antennas: vertical and horizontal polarization; concept of gain; common portable and mobile antennas; relationships between resonant length and frequency; concept of dipole antennas

T9A01
(C)
Page 4-16

T9A01

What is a beam antenna?
- A. An antenna built from aluminum I-beams
- B. An omnidirectional antenna invented by Clarence Beam
- C. An antenna that concentrates signals in one direction
- D. An antenna that reverses the phase of received signals

T9A02
(A)
Page 4-13

T9A02

Which of the following describes a type of antenna loading?
- A. Inserting an inductor in the radiating portion of the antenna to make it electrically longer
- B. Inserting a resistor in the radiating portion of the antenna to make it resonant
- C. Installing a spring in the base of a mobile vertical antenna to make it more flexible
- D. Strengthening the radiating elements of a beam antenna to better resist wind damage

T9A03
(B)
Page 4-12

T9A03

Which of the following describes a simple dipole oriented parallel to the Earth's surface?
- A. A ground-wave antenna
- B. A horizontally polarized antenna
- C. A rhombic antenna
- D. A vertically polarized antenna

T9A04
(A)
Page 4-15

T9A04

What is a disadvantage of the "rubber duck" antenna supplied with most handheld radio transceivers when compared to a full-sized quarter-wave antenna?
- A. It does not transmit or receive as effectively
- B. It transmits only circularly polarized signals
- C. If the rubber end cap is lost, it will unravel very easily
- D. All of these choices are correct

T9A05
(C)
Page 4-13

T9A05

How would you change a dipole antenna to make it resonant on a higher frequency?
- A. Lengthen it
- B. Insert coils in series with radiating wires
- C. Shorten it
- D. Add capacitive loading to the ends of the radiating wires

T9A06
(C)
Page 4-16

T9A06

What type of antennas are the quad, Yagi, and dish?
- A. Non-resonant antennas
- B. Log periodic antennas
- C. Directional antennas
- D. Isotropic antennas

T9A07

What is a disadvantage of using a handheld VHF transceiver, with its integral antenna, inside a vehicle?

    A. Signals might not propagate well due to the shielding effect of the vehicle
    B. It might cause the transceiver to overheat
    C. The SWR might decrease, decreasing the signal strength
    D. All of these choices are correct

T9A08

What is the approximate length, in inches, of a quarter-wavelength vertical antenna for 146 MHz?

    A. 112
    B. 50
    C. 19
    D. 12

T9A09

What is the approximate length, in inches, of a half-wavelength 6 meter dipole antenna?

    A. 6
    B. 50
    C. 112
    D. 236

T9A10

In which direction does a half-wave dipole antenna radiate the strongest signal?

    A. Equally in all directions
    B. Off the ends of the antenna
    C. Broadside to the antenna
    D. In the direction of the feed line

T9A11

What is the gain of an antenna?

    A. The additional power that is added to the transmitter power
    B. The additional power that is lost in the antenna when transmitting on a higher frequency
    C. The increase in signal strength in a specified direction compared to a reference antenna
    D. The increase in impedance on receive or transmit compared to a reference antenna

T9A12

What is an advantage of using a properly mounted 5/8 wavelength antenna for VHF or UHF mobile service?

    A. It has a lower radiation angle and more gain than a 1/4 wavelength antenna
    B. It has very high angle radiation for better communicating through a repeater
    C. It eliminates distortion caused by reflected signals
    D. It has 10 times the power gain of a 1/4 wavelength design

T9A07
(A)
Page 4-15

T9A08
(C)
Page 4-13

T9A09
(C)
Page 4-13

T9A10
(C)
Page 4-12

T9A11
(C)
Page 4-7

T9A12
(A)
Page 4-12

T9B — Feed lines: types, attenuation vs frequency, selecting; SWR concepts; Antenna tuners (couplers); RF Connectors: selecting, weather protection

T9B01
(B)
Page 4-11

T9B01
Why is it important to have low SWR when using coaxial cable feed line?
    A. To reduce television interference
    B. To reduce signal loss
    C. To prolong antenna life
    D. All of these choices are correct

T9B02
(B)
Page 4-9

T9B02
What is the impedance of most coaxial cables used in amateur radio installations?
    A. 8 ohms
    B. 50 ohms
    C. 600 ohms
    D. 12 ohms

T9B03
(A)
Page 4-9

T9B03
Why is coaxial cable the most common feed line selected for amateur radio antenna systems?
    A. It is easy to use and requires few special installation considerations
    B. It has less loss than any other type of feed line
    C. It can handle more power than any other type of feed line
    D. It is less expensive than any other type of feed line

T9B04
(A)
Page 4-19

T9B04
What is the major function of an antenna tuner (antenna coupler)?
    A. It matches the antenna system impedance to the transceiver's output impedance
    B. It helps a receiver automatically tune in weak stations
    C. It allows an antenna to be used on both transmit and receive
    D. It automatically selects the proper antenna for the frequency band being used

T9B05
(D)
Page 4-9

T9B05
In general, what happens as the frequency of a signal passing through coaxial cable is increased?
    A. The characteristic impedance decreases
    B. The loss decreases
    C. The characteristic impedance increases
    D. The loss increases

T9B06
(B)
Page 4-18

T9B06
Which of the following connectors is most suitable for frequencies above 400 MHz?
    A. A UHF (PL-259/SO-239) connector
    B. A Type N connector
    C. An RS-213 connector
    D. A DB-25 connector

T9B07
(C)
Page 4-18

T9B07
Which of the following is true of PL-259 type coax connectors?
    A. They are preferred for microwave operation
    B. They are watertight
    C. They are commonly used at HF frequencies
    D. They are a bayonet type connector

T9B08
Why should coax connectors exposed to the weather be sealed against water intrusion?
  A. To prevent an increase in feed line loss
  B. To prevent interference to telephones
  C. To keep the jacket from becoming loose
  D. All of these choices are correct

T9B09
What can cause erratic changes in SWR readings?
  A. The transmitter is being modulated
  B. A loose connection in an antenna or a feed line
  C. The transmitter is being over-modulated
  D. Interference from other stations is distorting your signal

T9B10
What is the electrical difference between RG-58 and RG-8 coaxial cable?
  A. There is no significant difference between the two types
  B. RG-58 cable has two shields
  C. RG-8 cable has less loss at a given frequency
  D. RG-58 cable can handle higher power levels

T9B11
Which of the following types of feed line has the lowest loss at VHF and UHF?
  A. 50-ohm flexible coax
  B. Multi-conductor unbalanced cable
  C. Air-insulated hard line
  D. 75-ohm flexible coax

T9B08
(A)
Page 4-18

T9B09
(B)
Page 4-11

T9B10
(C)
Page 4-17

T9B11
(C)
Page 4-9

SUBELEMENT T0

Electrical safety: AC and DC power circuits; antenna installation; RF hazards

[3 Exam Questions — 3 Groups]

T0A — Power circuits and hazards: hazardous voltages; fuses and circuit breakers; grounding; lightning protection; battery safety; electrical code compliance

T0A01
(B)
Page 9-3

T0A01
Which of the following is a safety hazard of a 12-volt storage battery?
A. Touching both terminals with the hands can cause electrical shock
B. Shorting the terminals can cause burns, fire, or an explosion
C. RF emissions from the battery
D. All of these choices are correct

T0A02
(D)
Page 9-2

T0A02
What health hazard is presented by electrical current flowing through the body?
A. It may cause injury by heating tissue
B. It may disrupt the electrical functions of cells
C. It may cause involuntary muscle contractions
D. All of these choices are correct

T0A03
(C)
Page 9-5

T0A03
In the United States, what is connected to the green wire in a three-wire electrical AC plug?
A. Neutral
B. Hot
C. Equipment ground
D. The white wire

T0A04
(B)
Page 3-12

T0A04
What is the purpose of a fuse in an electrical circuit?
A. To prevent power supply ripple from damaging a circuit
B. To interrupt power in case of overload
C. To limit current to prevent shocks
D. All of these choices are correct

T0A05
(C)
Page 3-12

T0A05
Why is it unwise to install a 20-ampere fuse in the place of a 5-ampere fuse?
A. The larger fuse would be likely to blow because it is rated for higher current
B. The power supply ripple would greatly increase
C. Excessive current could cause a fire
D. All of these choices are correct

T0A06
(D)
Page 9-4

T0A06
What is a good way to guard against electrical shock at your station?
A. Use three-wire cords and plugs for all AC powered equipment
B. Connect all AC powered station equipment to a common safety ground
C. Use a circuit protected by a ground-fault interrupter
D. All of these choices are correct

T0A07
Which of these precautions should be taken when installing devices for lightning protection in a coaxial cable feed line?
- A. Include a parallel bypass switch for each protector so that it can be switched out of the circuit when running high power
- B. Include a series switch in the ground line of each protector to prevent RF overload from inadvertently damaging the protector
- C. Keep the ground wires from each protector separate and connected to station ground
- D. Mount all of the protectors on a metal plate that is in turn connected to an external ground rod

T0A07
(D)
Page 9-5

T0A08
What safety equipment should always be included in home-built equipment that is powered from 120V AC power circuits?
- A. A fuse or circuit breaker in series with the AC hot conductor
- B. An AC voltmeter across the incoming power source
- C. An inductor in parallel with the AC power source
- D. A capacitor in series with the AC power source

T0A08
(A)
Page 9-5

T0A09
What should be done to all external ground rods or earth connections?
- A. Waterproof them with silicone caulk or electrical tape
- B. Keep them as far apart as possible
- C. Bond them together with heavy wire or conductive strap
- D. Tune them for resonance on the lowest frequency of operation

T0A09
(C)
Page 9-5

T0A10
What can happen if a lead-acid storage battery is charged or discharged too quickly?
- A. The battery could overheat, give off flammable gas, or explode
- B. The voltage can become reversed
- C. The memory effect will reduce the capacity of the battery
- D. All of these choices are correct

T0A10
(A)
Page 5-19

T0A11
What kind of hazard might exist in a power supply when it is turned off and disconnected?
- A. Static electricity could damage the grounding system
- B. Circulating currents inside the transformer might cause damage
- C. The fuse might blow if you remove the cover
- D. You might receive an electric shock from the charge stored in large capacitors

T0A11
(D)
Page 9-2

T0B — Antenna safety: tower safety and grounding; erecting an antenna support; safely installing an antenna

T0B01
When should members of a tower work team wear a hard hat and safety glasses?
- A. At all times except when climbing the tower
- B. At all times except when belted firmly to the tower
- C. At all times when any work is being done on the tower
- D. Only when the tower exceeds 30 feet in height

T0B01
(C)
Page 9-19

T0B02
(C)
Page 9-19

T0B02
What is a good precaution to observe before climbing an antenna tower?
  A. Make sure that you wear a grounded wrist strap
  B. Remove all tower grounding connections
  C. Put on a carefully inspected climbing harness(fall arrester)and safety glasses
  D. All of these choices are correct

T0B03
(D)
Page 9-20

T0B03
Under what circumstances is it safe to climb a tower without a helper or observer?
  A. When no electrical work is being performed
  B. When no mechanical work is being performed
  C. When the work being done is not more than 20 feet above the ground
  D. Never

T0B04
(C)
Page 9-18

T0B04
Which of the following is an important safety precaution to observe when putting up an antenna tower?
  A. Wear a ground strap connected to your wrist at all times
  B. Insulate the base of the tower to avoid lightning strikes
  C. Look for and stay clear of any overhead electrical wires
  D. All of these choices are correct

T0B05
(C)
Page 9-20

T0B05
What is the purpose of a gin pole?
  A. To temporarily replace guy wires
  B. To be used in place of a safety harness
  C. To lift tower sections or antennas
  D. To provide a temporary ground

T0B06
(D)
Page 9-18

T0B06
What is the minimum safe distance from a power line to allow when installing an antenna?
  A. Half the width of your property
  B. The height of the power line above ground
  C. 1/2 wavelength at the operating frequency
  D. Enough so that if the antenna falls unexpectedly, no part of it can come closer than 10 feet to the power wires

T0B07
(C)
Page 9-20

T0B07
Which of the following is an important safety rule to remember when using a crank-up tower?
  A. This type of tower must never be painted
  B. This type of tower must never be grounded
  C. This type of tower must not be climbed unless retracted or mechanical safety locking devices have been installed
  D. All of these choices are correct

T0B08
(C)
Page 9-18

T0B08
What is considered to be a proper grounding method for a tower?
  A. A single four-foot ground rod, driven into the ground no more than 12 inches from the base
  B. A ferrite-core RF choke connected between the tower and ground
  C. Separate eight-foot long ground rods for each tower leg, bonded to the tower and each other
  D. A connection between the tower base and a cold water pipe

T0B09
Why should you avoid attaching an antenna to a utility pole?
    A. The antenna will not work properly because of induced voltages
    B. The utility company will charge you an extra monthly fee
    C. The antenna could contact high-voltage power lines
    D. All of these choices are correct

T0B09
(C)
Page 9-18

T0B10
Which of the following is true when installing grounding conductors used for lightning protection?
    A. Only non-insulated wire must be used
    B. Wires must be carefully routed with precise right-angle bends
    C. Sharp bends must be avoided
    D. Common grounds must be avoided

T0B10
(C)
Page 9-5

T0B11
Which of the following establishes grounding requirements for an amateur radio tower or antenna?
    A. FCC Part 97 Rules
    B. Local electrical codes
    C. FAA tower lighting regulations
    D. UL recommended practices

T0B11
(B)
Page 9-5

T0B12
Which of the following is good practice when installing ground wires on a tower for lightning protection?
    A. Put a loop in the ground connection to prevent water damage to the ground system
    B. Make sure that all bends in the ground wires are clean, right-angle bends
    C. Ensure that connections are short and direct
    D. All of these choices are correct

T0B12
(C)
Page 9-5

T0B13
What is the purpose of a safety wire through a turnbuckle used to tension guy lines?
    A. Secure the guy if the turnbuckle breaks
    B. Prevent loosening of the guy line from vibration
    C. Prevent theft or vandalism
    D. Deter unauthorized climbing of the tower

T0B13
(B)
Page 9-18

T0C — RF hazards: radiation exposure; proximity to antennas; recognized safe power levels; exposure to others; radiation types; duty cycle

T0C01
What type of radiation are VHF and UHF radio signals?
    A. Gamma radiation
    B. Ionizing radiation
    C. Alpha radiation
    D. Non-ionizing radiation

T0C01
(D)
Page 9-11

T0C02
Which of the following frequencies has the lowest value for Maximum Permissible Exposure limit?
    A. 3.5 MHz
    B. 50 MHz
    C. 440 MHz
    D. 1296 MHz

T0C02
(B)
Page 9-12

T0C03
What is the maximum power level that an amateur radio station may use at VHF frequencies before an RF exposure evaluation is required?
    A. 1500 watts PEP transmitter output
    B. 1 watt forward power
    C. 50 watts PEP at the antenna
    D. 50 watts PEP reflected power

T0C04
What factors affect the RF exposure of people near an amateur station antenna?
    A. Frequency and power level of the RF field
    B. Distance from the antenna to a person
    C. Radiation pattern of the antenna
    D. All of these choices are correct

T0C05
Why do exposure limits vary with frequency?
    A. Lower frequency RF fields have more energy than higher frequency fields
    B. Lower frequency RF fields do not penetrate the human body
    C. Higher frequency RF fields are transient in nature
    D. The human body absorbs more RF energy at some frequencies than at others

T0C06
Which of the following is an acceptable method to determine that your station complies with FCC RF exposure regulations?
    A. By calculation based on FCC OET Bulletin 65
    B. By calculation based on computer modeling
    C. By measurement of field strength using calibrated equipment
    D. All of these choices are correct

T0C07
What could happen if a person accidentally touched your antenna while you were transmitting?
    A. Touching the antenna could cause television interference
    B. They might receive a painful RF burn
    C. They might develop radiation poisoning
    D. All of these choices are correct

T0C08
Which of the following actions might amateur operators take to prevent exposure to RF radiation in excess of FCC-supplied limits?
    A. Relocate antennas
    B. Relocate the transmitter
    C. Increase the duty cycle
    D. All of these choices are correct

T0C09
How can you make sure your station stays in compliance with RF safety regulations?
    A. By informing the FCC of any changes made in your station
    B. By re-evaluating the station whenever an item of equipment is changed
    C. By making sure your antennas have low SWR
    D. All of these choices are correct

T0C10

Why is duty cycle one of the factors used to determine safe RF radiation exposure levels?
    A. It affects the average exposure of people to radiation
    B. It affects the peak exposure of people to radiation
    C. It takes into account the antenna feed line loss
    D. It takes into account the thermal effects of the final amplifier

T0C10
(A)
Page 9-13

T0C11

What is the definition of duty cycle during the averaging time for RF exposure?
    A. The difference between the lowest power output and the highest power output of a transmitter
    B. The difference between the PEP and average power output of a transmitter
    C. The percentage of time that a transmitter is transmitting
    D. The percentage of time that a transmitter is not transmitting

T0C11
(C)
Page 9-13

T0C12

How does RF radiation differ from ionizing radiation (radioactivity)?
    A. RF radiation does not have sufficient energy to cause genetic damage
    B. RF radiation can only be detected with an RF dosimeter
    C. RF radiation is limited in range to a few feet
    D. RF radiation is perfectly safe

T0C12
(A)
Page 9-11

T0C13

If the averaging time for exposure is 6 minutes, how much power density is permitted if the signal is present for 3 minutes and absent for 3 minutes rather than being present for the entire 6 minutes?
    A. 3 times as much
    B. 1/2 as much
    C. 2 times as much
    D. There is no adjustment allowed for shorter exposure times

T0C13
(C)
Page 9-13

The ARRL Ham Radio License Manual

Index of Advertisers

Sophisticated Receivers

The **Icom IC-R8600** is a professional grade *DC to Daylight* receiver covering 10 kHz to 3000 MHz. Highlights include: D-STAR, NXDN, dPMR and APCO P25. 4.3 inch color TFT touch screen display with spectrum scope and waterfall. Hybrid FPGA/DSP superhet circuitry, I/Q out and more! Please visit: **www.universal-radio.com** for the full story on this amazing radio.

Advanced Transceivers

Universal is proud to offer the entire line of Icom amateur equipment, including their ground - breaking line of D-STAR digital transceivers.

✔ *Please note our new address below.*

Universal Radio
651-B Lakeview Plaza Blvd.
Worthington, OH 43085
◆ Orders: 800 431-3939
◆ Info: 614 866-4267
www.universal-radio.com

D-STAR

IC-7100
HF / 6M / 2M / 70CM

ID-4100A
2M / 70CM Analog/Digital
Terminal and Access Point Modes

ID-5100A
2M / 70CM Analog/Digital

ID-31A PLUS
70CM Analog/Digital
Terminal and Access Point Modes

ID-51A PLUS2
2M / 70CM Analog/Digital
Terminal and Access Point Modes

Information & Downloads
AMATEUR TOOL KIT | COMIC BOOKS | VIDEOS | WWW.ICOMAMERICA.COM
Electronic advertisements feature active links.

ICOM®

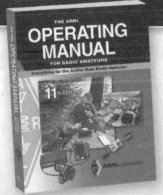

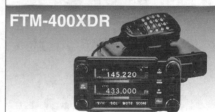

C4FM/FM 144/430 MHz Dual Band 5W
Digital Transceiver

FT-70DR

《 700 mW Loud and Clear audio,
Commercial Grade Specifications 》

C4FM/FM 144/430 MHz Dual Band 5 W
Digital Transceiver

FT2DR

《 Improved 66 ch GPS receiver included 》

System Fusion II

C4FM Digital
Pursuing Advanced Communications

C4FM/FM 144/430 MHz Dual Band 50 W
Digital Transceiver

FTM-100DR

《 Improved 66 ch GPS receiver included 》

C4FM/FM 144/430 MHz
Dual Band Dual Receive Digital Repeater

DR-2X

C4FM/FM 144/430 MHz Dual Band 50 W
Digital Transceiver

FTM-400XDR

《 Improved 66 ch GPS receiver included 》

C4FM/FM 144 MHz 65 W
Digital Transceiver

FTM-3200DR

《 Genuine 65 Watts High Power 》

CW/SSB/AM/FM/C4FM
HF/50/144/430 MHz Wide-Coverage
100 W All Mode Transceiver (144/430 MHz: 50 W)

FT-991 A

《 Real-Time Spectrum Scope included 》

C4FM/FM 430 MHz 55 W
Digital Transceiver   New

FTM-3207DR

《 Heavy Duty 55 Watts High Power 》

System Fusion II *Supports All C4FM Portables and Mobiles*

· Firmware updates will enable System Fusion II compatibility with all existing C4FM products.

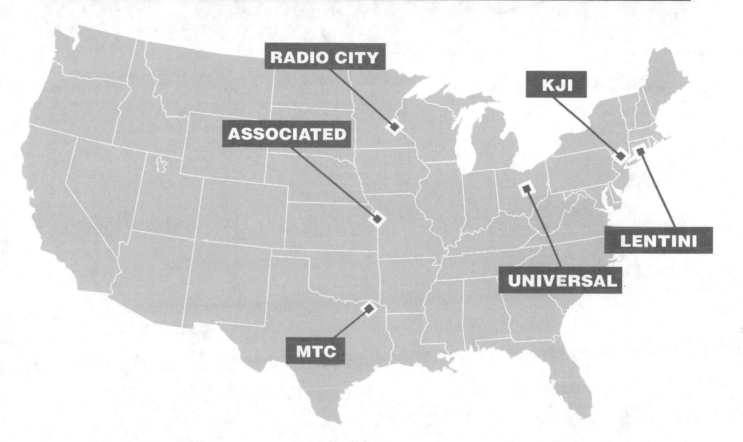